FAIRY TAIL
100 YEARS QUEST 4

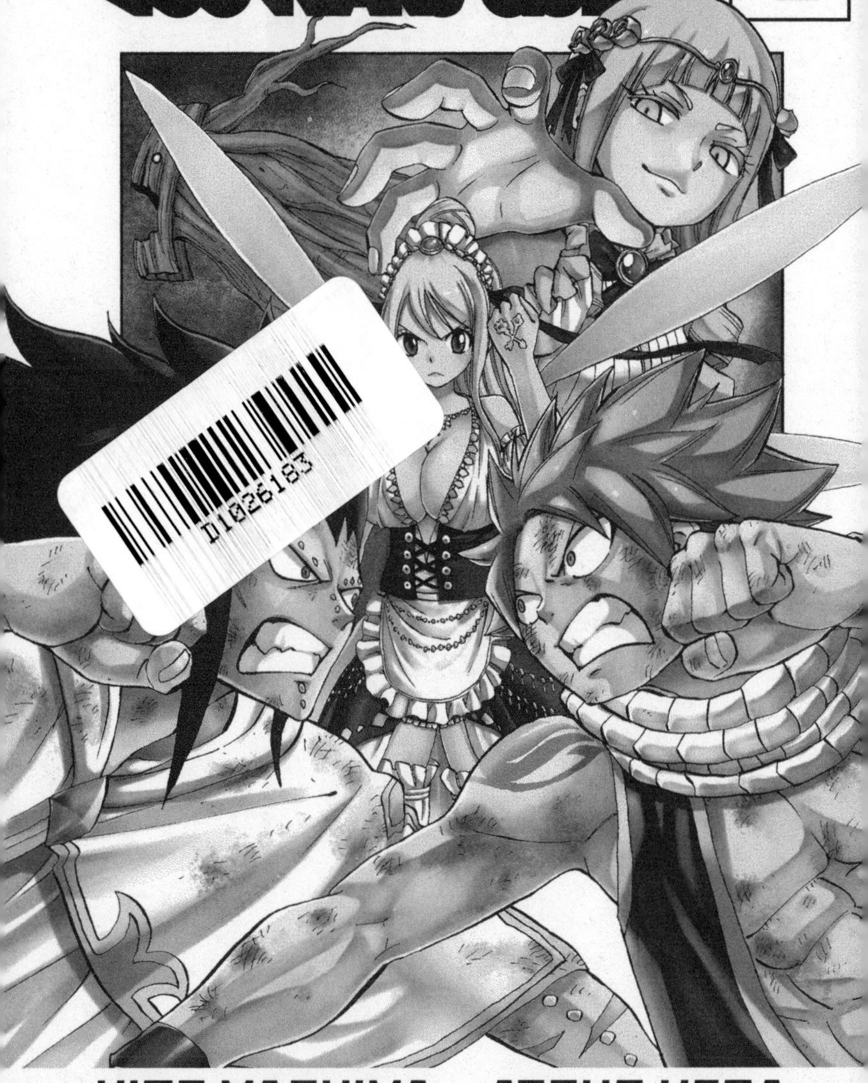

HIRO MASHIMA ATSUO UEDA

FAIRY TAIL 100 YEARS' QUEST 4 CONTENTS

FAIRY TAIL 100 YEARS QUEST

Chapter 28: White Ascendent

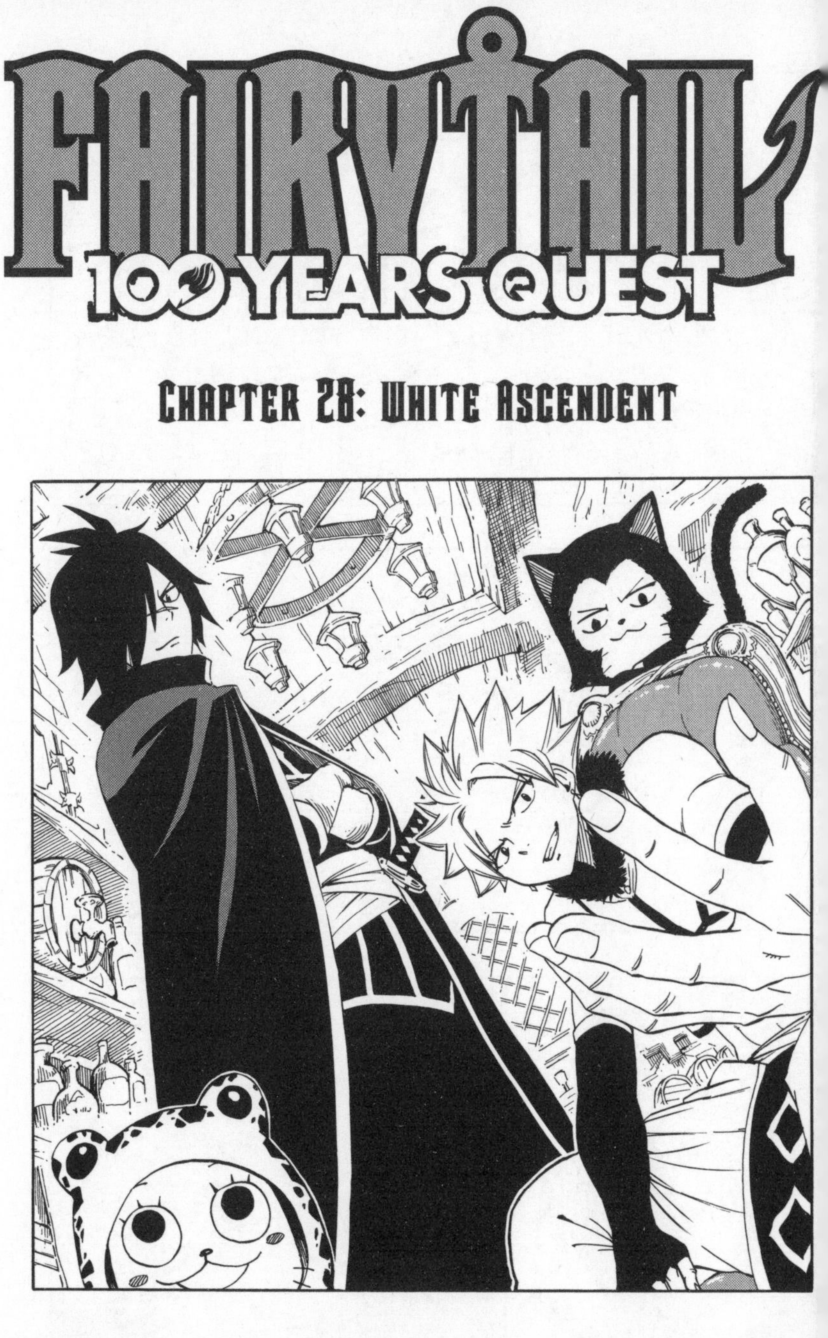

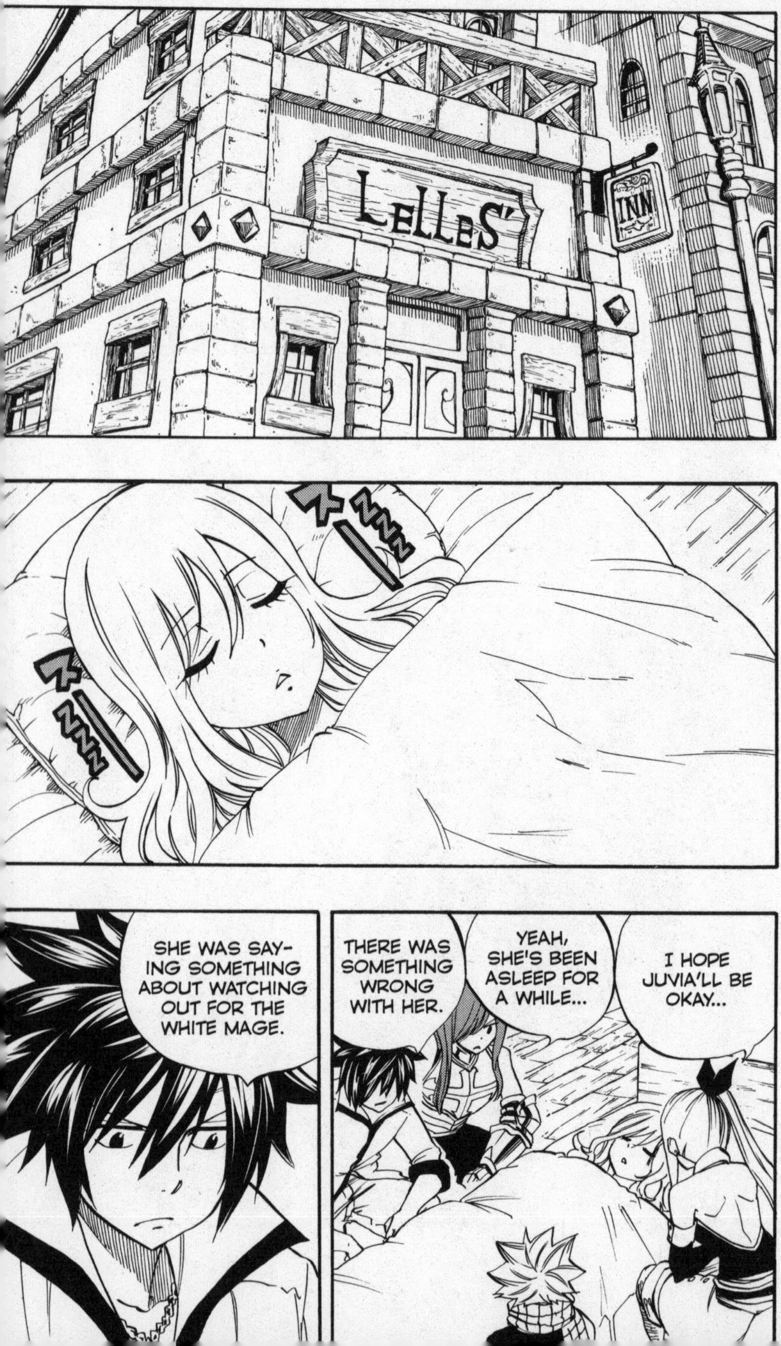
LELLES'
INN
I HOPE JUVIA'LL BE OKAY...
YEAH, SHE'S BEEN ASLEEP FOR A WHILE...
THERE WAS SOMETHING WRONG WITH HER.
SHE WAS SAY-ING SOMETHING ABOUT WATCHING OUT FOR THE WHITE MAGE.

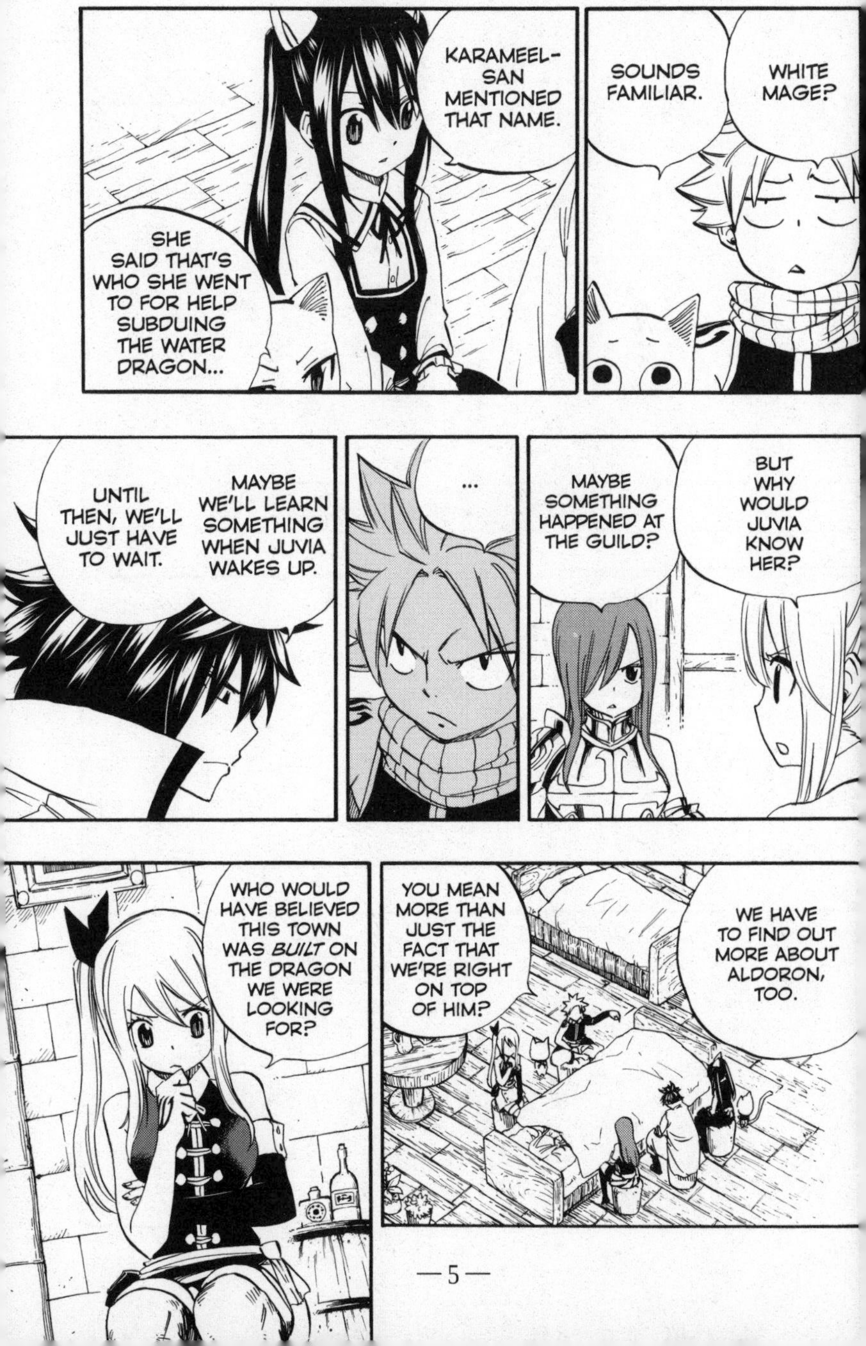
WHITE MAGE?
SOUNDS FAMILIAR.
KARAMEEL-SAN MENTIONED THAT NAME.
SHE SAID THAT'S WHO SHE WENT TO FOR HELP SUBDUING THE WATER DRAGON...
BUT WHY WOULD JUVIA KNOW HER?
MAYBE SOMETHING HAPPENED AT THE GUILD?
...
MAYBE WE'LL LEARN SOMETHING WHEN JUVIA WAKES UP.
UNTIL THEN, WE'LL JUST HAVE TO WAIT.
WE HAVE TO FIND OUT MORE ABOUT ALDORON, TOO.
YOU MEAN MORE THAN JUST THE FACT THAT WE'RE RIGHT ON TOP OF HIM?
WHO WOULD HAVE BELIEVED THIS TOWN WAS *BUILT* ON THE DRAGON WE WERE LOOKING FOR?

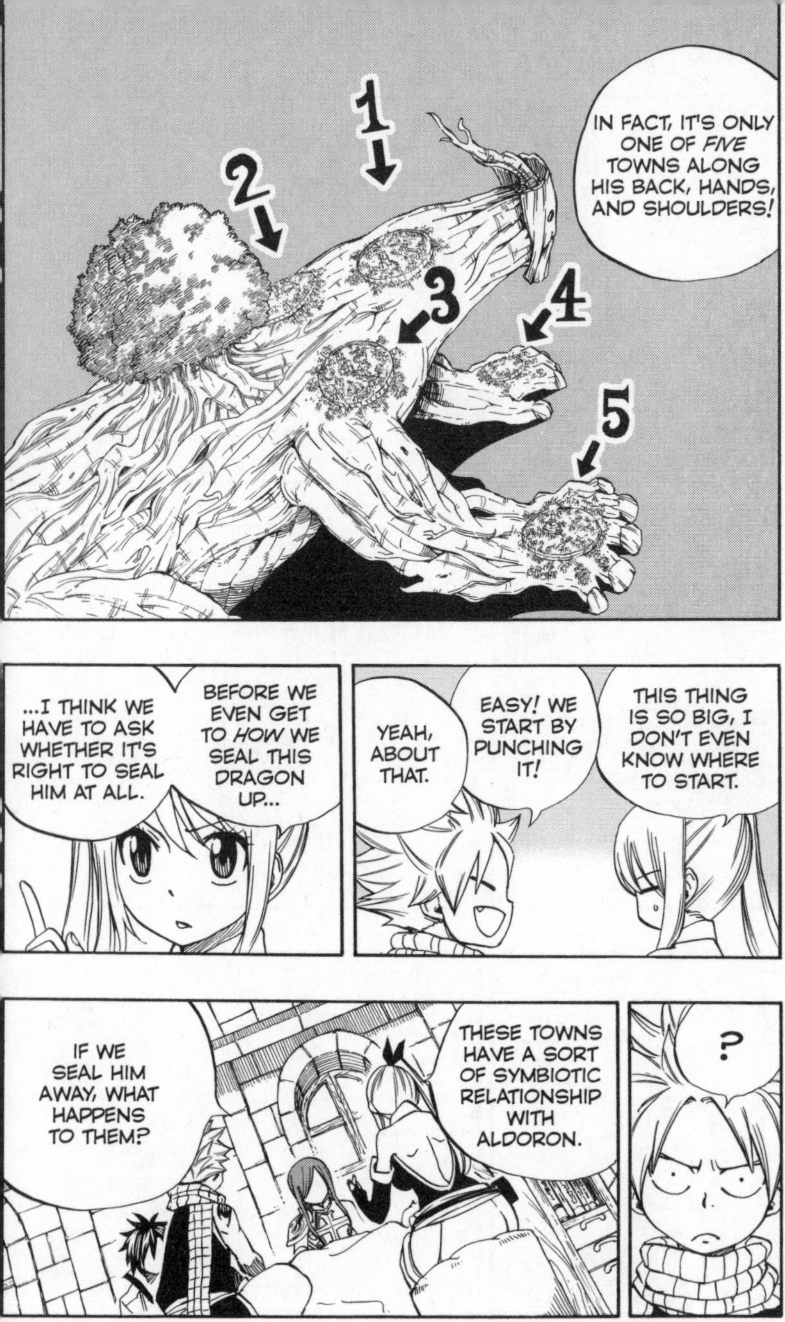

IN FACT, IT'S ONLY ONE OF *FIVE* TOWNS ALONG HIS BACK, HANDS, AND SHOULDERS!
1
2
3
4
5
THIS THING IS SO BIG, I DON'T EVEN KNOW WHERE TO START.
EASY! WE START BY PUNCHING IT!
YEAH, ABOUT THAT.
BEFORE WE EVEN GET TO *HOW* WE SEAL THIS DRAGON UP...
...I THINK WE HAVE TO ASK WHETHER IT'S RIGHT TO SEAL HIM AT ALL.
?
THESE TOWNS HAVE A SORT OF SYMBIOTIC RELATIONSHIP WITH ALDORON.
IF WE SEAL HIM AWAY, WHAT HAPPENS TO THEM?

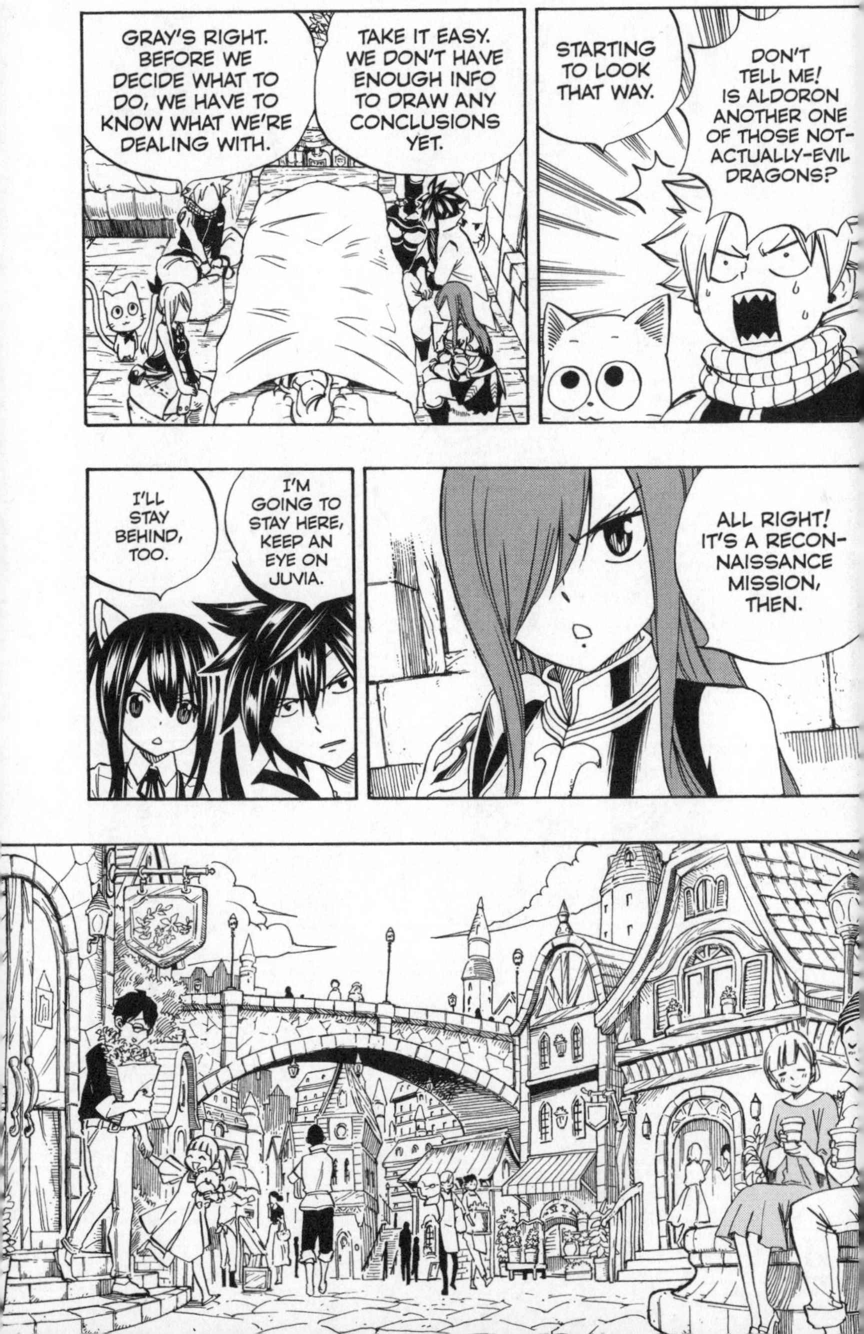
DON'T TELL ME! IS ALDORON ANOTHER ONE OF THOSE NOT-ACTUALLY-EVIL DRAGONS?
STARTING TO LOOK THAT WAY.
TAKE IT EASY. WE DON'T HAVE ENOUGH INFO TO DRAW ANY CONCLUSIONS YET.
GRAY'S RIGHT. BEFORE WE DECIDE WHAT TO DO, WE HAVE TO KNOW WHAT WE'RE DEALING WITH.
ALL RIGHT! IT'S A RECON-NAISSANCE MISSION, THEN.
I'M GOING TO STAY HERE, KEEP AN EYE ON JUVIA.
I'LL STAY BEHIND, TOO.

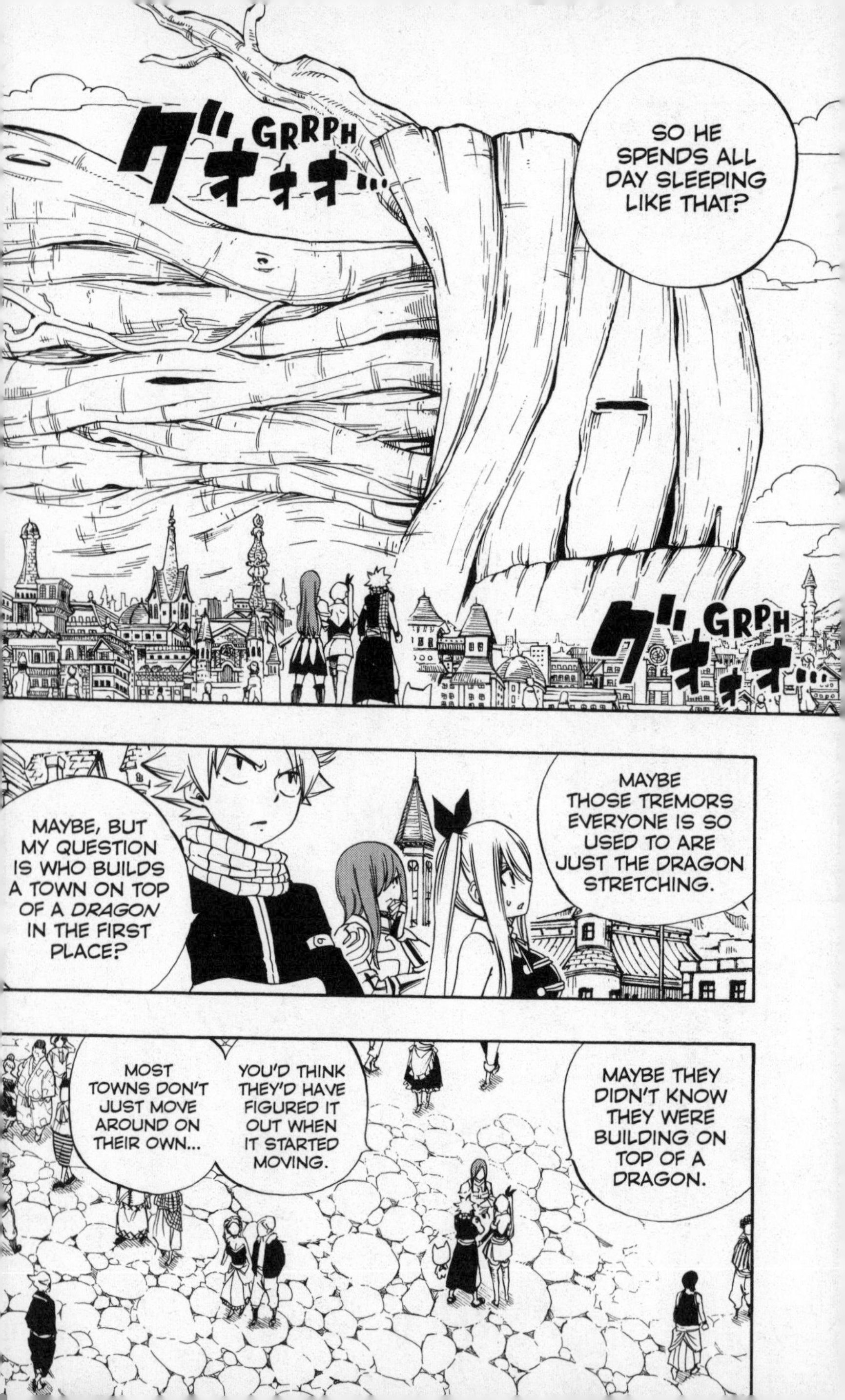
SO HE SPENDS ALL DAY SLEEPING LIKE THAT?
グオォオ… GRRPH
グオォオ… GRPH
MAYBE THOSE TREMORS EVERYONE IS SO USED TO ARE JUST THE DRAGON STRETCHING.
MAYBE, BUT MY QUESTION IS WHO BUILDS A TOWN ON TOP OF A *DRAGON* IN THE FIRST PLACE?
MAYBE THEY DIDN'T KNOW THEY WERE BUILDING ON TOP OF A DRAGON.
YOU'D THINK THEY'D HAVE FIGURED IT OUT WHEN IT STARTED MOVING.
MOST TOWNS DON'T JUST MOVE AROUND ON THEIR OWN...

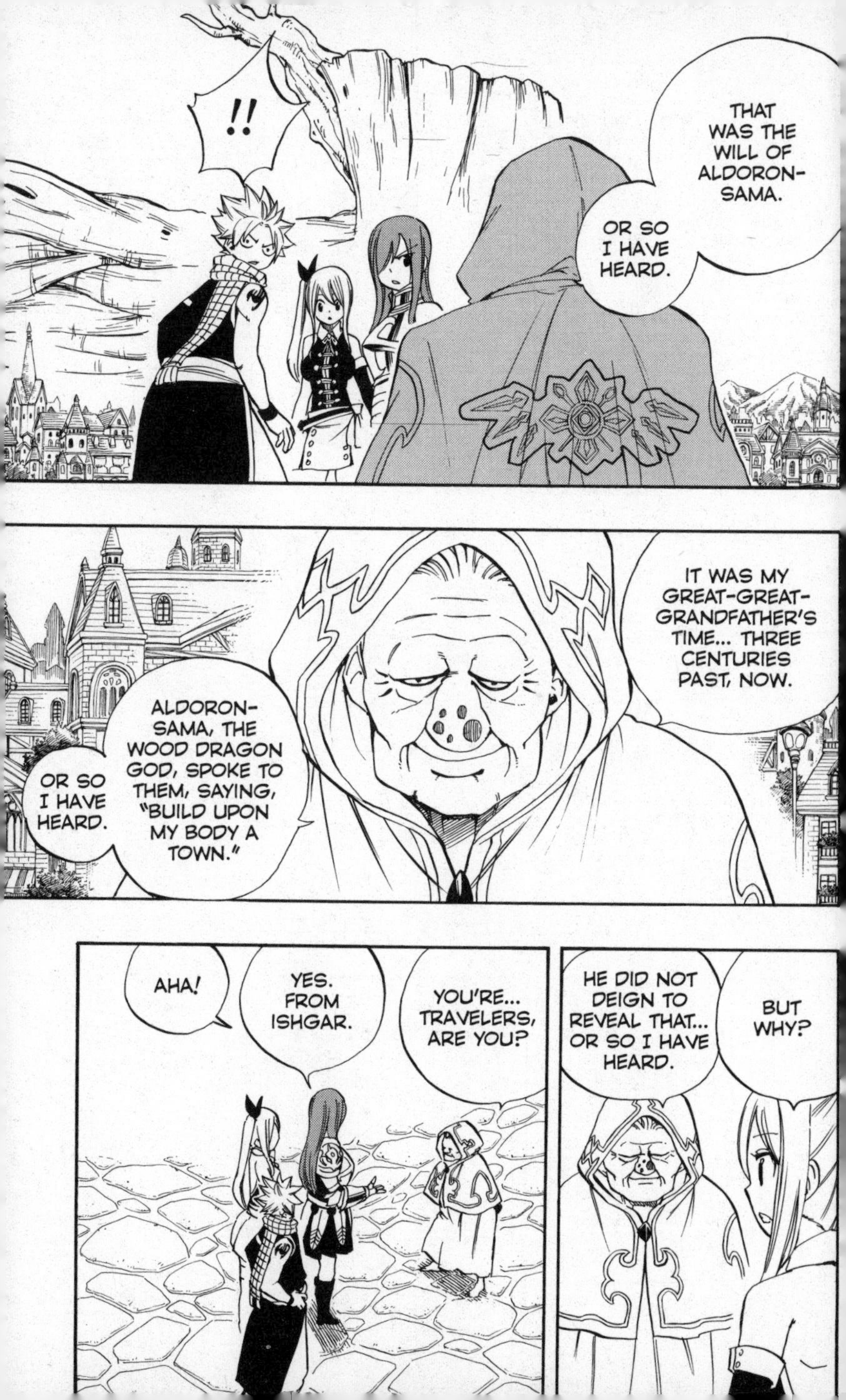
THAT WAS THE WILL OF ALDORON-SAMA.
OR SO I HAVE HEARD.
!!
IT WAS MY GREAT-GREAT-GRANDFATHER'S TIME... THREE CENTURIES PAST, NOW.
ALDORON-SAMA, THE WOOD DRAGON GOD, SPOKE TO THEM, SAYING, "BUILD UPON MY BODY A TOWN."
OR SO I HAVE HEARD.
BUT WHY?
HE DID NOT DEIGN TO REVEAL THAT... OR SO I HAVE HEARD.
YOU'RE... TRAVELERS, ARE YOU?
YES. FROM ISHGAR.
AHA!

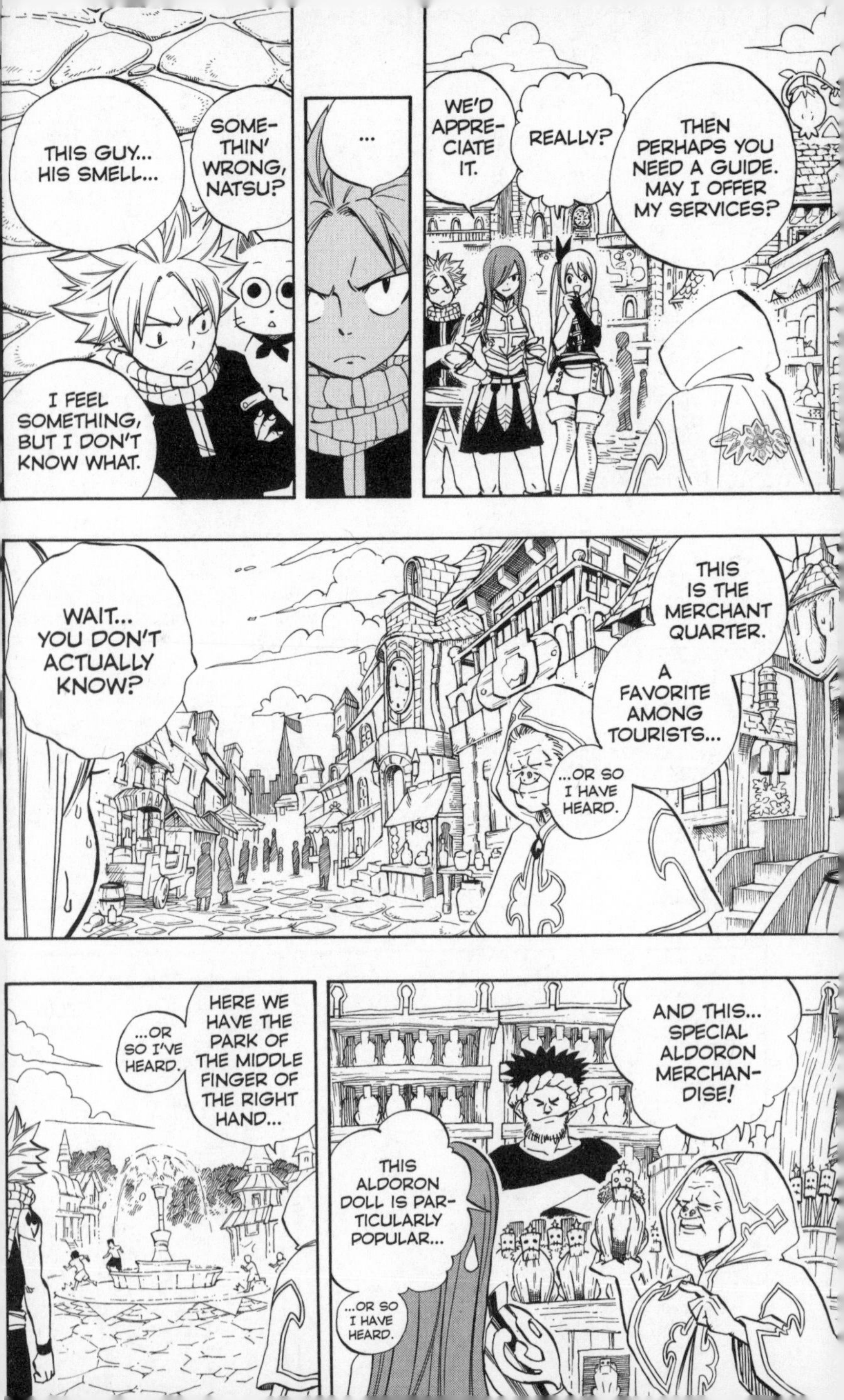
THEN PERHAPS YOU NEED A GUIDE. MAY I OFFER MY SERVICES?
REALLY?
WE'D APPRE-CIATE IT.
...
SOME-THIN' WRONG, NATSU?
THIS GUY... HIS SMELL...
I FEEL SOMETHING, BUT I DON'T KNOW WHAT.
THIS IS THE MERCHANT QUARTER.
A FAVORITE AMONG TOURISTS...
...OR SO I HAVE HEARD.
WAIT... YOU DON'T ACTUALLY KNOW?
AND THIS... SPECIAL ALDORON MERCHAN-DISE!
THIS ALDORON DOLL IS PAR-TICULARLY POPULAR...
...OR SO I HAVE HEARD.
HERE WE HAVE THE PARK OF THE MIDDLE FINGER OF THE RIGHT HAND...
...OR SO I'VE HEARD.

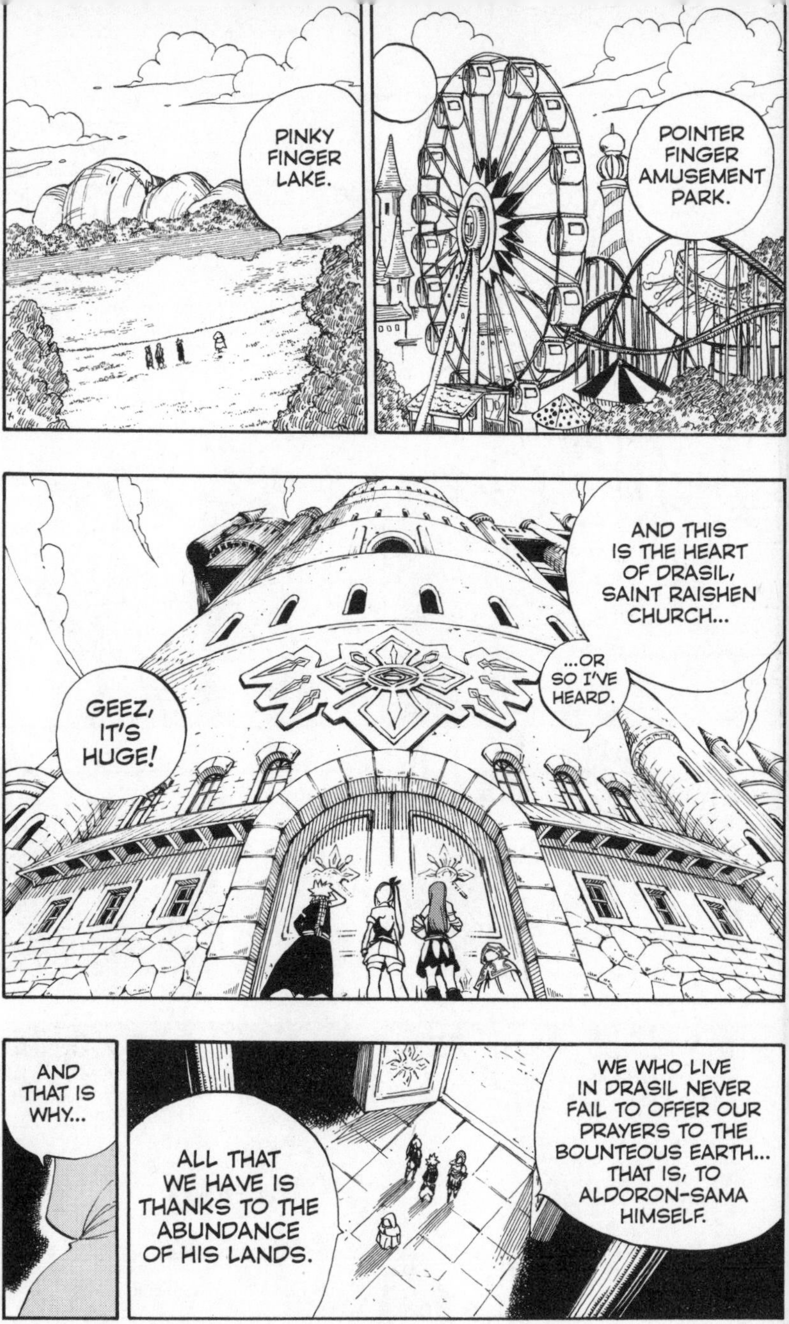
POINTER FINGER AMUSEMENT PARK.
PINKY FINGER LAKE.
AND THIS IS THE HEART OF DRASIL, SAINT RAISHEN CHURCH...
...OR SO I'VE HEARD.
GEEZ, IT'S HUGE!
WE WHO LIVE IN DRASIL NEVER FAIL TO OFFER OUR PRAYERS TO THE BOUNTEOUS EARTH... THAT IS, TO ALDORON-SAMA HIMSELF.
ALL THAT WE HAVE IS THANKS TO THE ABUNDANCE OF HIS LANDS.
AND THAT IS WHY...

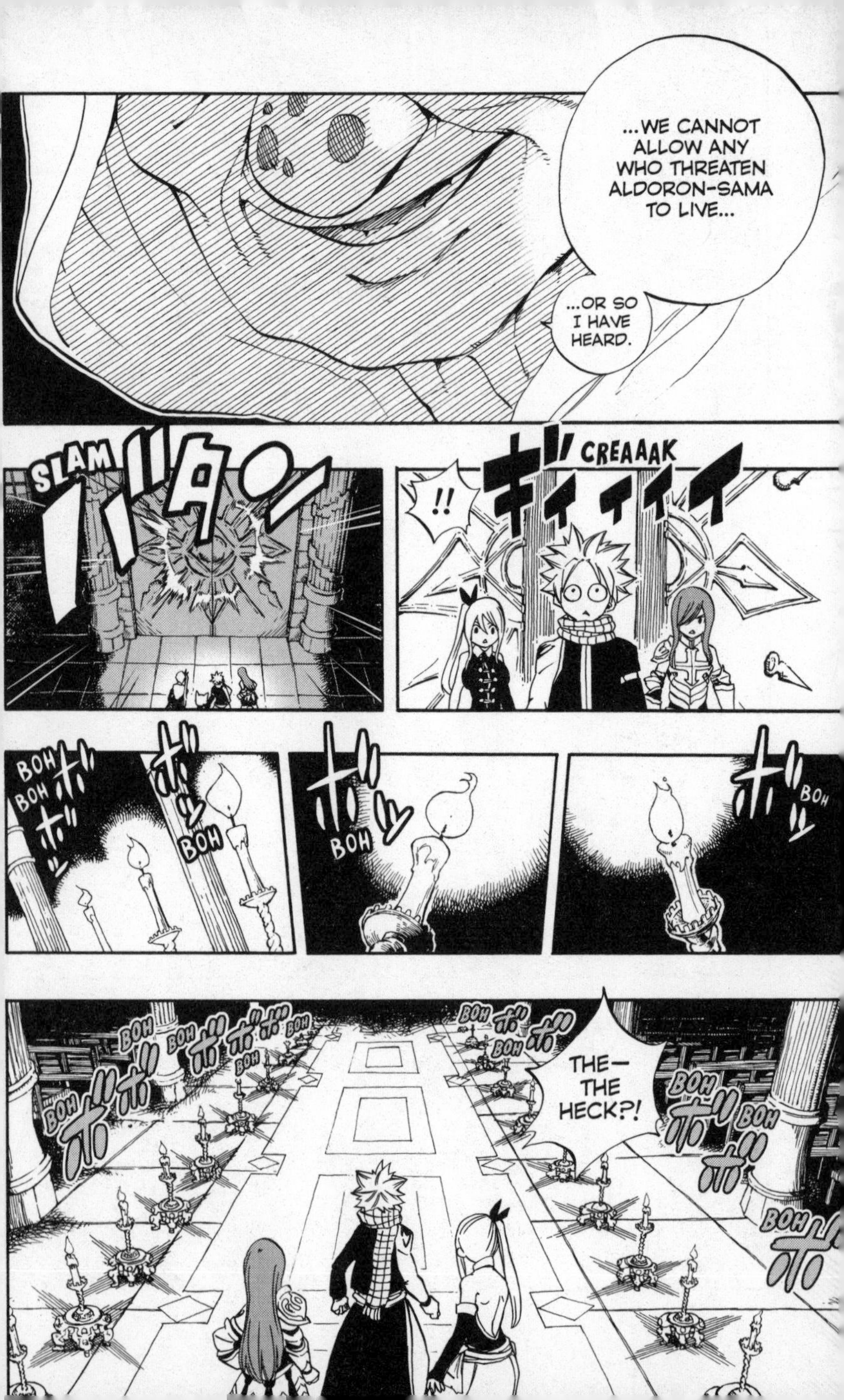
...WE CANNOT ALLOW ANY WHO THREATEN ALDORON-SAMA TO LIVE...
...OR SO I HAVE HEARD.
CREAAAK
!!
SLAM
BOH
BOH
BOH BOH
BOH
THE— THE HECK?!
BOH BOH
BOH
BOH
BOH BOH
BOH
BOH BOH
BOH

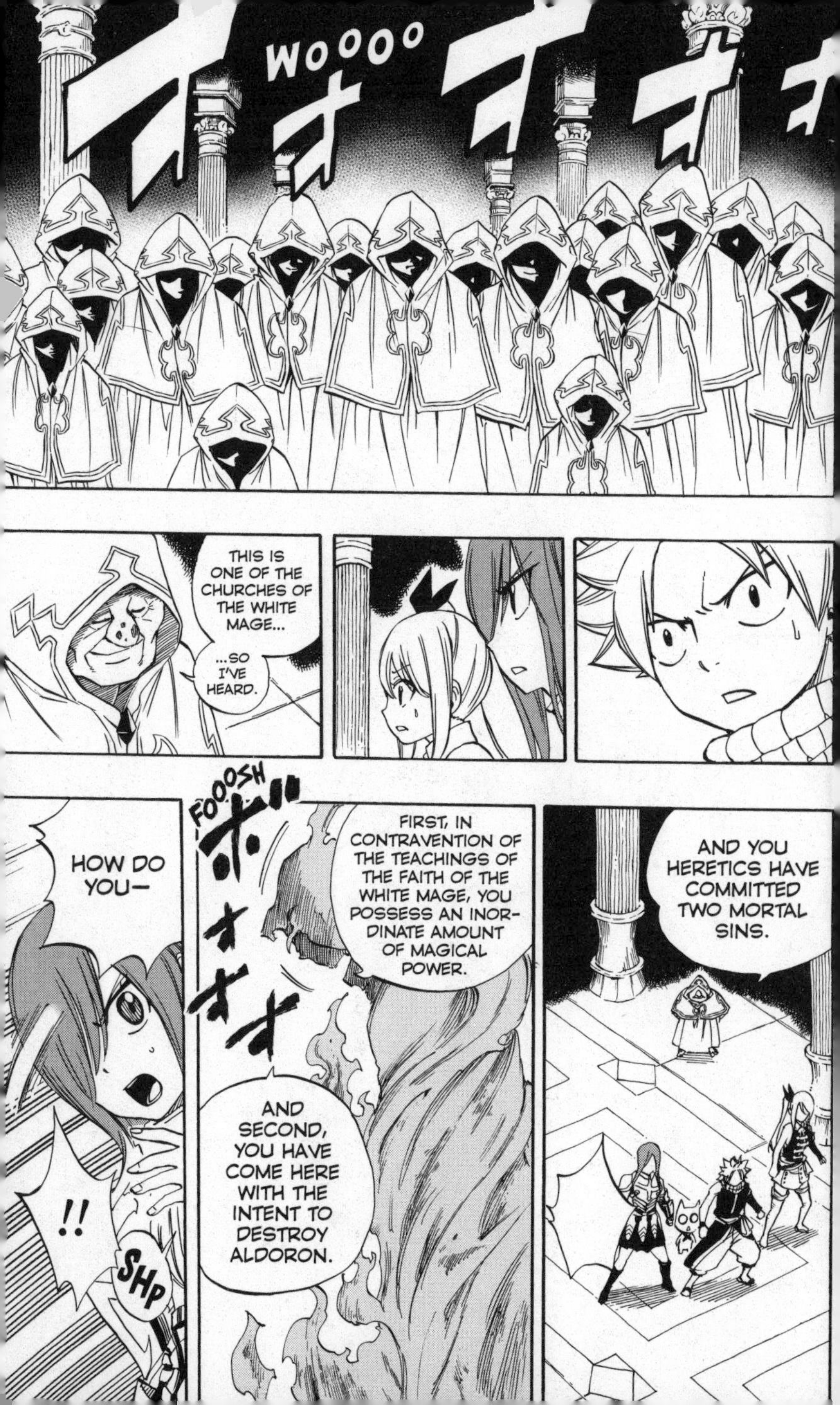
WOOOO
THIS IS ONE OF THE CHURCHES OF THE WHITE MAGE...
...SO I'VE HEARD.
AND YOU HERETICS HAVE COMMITTED TWO MORTAL SINS.
FOOOSH
FIRST, IN CONTRAVENTION OF THE TEACHINGS OF THE FAITH OF THE WHITE MAGE, YOU POSSESS AN INORDINATE AMOUNT OF MAGICAL POWER.
AND SECOND, YOU HAVE COME HERE WITH THE INTENT TO DESTROY ALDORON.
HOW DO YOU—
!!
SHP

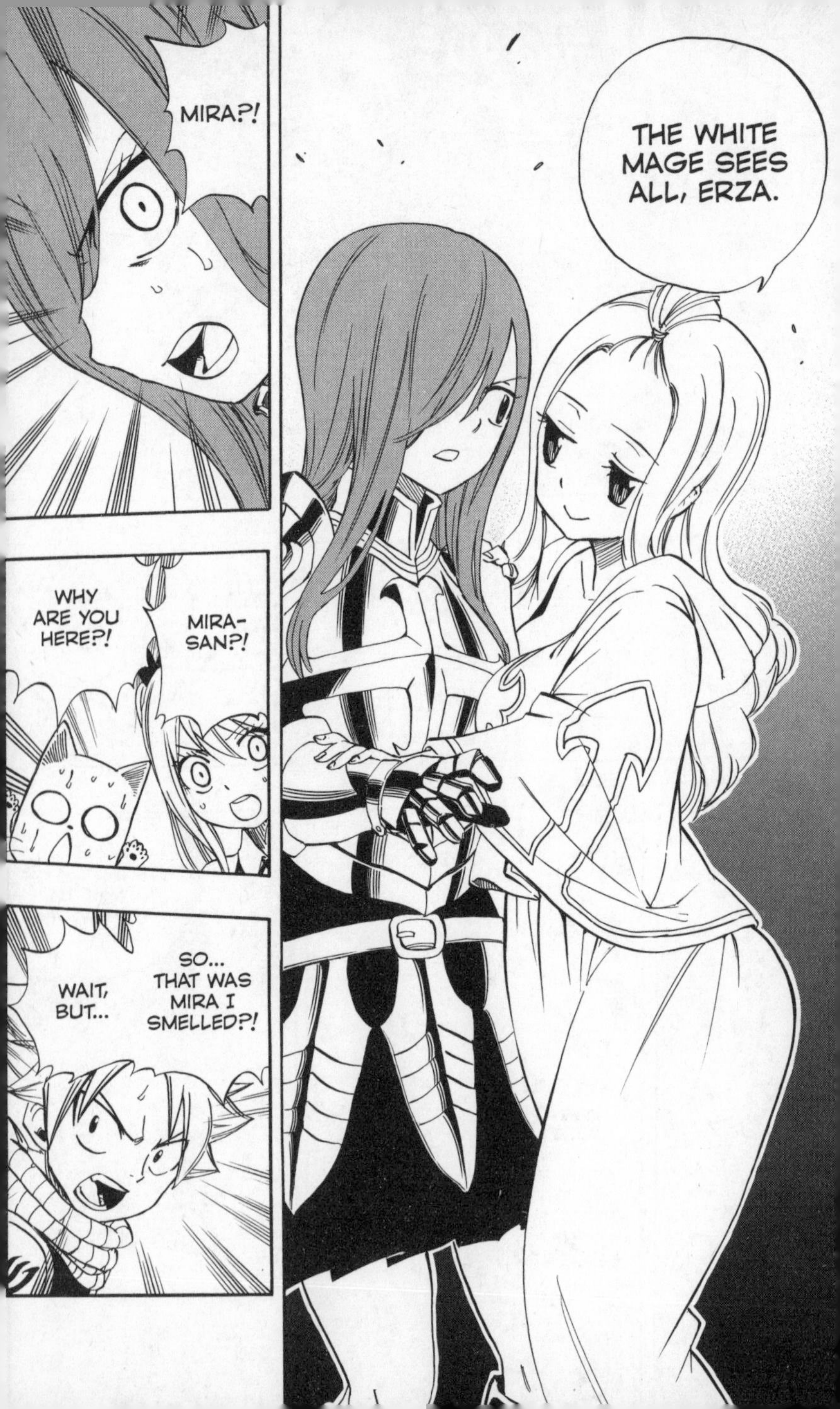
THE WHITE MAGE SEES ALL, ERZA.
MIRA?!
MIRA-SAN?!
WHY ARE YOU HERE?!
SO... THAT WAS MIRA I SMELLED?!
WAIT, BUT...

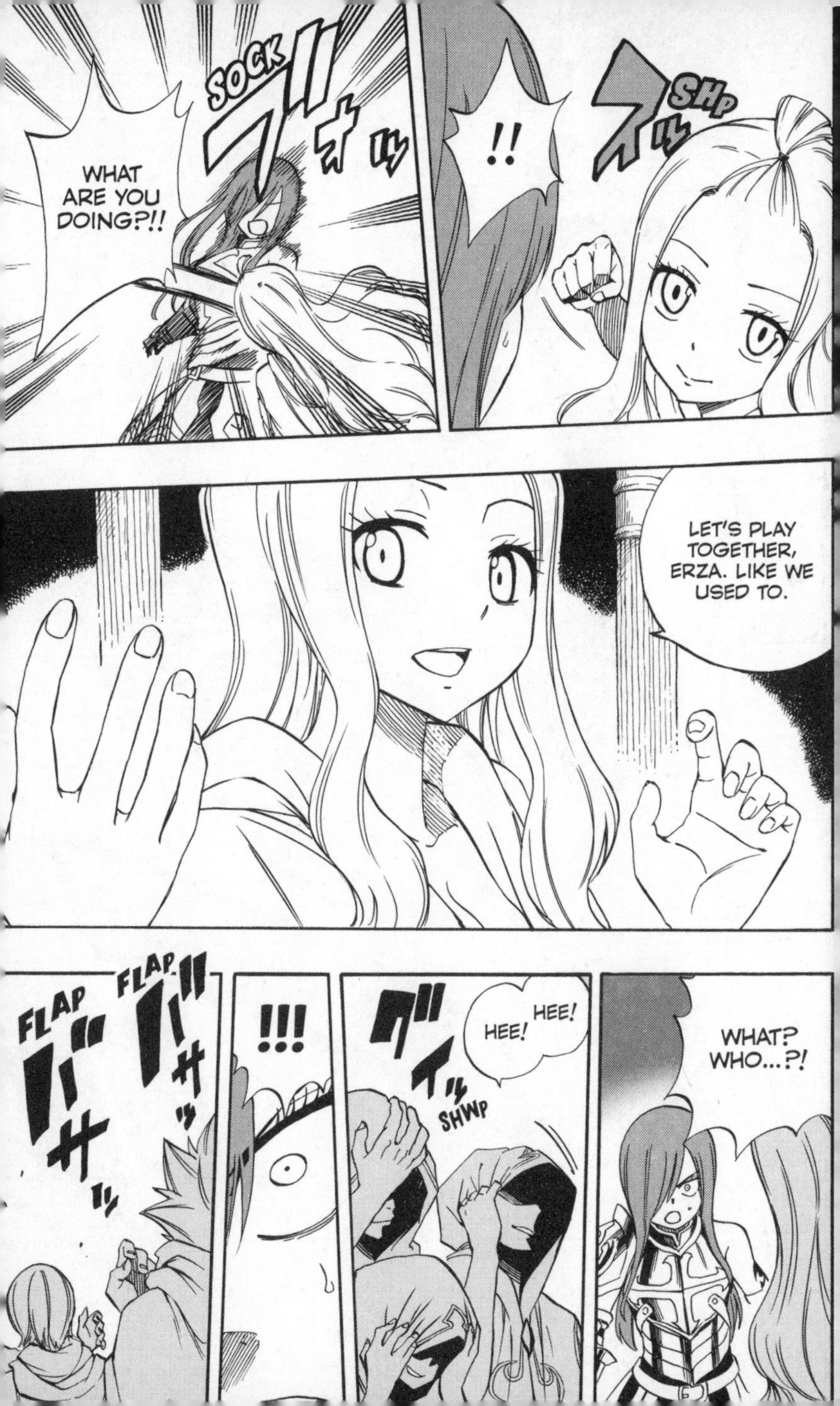
SHP
!!
SOCK
WHAT ARE YOU DOING?!!
LET'S PLAY TOGETHER, ERZA. LIKE WE USED TO.
WHAT? WHO...?!
HEE! HEE!
SHWP
!!!
FLAP-
FLAP

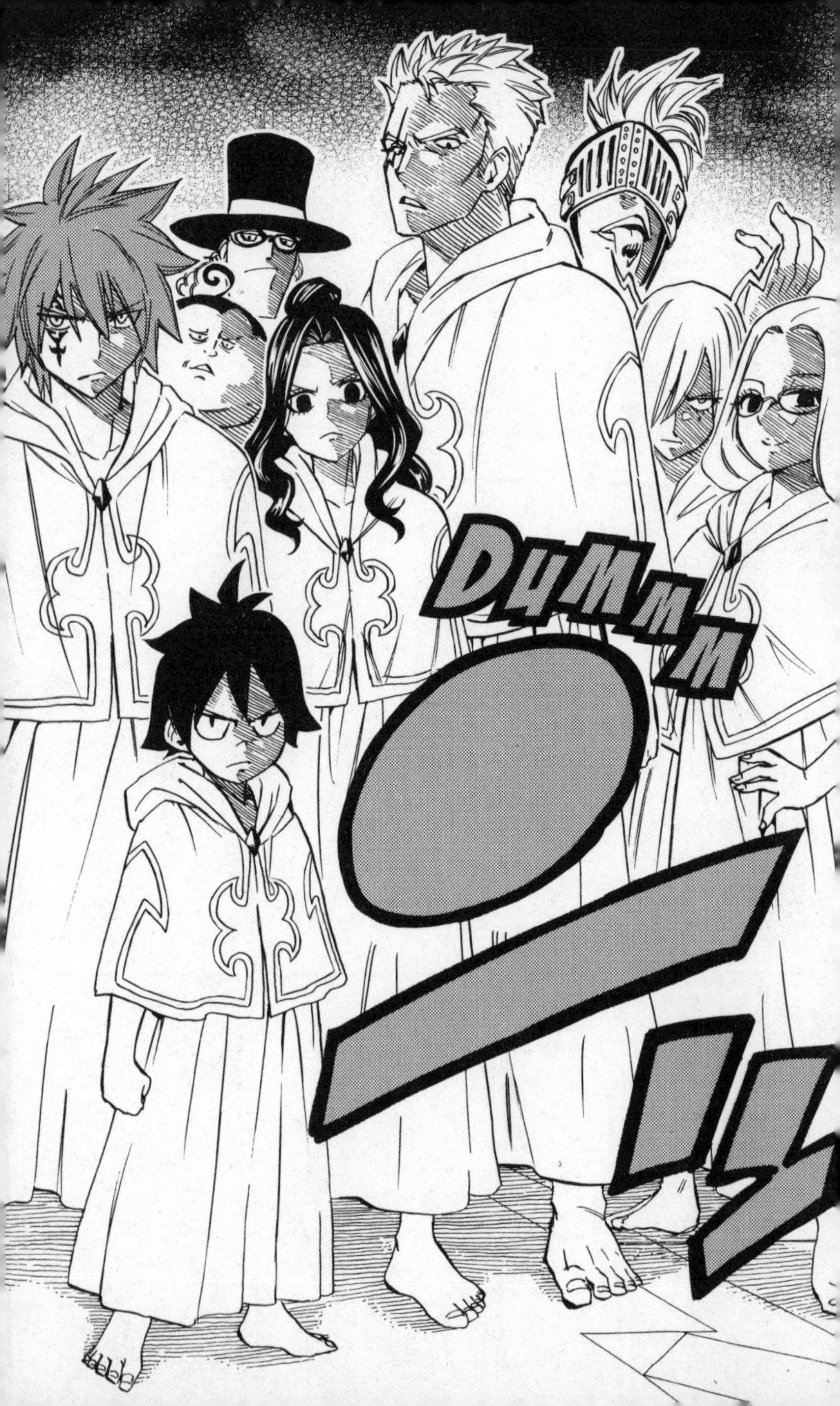
DUMMM

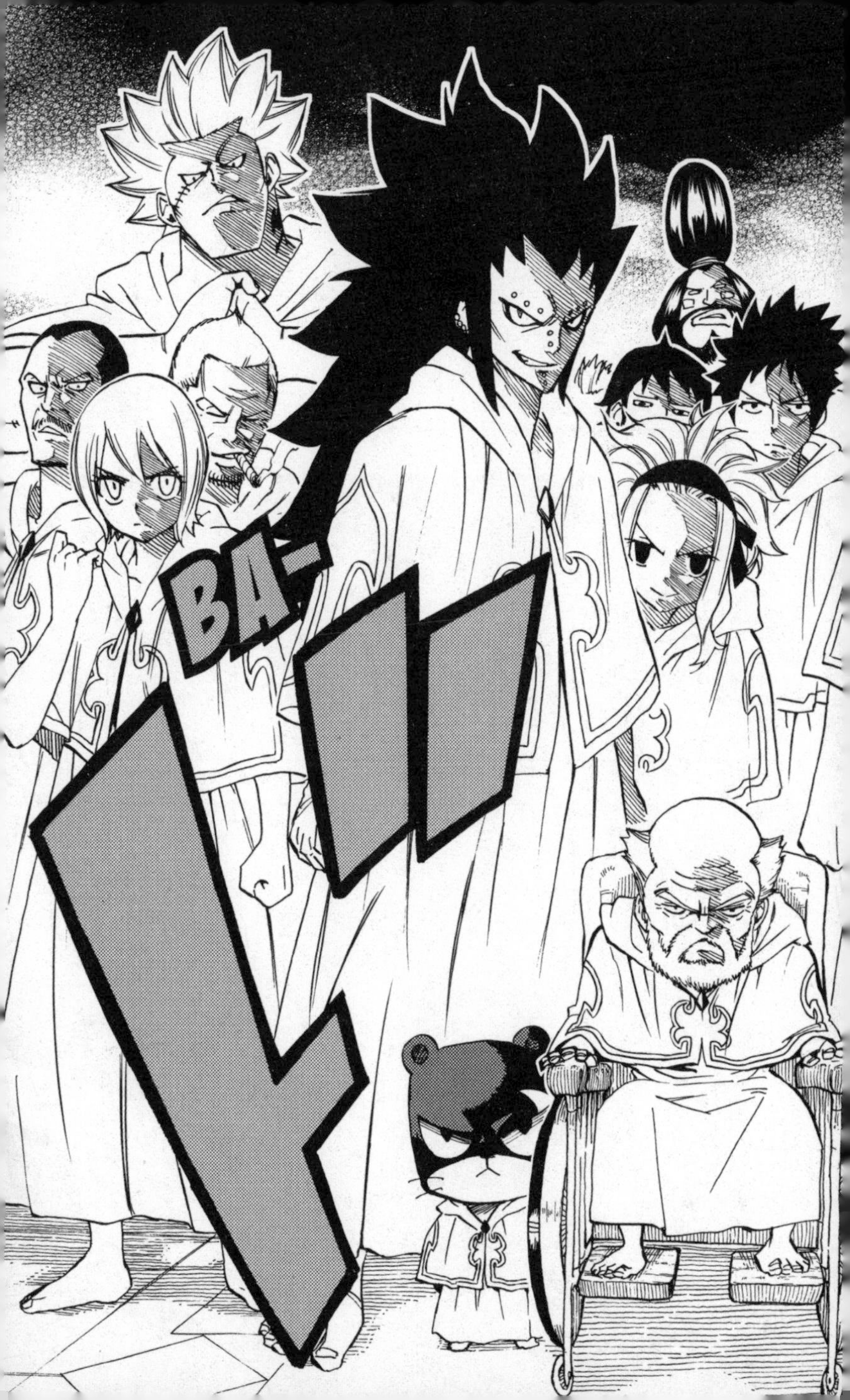
BA-

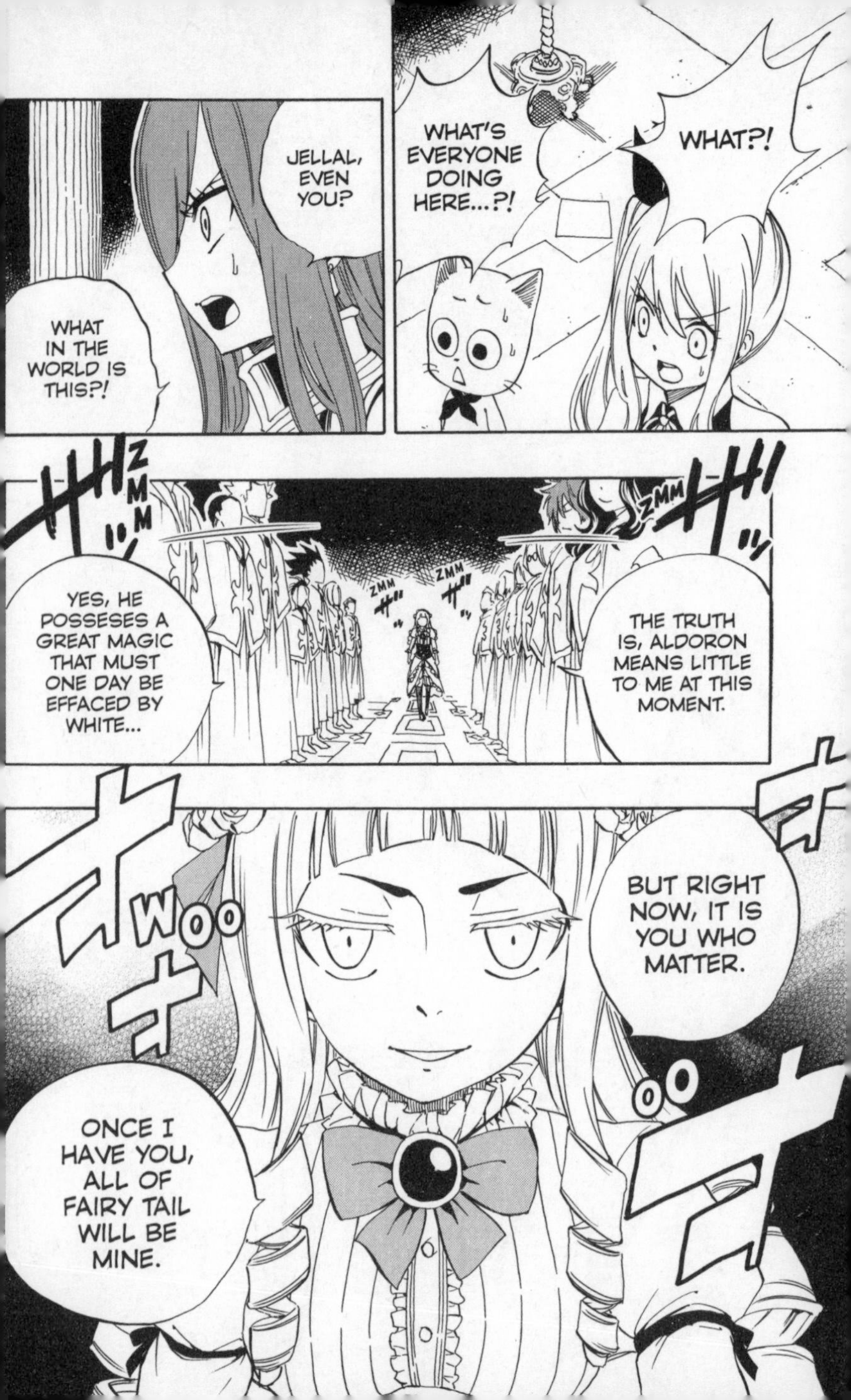
WHAT?!
WHAT'S EVERYONE DOING HERE...?!
JELLAL, EVEN YOU?
WHAT IN THE WORLD IS THIS?!
ZMM
ZMM
ZMM
ZMM
THE TRUTH IS, ALDORON MEANS LITTLE TO ME AT THIS MOMENT.
YES, HE POSSESSES A GREAT MAGIC THAT MUST ONE DAY BE EFFACED BY WHITE...
OO
BUT RIGHT NOW, IT IS YOU WHO MATTER.
WOO
ONCE I HAVE YOU, ALL OF FAIRY TAIL WILL BE MINE.

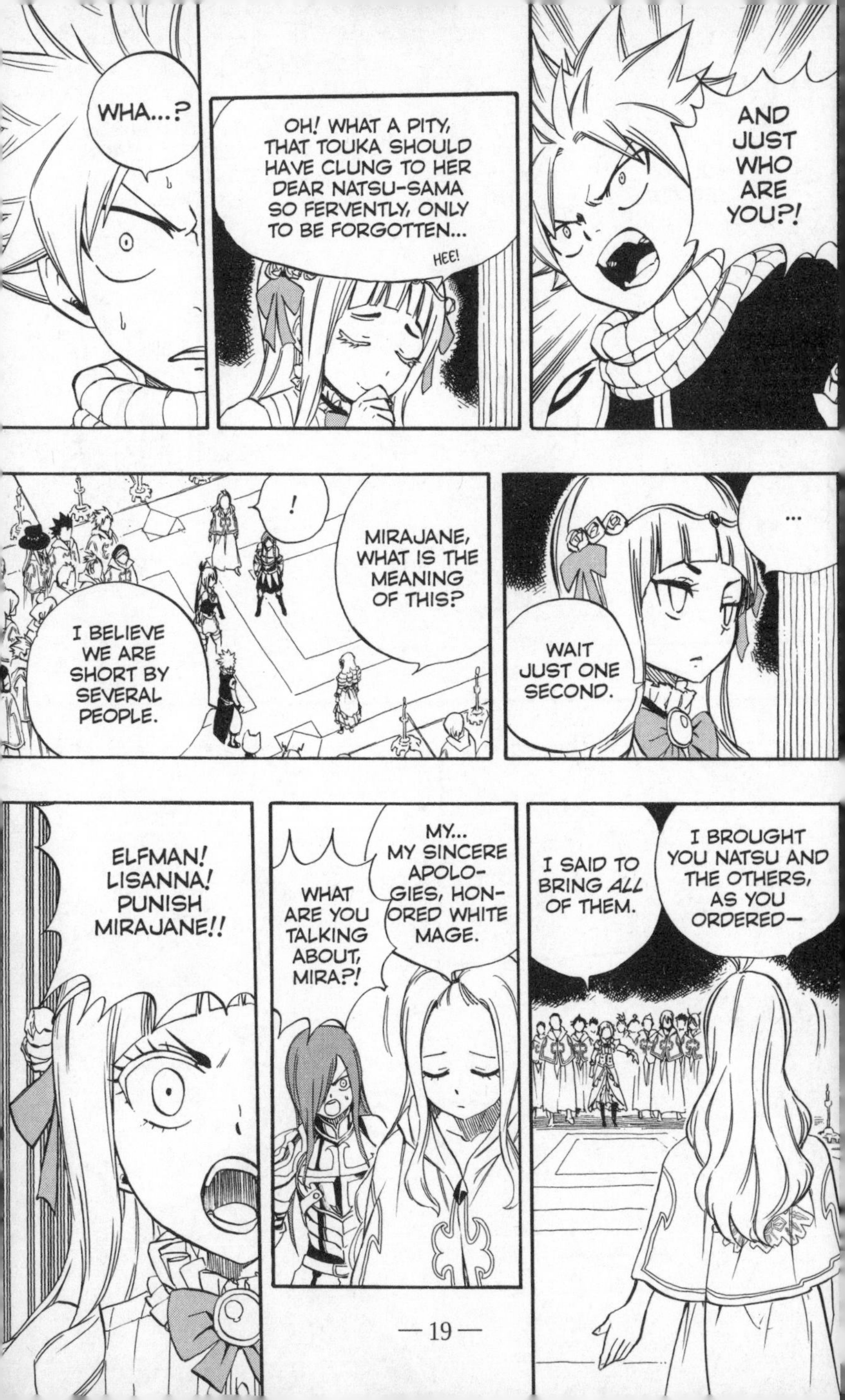
AND JUST WHO ARE YOU?!
OH! WHAT A PITY, THAT TOUKA SHOULD HAVE CLUNG TO HER DEAR NATSU-SAMA SO FERVENTLY, ONLY TO BE FORGOTTEN...
HEE!
WHA...?
...
WAIT JUST ONE SECOND.
MIRAJANE, WHAT IS THE MEANING OF THIS?
!
I BELIEVE WE ARE SHORT BY SEVERAL PEOPLE.
I BROUGHT YOU NATSU AND THE OTHERS, AS YOU ORDERED—
I SAID TO BRING *ALL* OF THEM.
MY... MY SINCERE APOLOGIES, HONORED WHITE MAGE.
WHAT ARE YOU TALKING ABOUT, MIRA?!
ELFMAN! LISANNA! PUNISH MIRAJANE!!

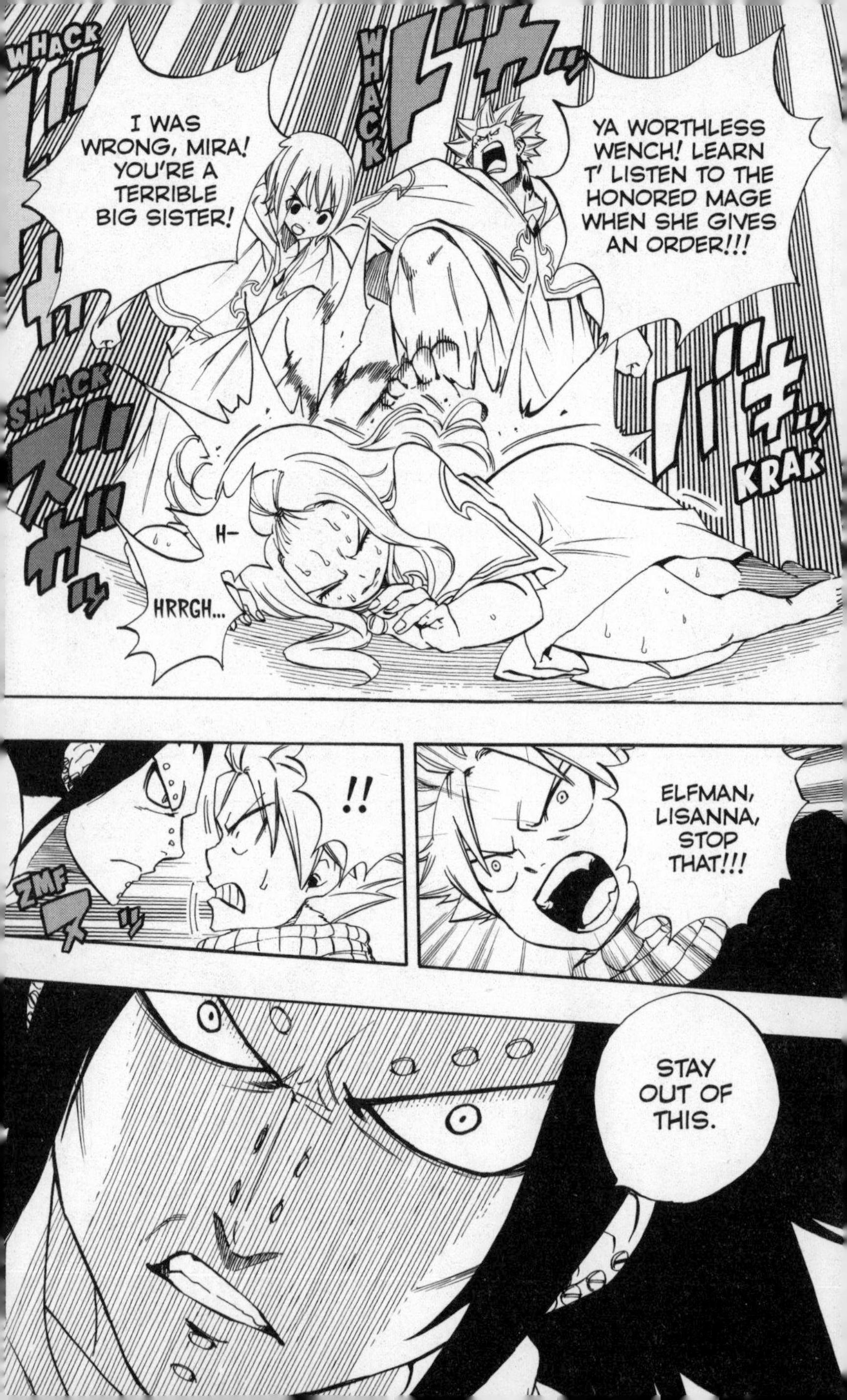
WHACK
YA WORTHLESS WENCH! LEARN T' LISTEN TO THE HONORED MAGE WHEN SHE GIVES AN ORDER!!!
WHACK
I WAS WRONG, MIRA! YOU'RE A TERRIBLE BIG SISTER!
KRAK
SMACK
H-
HRRGH...
ELFMAN, LISANNA, STOP THAT!!!
!!
ZMF
STAY OUT OF THIS.

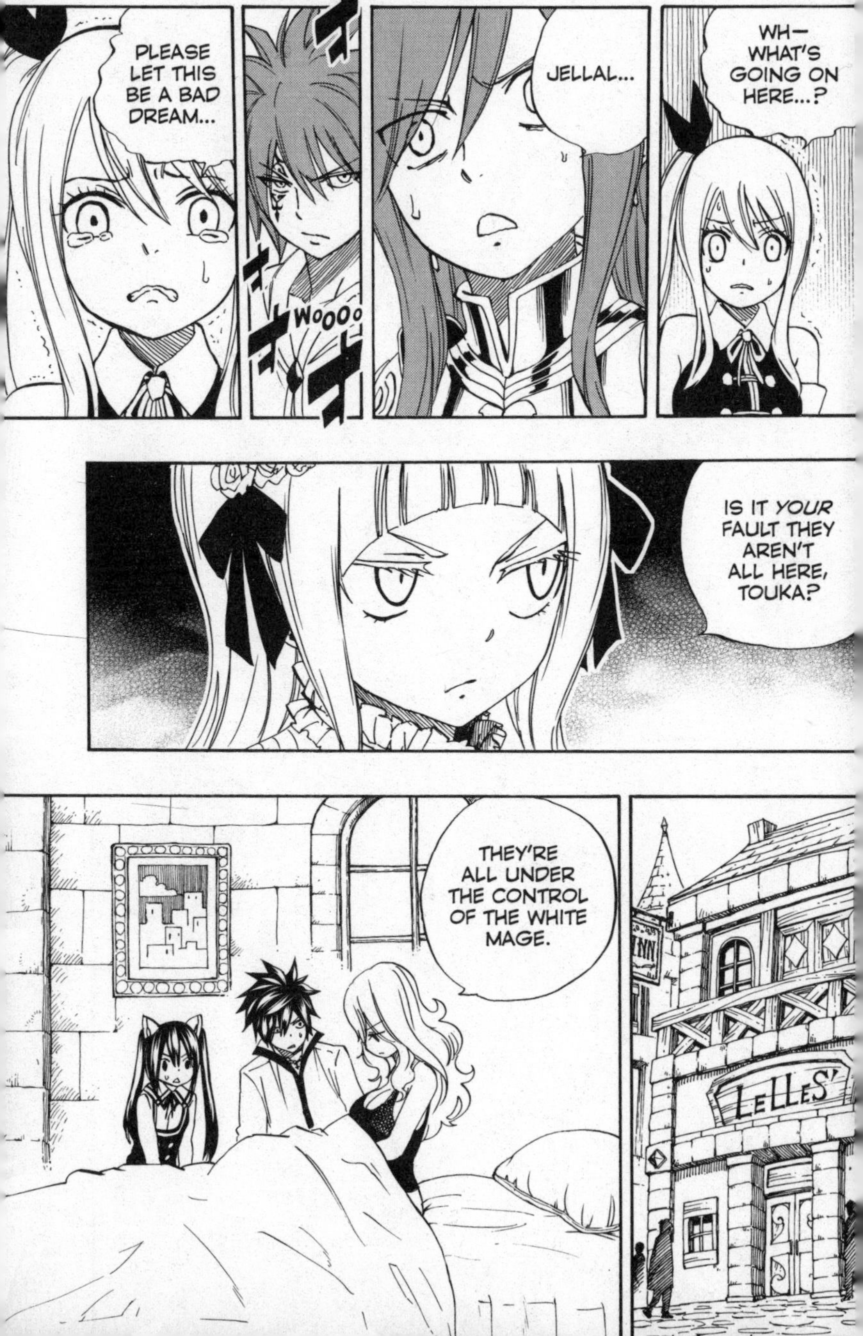
WH— WHAT'S GOING ON HERE...?
JELLAL...
WOOOO
PLEASE LET THIS BE A BAD DREAM...
IS IT *YOUR* FAULT THEY AREN'T ALL HERE, TOUKA?
LELLES'
THEY'RE ALL UNDER THE CONTROL OF THE WHITE MAGE.

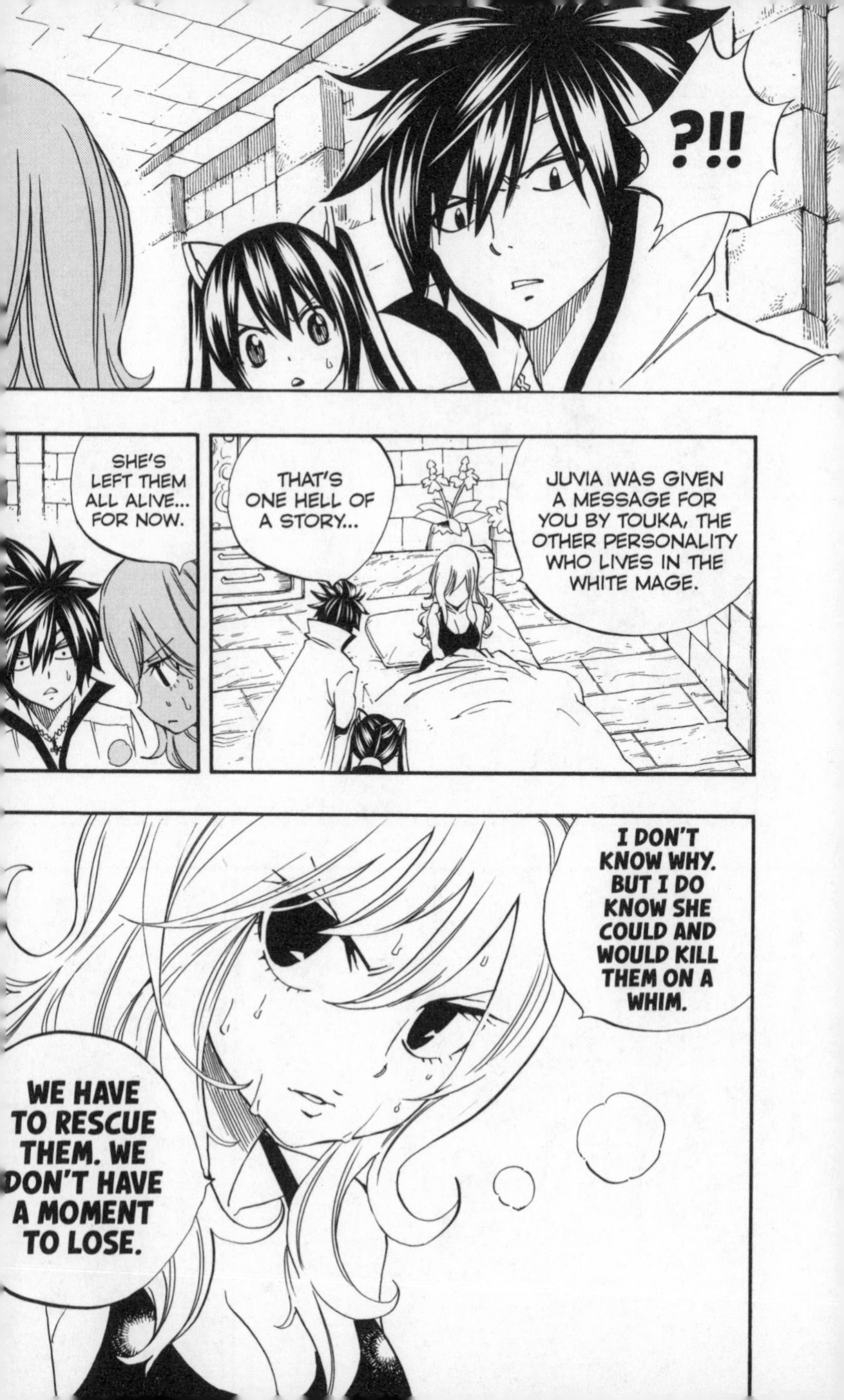
?!!
JUVIA WAS GIVEN A MESSAGE FOR YOU BY TOUKA, THE OTHER PERSONALITY WHO LIVES IN THE WHITE MAGE.
THAT'S ONE HELL OF A STORY...
SHE'S LEFT THEM ALL ALIVE... FOR NOW.
I DON'T KNOW WHY. BUT I DO KNOW SHE COULD AND WOULD KILL THEM ON A WHIM.
WE HAVE TO RESCUE THEM. WE DON'T HAVE A MOMENT TO LOSE.

FAIRY TAIL 100 YEARS QUEST

Chapter 29: Whiteout

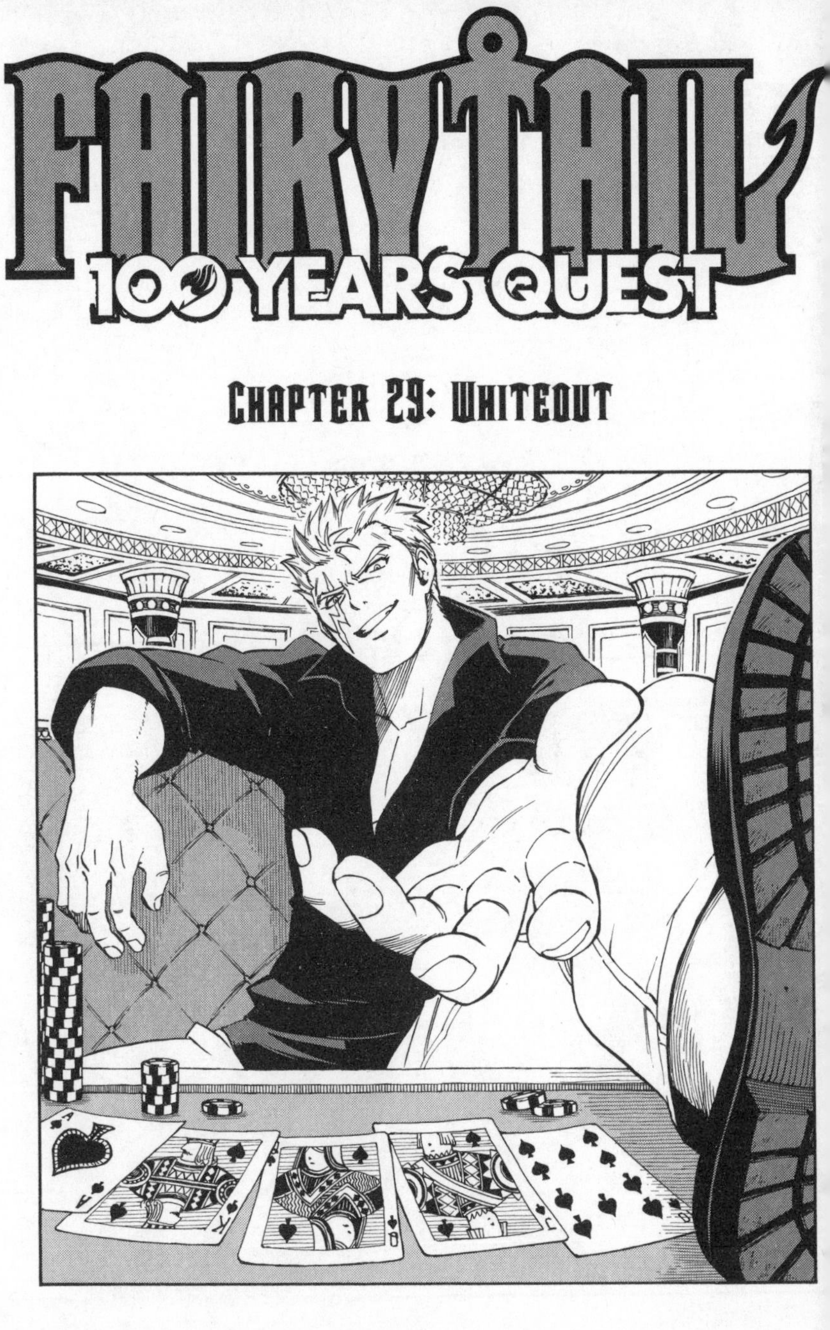

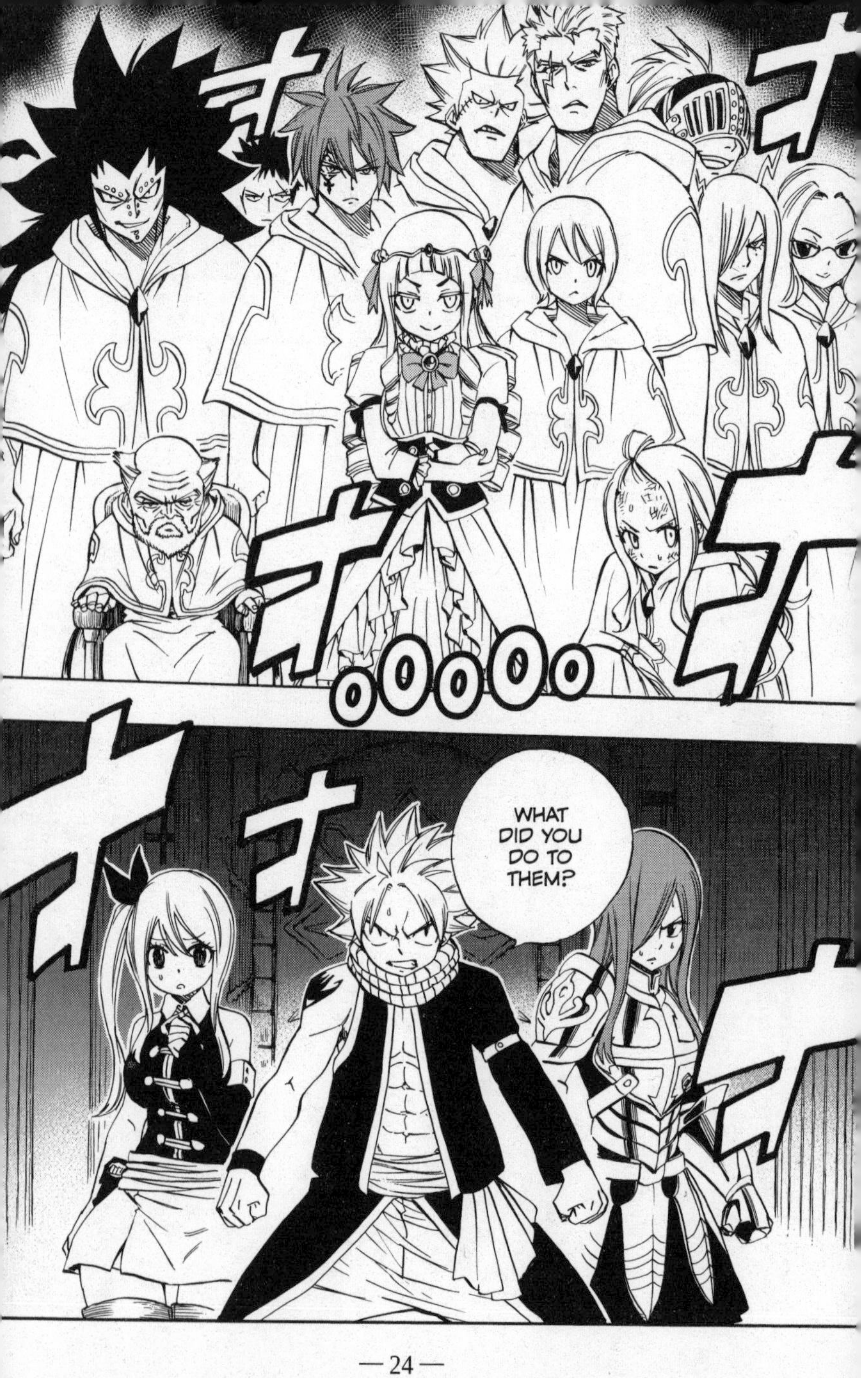
OOOOO
WHAT DID YOU DO TO THEM?

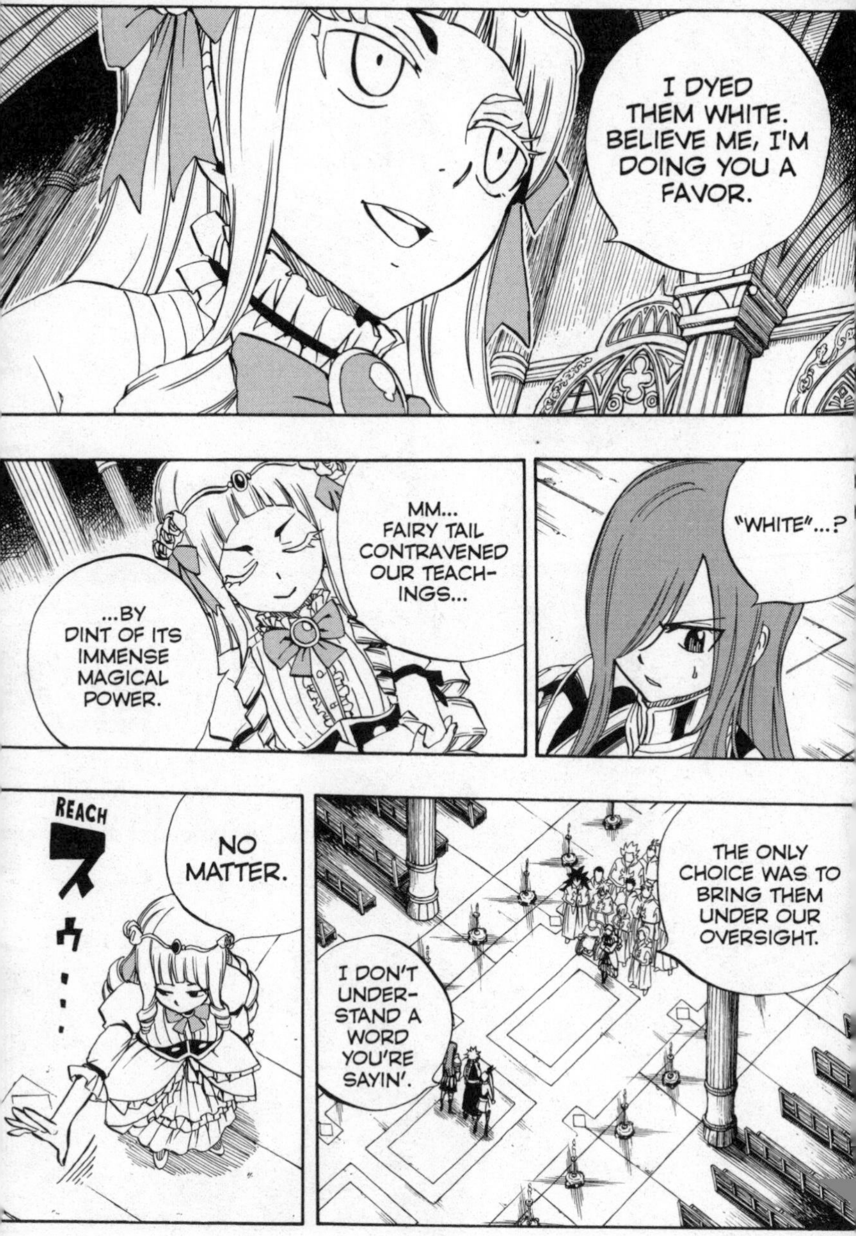
I DYED THEM WHITE. BELIEVE ME, I'M DOING YOU A FAVOR.
"WHITE"...?
MM... FAIRY TAIL CONTRAVENED OUR TEACHINGS...
...BY DINT OF ITS IMMENSE MAGICAL POWER.
THE ONLY CHOICE WAS TO BRING THEM UNDER OUR OVERSIGHT.
I DON'T UNDERSTAND A WORD YOU'RE SAYIN'.
NO MATTER.
REACH
スウ...

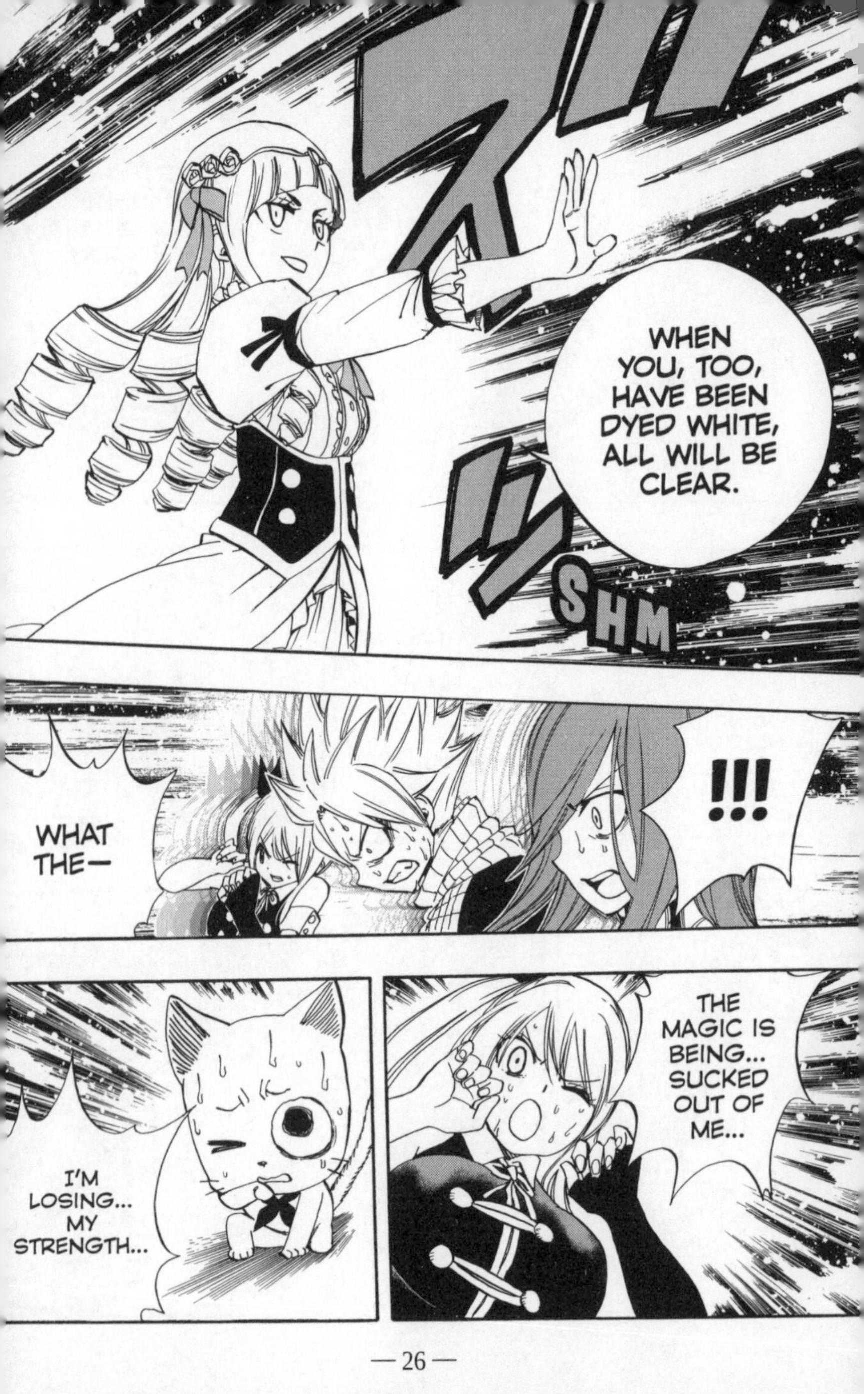
WHEN YOU, TOO, HAVE BEEN DYED WHITE, ALL WILL BE CLEAR.
SHM
!!!
WHAT THE—
THE MAGIC IS BEING... SUCKED OUT OF ME...
I'M LOSING... MY STRENGTH...

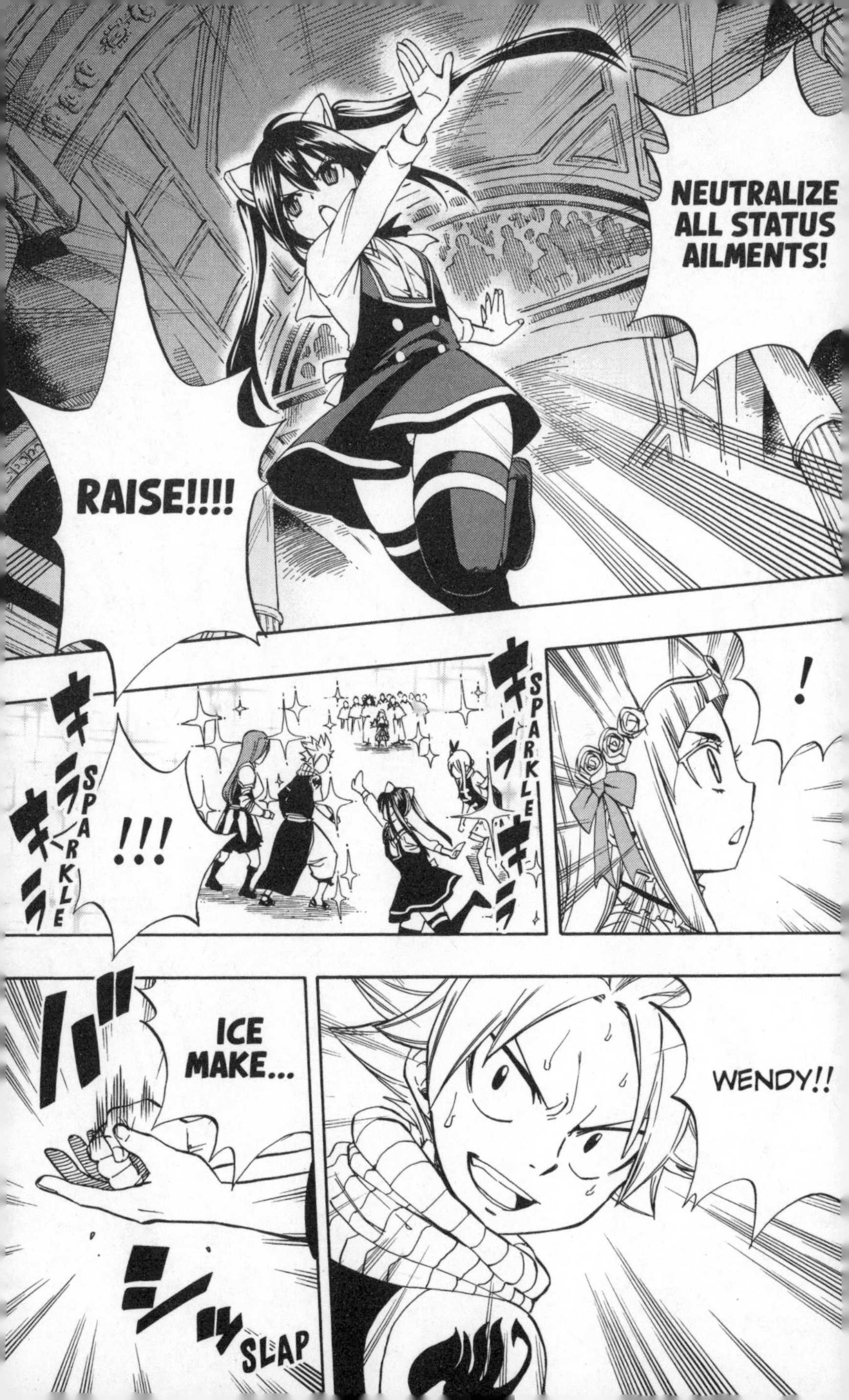
NEUTRALIZE ALL STATUS AILMENTS!
RAISE!!!!
!
キラキラ
SPARKLE
!!!
キラキラ
SPARKLE
WENDY!!
バ
ICE MAKE...
ビシッ
SLAP

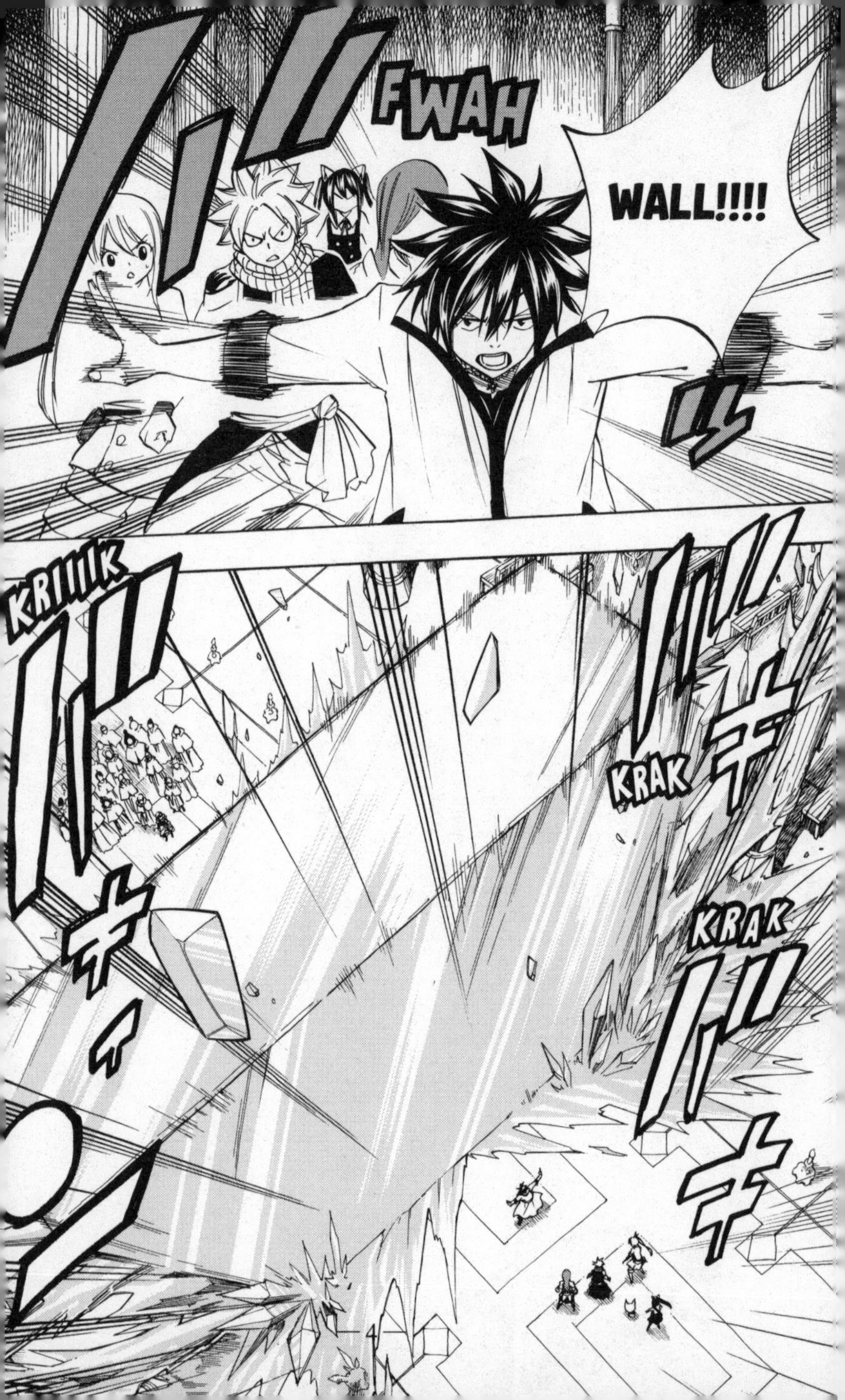
WALL!!!!
FWAH
KRAK
KRAK
KRIIIIK

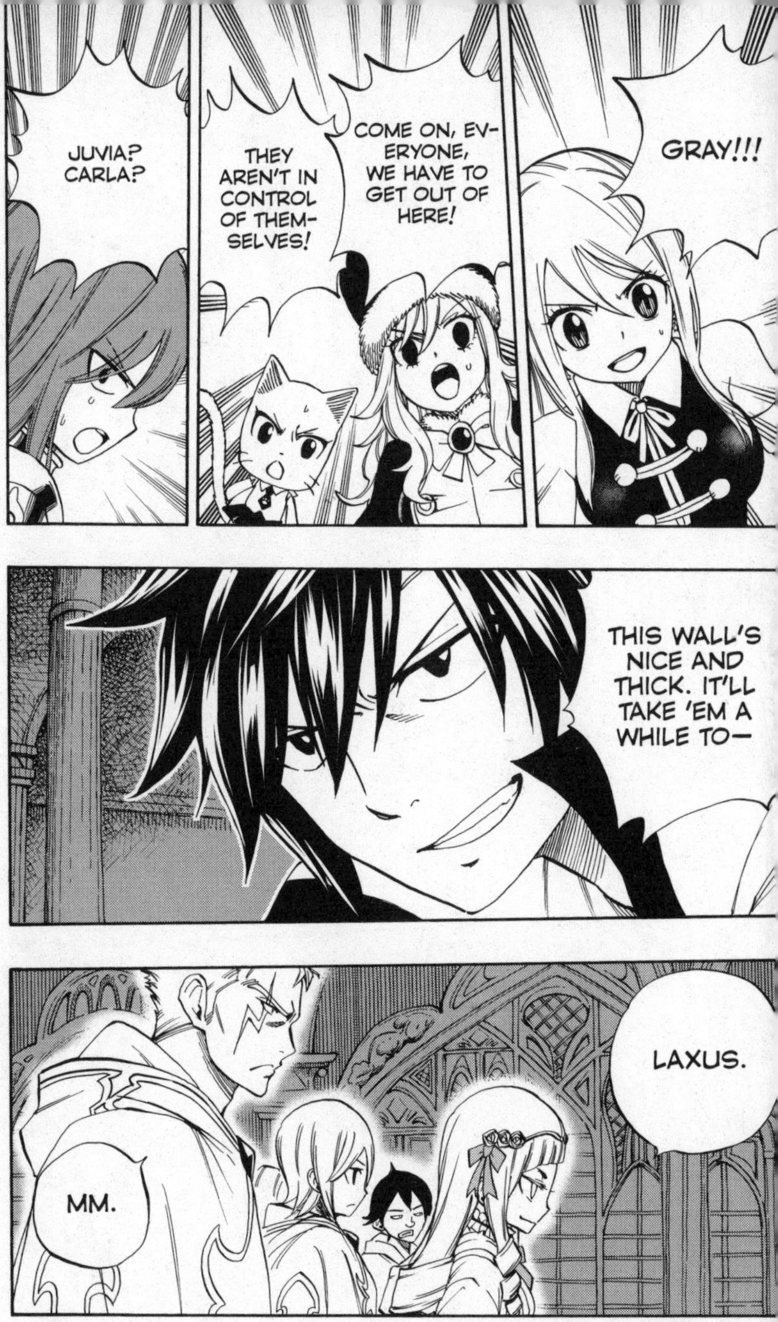
GRAY!!!
COME ON, EV-ERYONE, WE HAVE TO GET OUT OF HERE!
THEY AREN'T IN CONTROL OF THEM-SELVES!
JUVIA? CARLA?
THIS WALL'S NICE AND THICK. IT'LL TAKE 'EM A WHILE TO—
LAXUS.
MM.

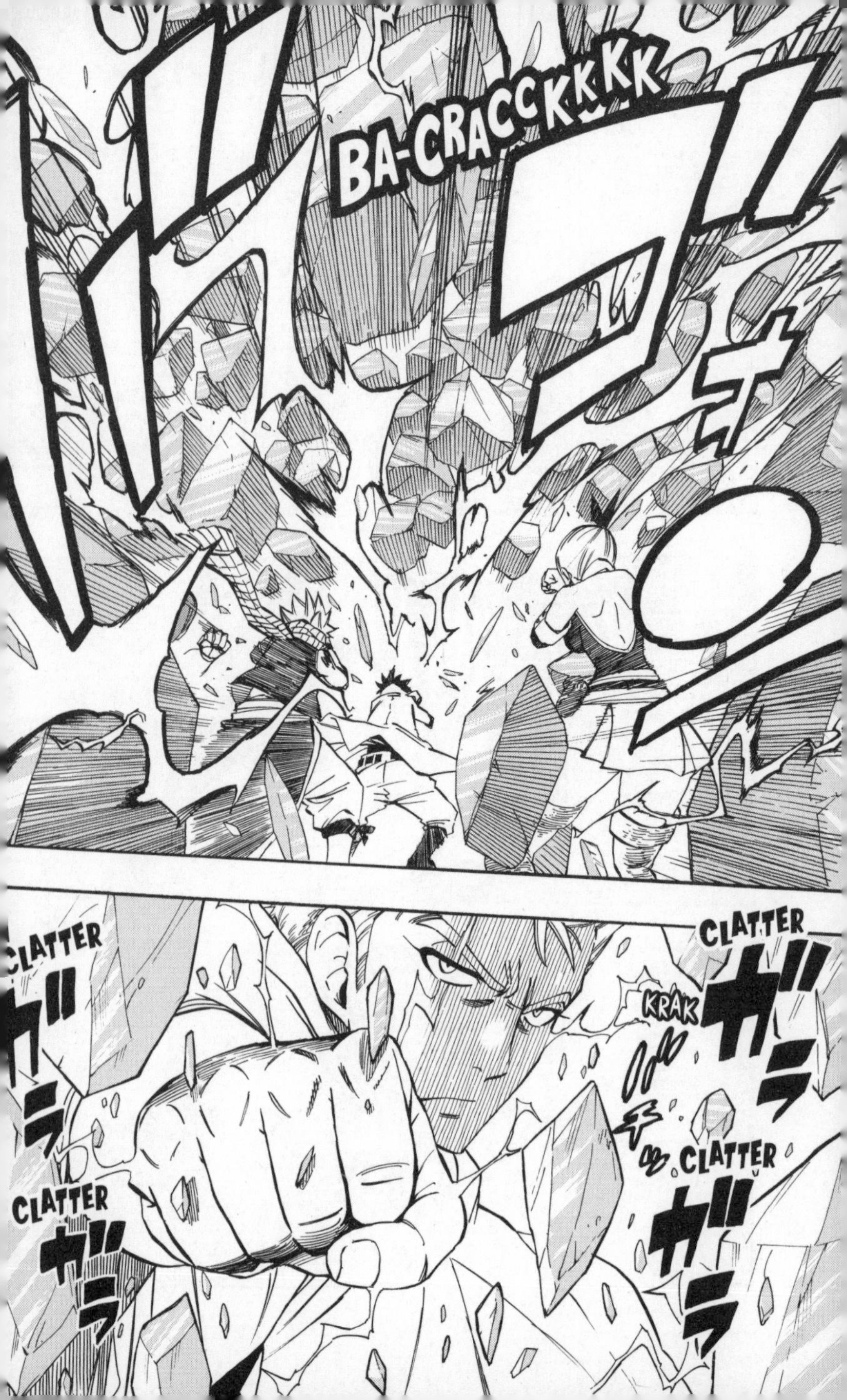
BA-CRACCKKKK
CLATTER
KRAK
CLATTER
CLATTER
CLATTER

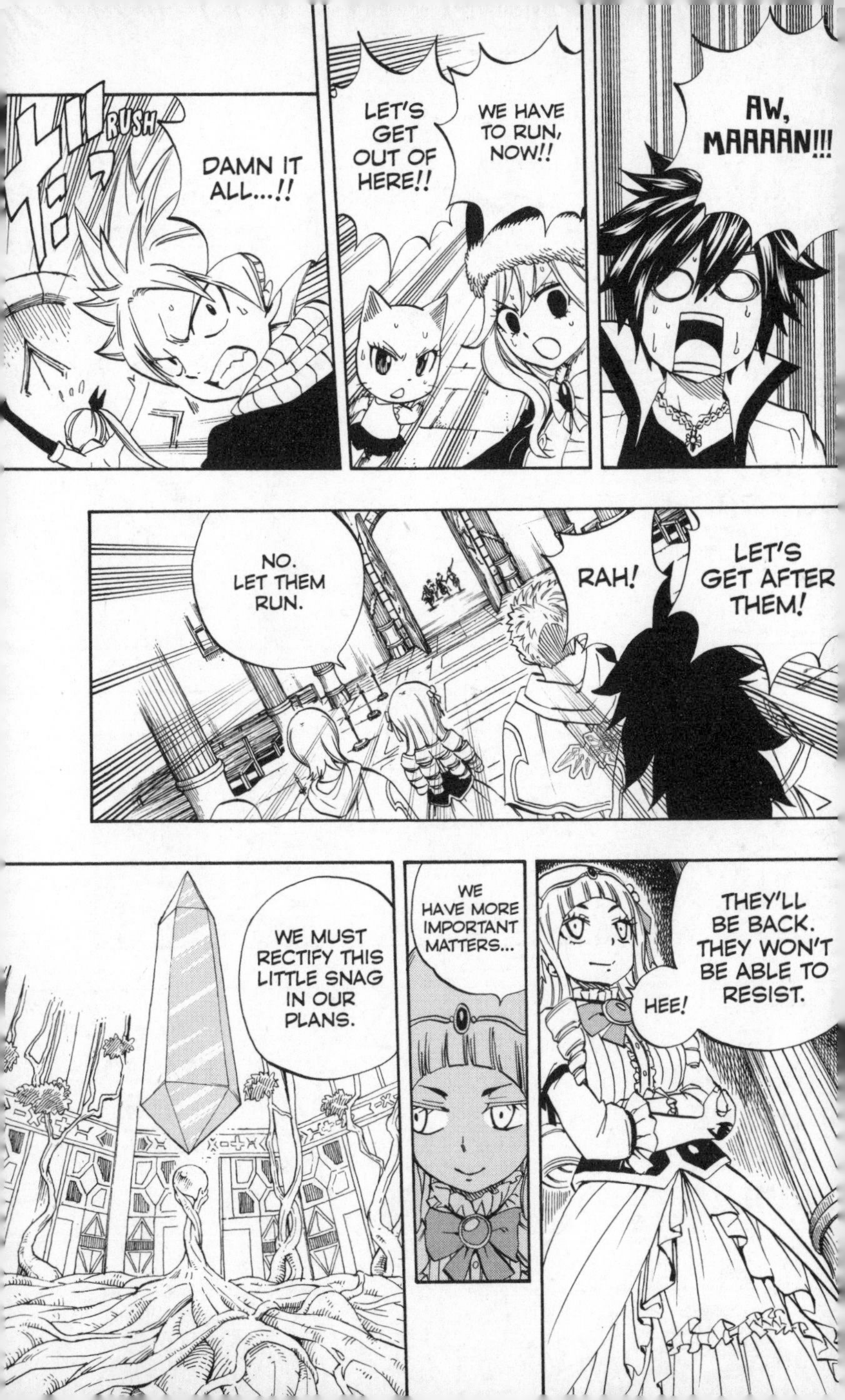
AW, MAAAAN!!!
WE HAVE TO RUN, NOW!!
LET'S GET OUT OF HERE!!
RUSH
DAMN IT ALL...!!
LET'S GET AFTER THEM!
RAH!
NO. LET THEM RUN.
THEY'LL BE BACK. THEY WON'T BE ABLE TO RESIST.
HEE!
WE HAVE MORE IMPORTANT MATTERS...
WE MUST RECTIFY THIS LITTLE SNAG IN OUR PLANS.

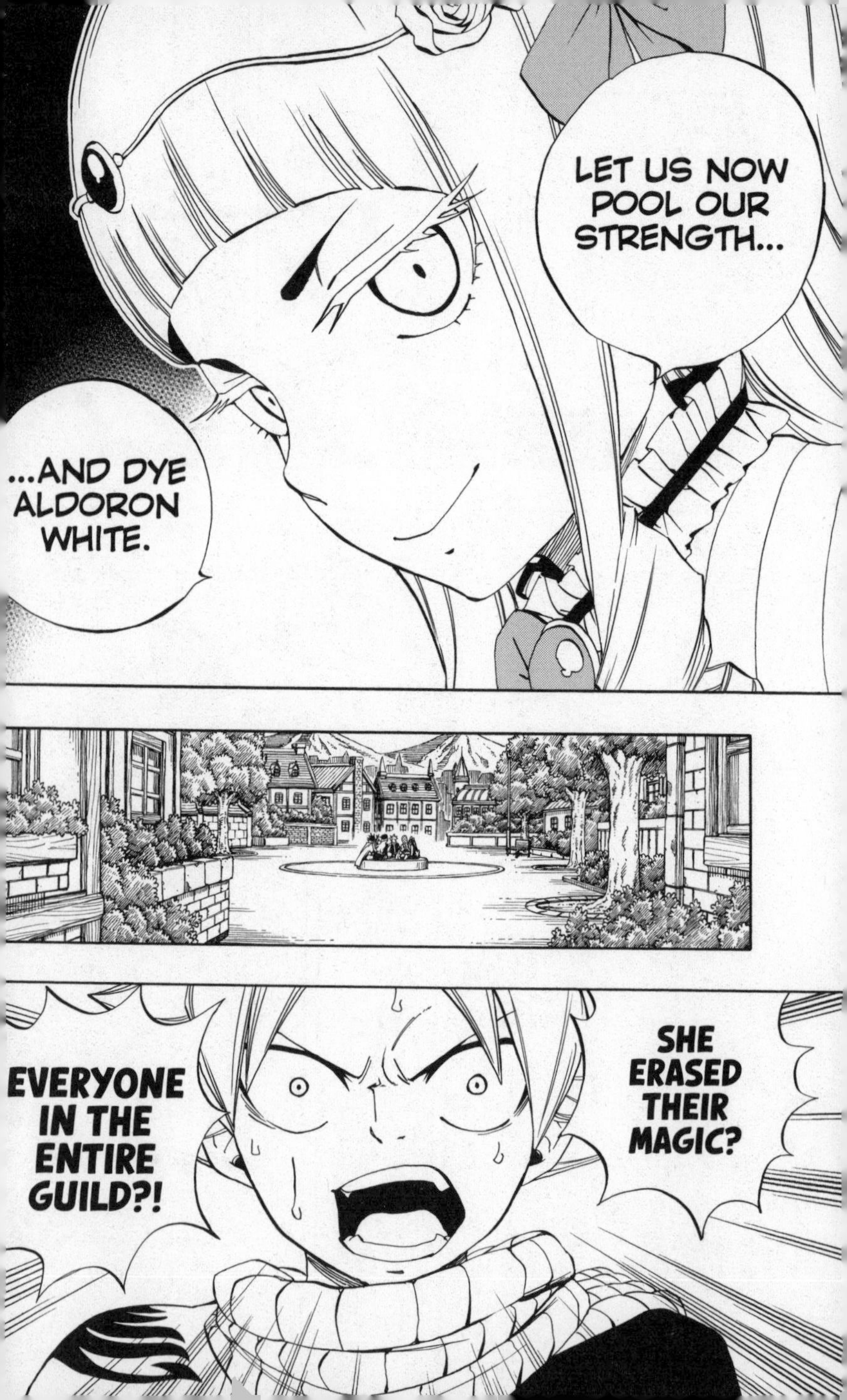
LET US NOW POOL OUR STRENGTH...
...AND DYE ALDORON WHITE.
SHE ERASED THEIR MAGIC?
EVERYONE IN THE ENTIRE GUILD?!

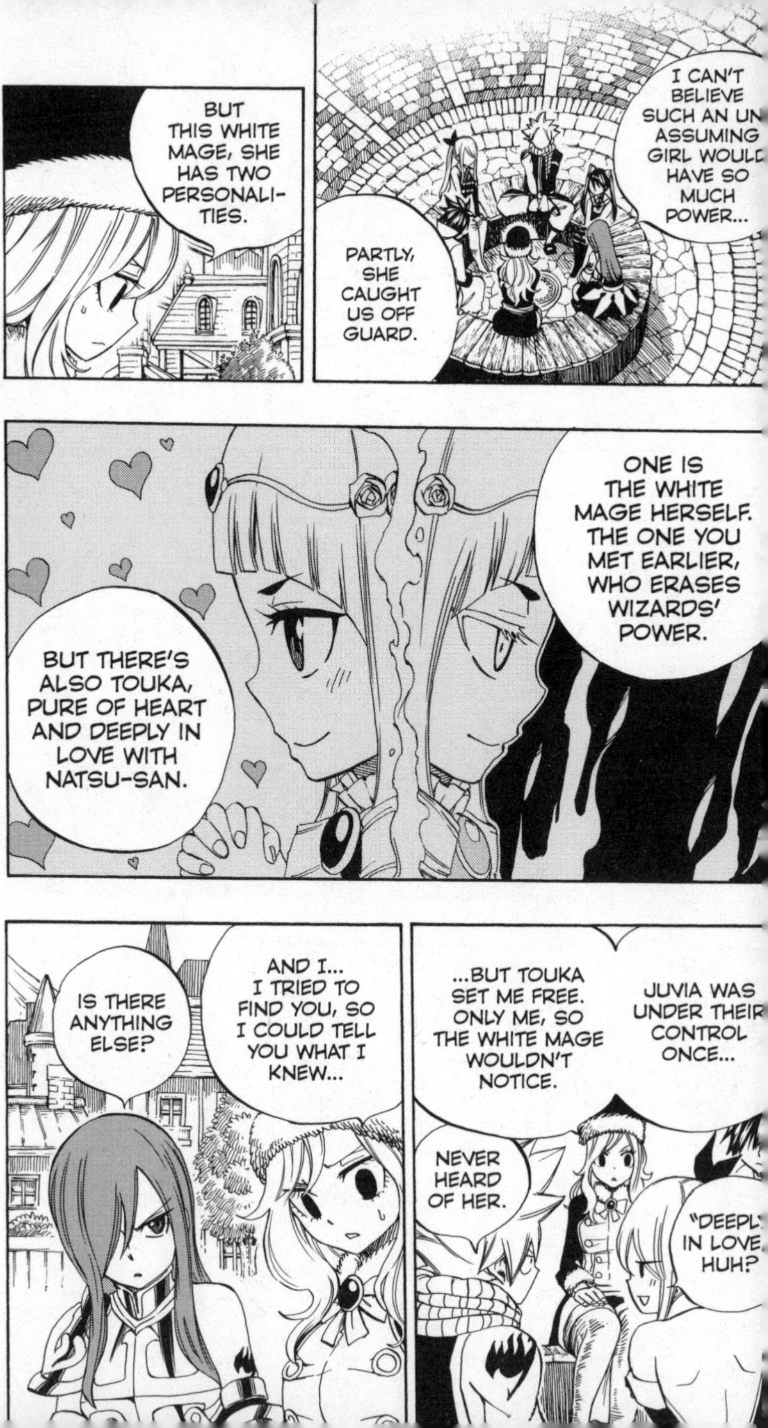
I CAN'T BELIEVE SUCH AN UN-ASSUMING GIRL WOULD HAVE SO MUCH POWER...
PARTLY, SHE CAUGHT US OFF GUARD.
BUT THIS WHITE MAGE, SHE HAS TWO PERSONALI-TIES.
ONE IS THE WHITE MAGE HERSELF. THE ONE YOU MET EARLIER, WHO ERASES WIZARDS' POWER.
BUT THERE'S ALSO TOUKA, PURE OF HEART AND DEEPLY IN LOVE WITH NATSU-SAN.
JUVIA WAS UNDER THEIR CONTROL ONCE...
...BUT TOUKA SET ME FREE. ONLY ME, SO THE WHITE MAGE WOULDN'T NOTICE.
"DEEPLY IN LOVE," HUH?
NEVER HEARD OF HER.
AND I... I TRIED TO FIND YOU, SO I COULD TELL YOU WHAT I KNEW...
IS THERE ANYTHING ELSE?

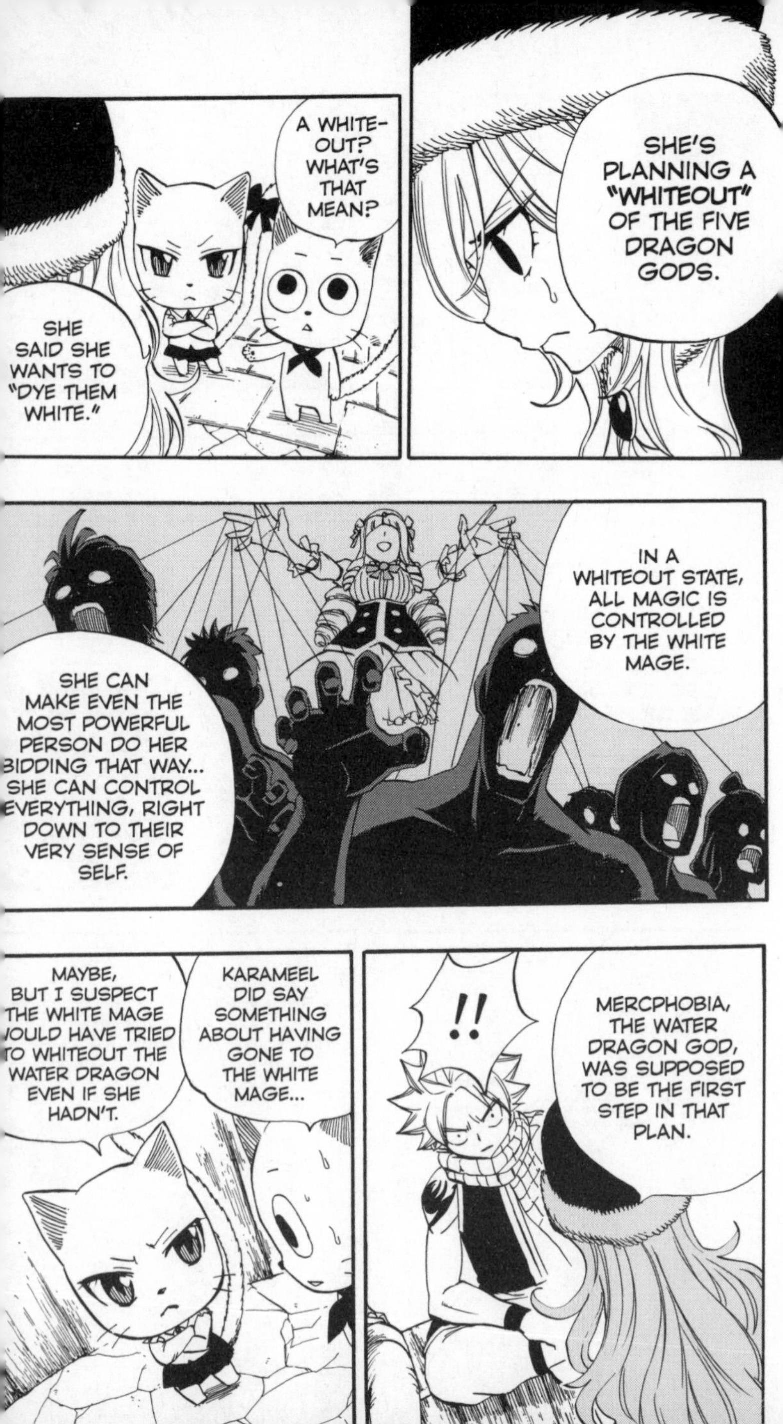

SHE'S PLANNING A "WHITEOUT" OF THE FIVE DRAGON GODS.
A WHITE-OUT? WHAT'S THAT MEAN?
SHE SAID SHE WANTS TO "DYE THEM WHITE."
IN A WHITEOUT STATE, ALL MAGIC IS CONTROLLED BY THE WHITE MAGE.
SHE CAN MAKE EVEN THE MOST POWERFUL PERSON DO HER BIDDING THAT WAY... SHE CAN CONTROL EVERYTHING, RIGHT DOWN TO THEIR VERY SENSE OF SELF.
MERCPHOBIA, THE WATER DRAGON GOD, WAS SUPPOSED TO BE THE FIRST STEP IN THAT PLAN.
!!
KARAMEEL DID SAY SOMETHING ABOUT HAVING GONE TO THE WHITE MAGE...
MAYBE, BUT I SUSPECT THE WHITE MAGE WOULD HAVE TRIED TO WHITEOUT THE WATER DRAGON EVEN IF SHE HADN'T.

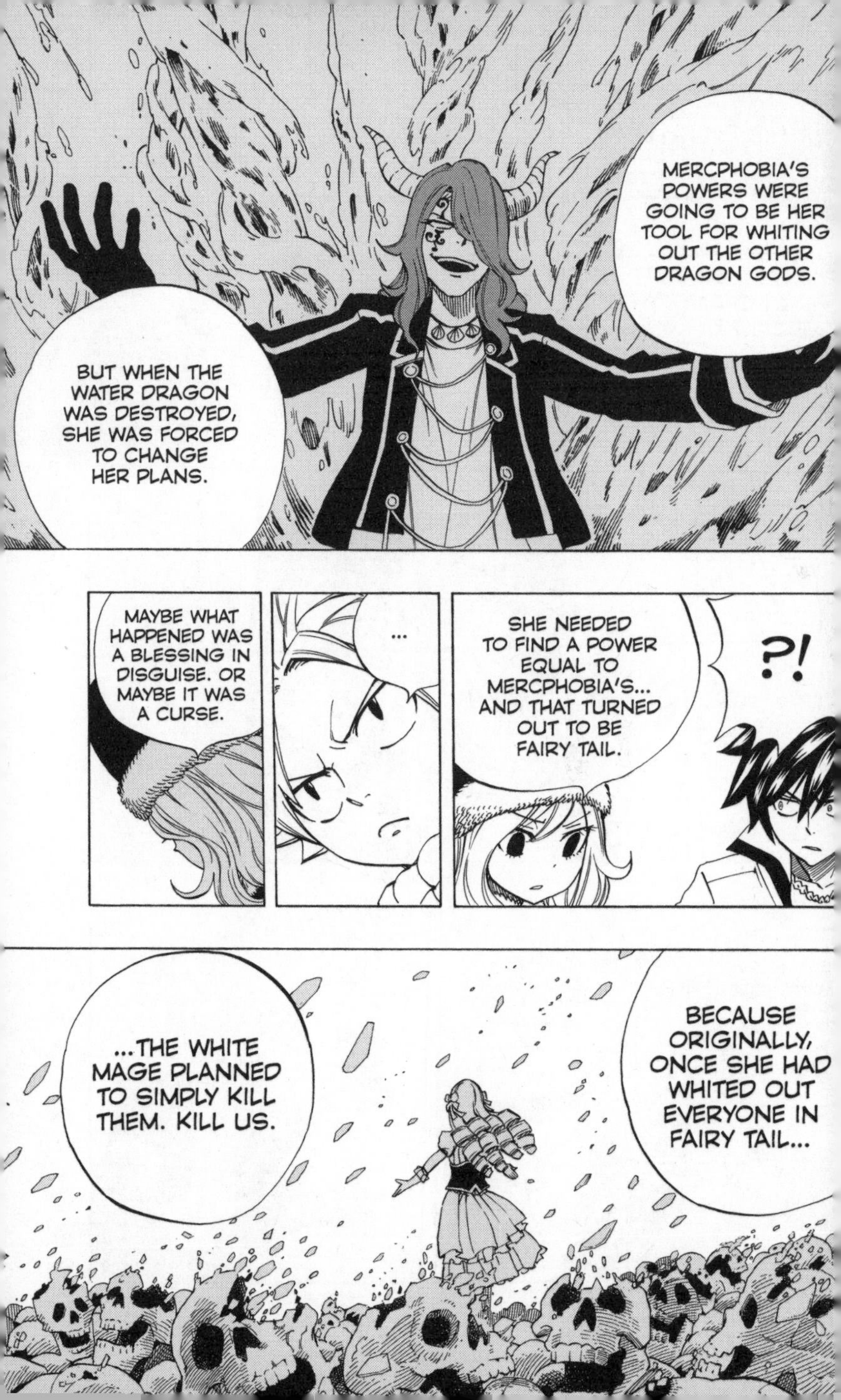
MERCPHOBIA'S POWERS WERE GOING TO BE HER TOOL FOR WHITING OUT THE OTHER DRAGON GODS.
BUT WHEN THE WATER DRAGON WAS DESTROYED, SHE WAS FORCED TO CHANGE HER PLANS.
?!
SHE NEEDED TO FIND A POWER EQUAL TO MERCPHOBIA'S... AND THAT TURNED OUT TO BE FAIRY TAIL.
...
MAYBE WHAT HAPPENED WAS A BLESSING IN DISGUISE. OR MAYBE IT WAS A CURSE.
BECAUSE ORIGINALLY, ONCE SHE HAD WHITED OUT EVERYONE IN FAIRY TAIL...
...THE WHITE MAGE PLANNED TO SIMPLY KILL THEM. KILL US.

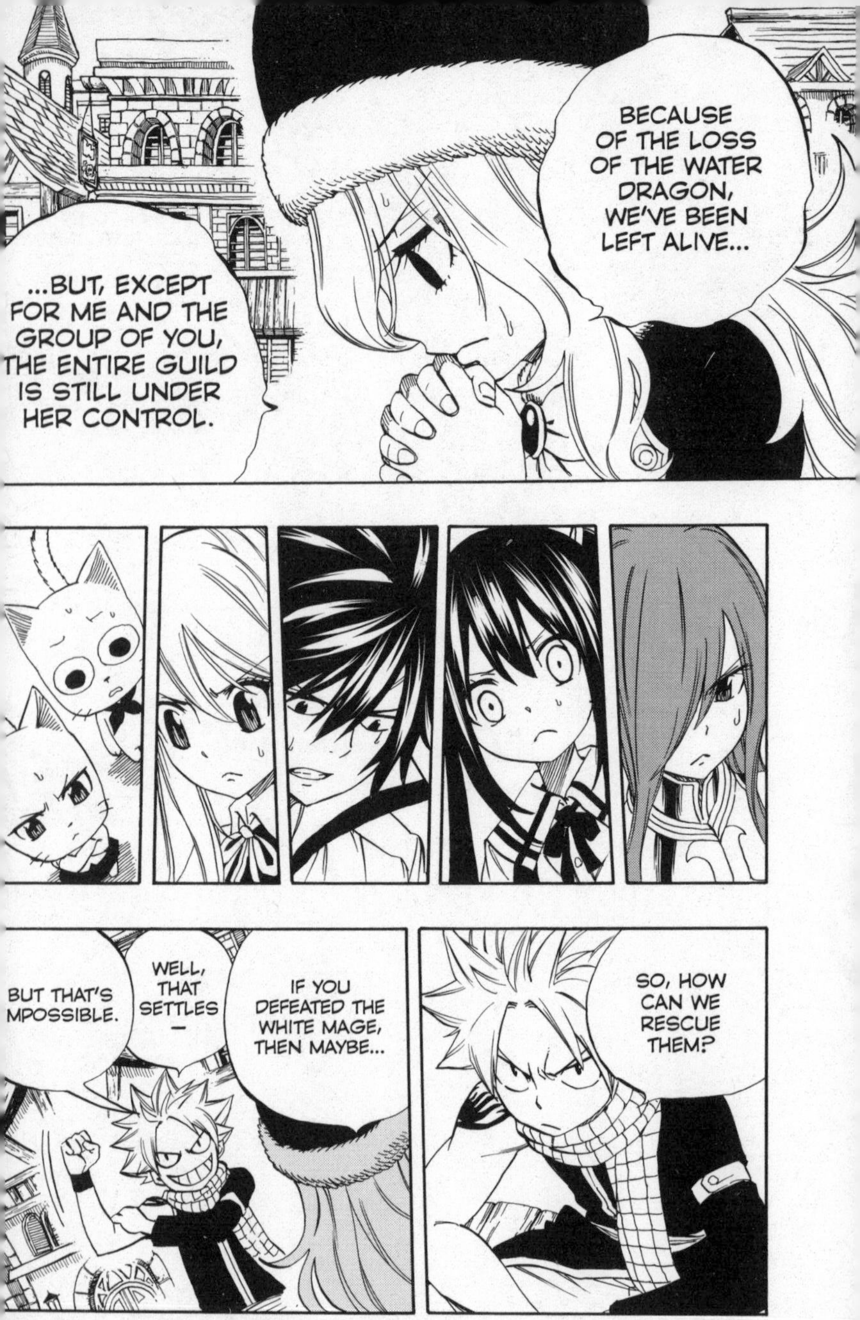
BECAUSE OF THE LOSS OF THE WATER DRAGON, WE'VE BEEN LEFT ALIVE...
...BUT, EXCEPT FOR ME AND THE GROUP OF YOU, THE ENTIRE GUILD IS STILL UNDER HER CONTROL.
SO, HOW CAN WE RESCUE THEM?
IF YOU DEFEATED THE WHITE MAGE, THEN MAYBE...
WELL, THAT SETTLES —
BUT THAT'S MPOSSIBLE.

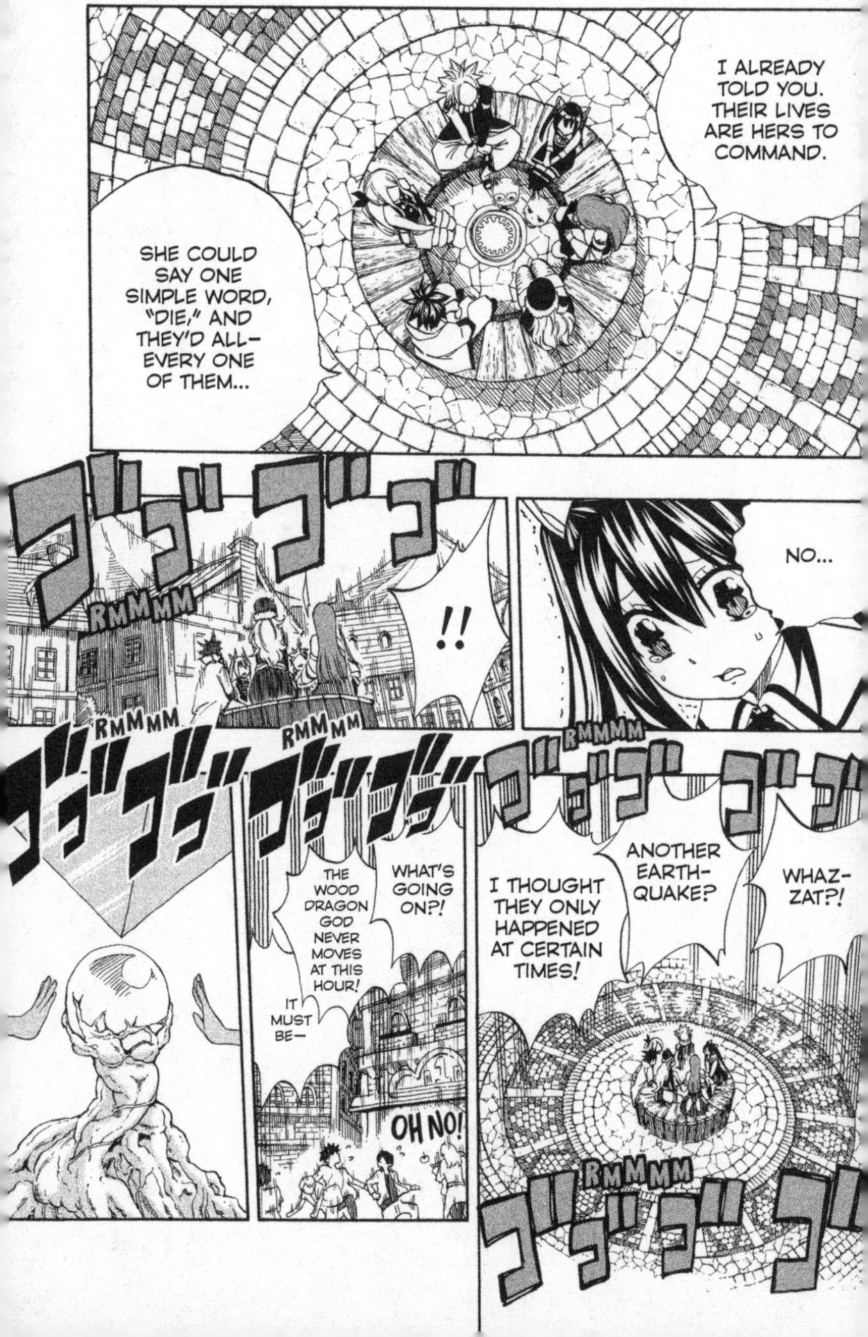
I ALREADY TOLD YOU. THEIR LIVES ARE HERS TO COMMAND.
SHE COULD SAY ONE SIMPLE WORD, "DIE," AND THEY'D ALL— EVERY ONE OF THEM...
NO...
RMMMM
RMMMM
!!
RMMMM
WHAZ-ZAT?!
ANOTHER EARTH-QUAKE?
I THOUGHT THEY ONLY HAPPENED AT CERTAIN TIMES!
RMMMM
RMMMM
WHAT'S GOING ON?!
THE WOOD DRAGON GOD NEVER MOVES AT THIS HOUR!
IT MUST BE—
OH NO!
RMMMM

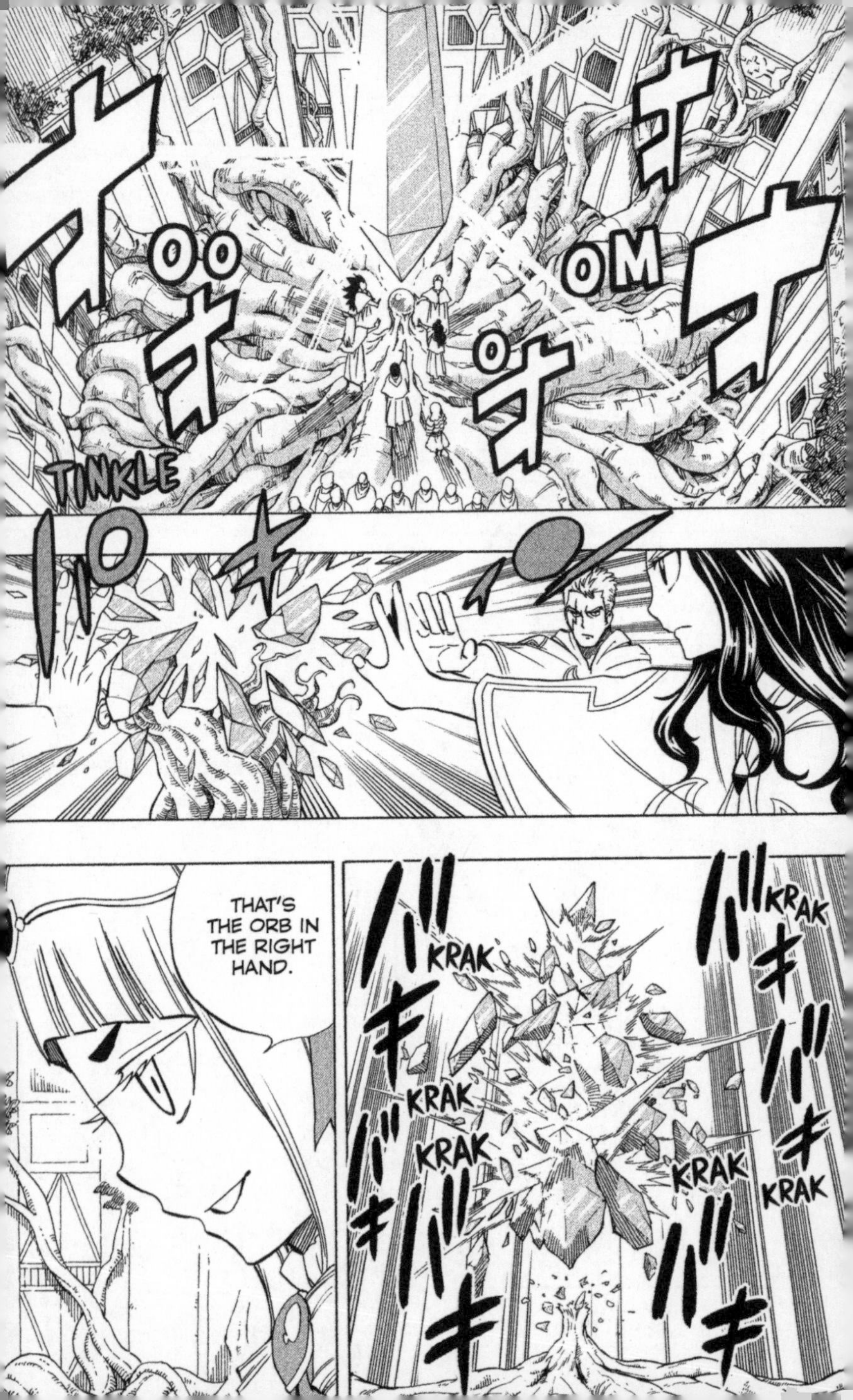
OO
OM
TINKLE
KRAK
KRAK
KRAK
KRAK
KRAK
KRAK
THAT'S THE ORB IN THE RIGHT HAND.

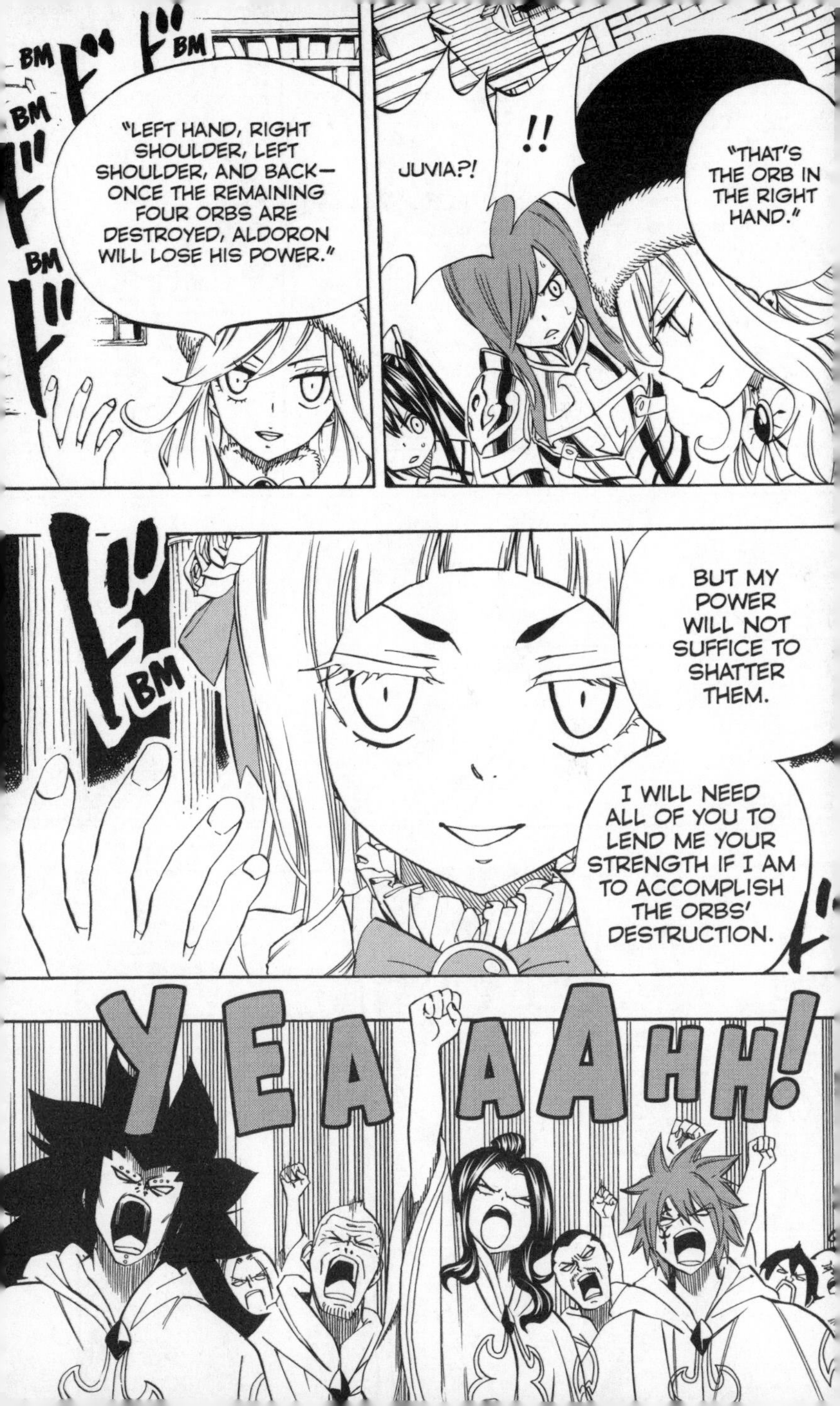
"THAT'S THE ORB IN THE RIGHT HAND."
!!
JUVIA?!
BM
BM
BM
BM
"LEFT HAND, RIGHT SHOULDER, LEFT SHOULDER, AND BACK—ONCE THE REMAINING FOUR ORBS ARE DESTROYED, ALDORON WILL LOSE HIS POWER."
BUT MY POWER WILL NOT SUFFICE TO SHATTER THEM.
BM
I WILL NEED ALL OF YOU TO LEND ME YOUR STRENGTH IF I AM TO ACCOMPLISH THE ORBS' DESTRUCTION.
YEAAAHH!

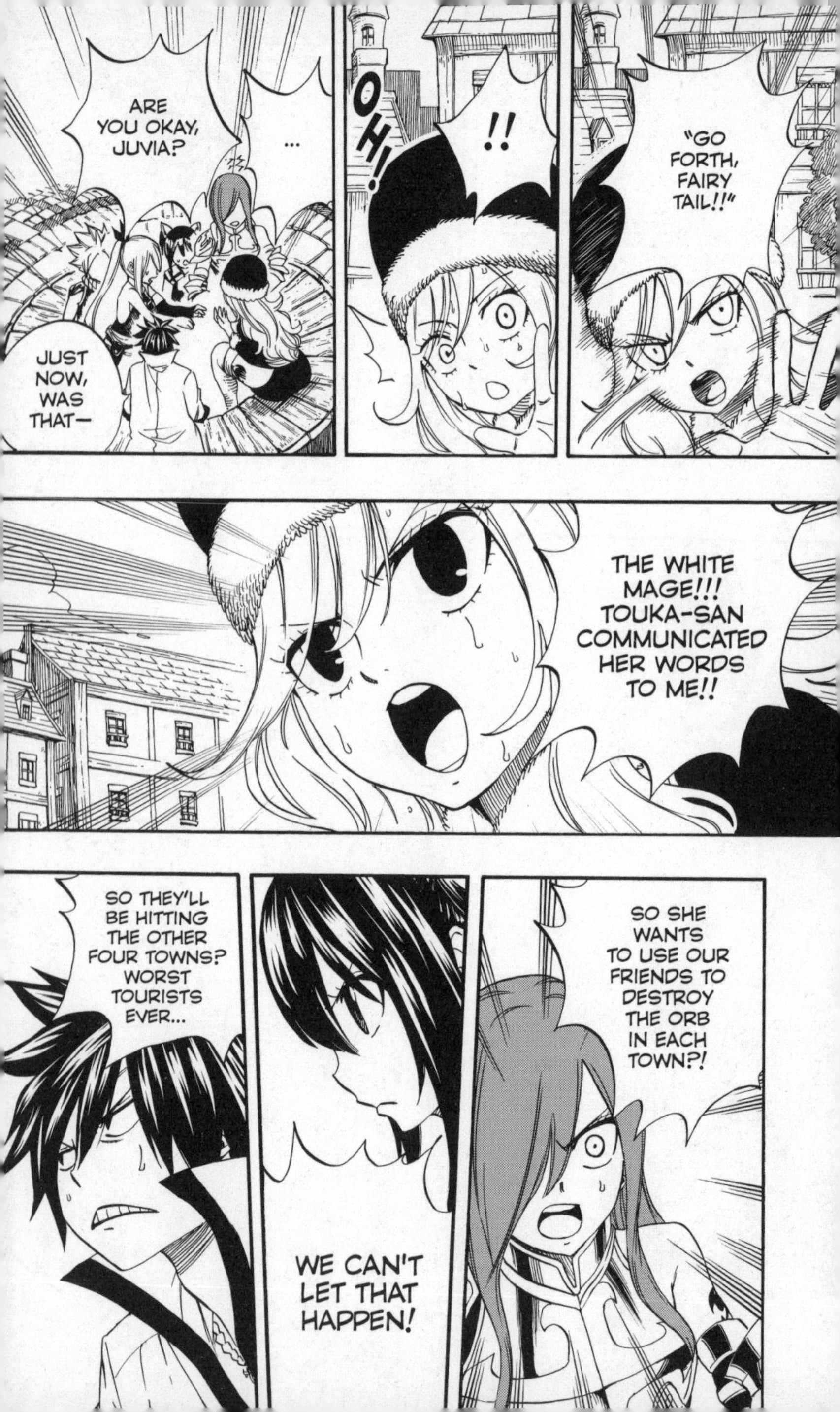
"GO FORTH, FAIRY TAIL!!"
OH!
!!
ARE YOU OKAY, JUVIA?
...
JUST NOW, WAS THAT—
THE WHITE MAGE!!! TOUKA-SAN COMMUNICATED HER WORDS TO ME!!
SO SHE WANTS TO USE OUR FRIENDS TO DESTROY THE ORB IN EACH TOWN?!
WE CAN'T LET THAT HAPPEN!
SO THEY'LL BE HITTING THE OTHER FOUR TOWNS? WORST TOURISTS EVER...

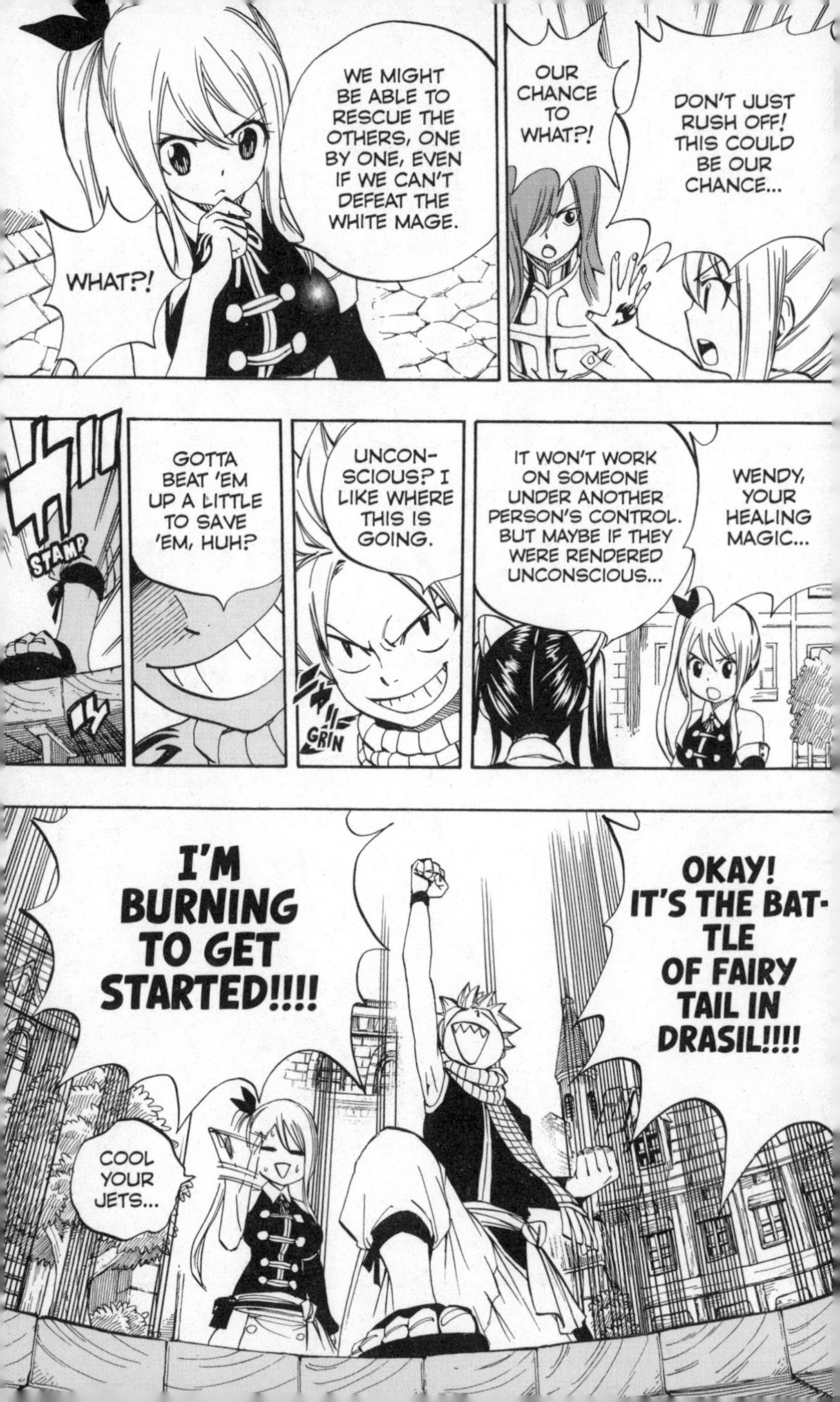
DON'T JUST RUSH OFF! THIS COULD BE OUR CHANCE...
OUR CHANCE TO WHAT?!
WE MIGHT BE ABLE TO RESCUE THE OTHERS, ONE BY ONE, EVEN IF WE CAN'T DEFEAT THE WHITE MAGE.
WHAT?!
WENDY, YOUR HEALING MAGIC...
IT WON'T WORK ON SOMEONE UNDER ANOTHER PERSON'S CONTROL. BUT MAYBE IF THEY WERE RENDERED UNCONSCIOUS...
UNCON-SCIOUS? I LIKE WHERE THIS IS GOING.
GRIN
GOTTA BEAT 'EM UP A LITTLE TO SAVE 'EM, HUH?
STAMP
OKAY! IT'S THE BAT-TLE OF FAIRY TAIL IN DRASIL!!!!
I'M BURNING TO GET STARTED!!!!
COOL YOUR JETS...

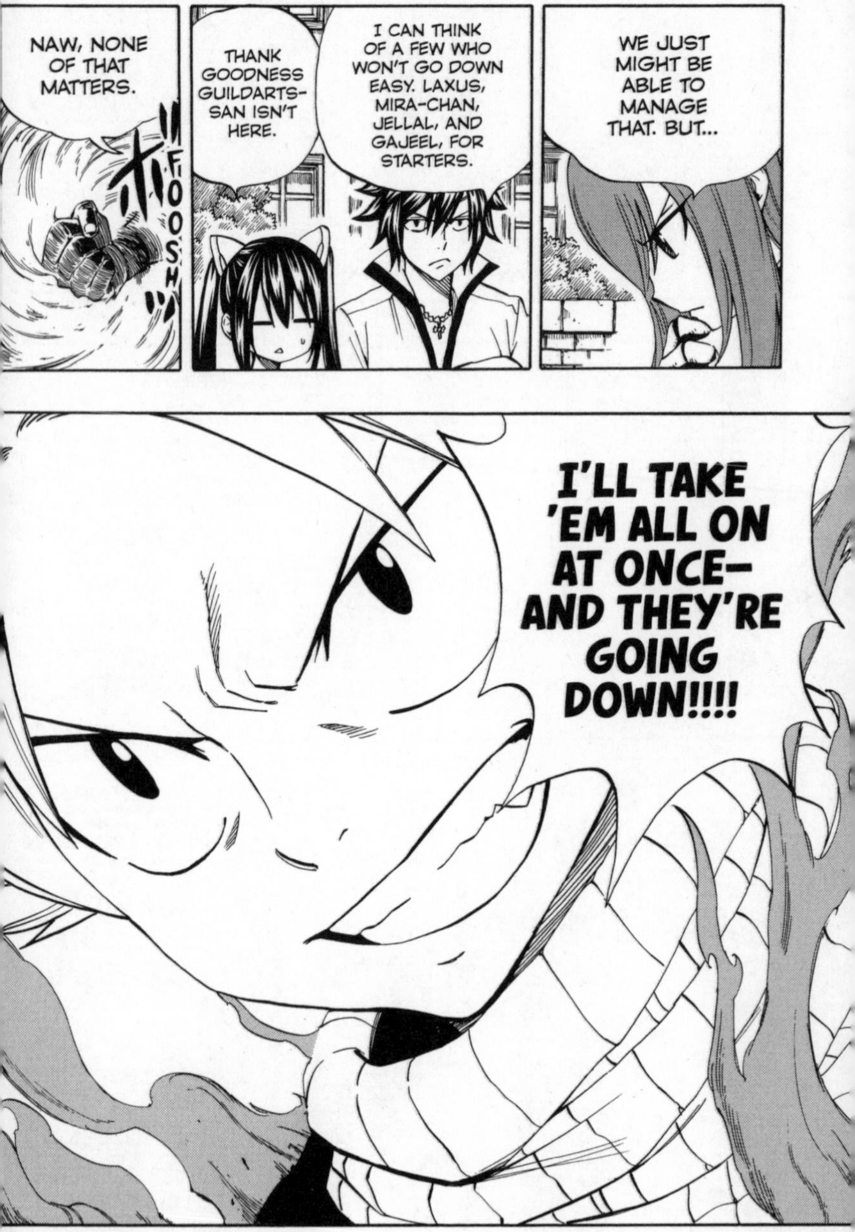
WE JUST MIGHT BE ABLE TO MANAGE THAT. BUT...
I CAN THINK OF A FEW WHO WON'T GO DOWN EASY. LAXUS, MIRA-CHAN, JELLAL, AND GAJEEL, FOR STARTERS.
THANK GOODNESS GUILDARTS-SAN ISN'T HERE.
NAW, NONE OF THAT MATTERS.
FOOSH
I'LL TAKE 'EM ALL ON AT ONCE– AND THEY'RE GOING DOWN!!!!

FAIRY TAIL
100 YEARS QUEST

Chapter 38: Fun with Fighting

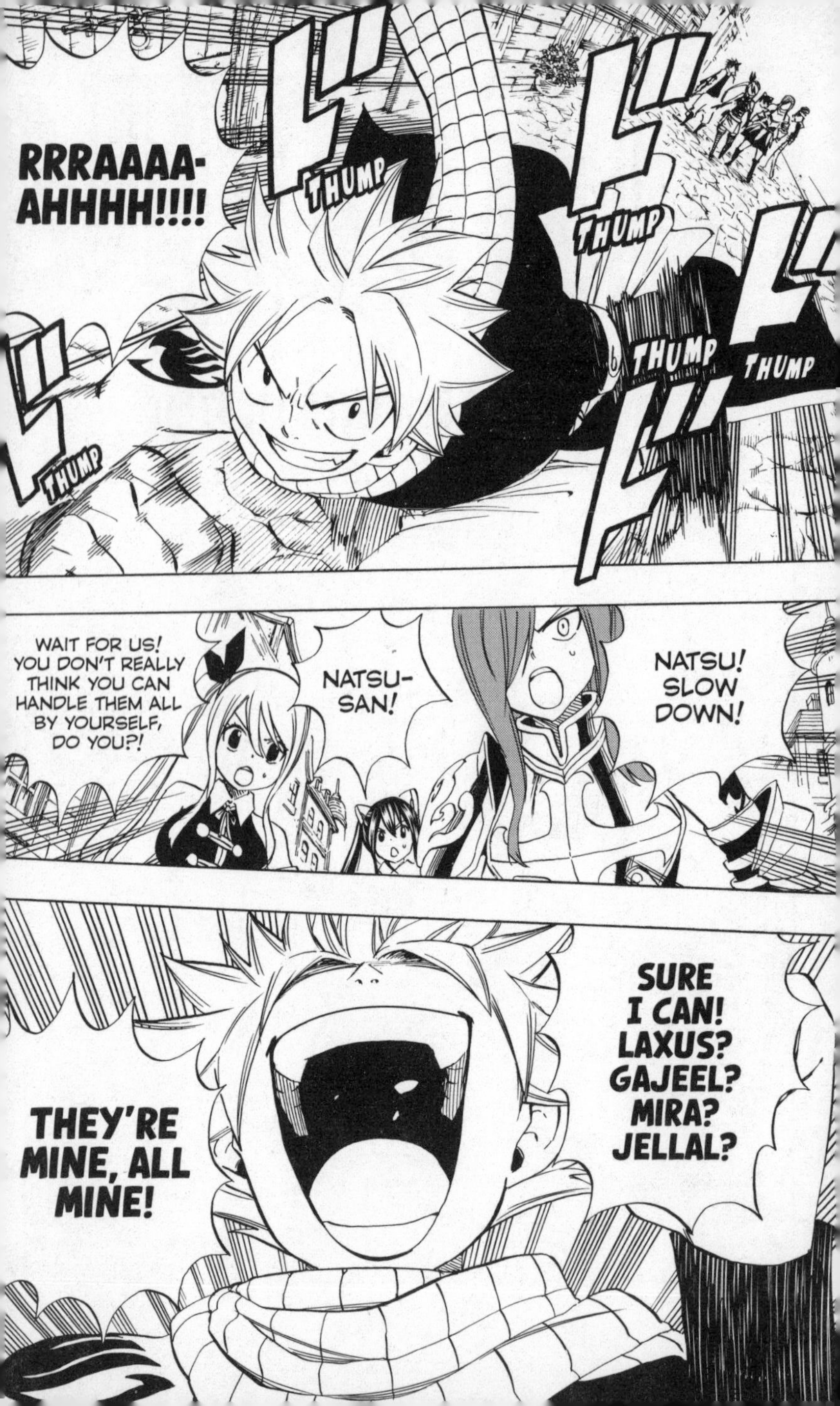
THUMP
THUMP
THUMP
THUMP
RRRAAAA-AHHHH!!!!
THUMP
NATSU! SLOW DOWN!
NATSU-SAN!
WAIT FOR US! YOU DON'T REALLY THINK YOU CAN HANDLE THEM ALL BY YOURSELF, DO YOU?!
SURE I CAN! LAXUS? GAJEEL? MIRA? JELLAL?
THEY'RE MINE, ALL MINE!

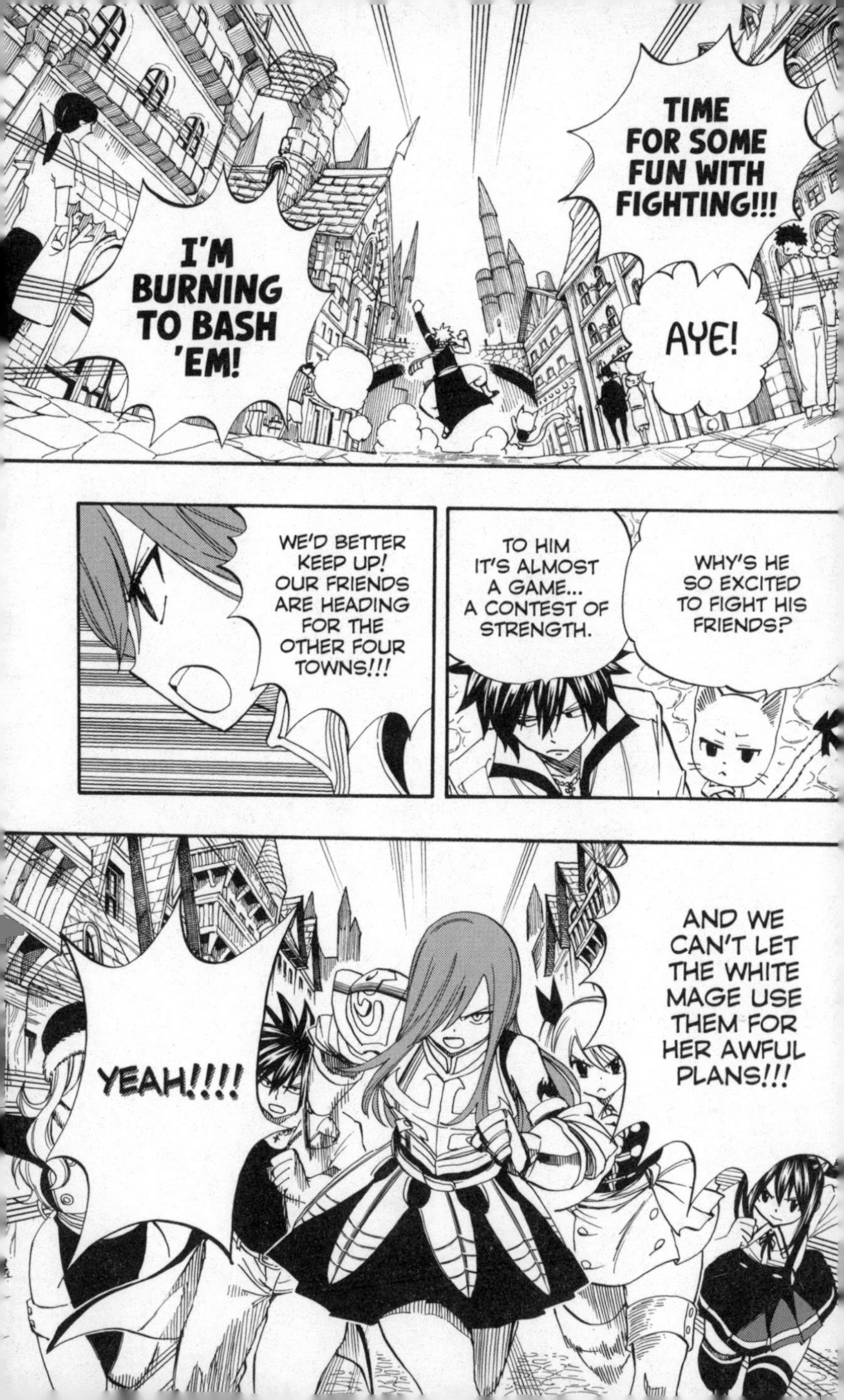
TIME FOR SOME FUN WITH FIGHTING!!!
I'M BURNING TO BASH 'EM!
AYE!
WHY'S HE SO EXCITED TO FIGHT HIS FRIENDS?
TO HIM IT'S ALMOST A GAME... A CONTEST OF STRENGTH.
WE'D BETTER KEEP UP! OUR FRIENDS ARE HEADING FOR THE OTHER FOUR TOWNS!!!
AND WE CAN'T LET THE WHITE MAGE USE THEM FOR HER AWFUL PLANS!!!
YEAH!!!!

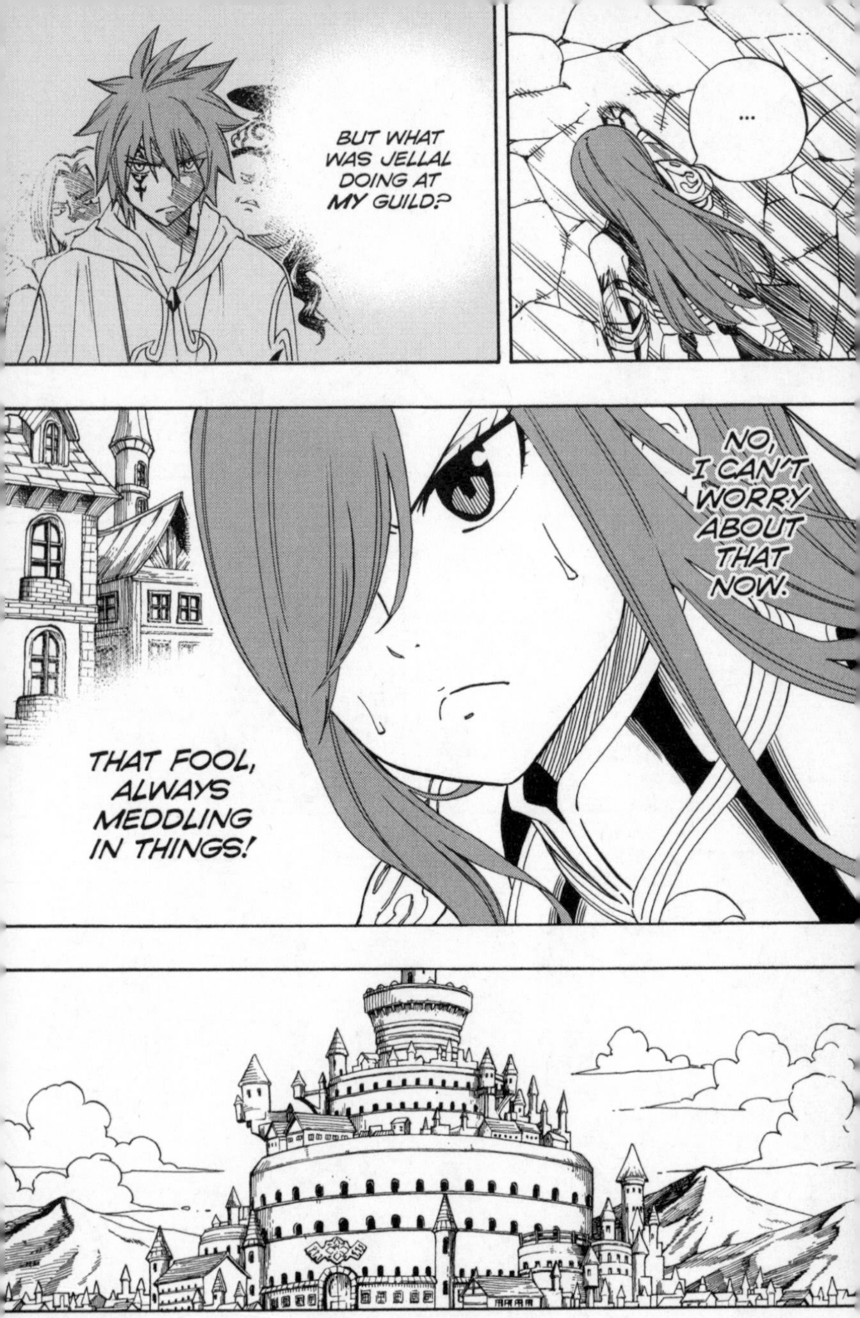
...
BUT WHAT WAS JELLAL DOING AT MY GUILD?
NO, I CAN'T WORRY ABOUT THAT NOW.
THAT FOOL, ALWAYS MEDDLING IN THINGS!

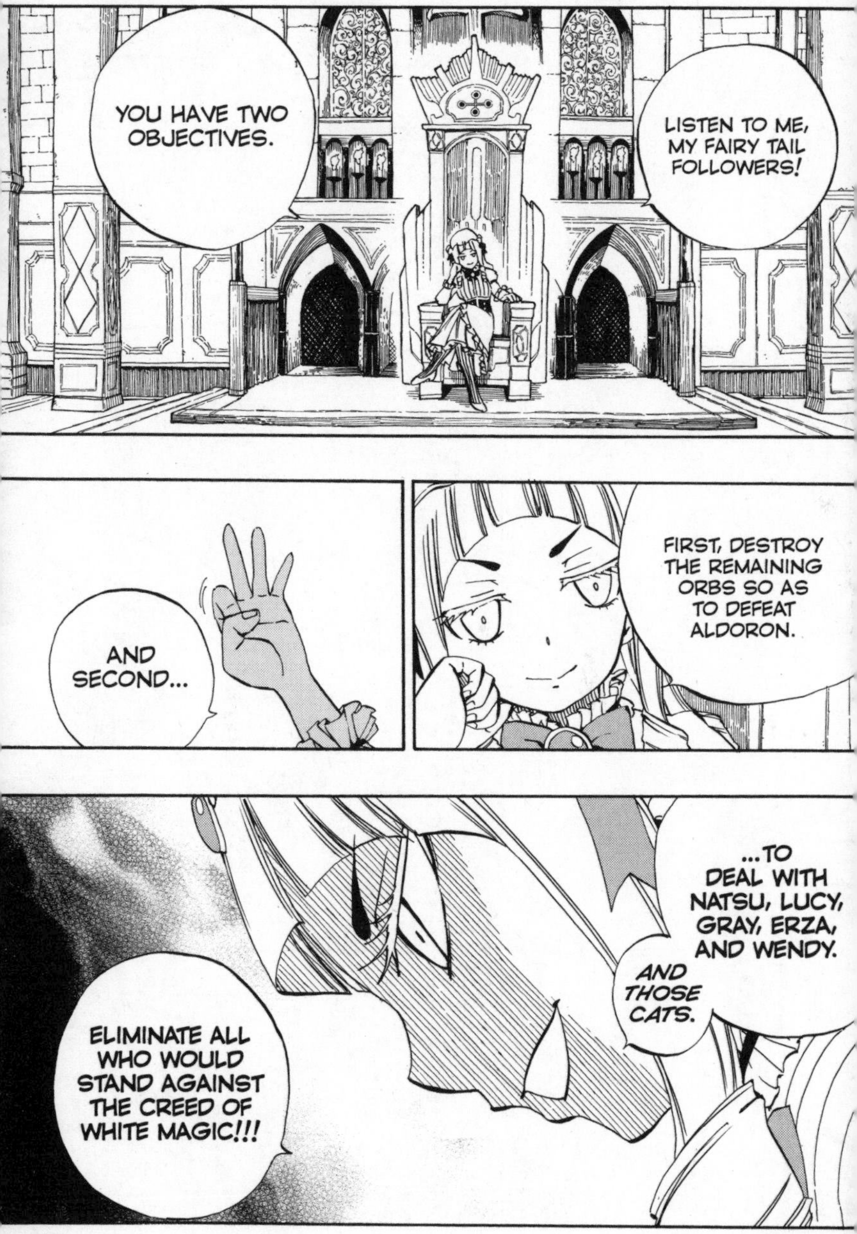
LISTEN TO ME, MY FAIRY TAIL FOLLOWERS!
YOU HAVE TWO OBJECTIVES.
FIRST, DESTROY THE REMAINING ORBS SO AS TO DEFEAT ALDORON.
AND SECOND...
...TO DEAL WITH NATSU, LUCY, GRAY, ERZA, AND WENDY.
AND THOSE CATS.
ELIMINATE ALL WHO WOULD STAND AGAINST THE CREED OF WHITE MAGIC!!!

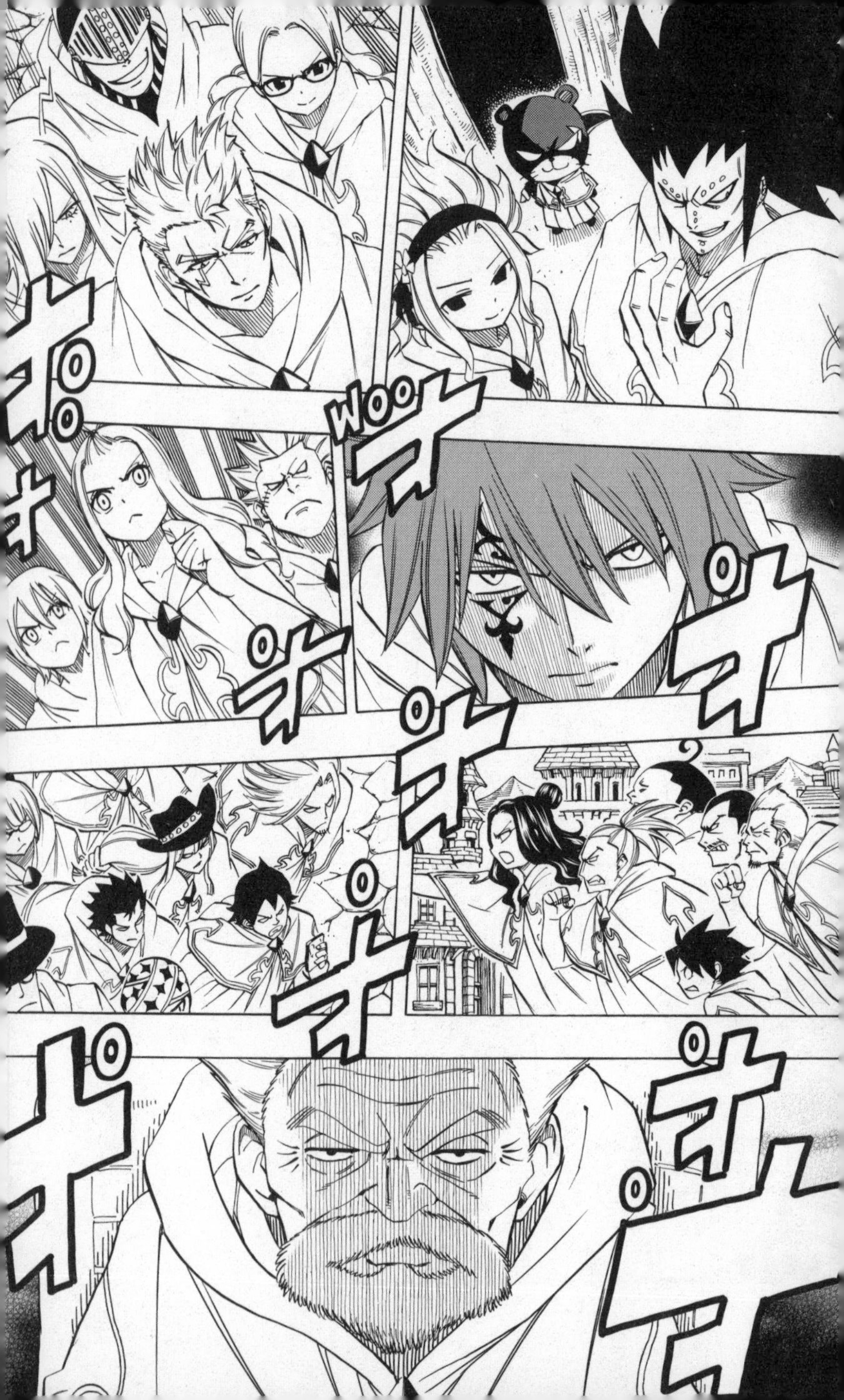
WOO

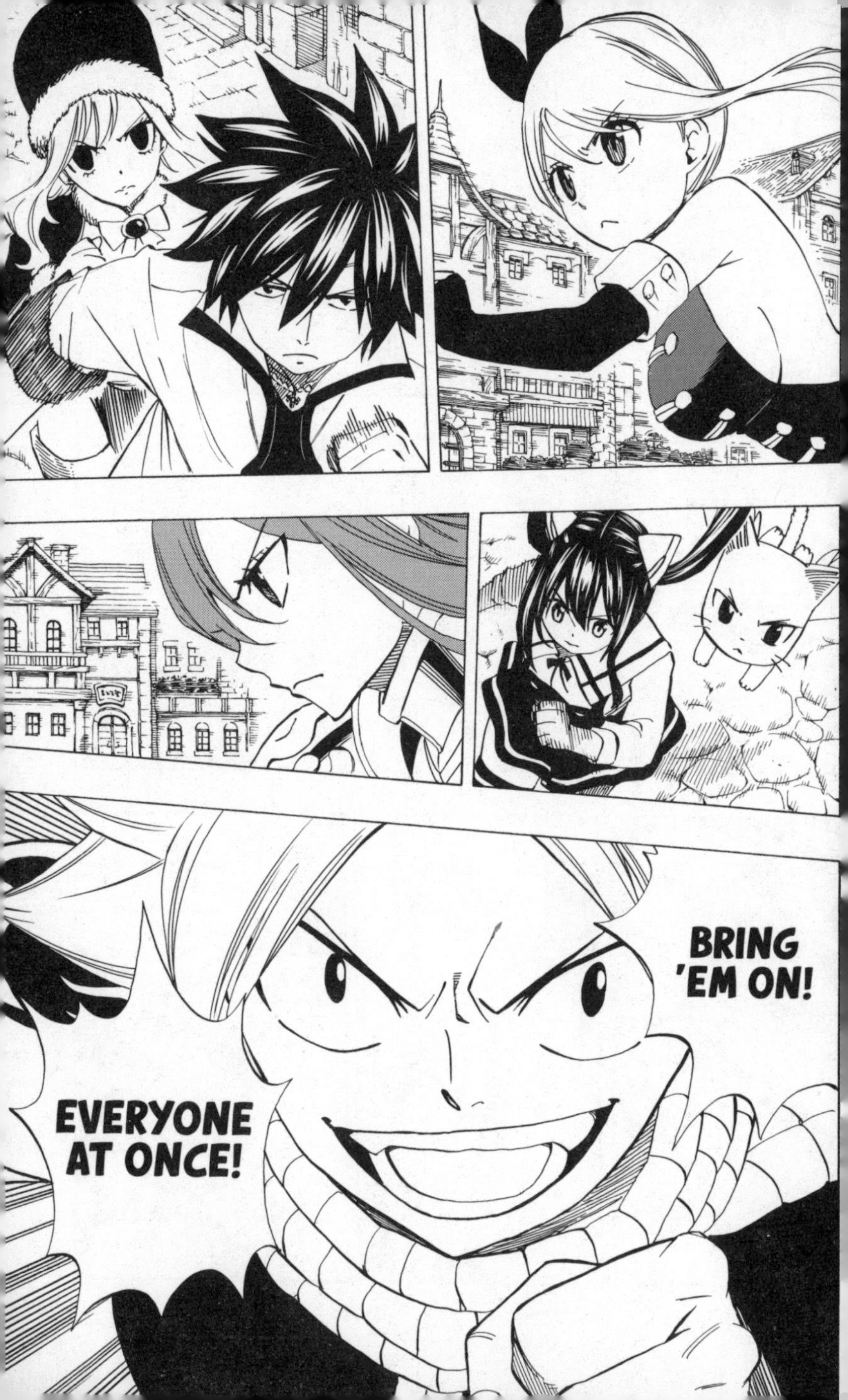
BRING 'EM ON!
EVERYONE AT ONCE!

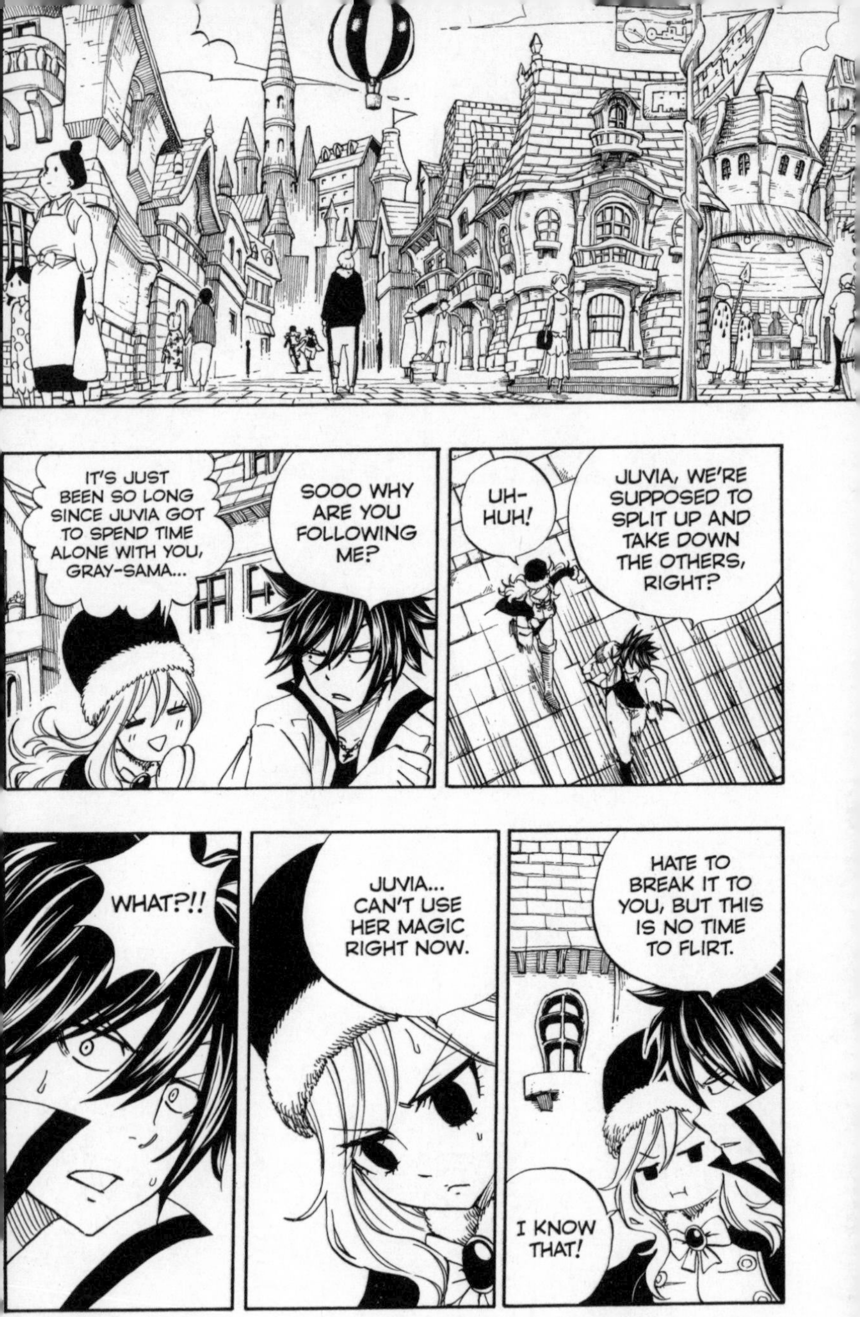

JUVIA, WE'RE SUPPOSED TO SPLIT UP AND TAKE DOWN THE OTHERS, RIGHT?
UH-HUH!
SOOO WHY ARE YOU FOLLOWING ME?
IT'S JUST BEEN SO LONG SINCE JUVIA GOT TO SPEND TIME ALONE WITH YOU, GRAY-SAMA...
HATE TO BREAK IT TO YOU, BUT THIS IS NO TIME TO FLIRT.
I KNOW THAT!
JUVIA... CAN'T USE HER MAGIC RIGHT NOW.
WHAT?!!

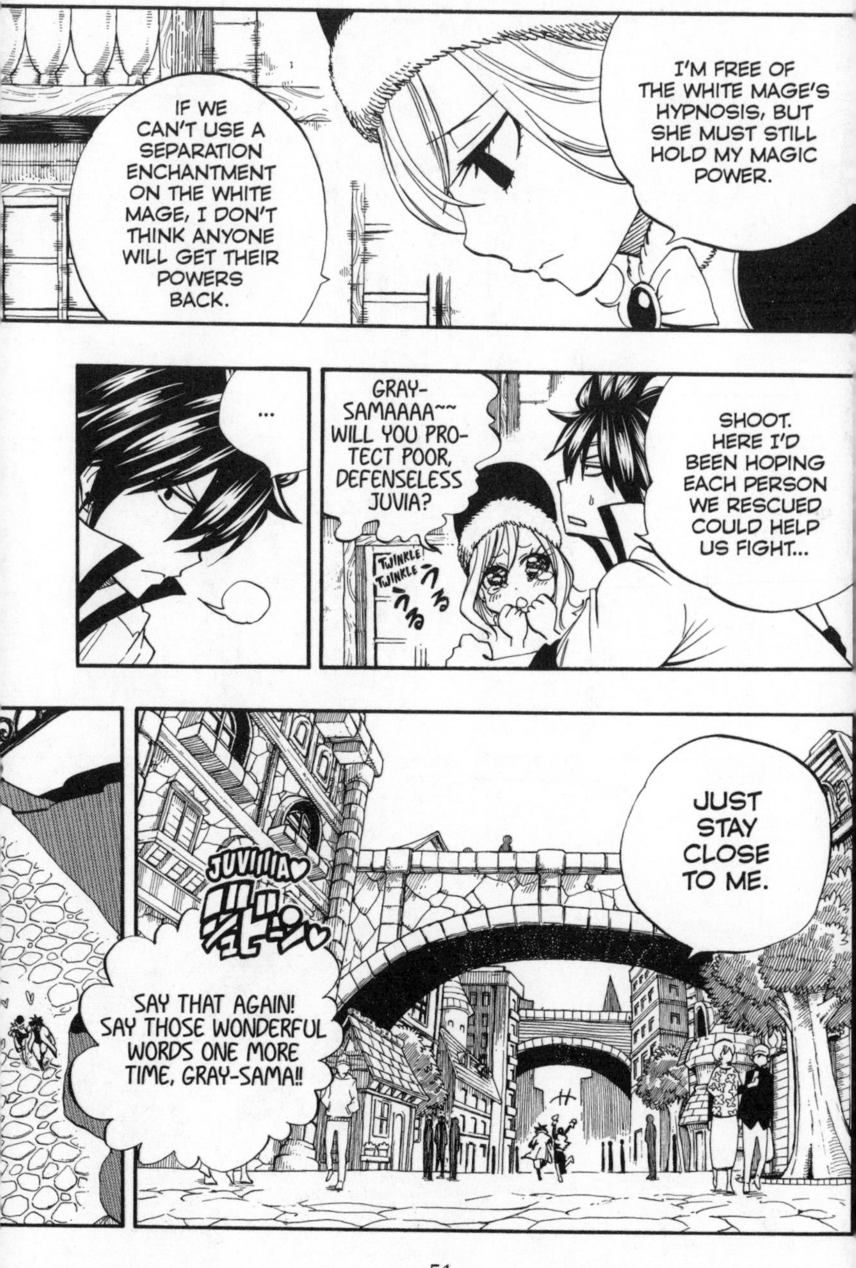
I'M FREE OF THE WHITE MAGE'S HYPNOSIS, BUT SHE MUST STILL HOLD MY MAGIC POWER.
IF WE CAN'T USE A SEPARATION ENCHANTMENT ON THE WHITE MAGE, I DON'T THINK ANYONE WILL GET THEIR POWERS BACK.
SHOOT. HERE I'D BEEN HOPING EACH PERSON WE RESCUED COULD HELP US FIGHT...
GRAY-SAMAAAA~~ WILL YOU PROTECT POOR, DEFENSELESS JUVIA?
TWINKLE TWINKLE
...
JUST STAY CLOSE TO ME.
JUVIIIIA♥
SAY THAT AGAIN! SAY THOSE WONDERFUL WORDS ONE MORE TIME, GRAY-SAMA!!

LOOKIT THE LITTLE LOVEBIRDS!
JEALOUS!
LOVE! BIRDS!
JEALOUS BODY!
A BODY GETS JEALOUS, BABY!
BICK-SLOW!!
!
TAKES YA BACK, DOESN'T IT, GRAY?
TELL ME YOU HAVEN'T FORGOTTEN....
...THE BATTLE OF FAIRY TAIL?
REMEMBER HOW I BEAT THE STUFFING OUT OF YOU?

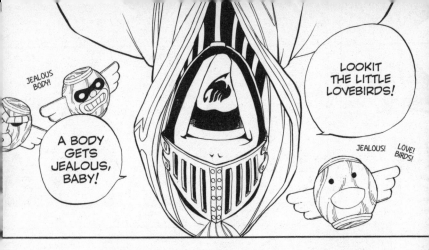

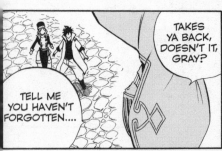

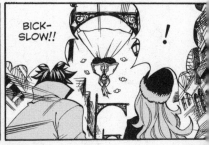

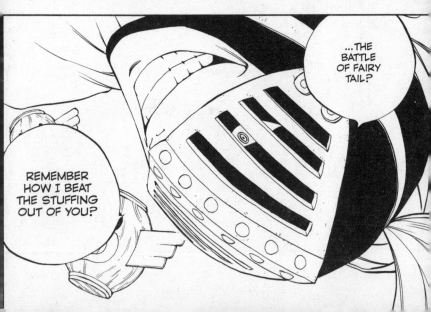

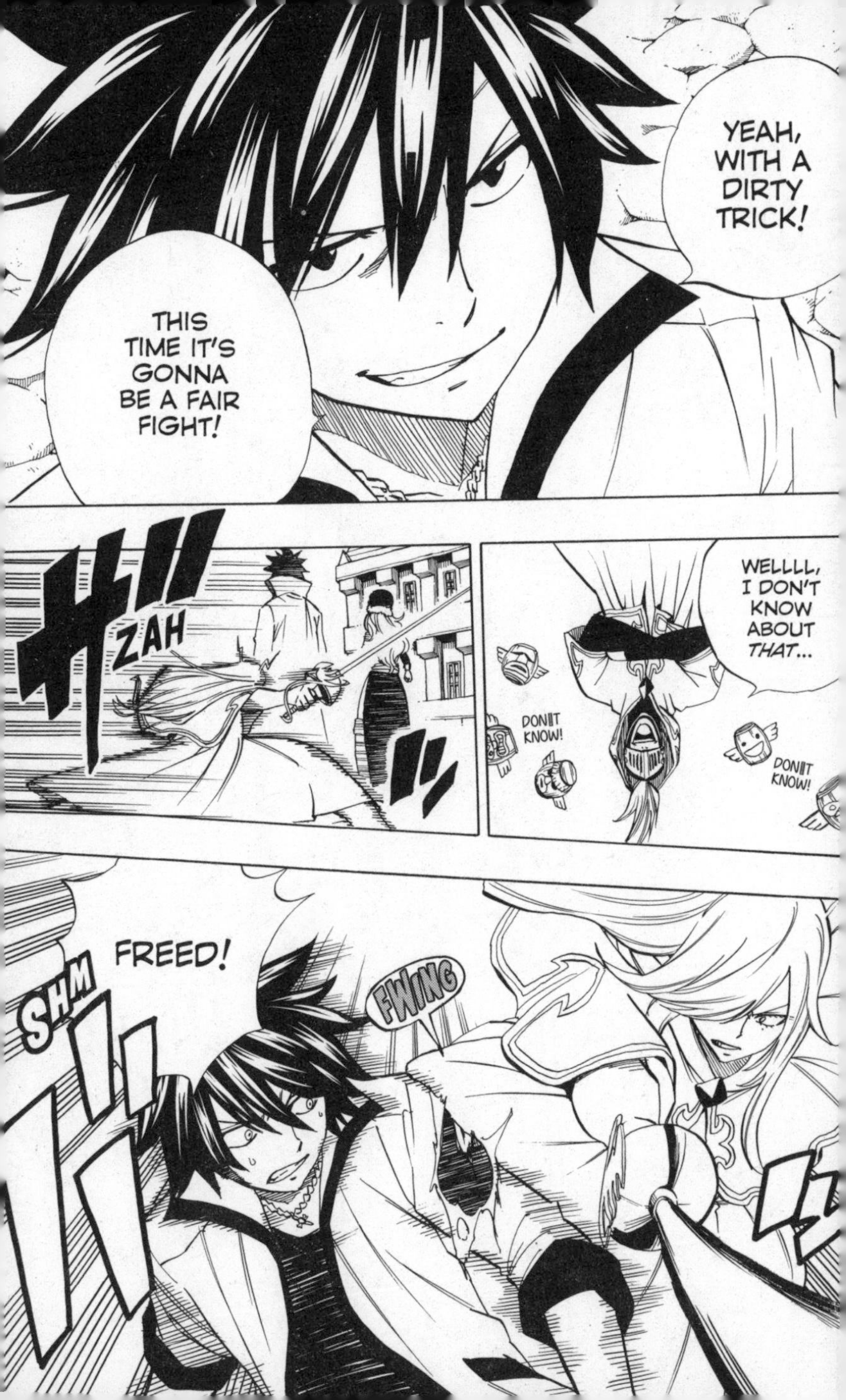
YEAH, WITH A DIRTY TRICK!
THIS TIME IT'S GONNA BE A FAIR FIGHT!
WELLLL, I DON'T KNOW ABOUT *THAT*...
DON'T KNOW!
DON'T KNOW!
ZAH
FREED!
FWING
SHM

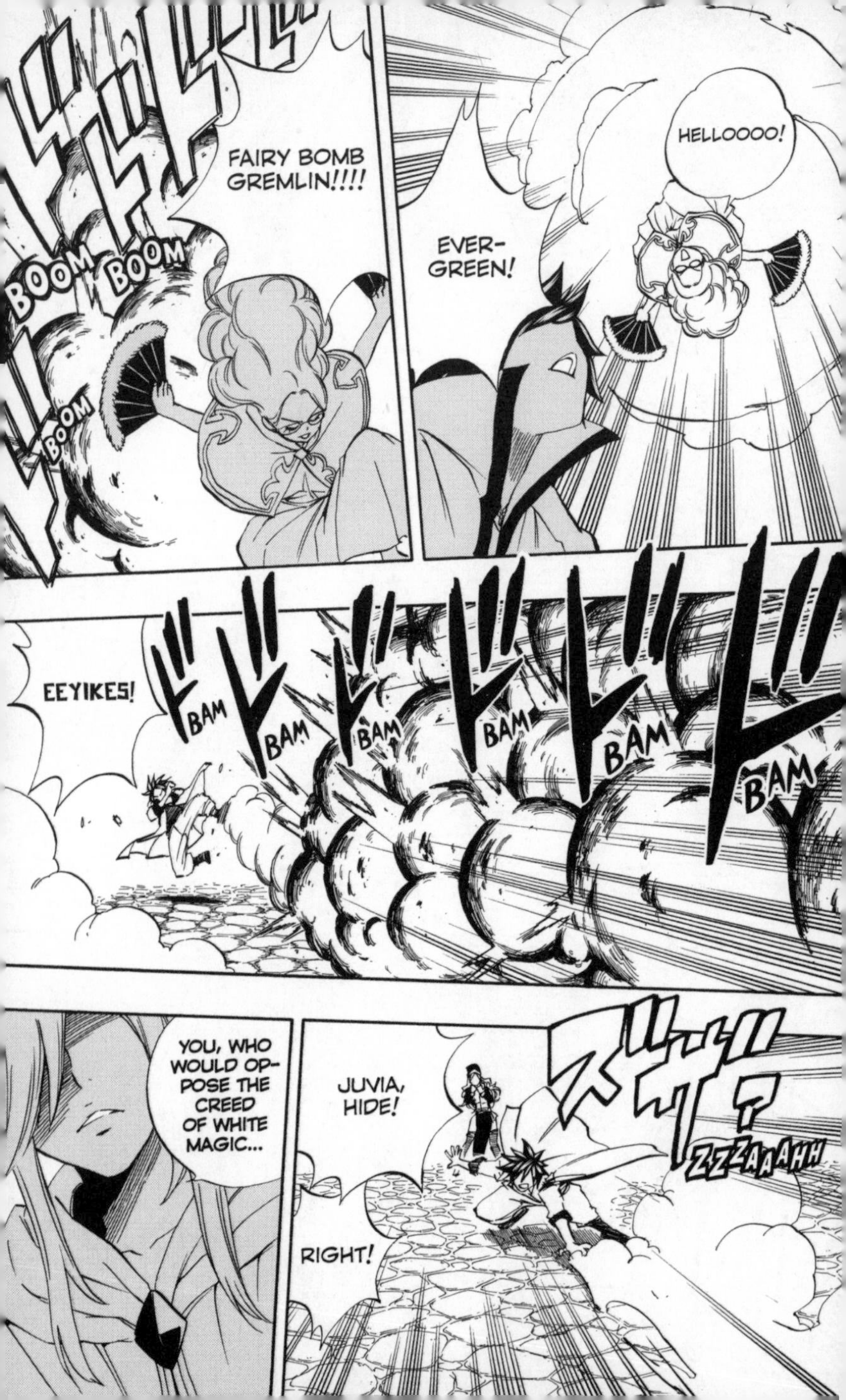
HELLOOOO!
EVER-GREEN!
FAIRY BOMB GREMLIN!!!!
BOOM
BOOM
BOOM
BAM
BAM
BAM
BAM
BAM
BAM
EEYIKES!
ZZZAAAHH
JUVIA, HIDE!
RIGHT!
YOU, WHO WOULD OPPOSE THE CREED OF WHITE MAGIC...

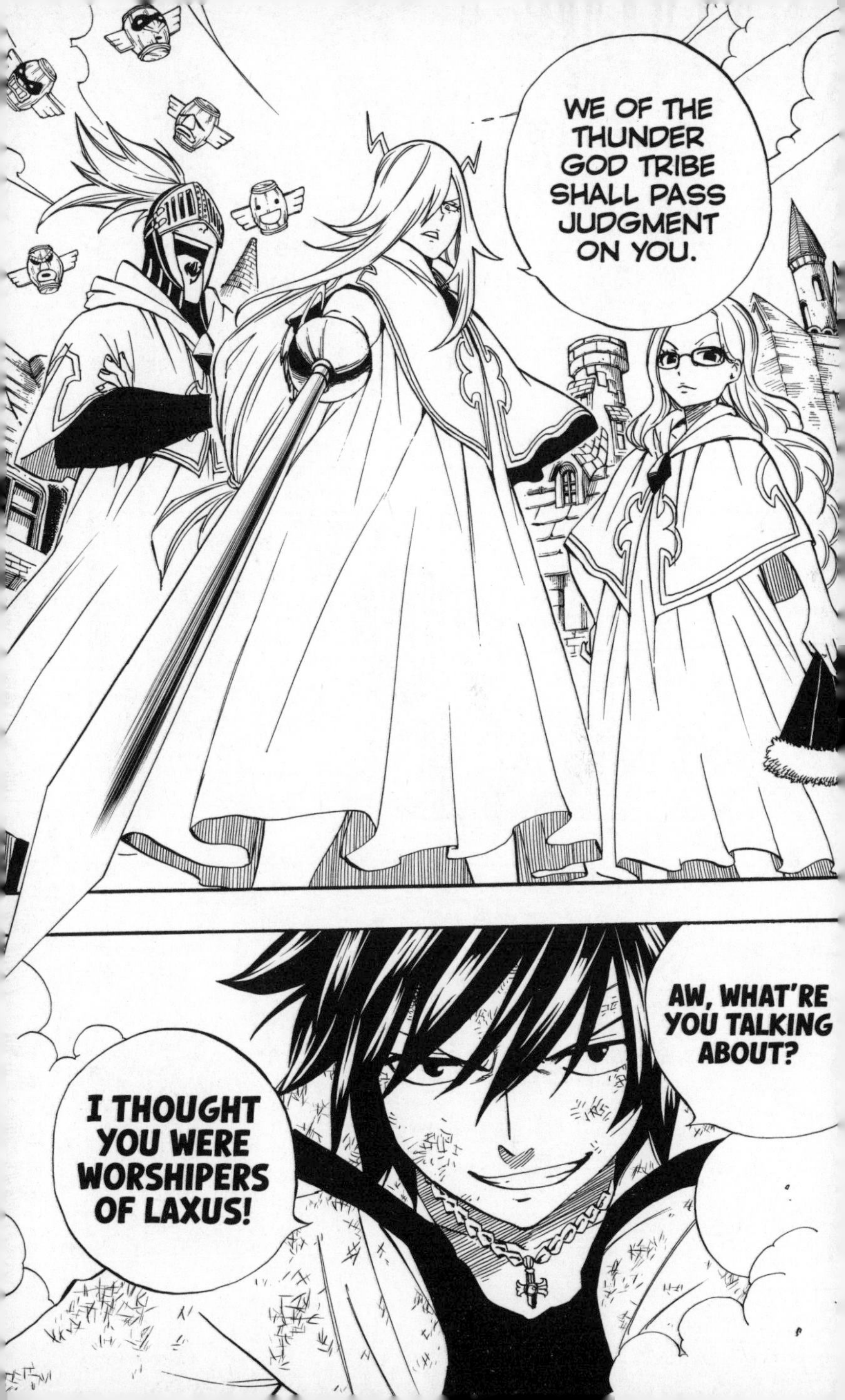
WE OF THE THUNDER GOD TRIBE SHALL PASS JUDGMENT ON YOU.
AW, WHAT'RE YOU TALKING ABOUT?
I THOUGHT YOU WERE WORSHIPERS OF LAXUS!

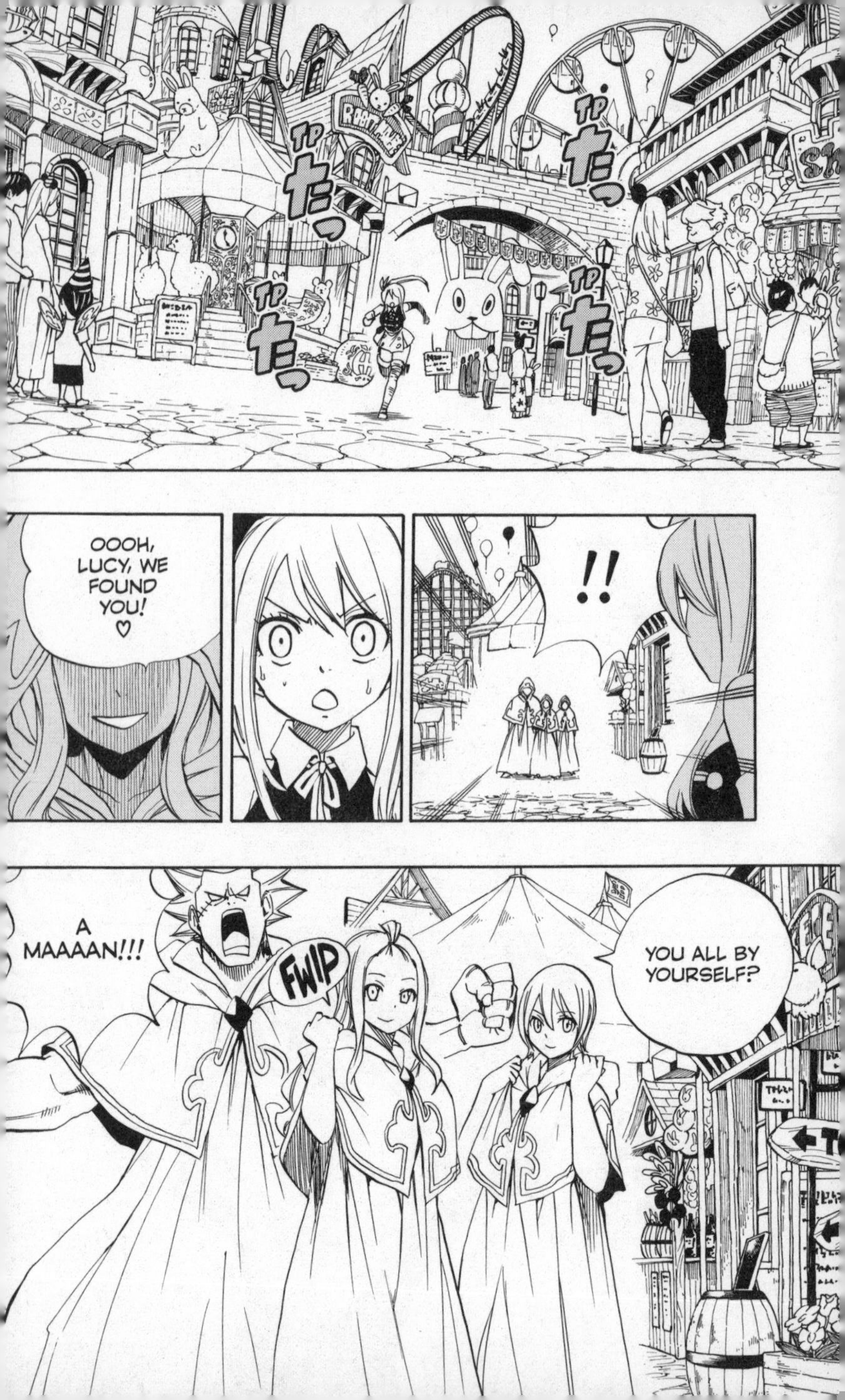

TP たっ
TP たっ
TP たっ
TP たっ
!!
OOOH, LUCY, WE FOUND YOU! ♡
YOU ALL BY YOURSELF?
FWIP
A MAAAAN!!!

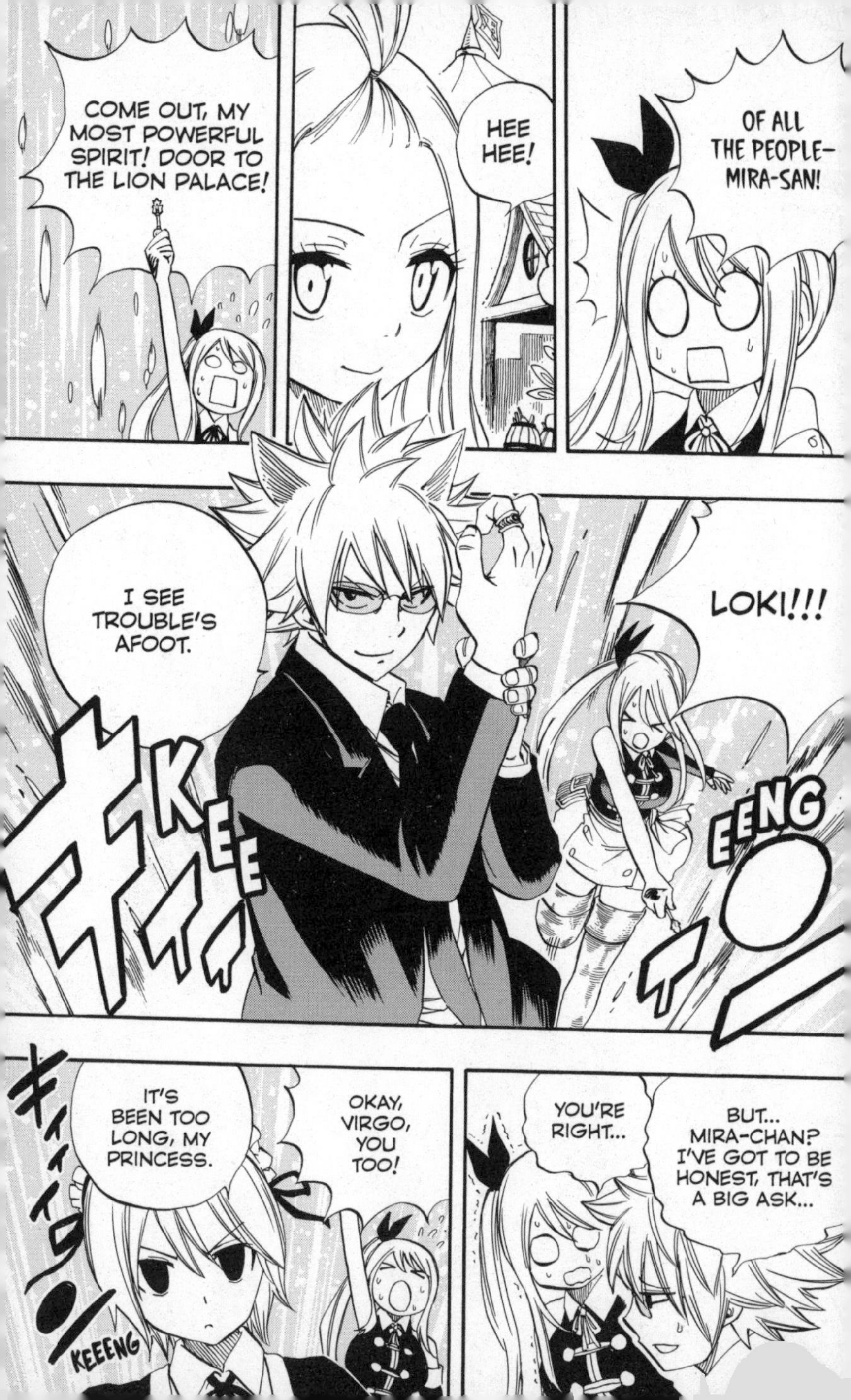

OF ALL THE PEOPLE— MIRA-SAN!
HEE HEE!
COME OUT, MY MOST POWERFUL SPIRIT! DOOR TO THE LION PALACE!
LOKI!!!
I SEE TROUBLE'S AFOOT.
EENG
KEE
BUT... MIRA-CHAN? I'VE GOT TO BE HONEST, THAT'S A BIG ASK...
YOU'RE RIGHT...
OKAY, VIRGO, YOU TOO!
IT'S BEEN TOO LONG, MY PRINCESS.
KEEENG

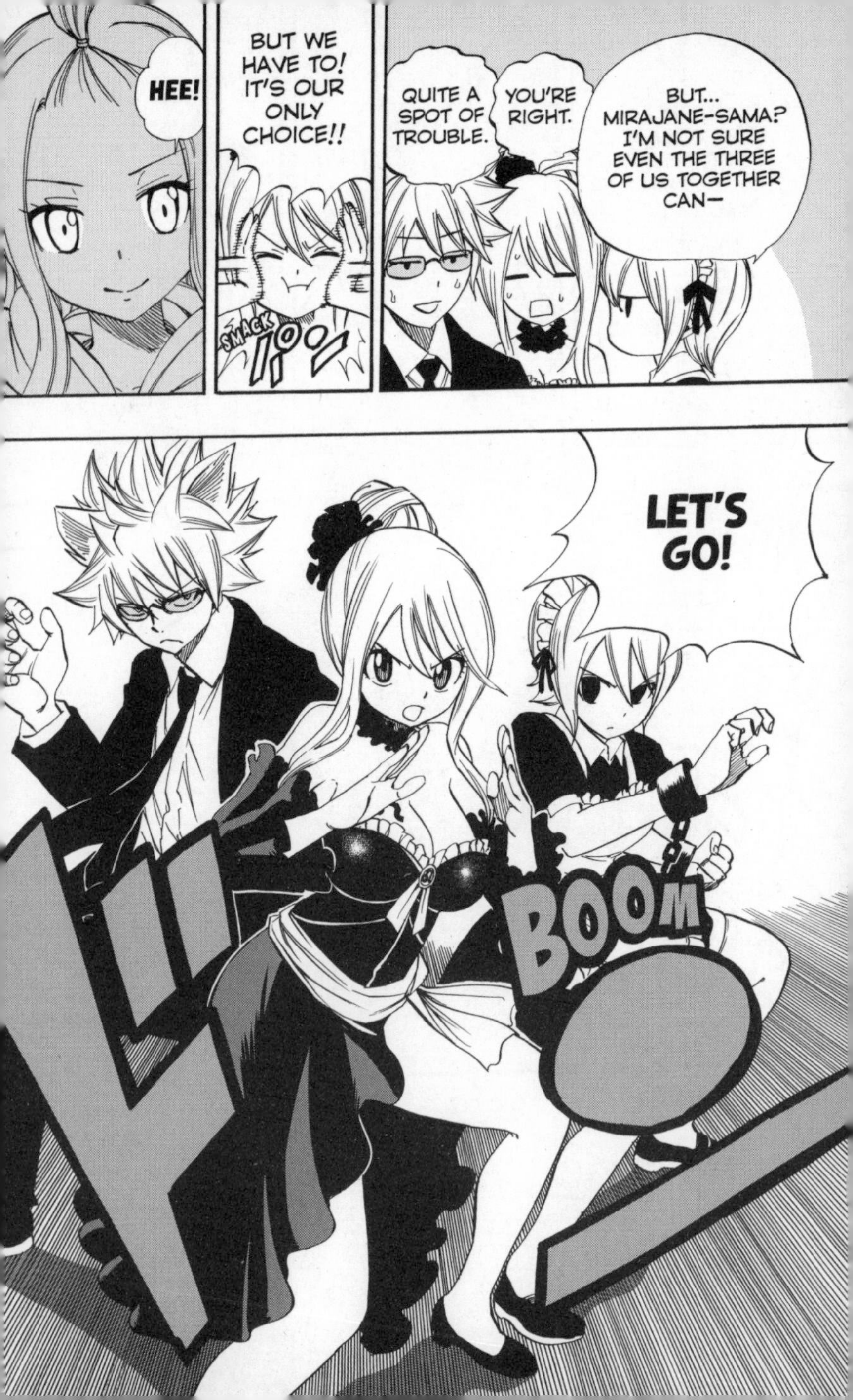
BUT... MIRAJANE-SAMA? I'M NOT SURE EVEN THE THREE OF US TOGETHER CAN—
YOU'RE RIGHT.
QUITE A SPOT OF TROUBLE.
BUT WE HAVE TO! IT'S OUR ONLY CHOICE!!
SMACK
HEE!
LET'S GO!
BOOM

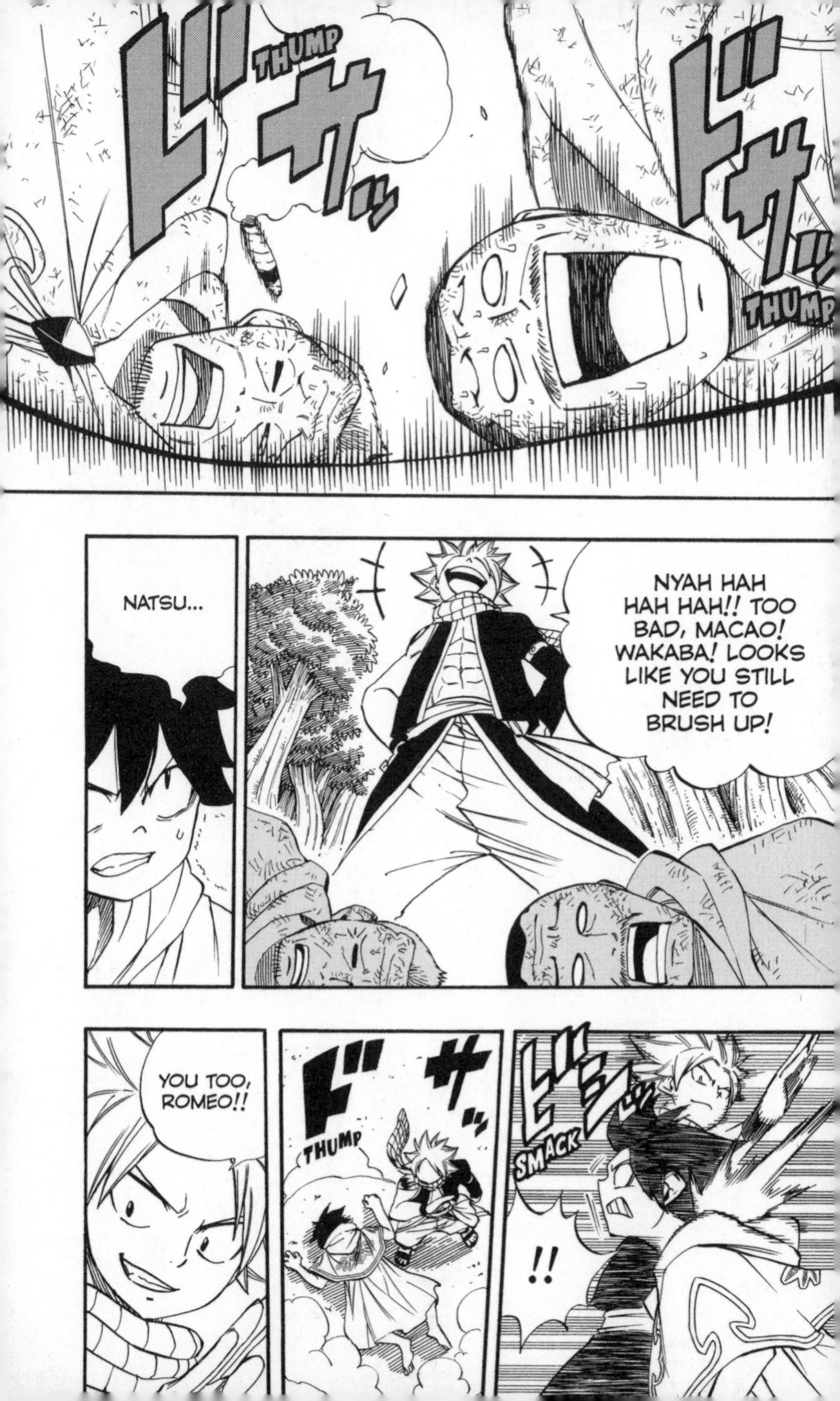
THUMP
THUMP
NYAH HAH HAH HAH!! TOO BAD, MACAO! WAKABA! LOOKS LIKE YOU STILL NEED TO BRUSH UP!
NATSU...
SMACK
!!
THUMP
YOU TOO, ROMEO!!

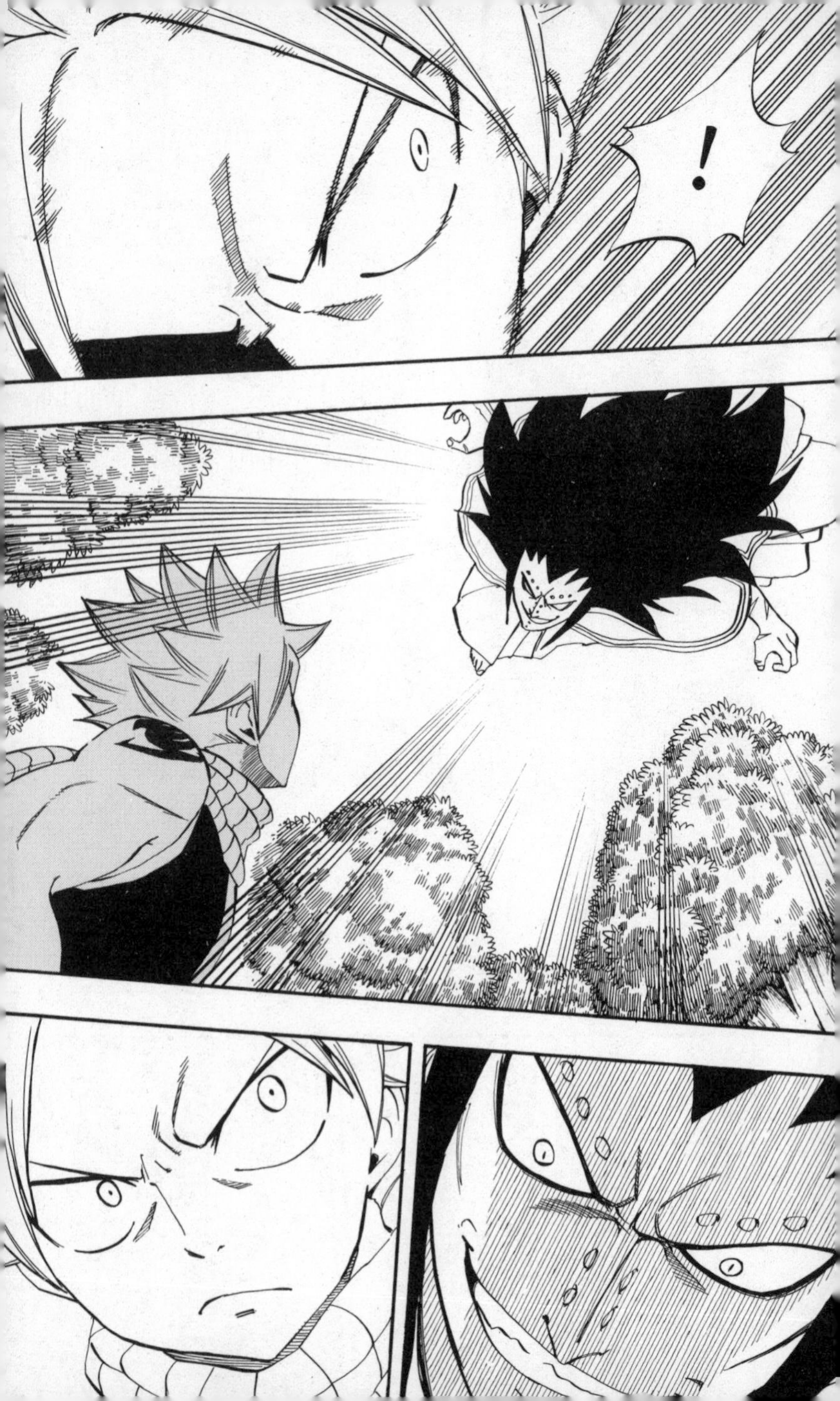
!

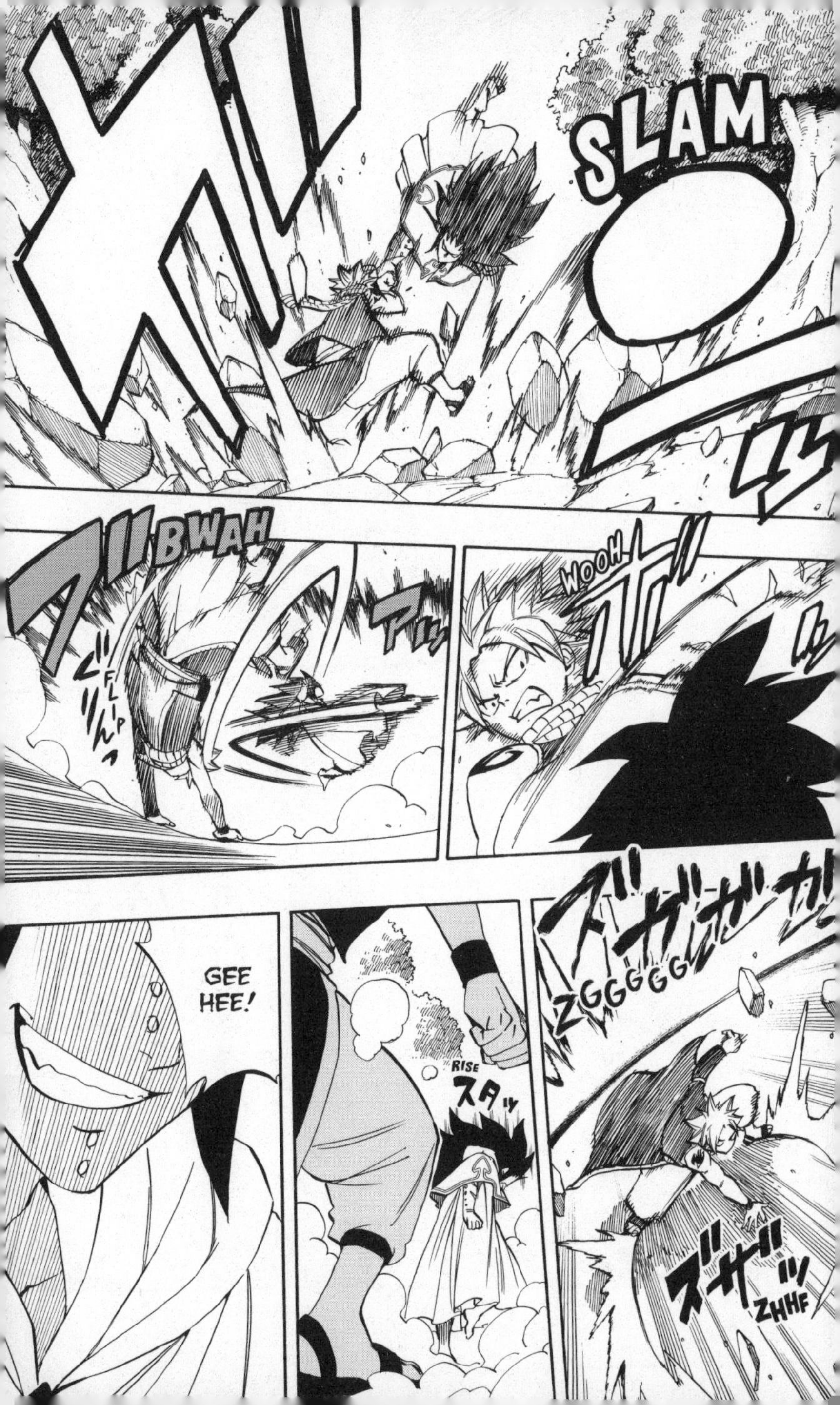
SLAM
WOOH
BWAH
FLIP
ZGGGGG
ZHHF
RISE
スタッ
GEE HEE!

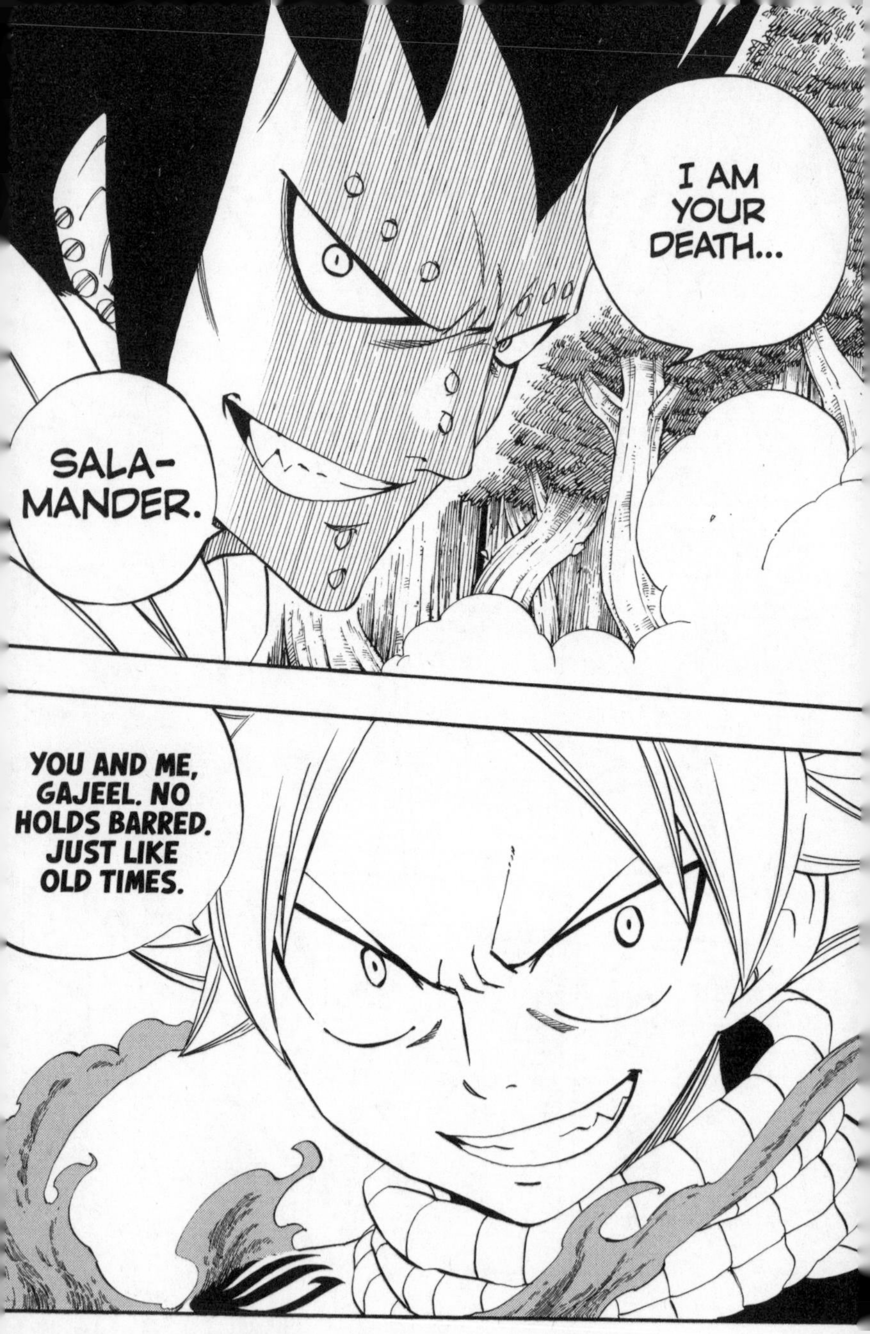
I AM YOUR DEATH...
SALA-MANDER.
YOU AND ME, GAJEEL. NO HOLDS BARRED. JUST LIKE OLD TIMES.

FAIRY TAIL 100 YEARS QUEST

Chapter 31: Fairy Face-Off

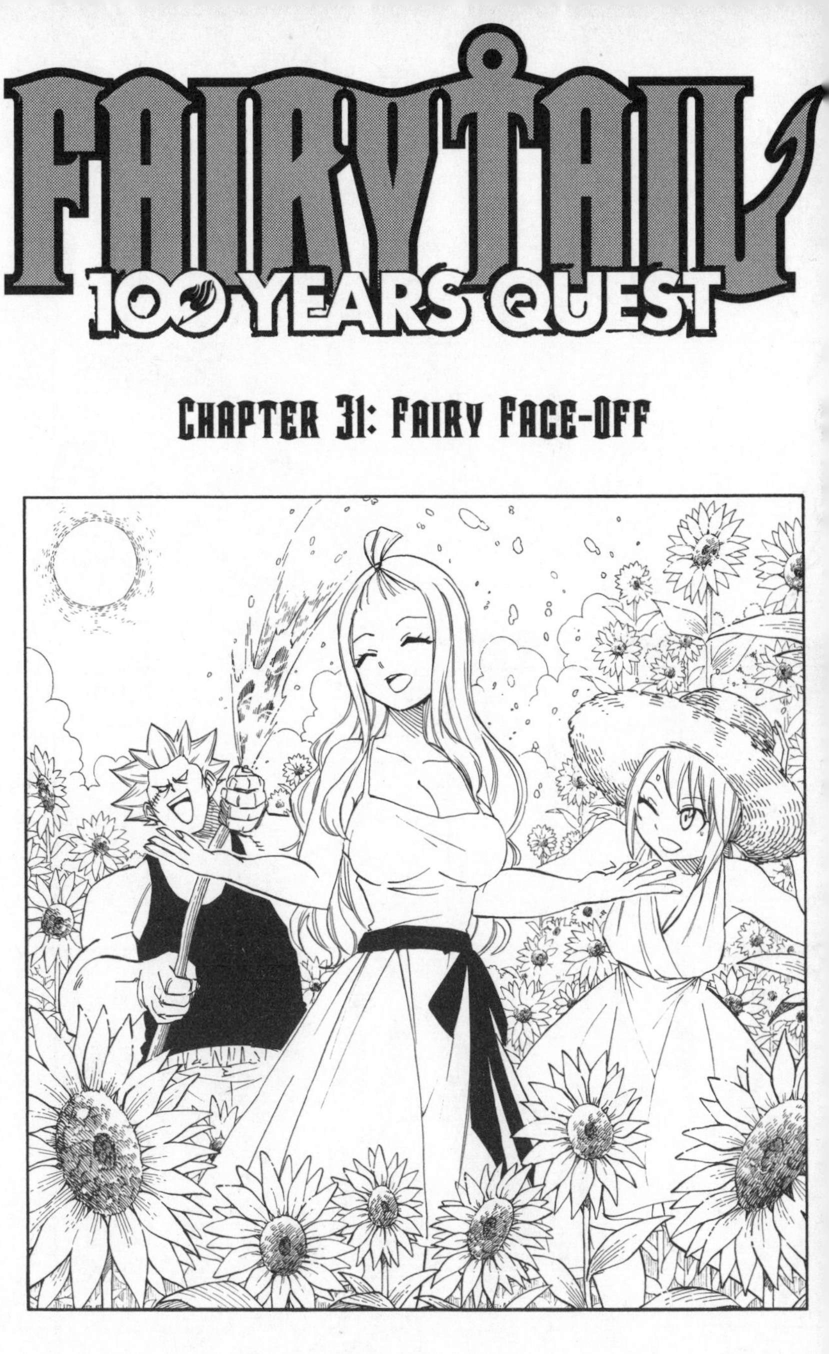

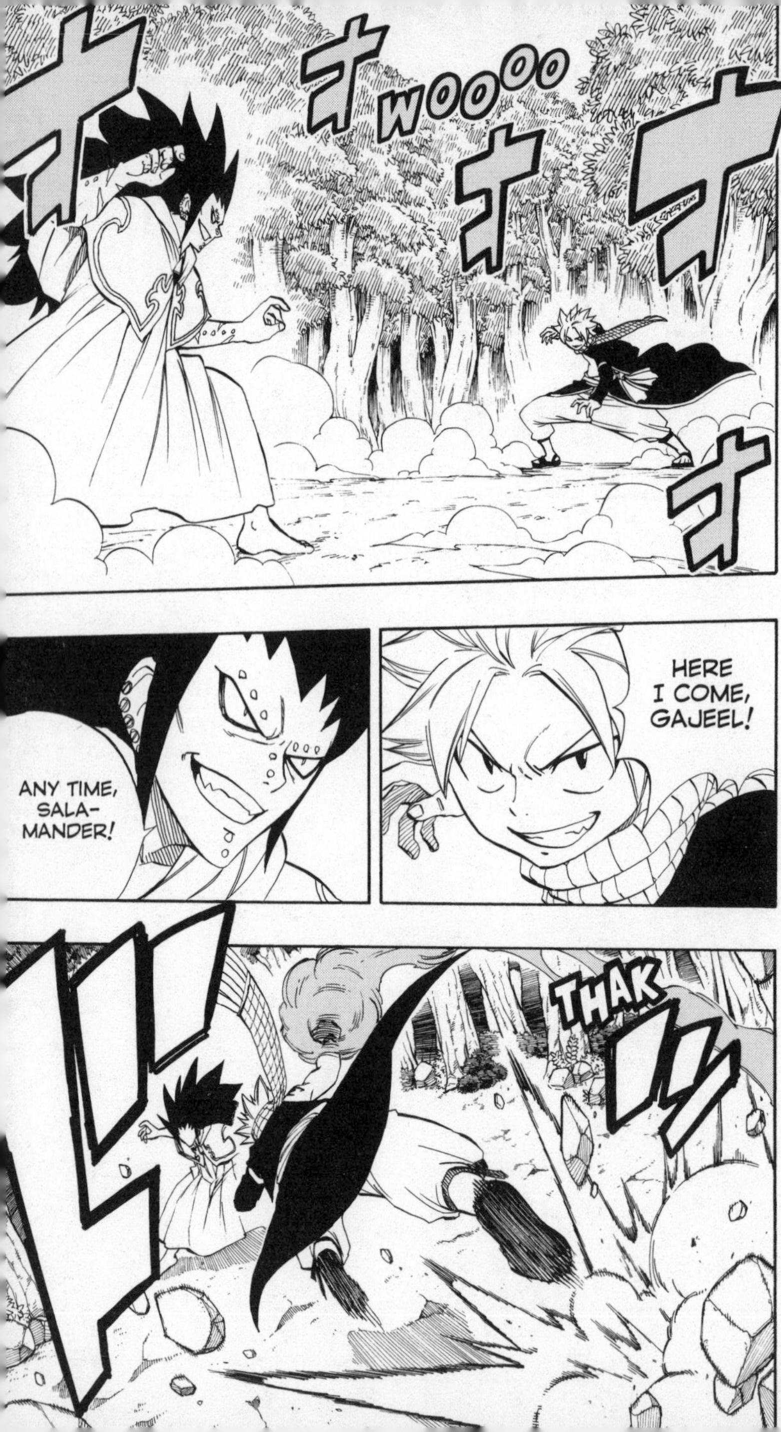
WOOOO
HERE I COME, GAJEEL!
ANY TIME, SALA-MANDER!
THAK

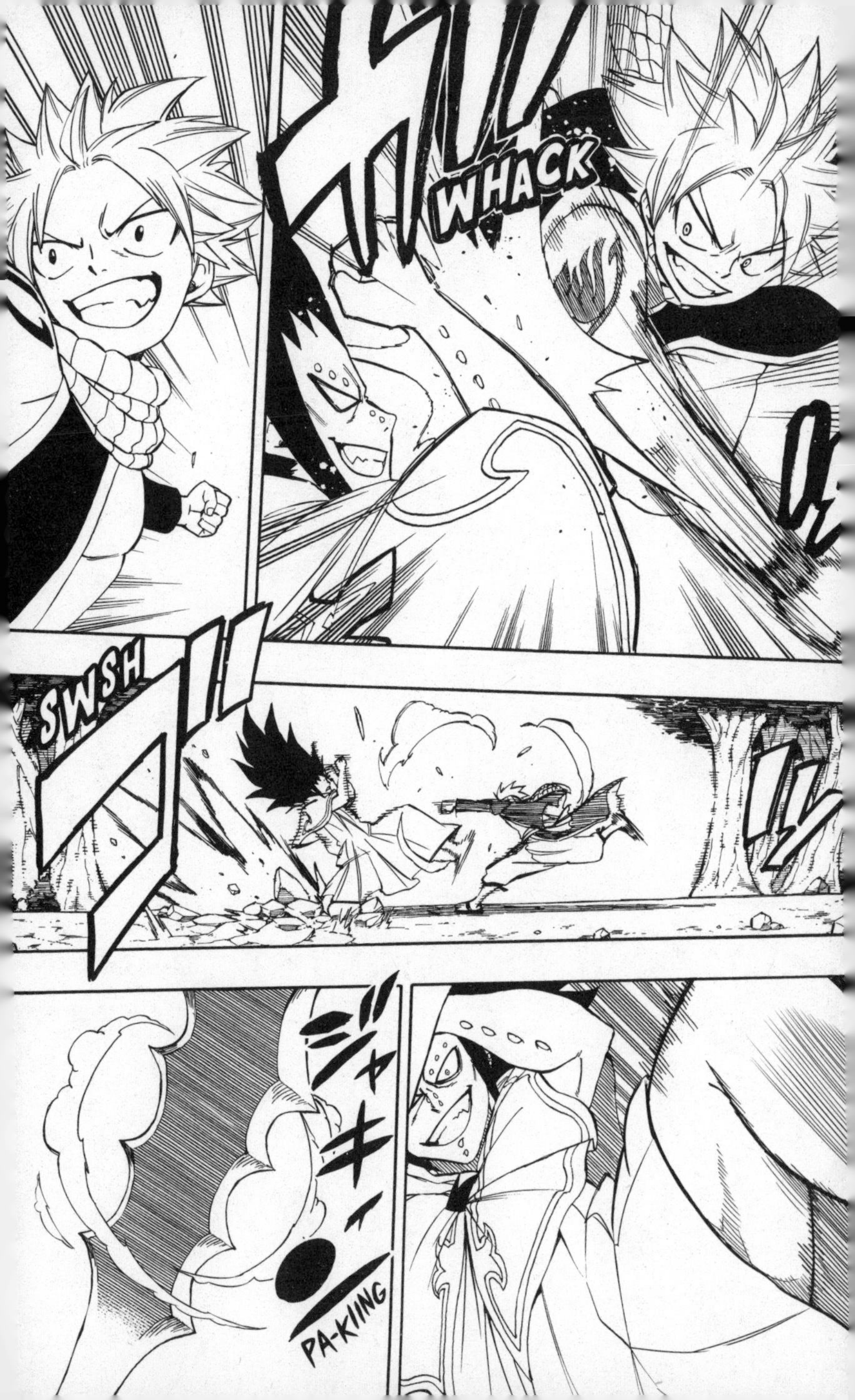
WHACK
SWSH
PA-KIING

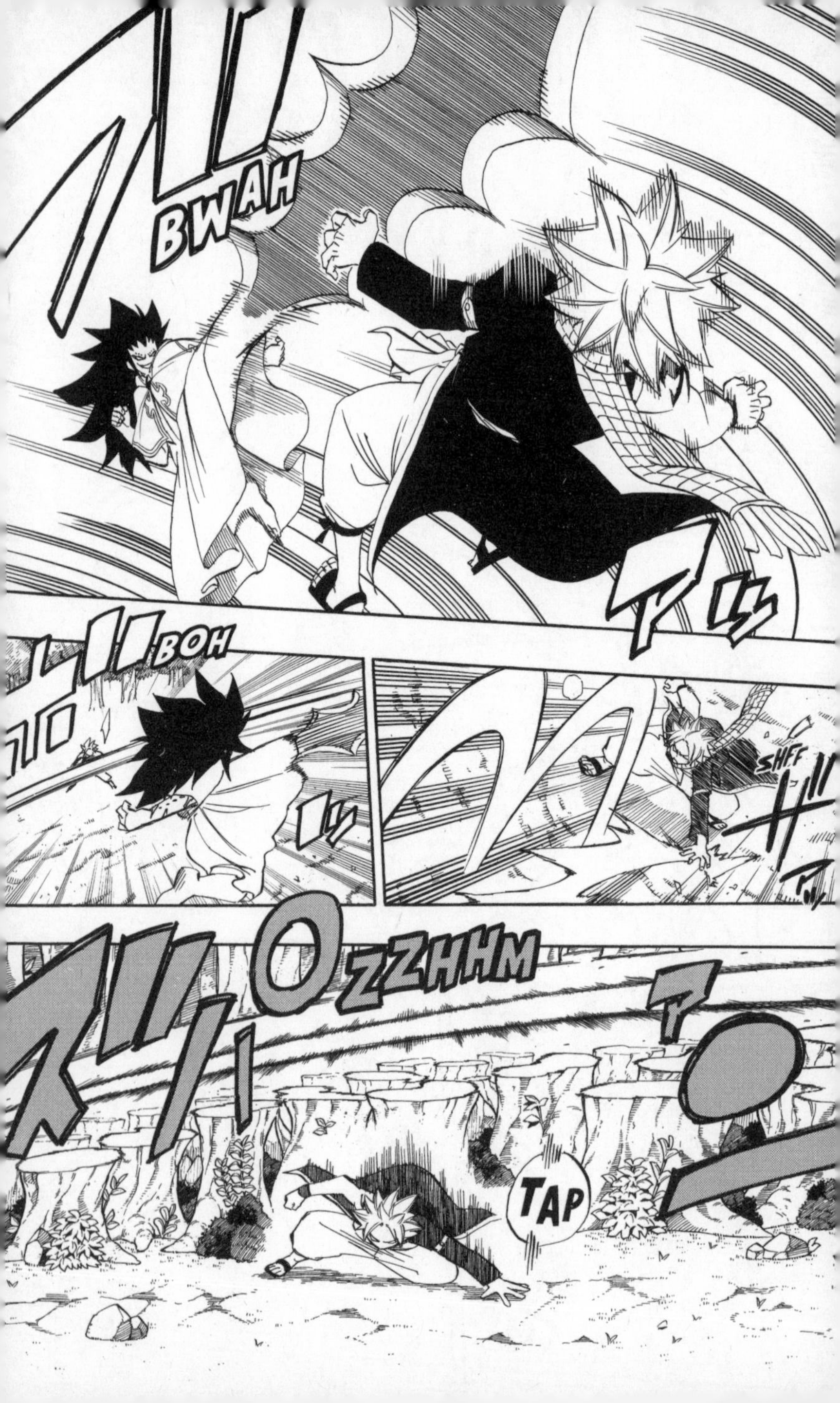
BWAH
SHFF
BOH
OZZHHM
TAP

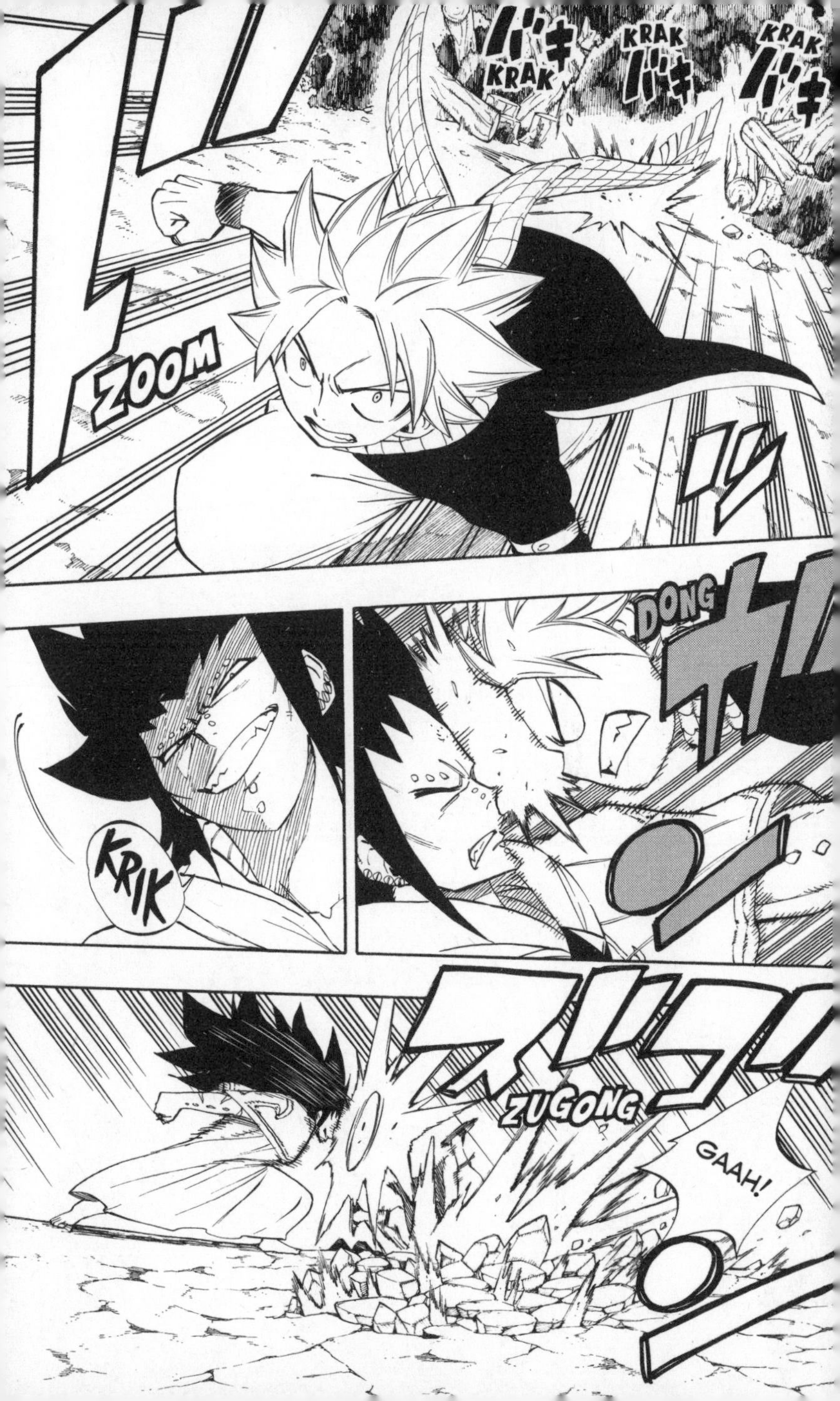
KRAK
KRAK
KRAK
ZOOM
DONG
KRIK
ZUGONG
GAAH!

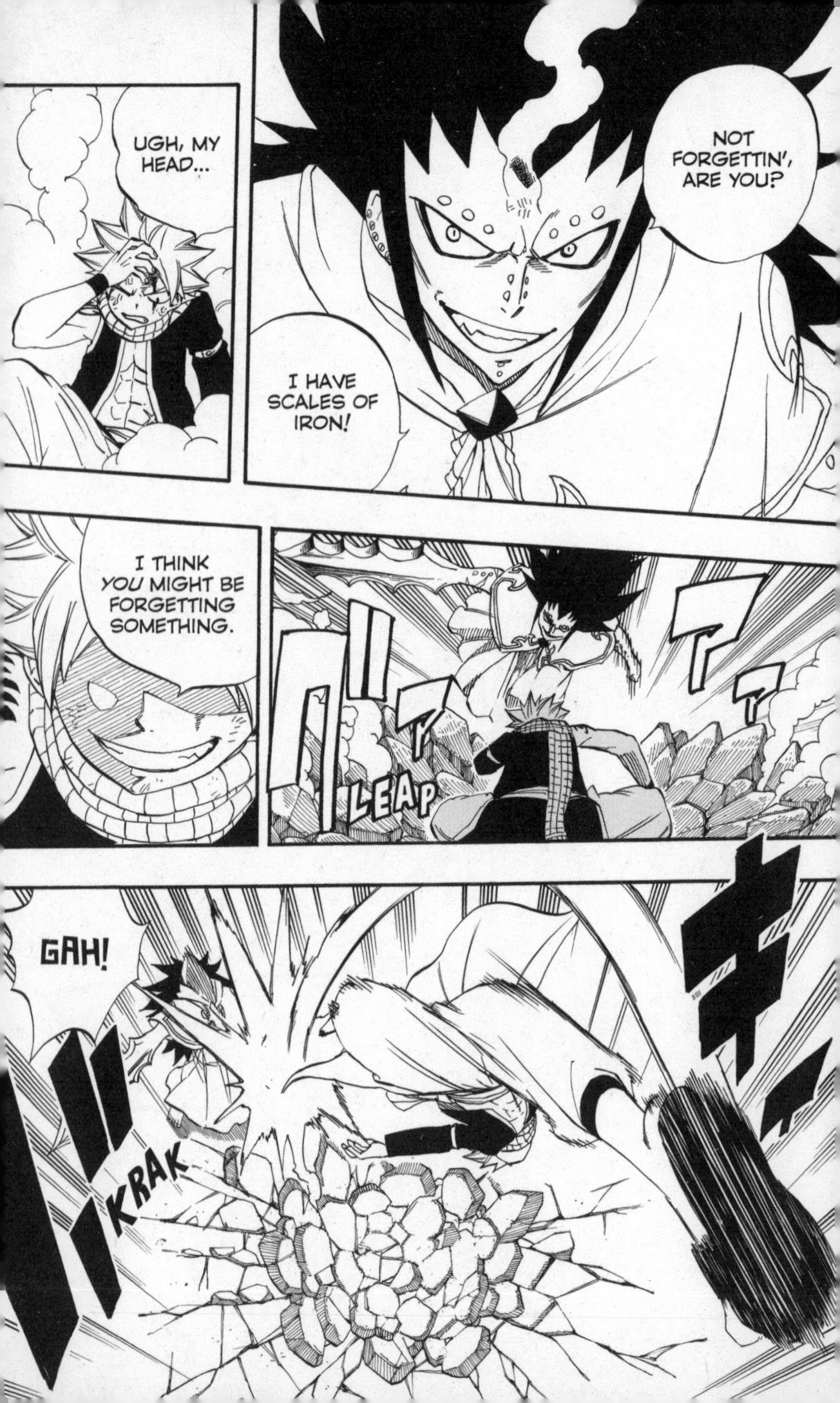
UGH, MY HEAD...
NOT FORGETTIN', ARE YOU?
I HAVE SCALES OF IRON!
I THINK *YOU* MIGHT BE FORGETTING SOMETHING.
LEAP
GAH!
KRAK

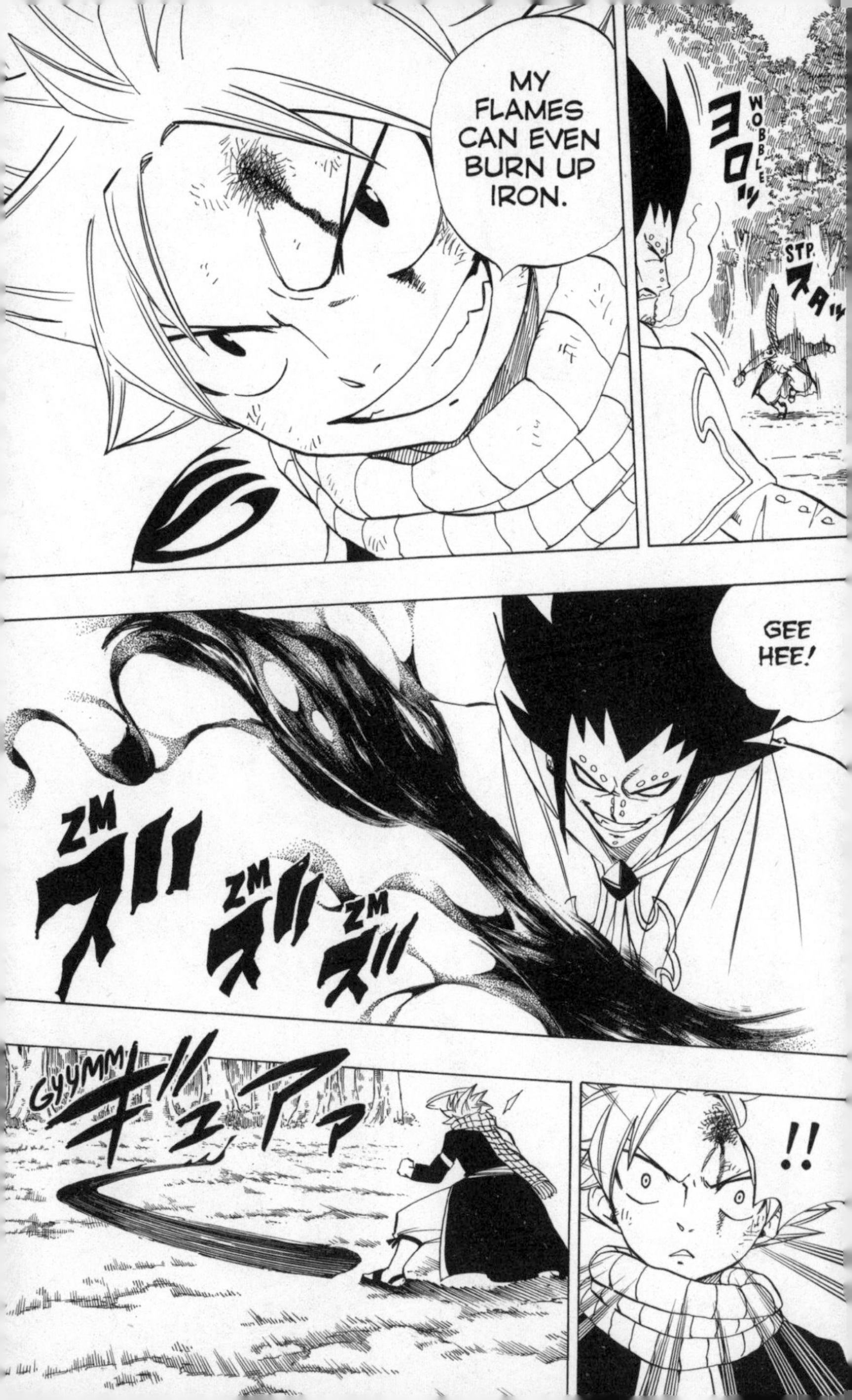
WOBBLE
STP.
MY FLAMES CAN EVEN BURN UP IRON.
GEE HEE!
ZM
ZM
ZM
!!
GYYMM

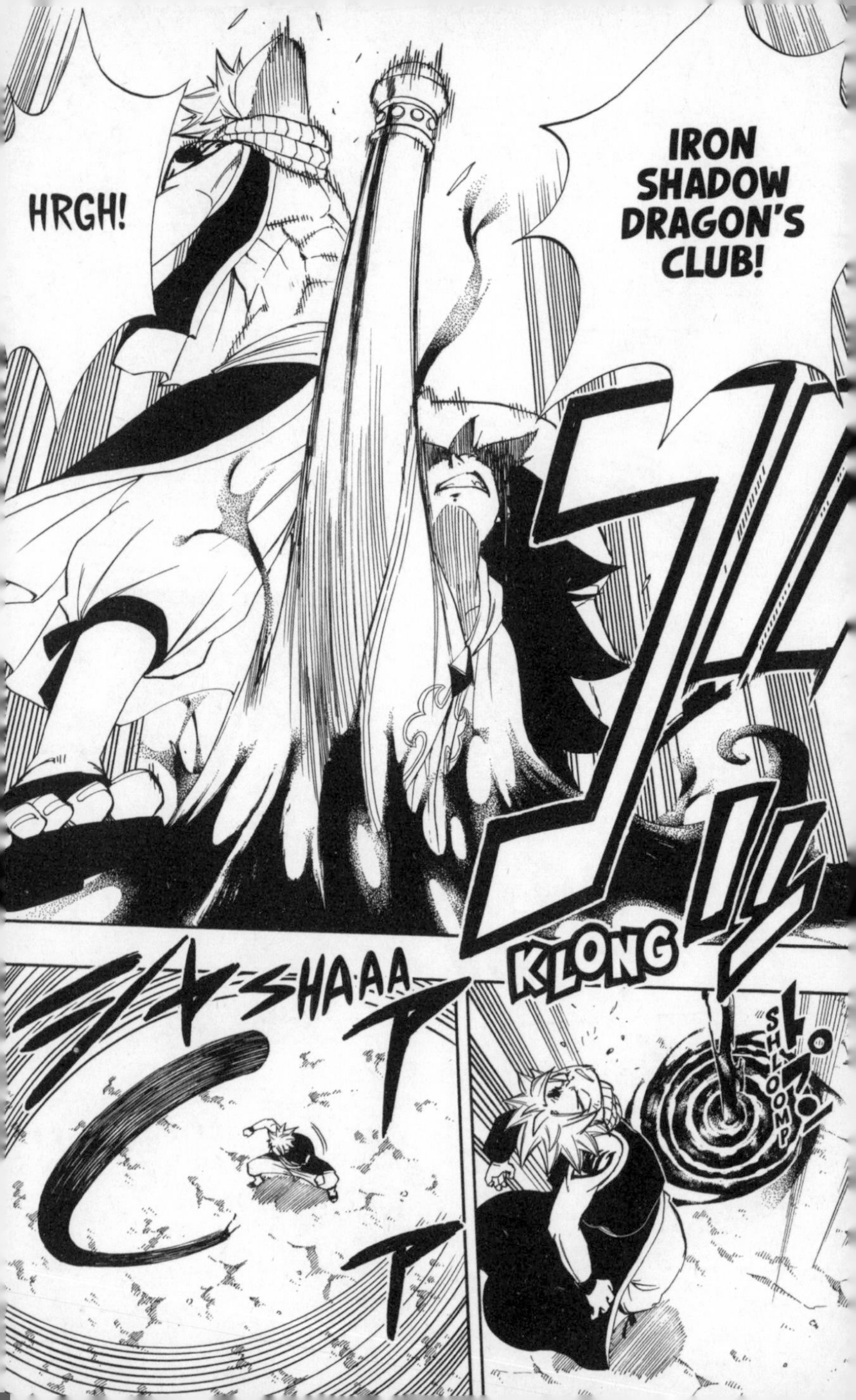
IRON SHADOW DRAGON'S CLUB!
HRGH!
KLONG
SHLOOMP
SHAAA

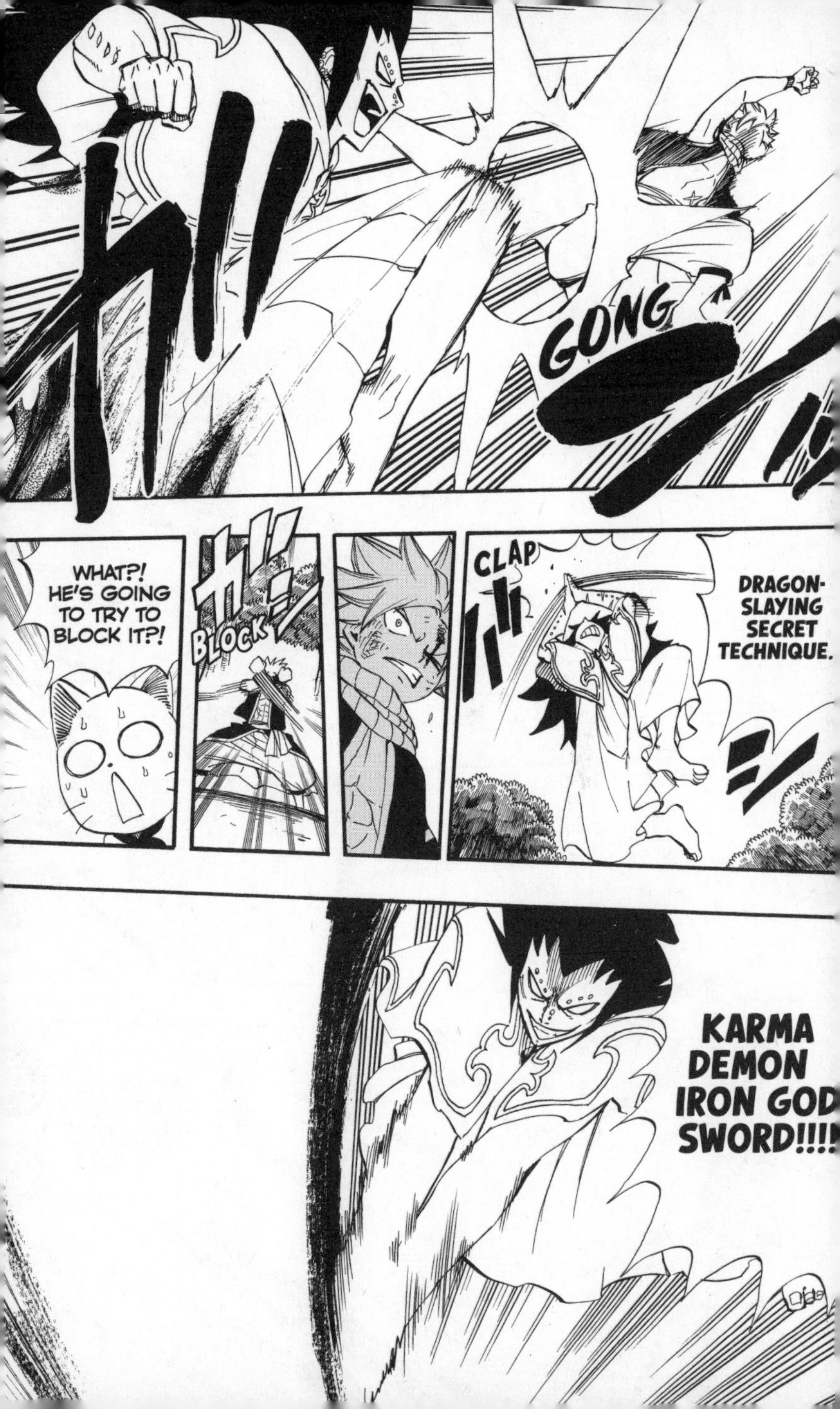
GONG
DRAGON-SLAYING SECRET TECHNIQUE.
CLAP
BLOCK
WHAT?! HE'S GOING TO TRY TO BLOCK IT?!
KARMA DEMON IRON GOD SWORD!!!!

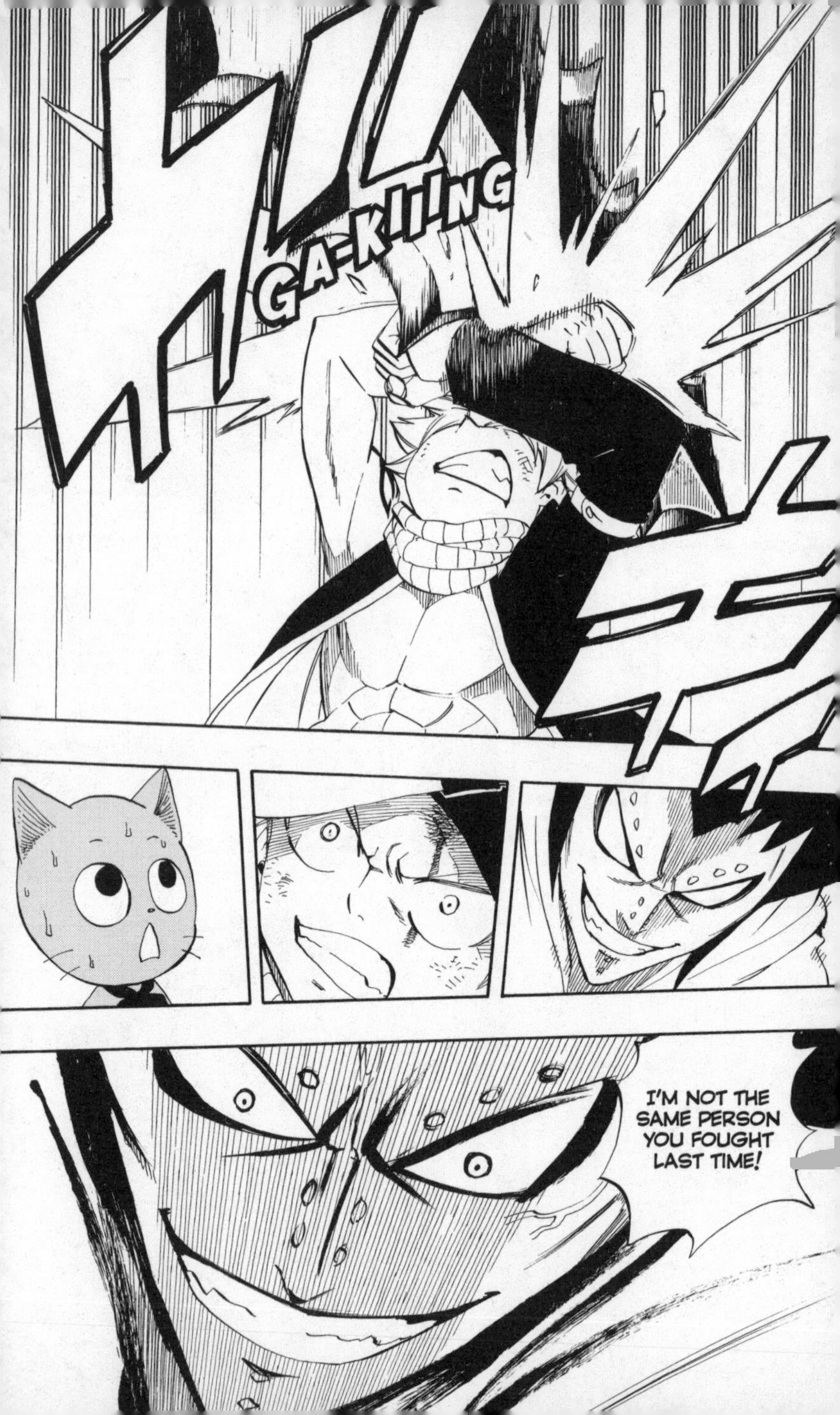
GA-KIIING
I'M NOT THE SAME PERSON YOU FOUGHT LAST TIME!

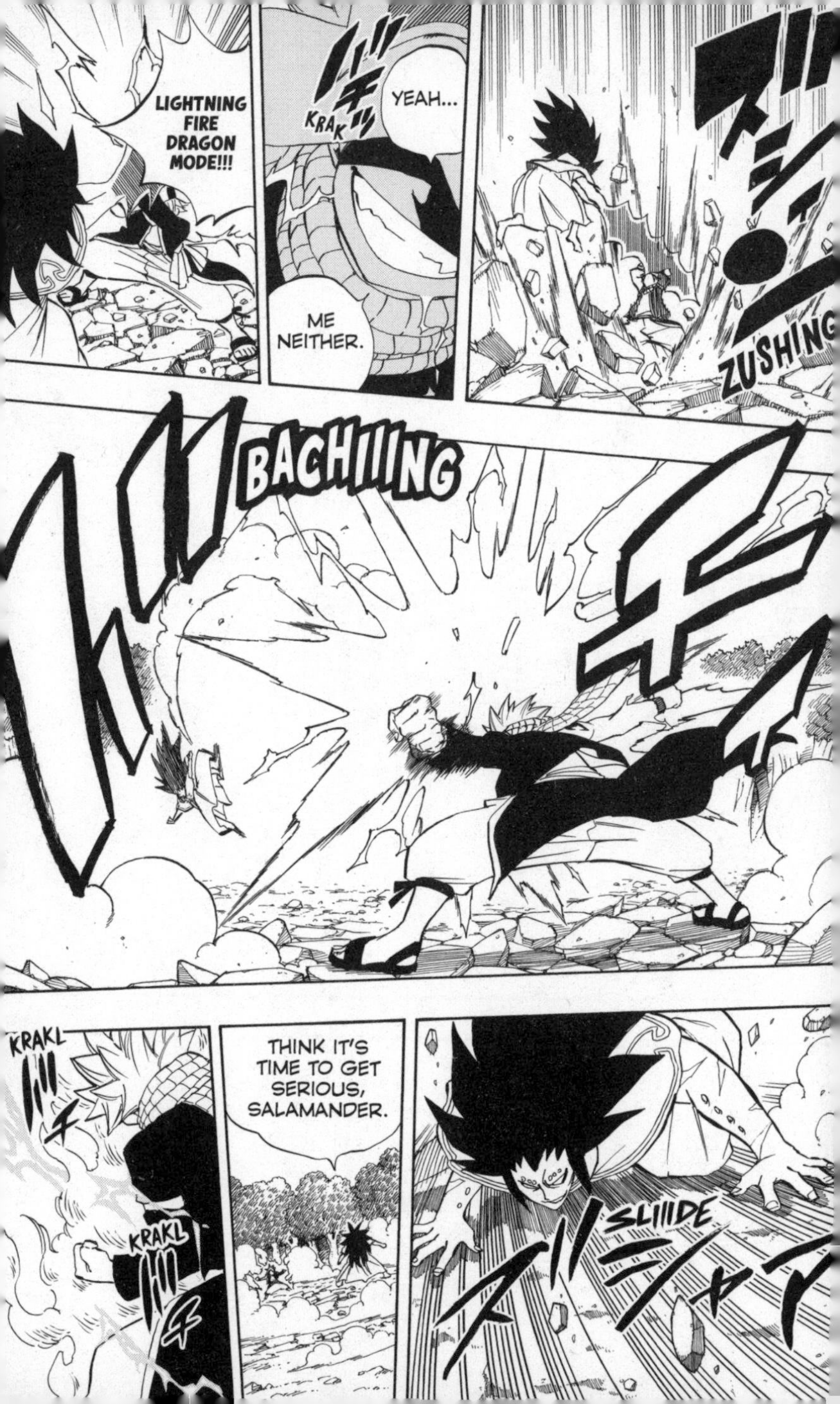
ZUSHING
KRAK
YEAH...
ME NEITHER.
LIGHTNING FIRE DRAGON MODE!!!
BACHIIIING
SLIIIDE
THINK IT'S TIME TO GET SERIOUS, SALAMANDER.
KRAKL
KRAKL

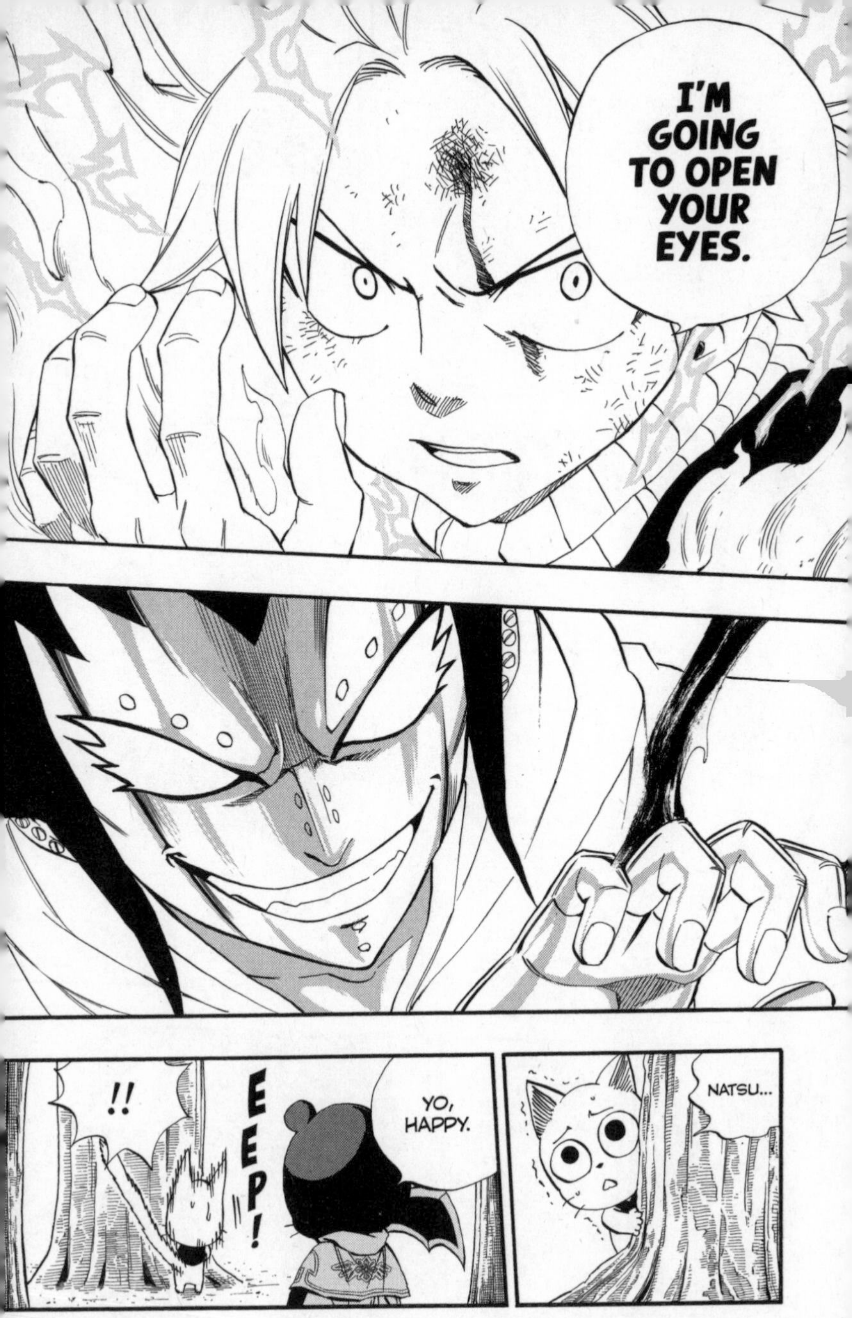
I'M GOING TO OPEN YOUR EYES.
NATSU...
YO, HAPPY.
EEP!
!!

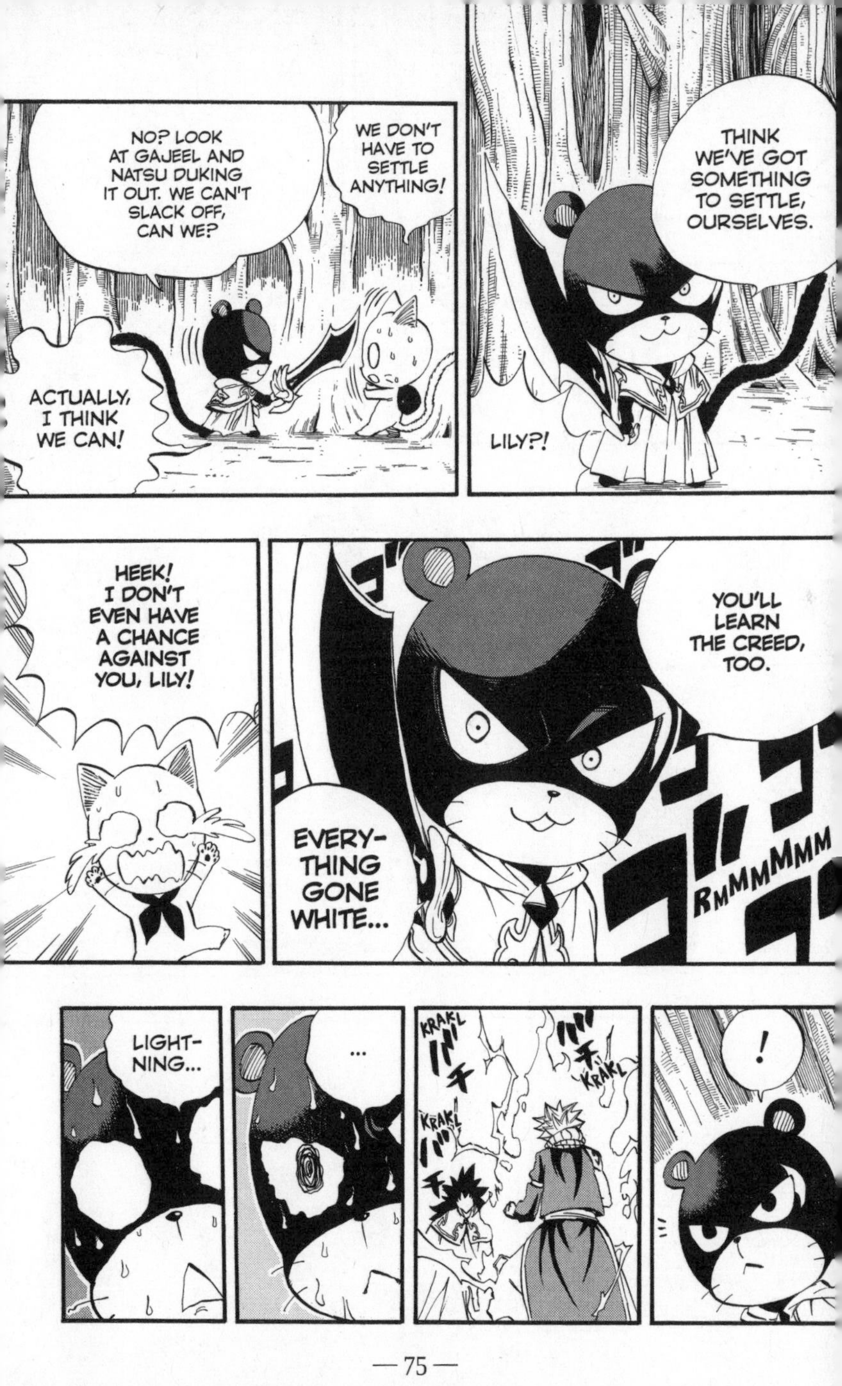
THINK WE'VE GOT SOMETHING TO SETTLE, OURSELVES.
LILY?!
WE DON'T HAVE TO SETTLE ANYTHING!
NO? LOOK AT GAJEEL AND NATSU DUKING IT OUT. WE CAN'T SLACK OFF, CAN WE?
ACTUALLY, I THINK WE CAN!
YOU'LL LEARN THE CREED, TOO.
RMMMMMM
EVERY-THING GONE WHITE...
HEEK! I DON'T EVEN HAVE A CHANCE AGAINST YOU, LILY!
!
KRAKL
KRAKL
KRAKL
...
LIGHT-NING...

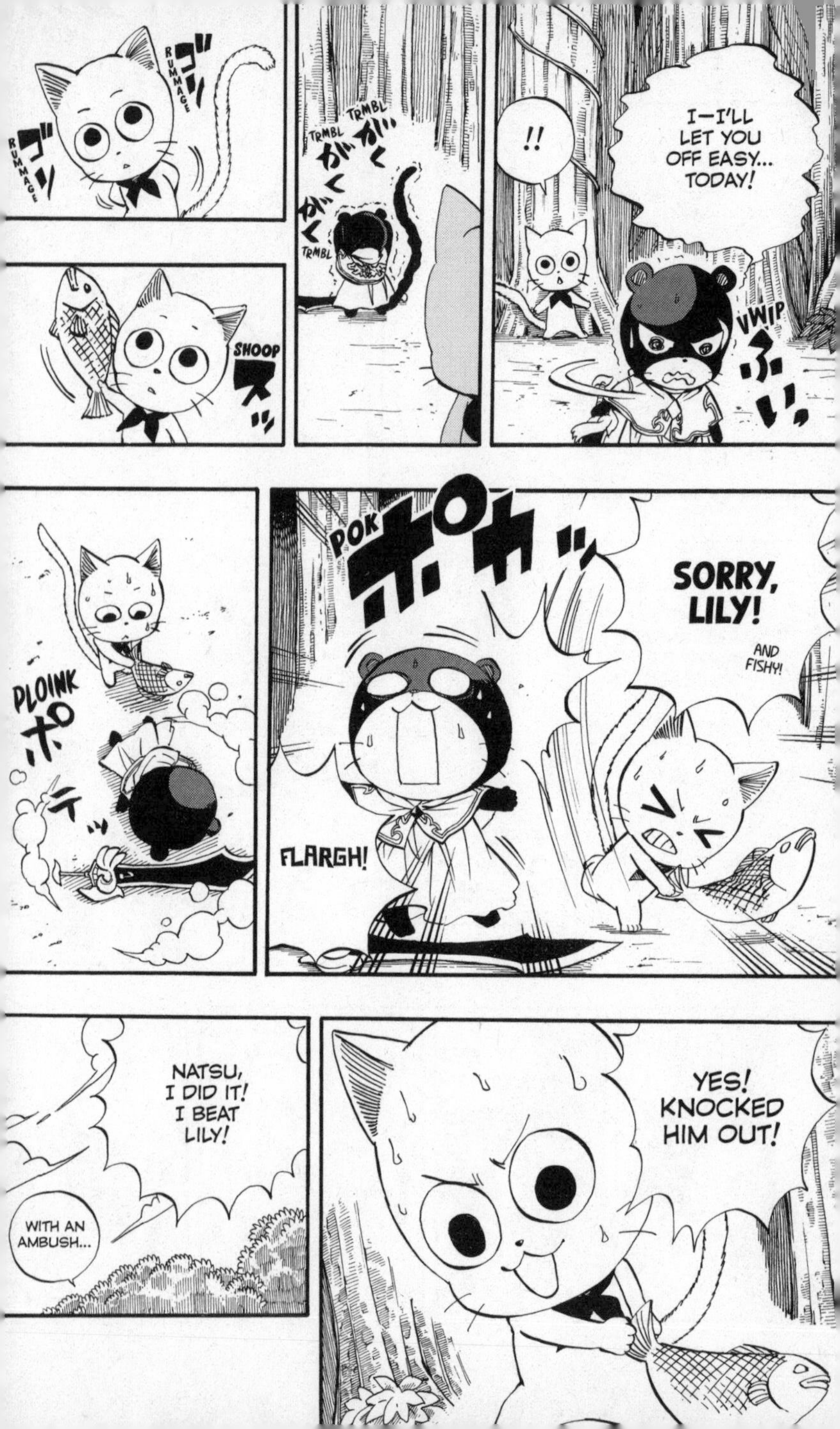
I-I'LL LET YOU OFF EASY... TODAY!
!!
VWIP
ふぃ
TRMBL
がくがく
TRMBL
がくがく
TRMBL
RUMMAGE
ゴソ
RUMMAGE
ゴソ
SHOOP
スッ
POK
ポカッ
SORRY, LILY!
AND FISHY!
FLARGH!
PLOINK
ポテッ
YES! KNOCKED HIM OUT!
NATSU, I DID IT! I BEAT LILY!
WITH AN AMBUSH...

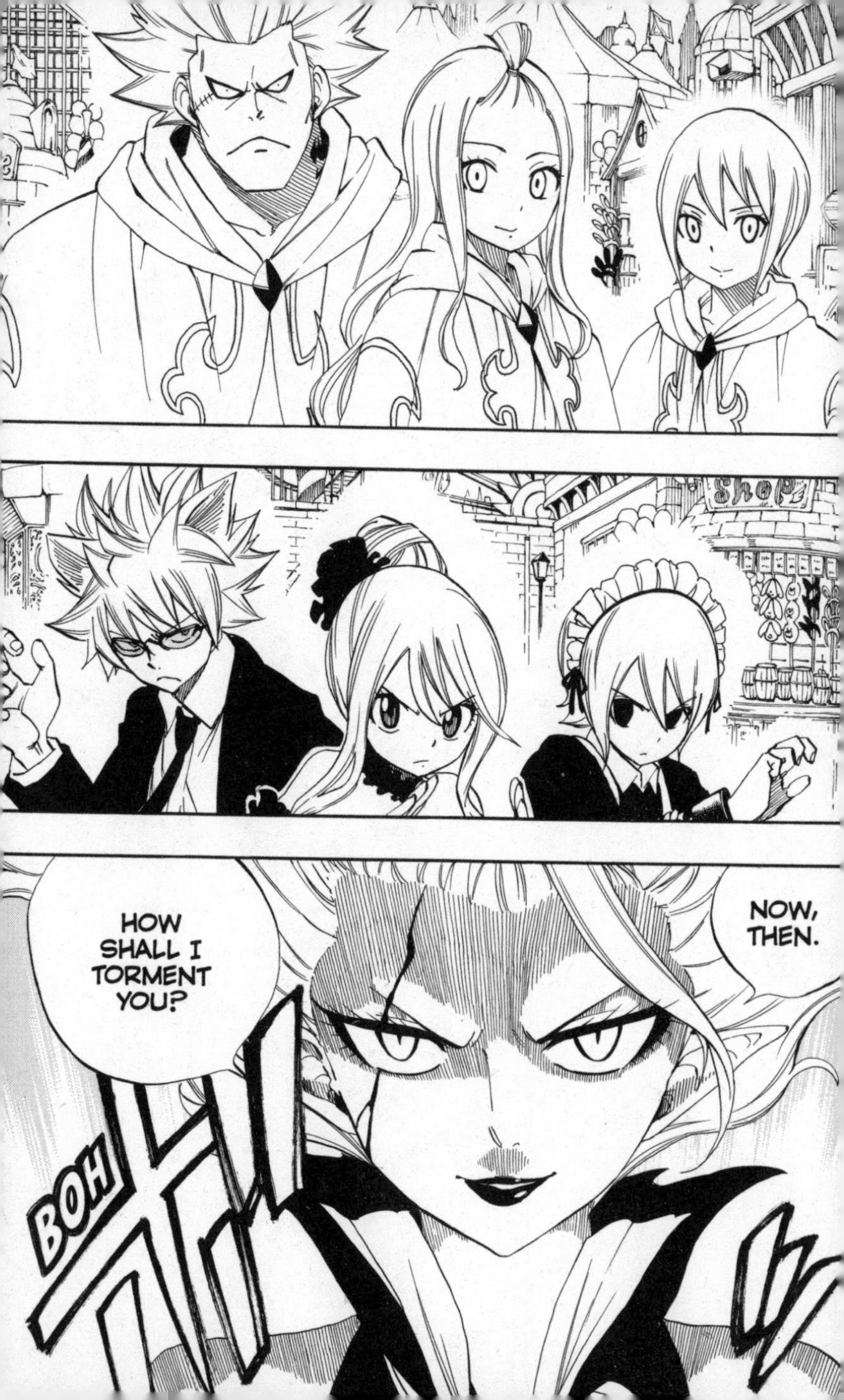
Shop
NOW, THEN.
HOW SHALL I TORMENT YOU?
BOH

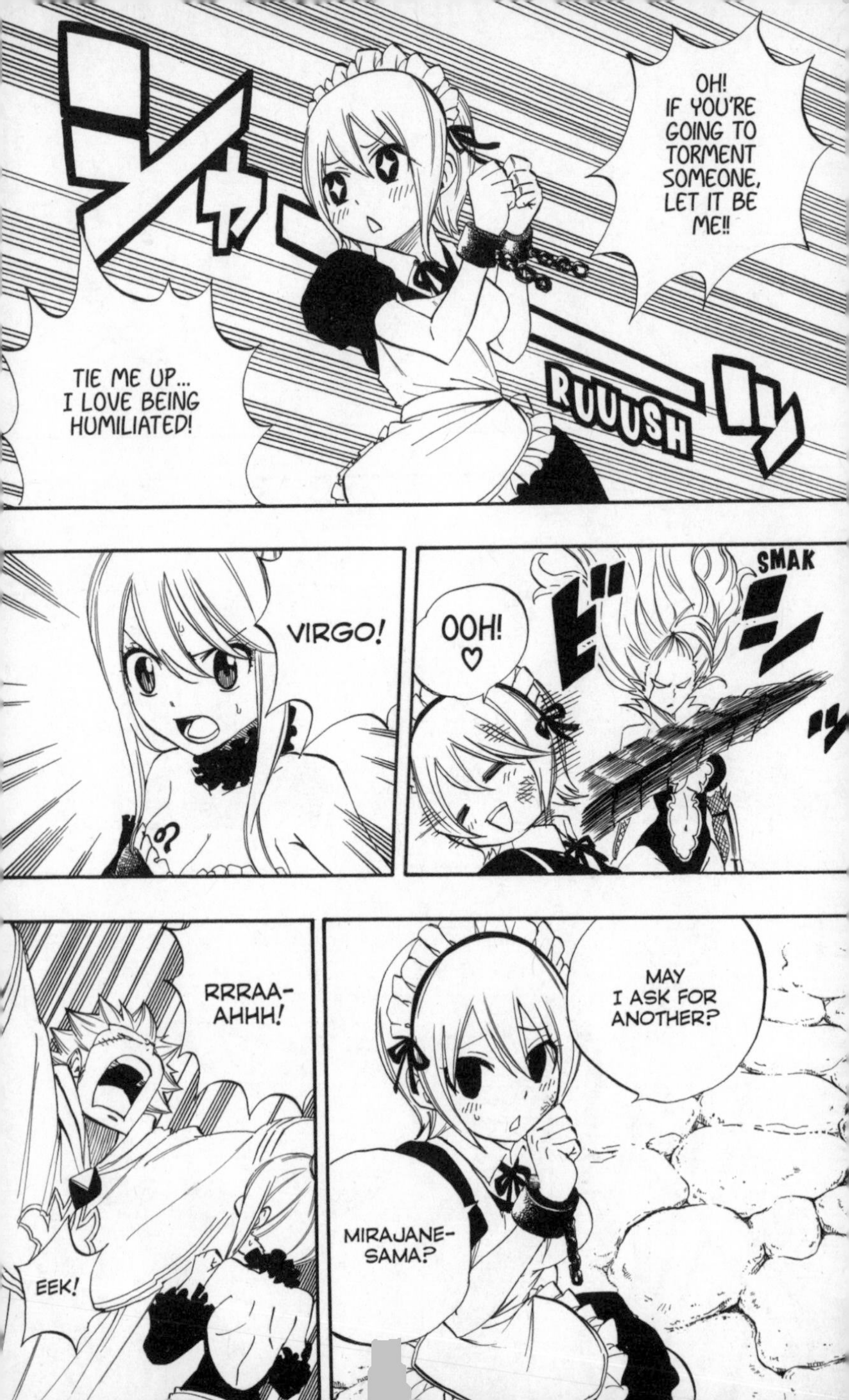
OH! IF YOU'RE GOING TO TORMENT SOMEONE, LET IT BE ME!!
RUUUSH
TIE ME UP... I LOVE BEING HUMILIATED!
SMAK
OOH! ♡
VIRGO!
MAY I ASK FOR ANOTHER?
MIRAJANE-SAMA?
RRRAA-AHHH!
EEK!

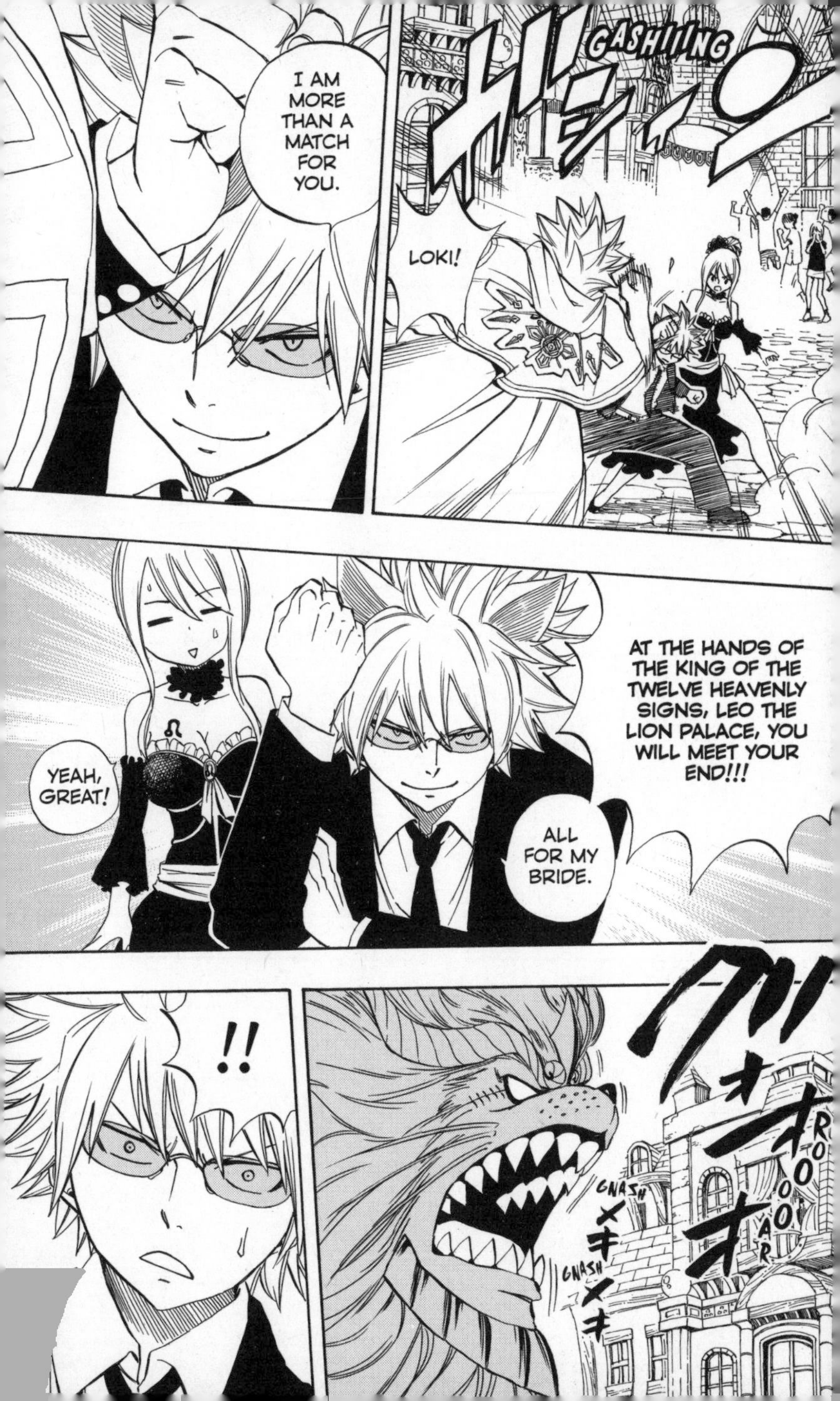
GASHIIING
LOKI!
I AM MORE THAN A MATCH FOR YOU.
AT THE HANDS OF THE KING OF THE TWELVE HEAVENLY SIGNS, LEO THE LION PALACE, YOU WILL MEET YOUR END!!!
ALL FOR MY BRIDE.
YEAH, GREAT!
ROOOOAR
GNASH
GNASH
!!

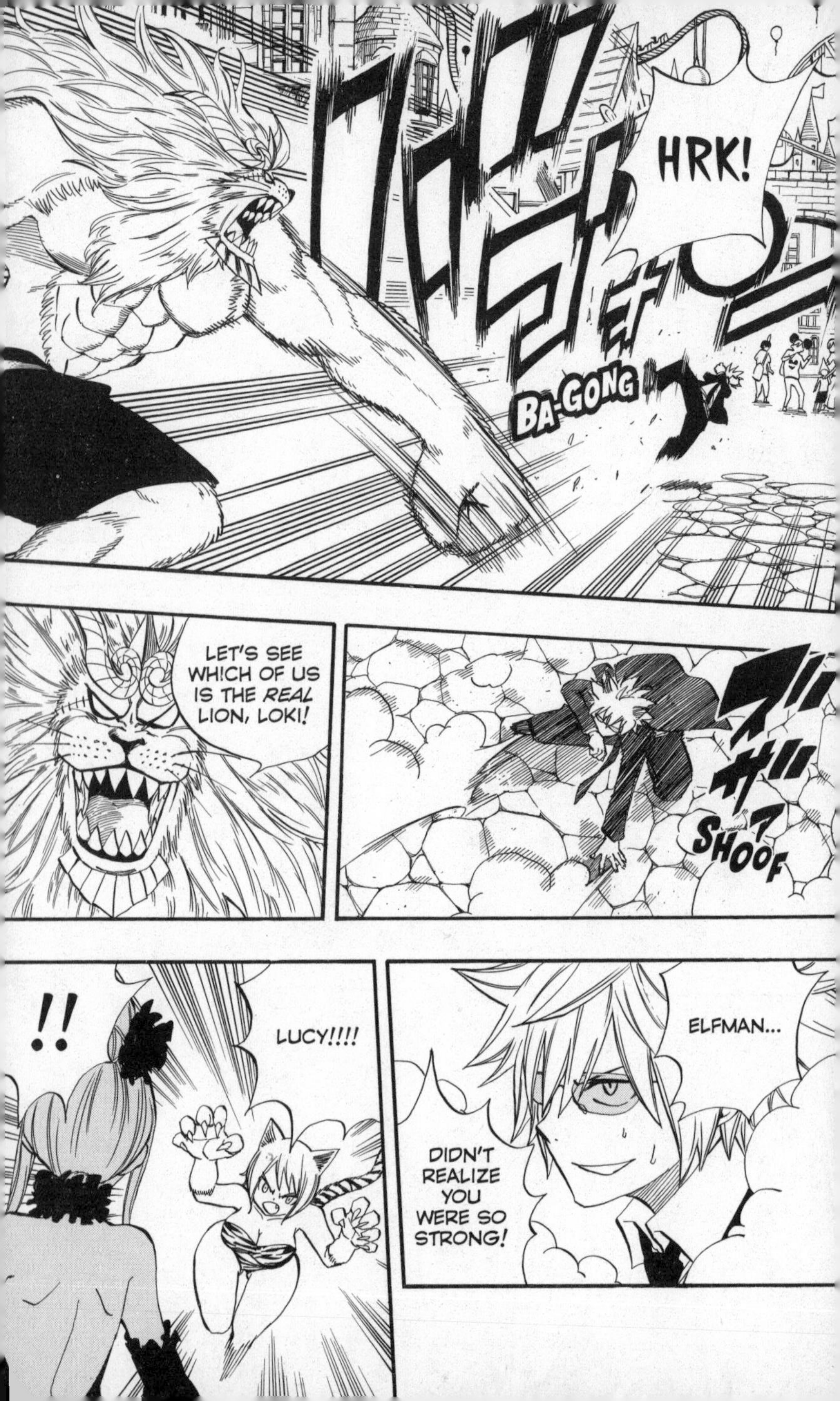

HRK!
BA-GONG
SHOOF
LET'S SEE WHICH OF US IS THE *REAL* LION, LOKI!
ELFMAN...
DIDN'T REALIZE YOU WERE SO STRONG!
LUCY!!!!
!!

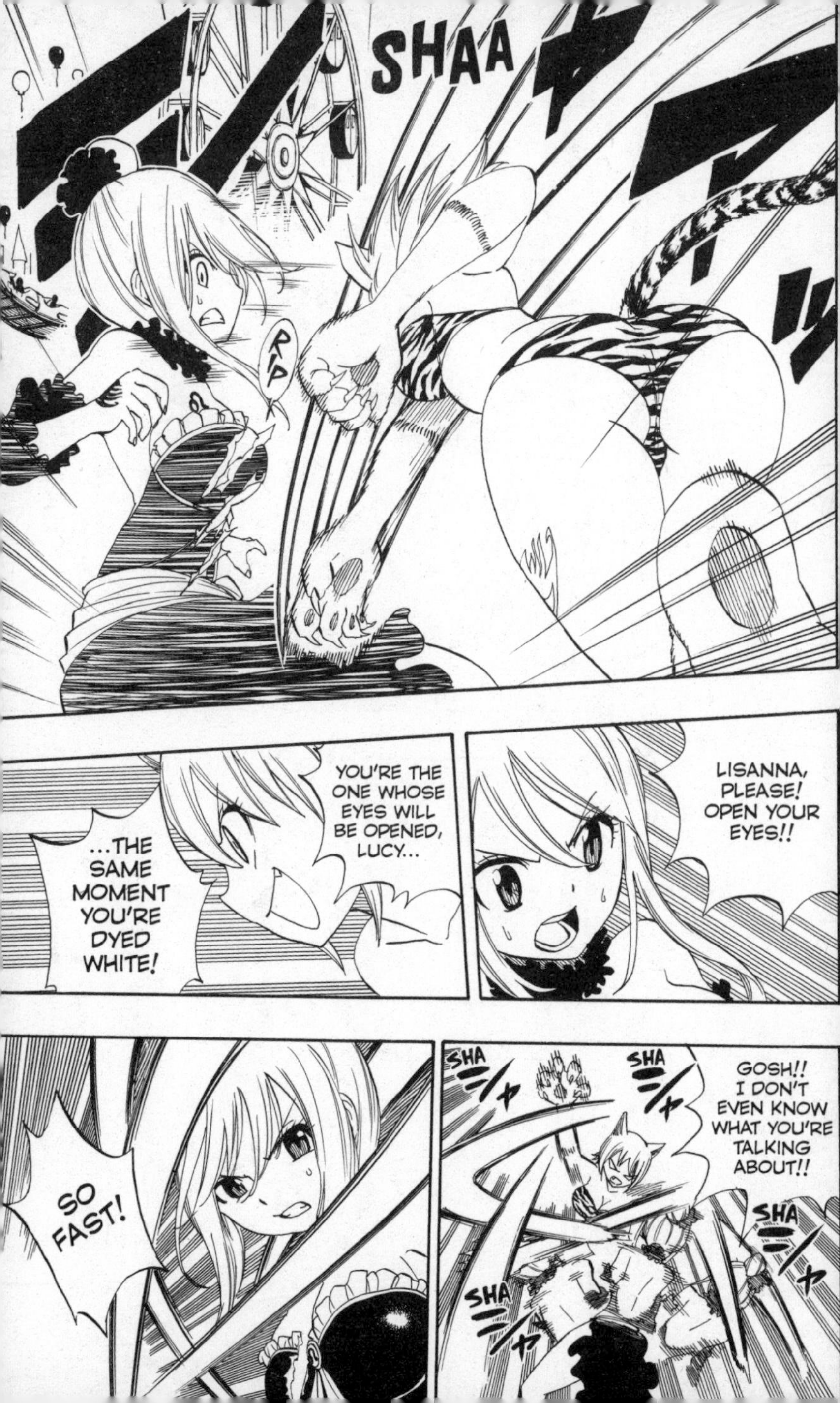
SHAA
RIP
LISANNA, PLEASE! OPEN YOUR EYES!!
YOU'RE THE ONE WHOSE EYES WILL BE OPENED, LUCY...
...THE SAME MOMENT YOU'RE DYED WHITE!
SHA
SHA
GOSH!! I DON'T EVEN KNOW WHAT YOU'RE TALKING ABOUT!!
SHA
SHA
SO FAST!

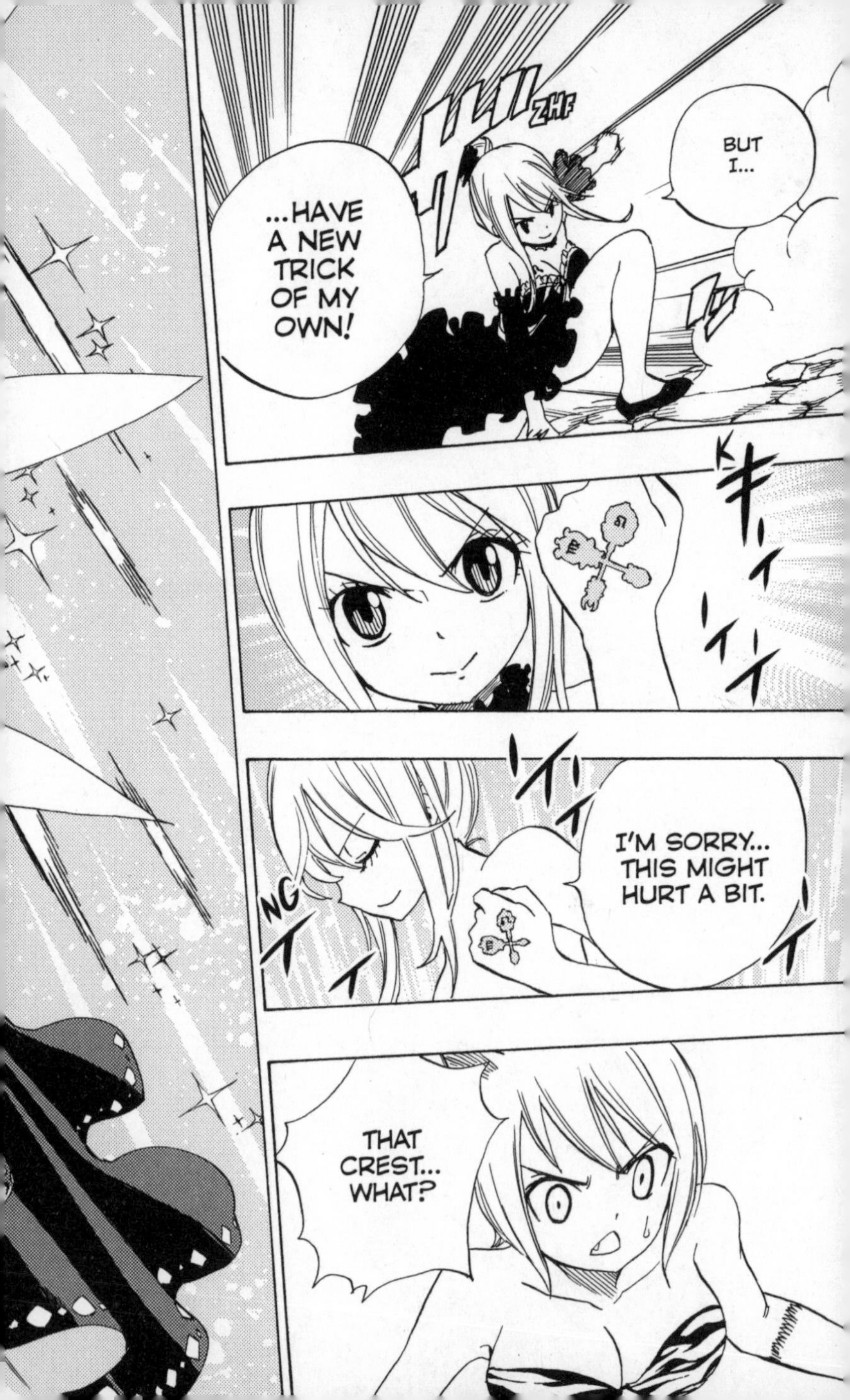
BUT I...
ZHF
...HAVE A NEW TRICK OF MY OWN!
K
I'M SORRY... THIS MIGHT HURT A BIT.
NG
THAT CREST... WHAT?

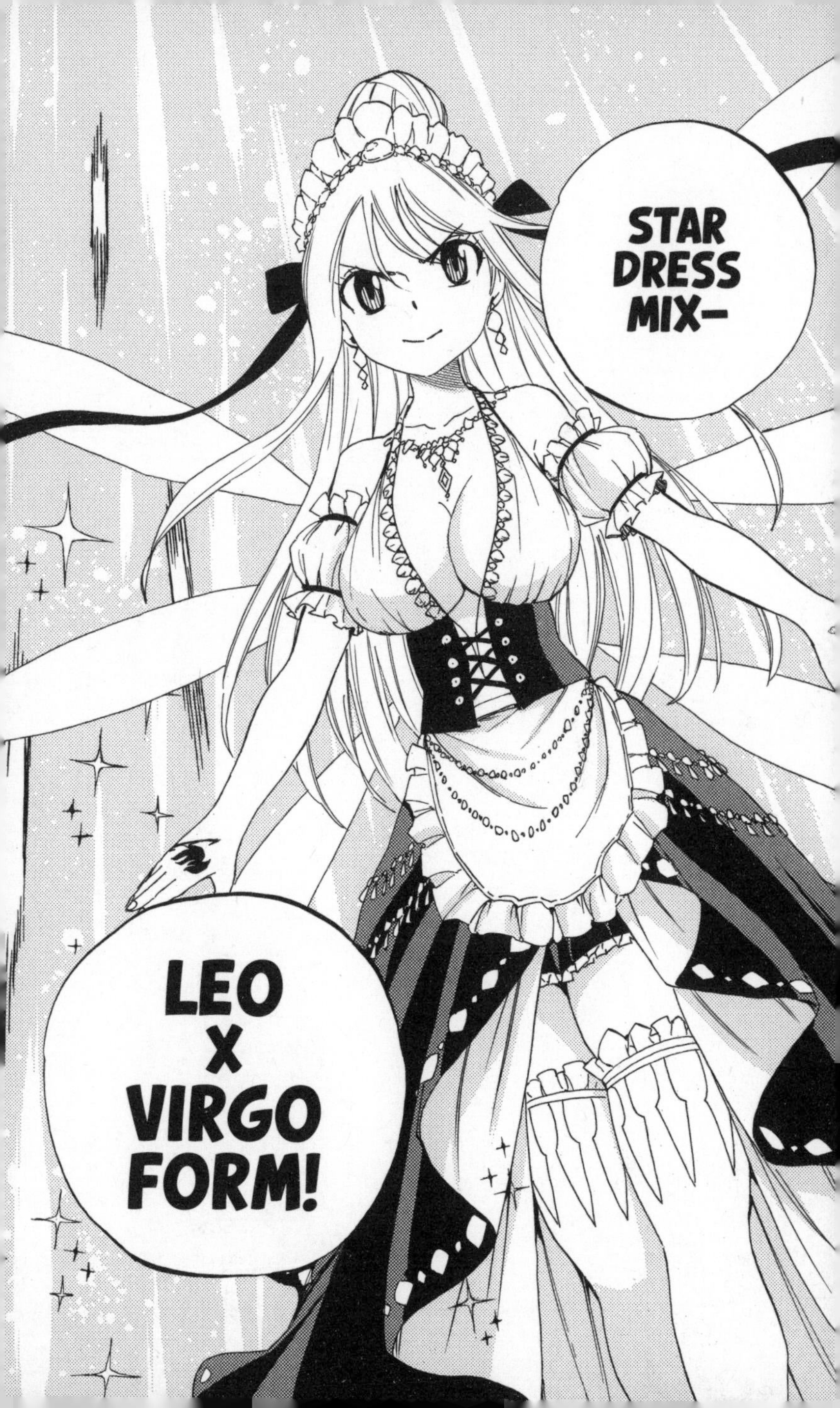
STAR DRESS MIX—
LEO X VIRGO FORM!

FAIRY TAIL 100 YEARS QUEST

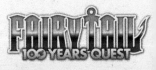

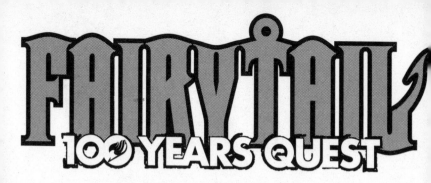

FAIRY TAIL
100 YEARS QUEST

Chapter 32: Star Dress Mix

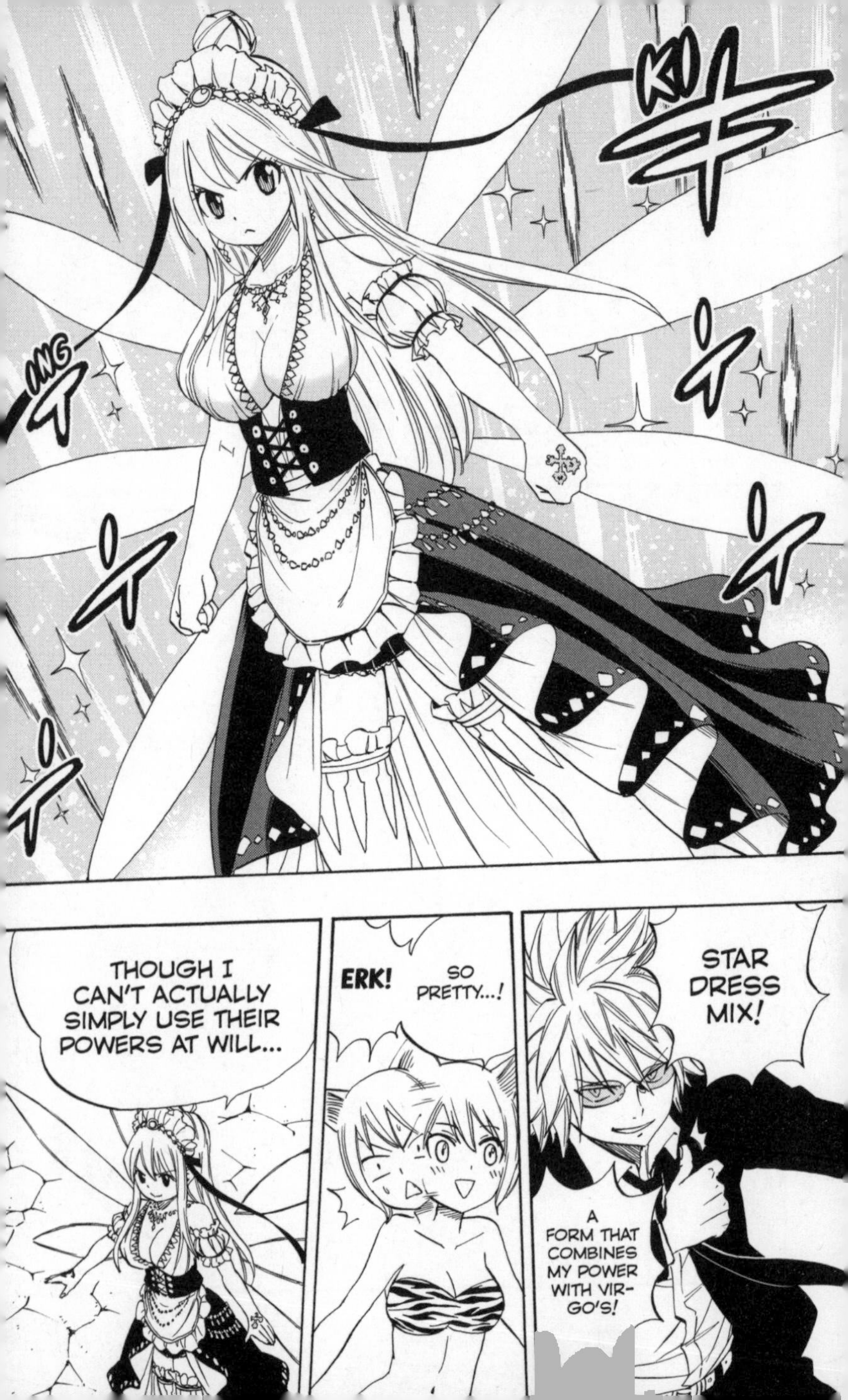
KI
ING
STAR DRESS MIX!
A FORM THAT COMBINES MY POWER WITH VIR-GO'S!
SO PRETTY...!
ERK!
THOUGH I CAN'T ACTUALLY SIMPLY USE THEIR POWERS AT WILL...

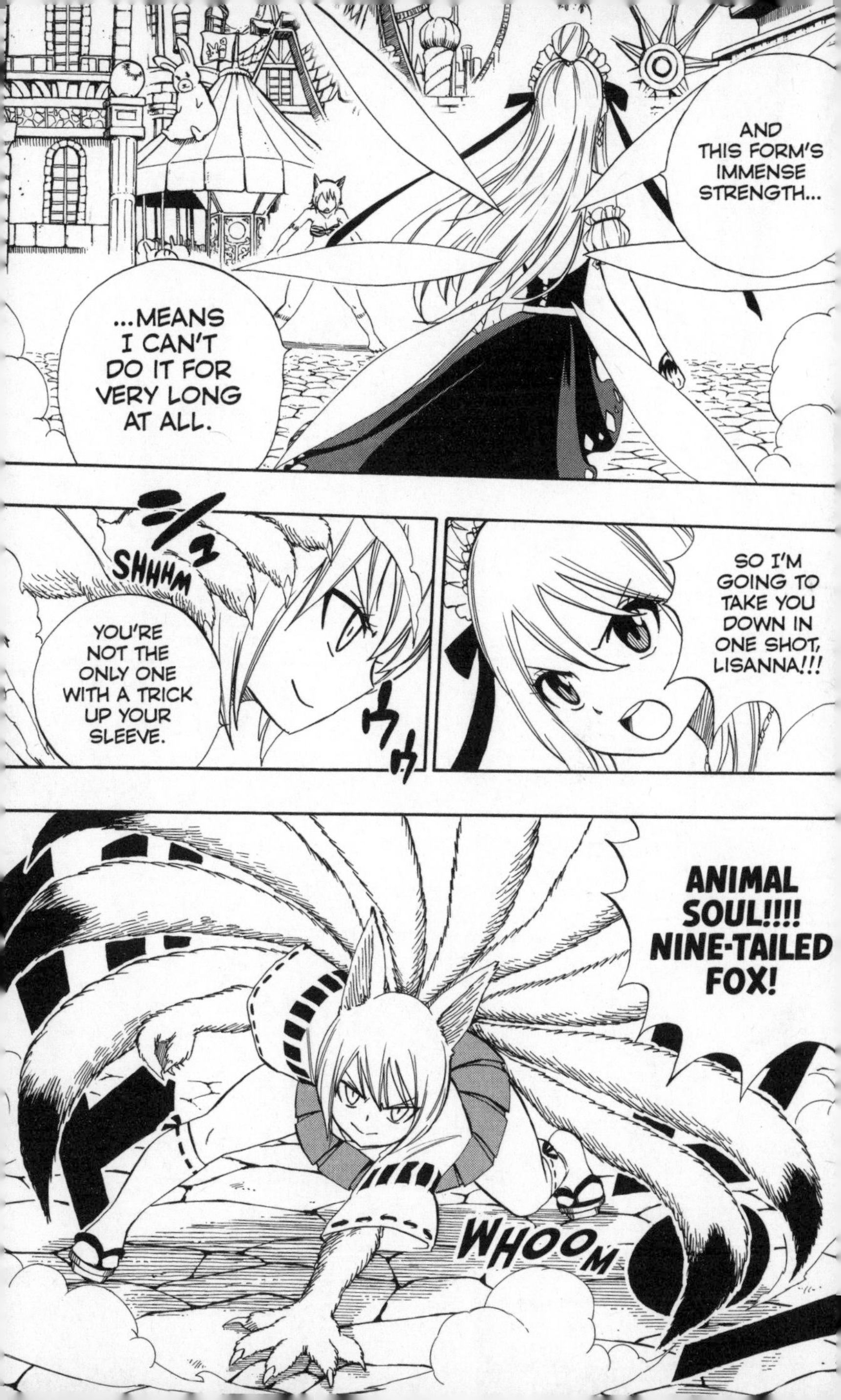
AND THIS FORM'S IMMENSE STRENGTH...
...MEANS I CAN'T DO IT FOR VERY LONG AT ALL.
SO I'M GOING TO TAKE YOU DOWN IN ONE SHOT, LISANNA!!!
SHHHM
YOU'RE NOT THE ONLY ONE WITH A TRICK UP YOUR SLEEVE.
ANIMAL SOUL!!!! NINE-TAILED FOX!
WHOOM

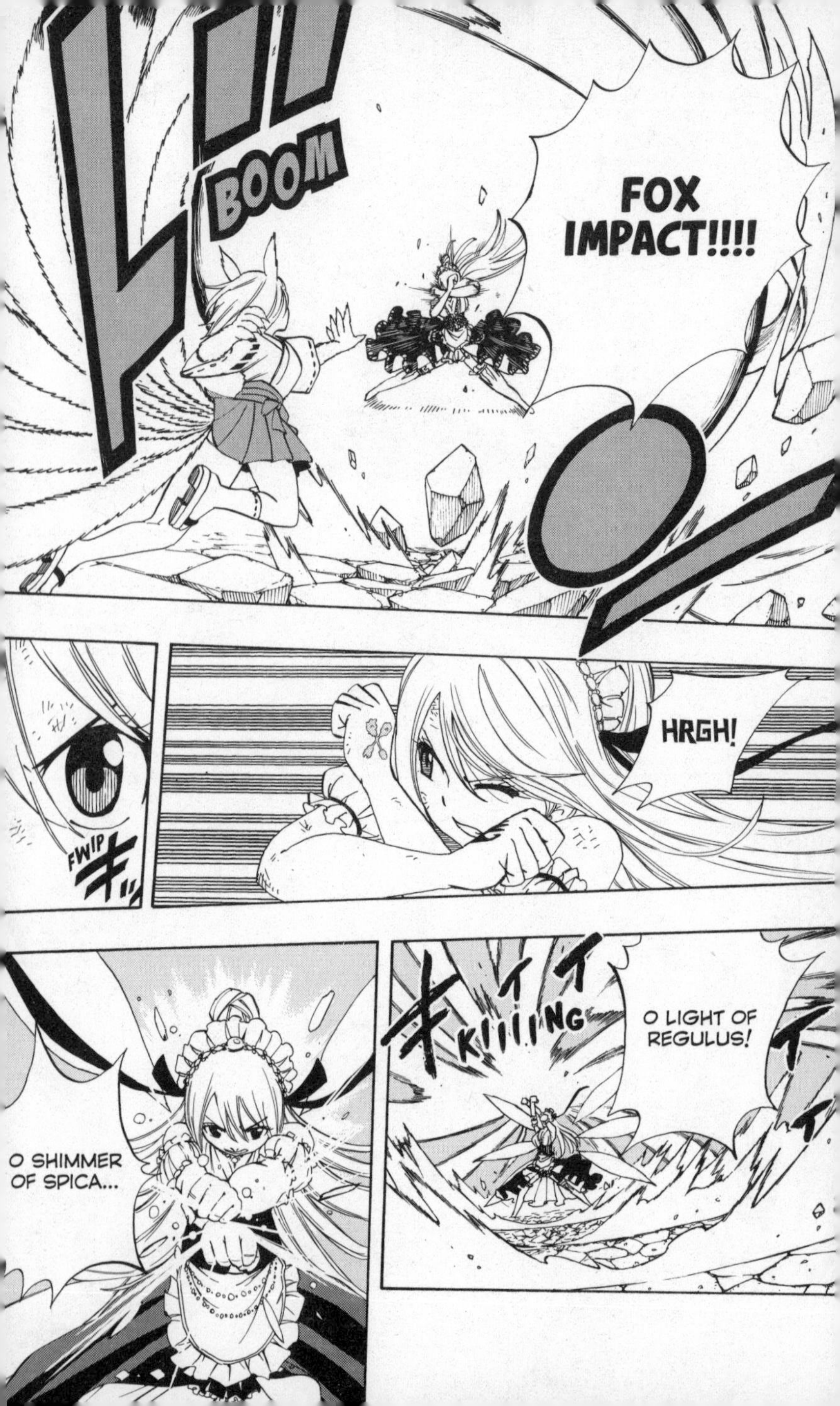
FOX IMPACT!!!!
BOOM
HRGH!
FWIP
O LIGHT OF REGULUS!
KIIIING
O SHIMMER OF SPICA...

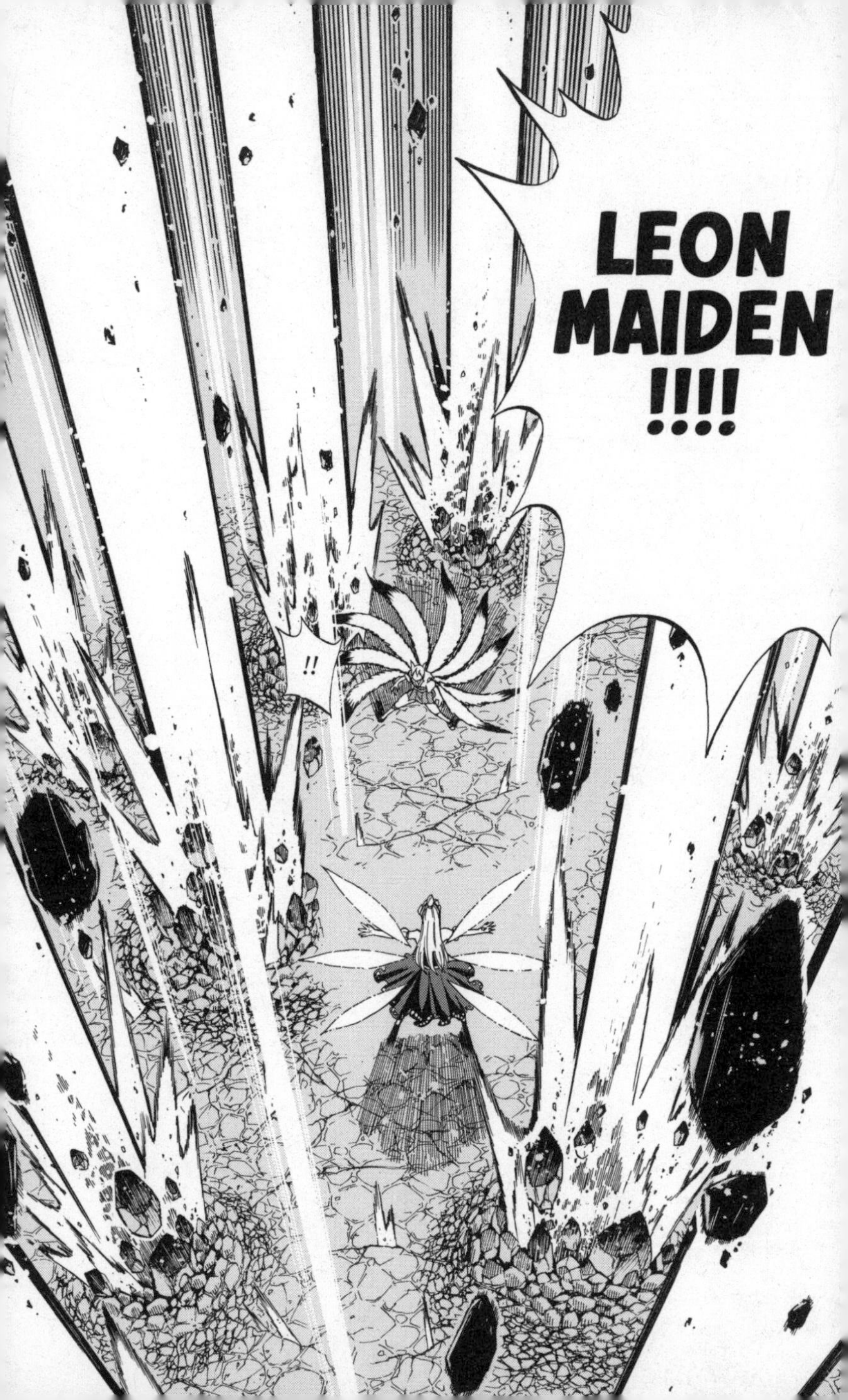
LEON MAIDEN !!!!
!!

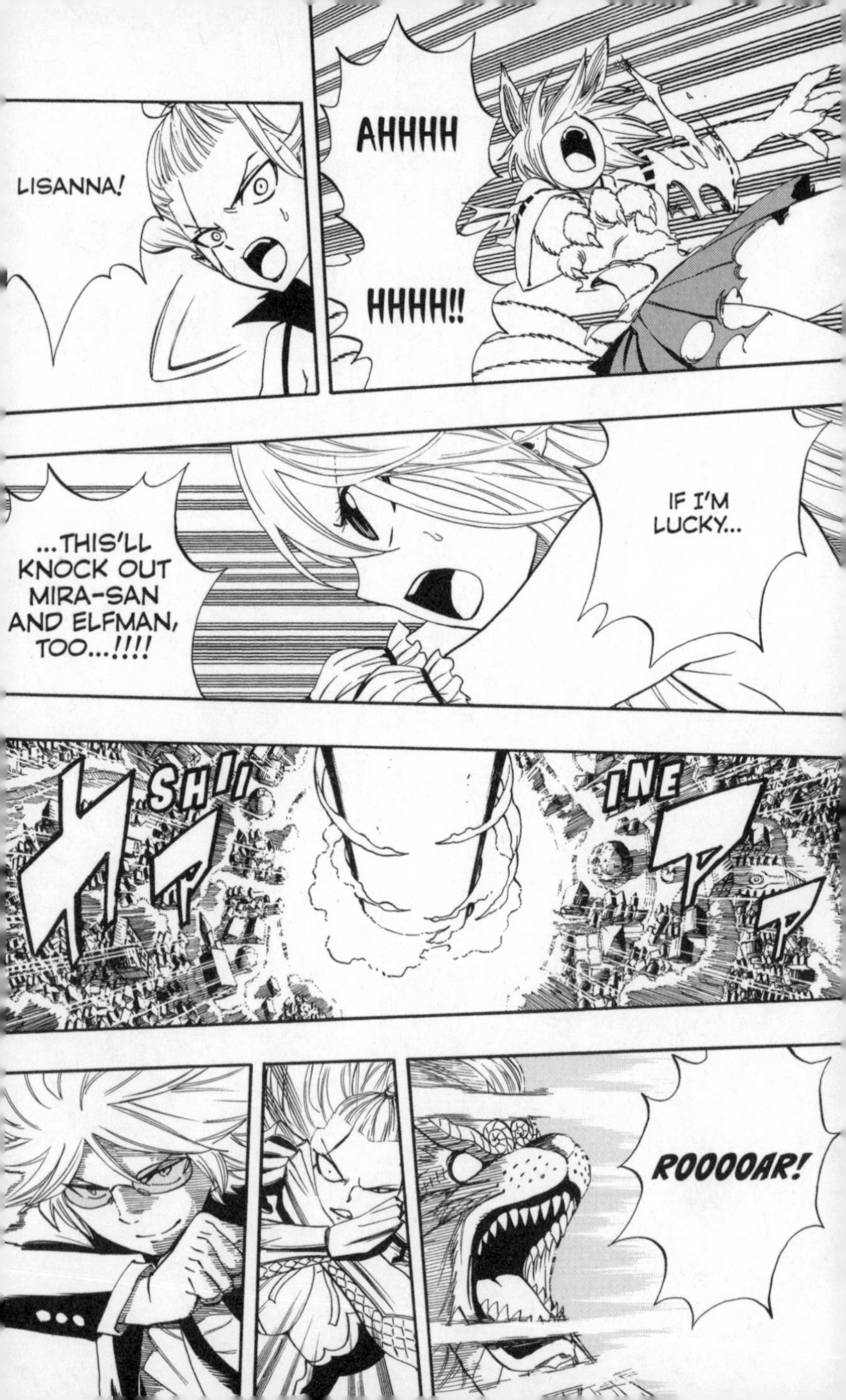
AHHHH
HHHH!!
LISANNA!
IF I'M LUCKY...
...THIS'LL KNOCK OUT MIRA-SAN AND ELFMAN, TOO...!!!!
SHI
INE
ROOOOAR!

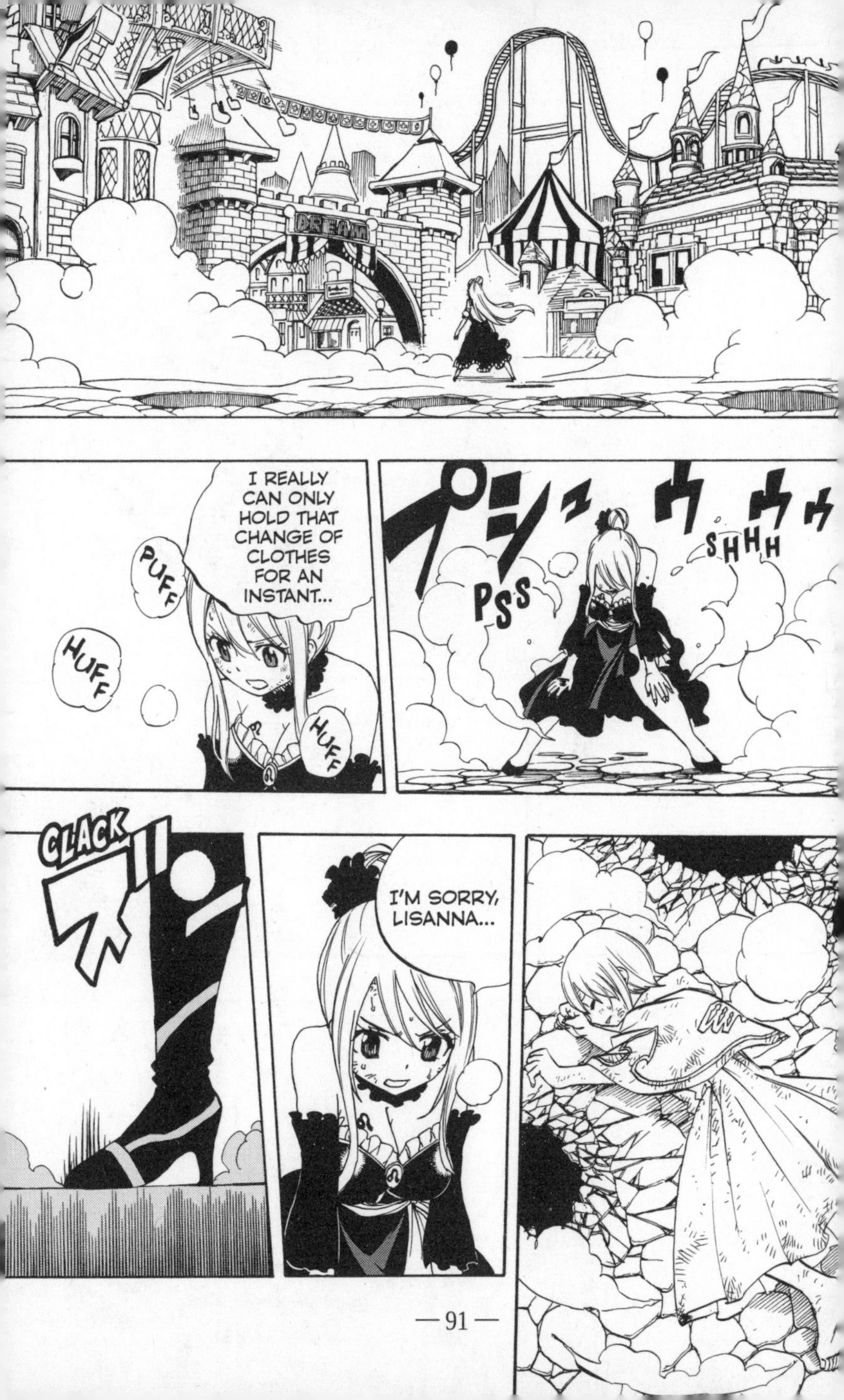
DREAM
プシュウウゥ
SHHH
PSS
I REALLY CAN ONLY HOLD THAT CHANGE OF CLOTHES FOR AN INSTANT...
PUFF
HUFF
HUFF
I'M SORRY, LISANNA...
CLACK

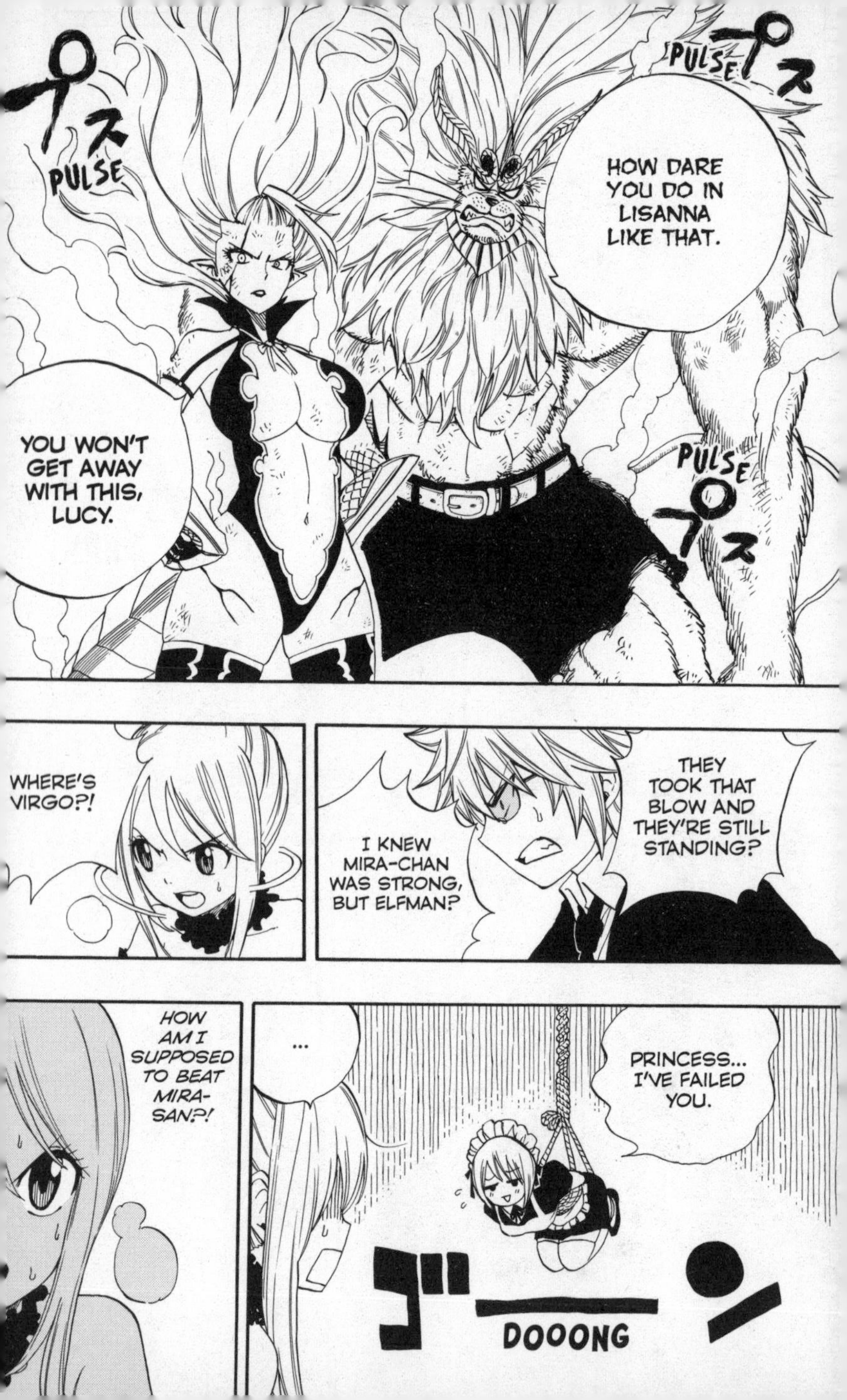
PULSE
HOW DARE YOU DO IN LISANNA LIKE THAT.
PULSE
PULSE
YOU WON'T GET AWAY WITH THIS, LUCY.
THEY TOOK THAT BLOW AND THEY'RE STILL STANDING?
I KNEW MIRA-CHAN WAS STRONG, BUT ELFMAN?
WHERE'S VIRGO?!
PRINCESS... I'VE FAILED YOU.
...
DOOONG
HOW AM I SUPPOSED TO BEAT MIRA-SAN?!

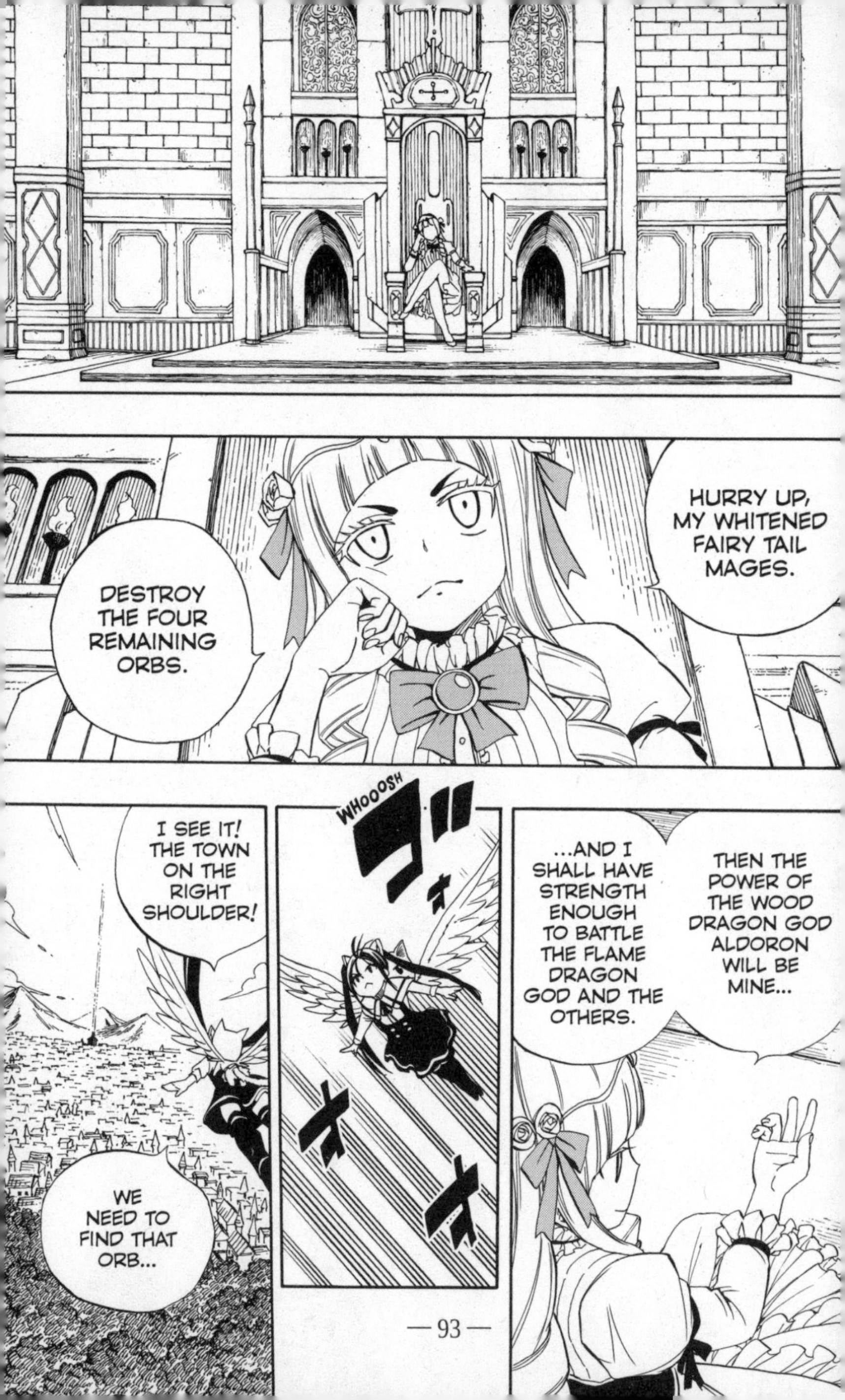
HURRY UP, MY WHITENED FAIRY TAIL MAGES.
DESTROY THE FOUR REMAINING ORBS.
THEN THE POWER OF THE WOOD DRAGON GOD ALDORON WILL BE MINE...
...AND I SHALL HAVE STRENGTH ENOUGH TO BATTLE THE FLAME DRAGON GOD AND THE OTHERS.
WHOOOSH
I SEE IT! THE TOWN ON THE RIGHT SHOULDER!
WE NEED TO FIND THAT ORB...

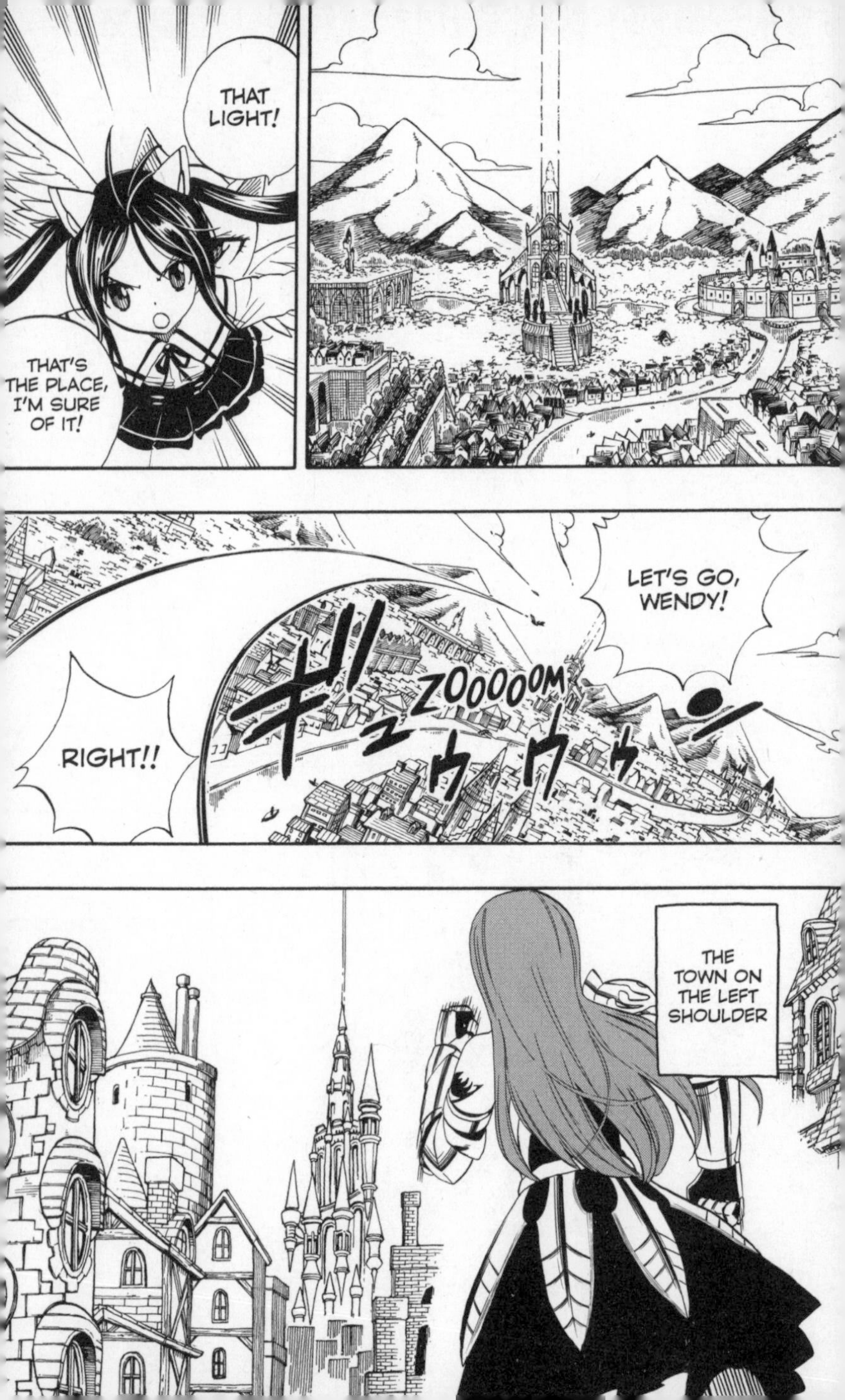
THAT LIGHT!
THAT'S THE PLACE, I'M SURE OF IT!
LET'S GO, WENDY!
ZOOOOOM
RIGHT!!
THE TOWN ON THE LEFT SHOULDER

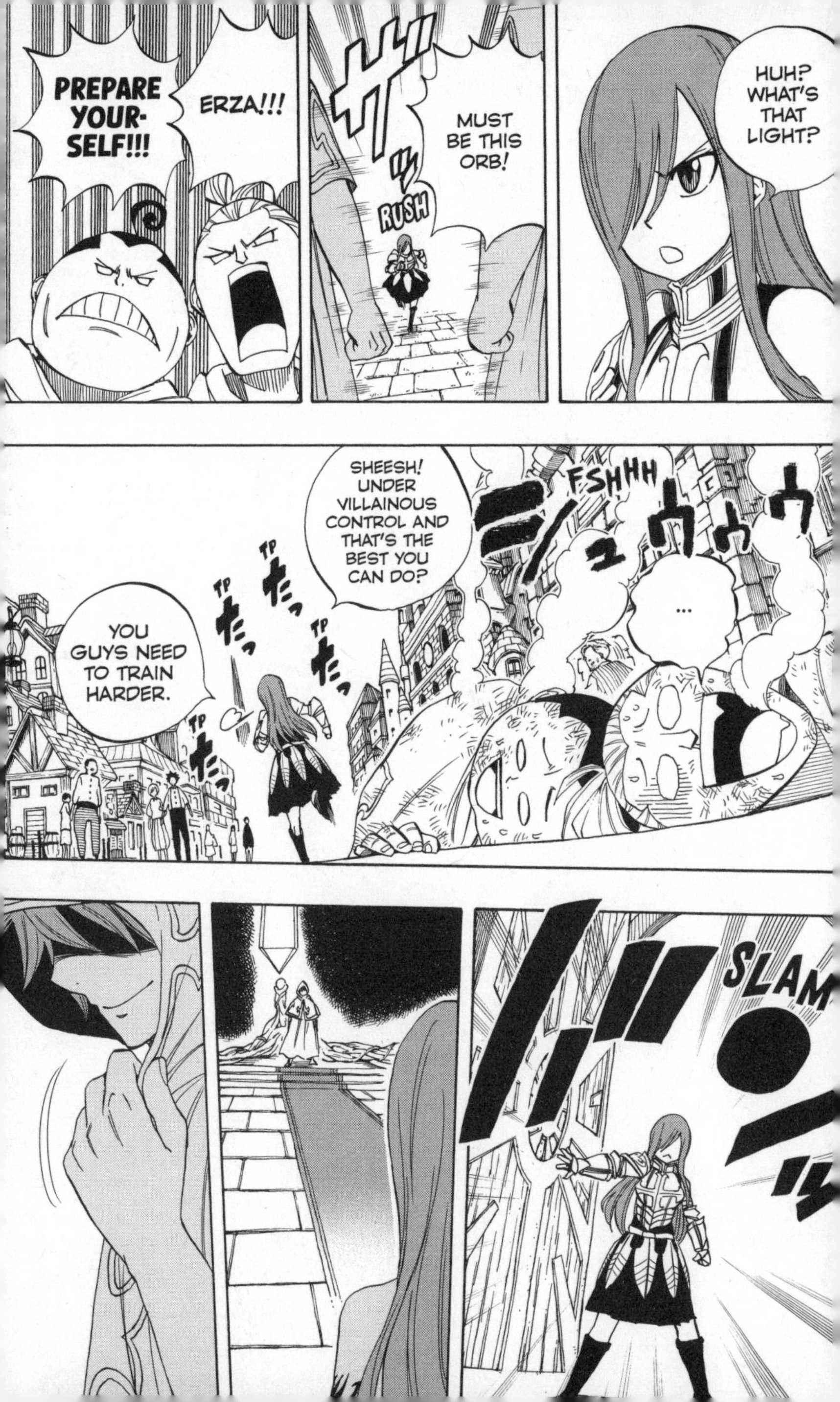
HUH? WHAT'S THAT LIGHT?
MUST BE THIS ORB!
RUSH
ERZA!!!
PREPARE YOUR-SELF!!!
FSHHH
...
SHEESH! UNDER VILLAINOUS CONTROL AND THAT'S THE BEST YOU CAN DO?
TP
TP
TP
YOU GUYS NEED TO TRAIN HARDER.
TP
SLAM

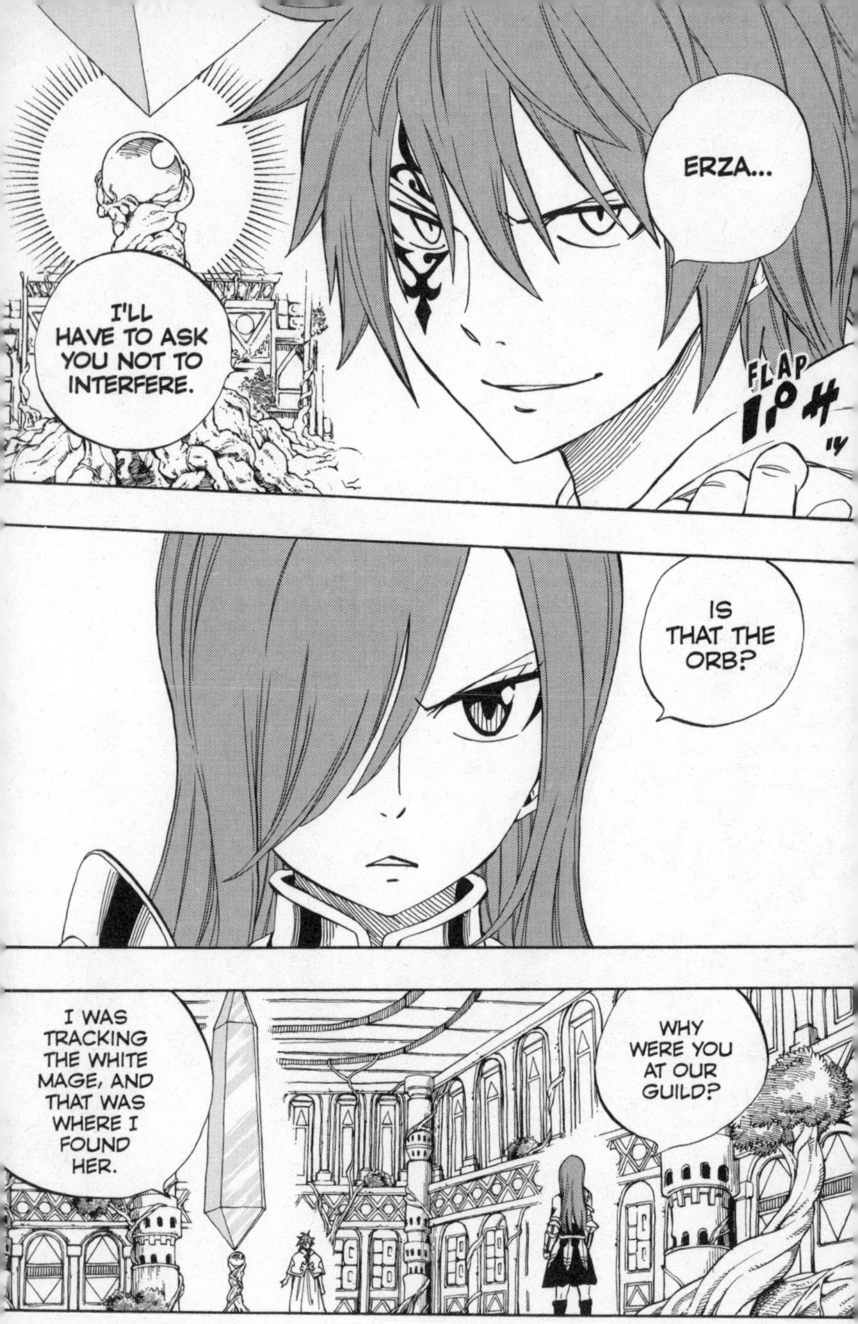
ERZA...
FLAP
I'LL HAVE TO ASK YOU NOT TO INTERFERE.
IS THAT THE ORB?
WHY WERE YOU AT OUR GUILD?
I WAS TRACKING THE WHITE MAGE, AND THAT WAS WHERE I FOUND HER.

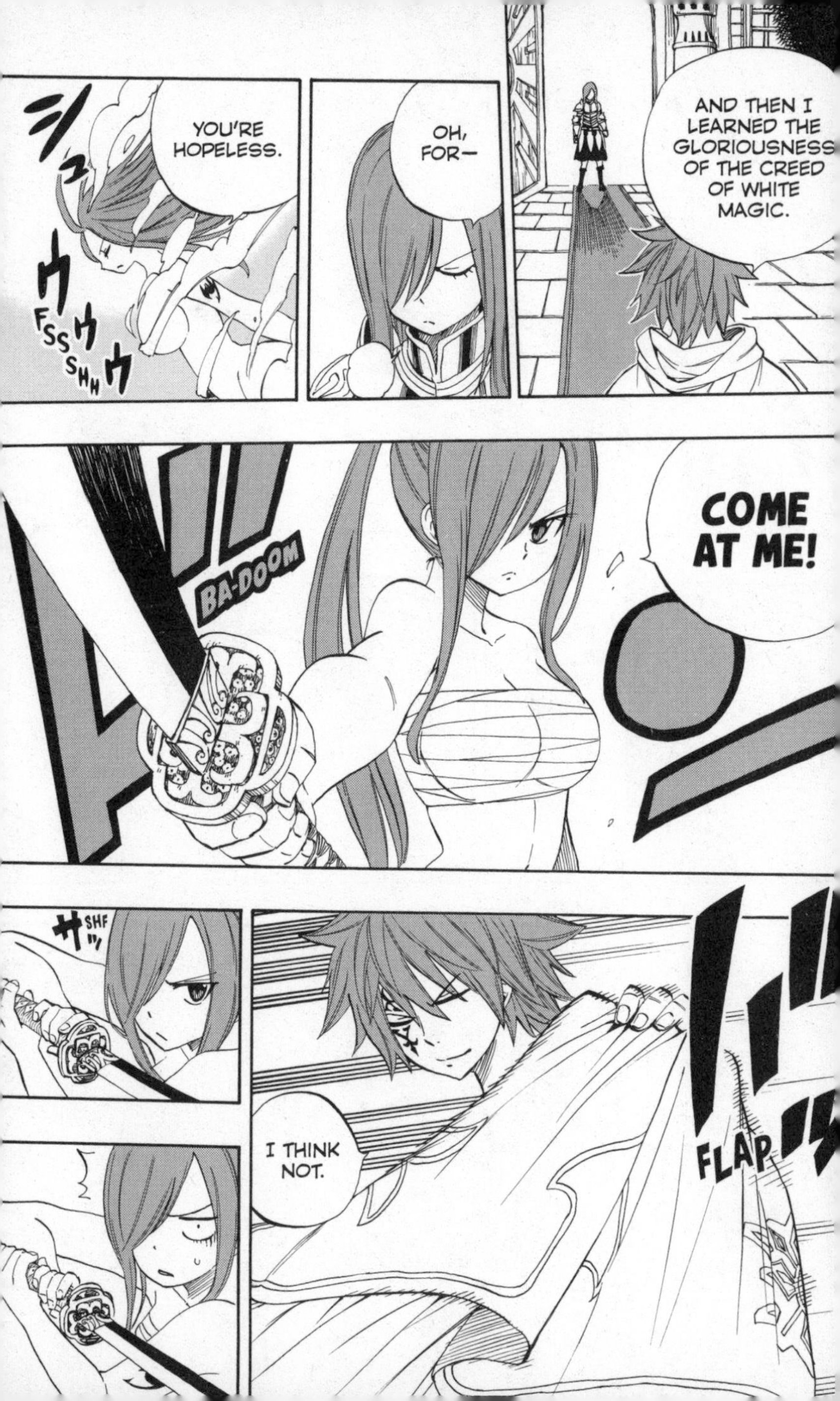

AND THEN I LEARNED THE GLORIOUSNESS OF THE CREED OF WHITE MAGIC.
OH, FOR—
YOU'RE HOPELESS.
FSSSHH
COME AT ME!
BA-DOOM
FLAP
I THINK NOT.
SHF

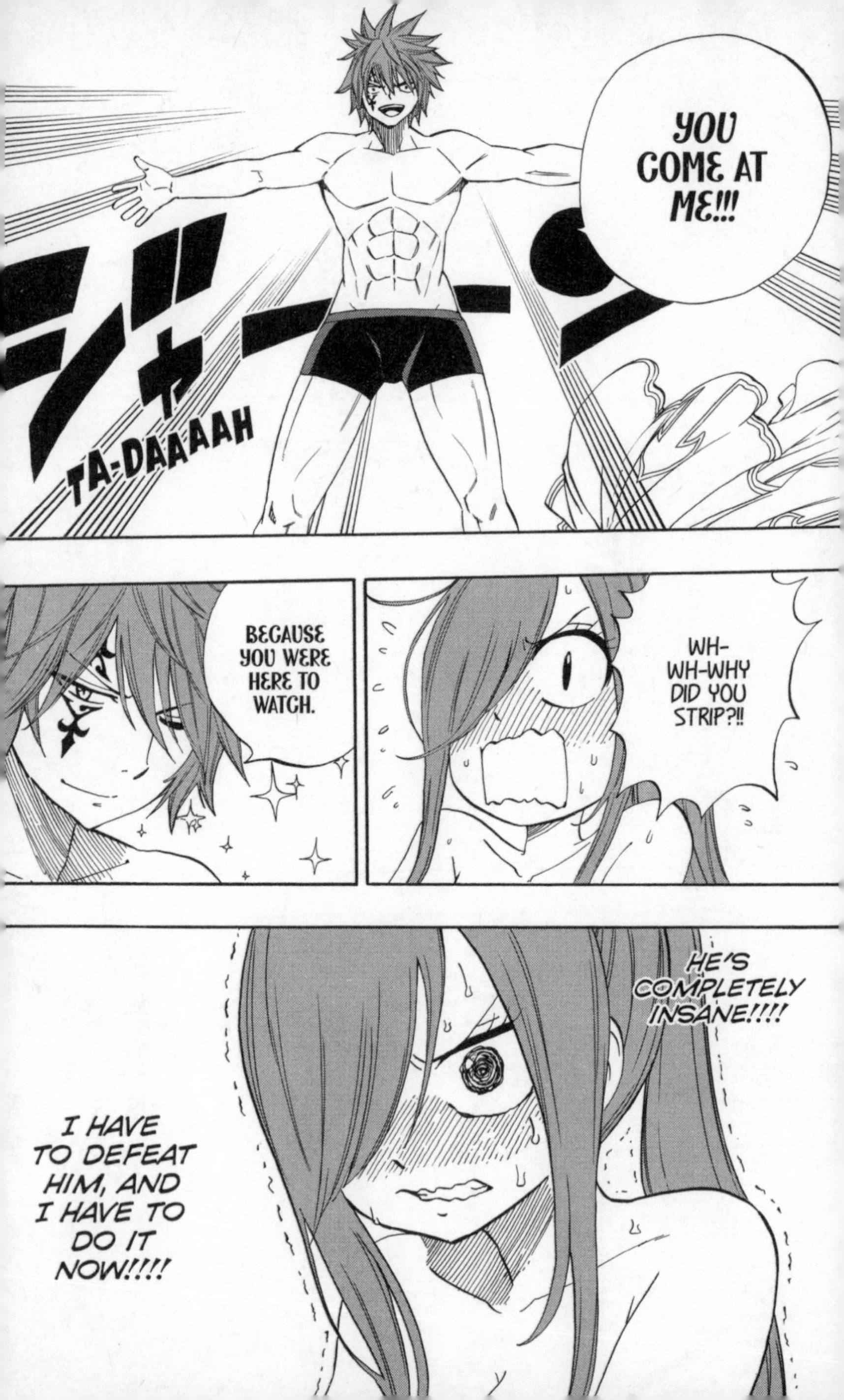
YOU COME AT ME!!!
TA-DAAAAH
WH- WH-WHY DID YOU STRIP?!!
BECAUSE YOU WERE HERE TO WATCH.
HE'S COMPLETELY INSANE!!!!
I HAVE TO DEFEAT HIM, AND I HAVE TO DO IT NOW!!!!

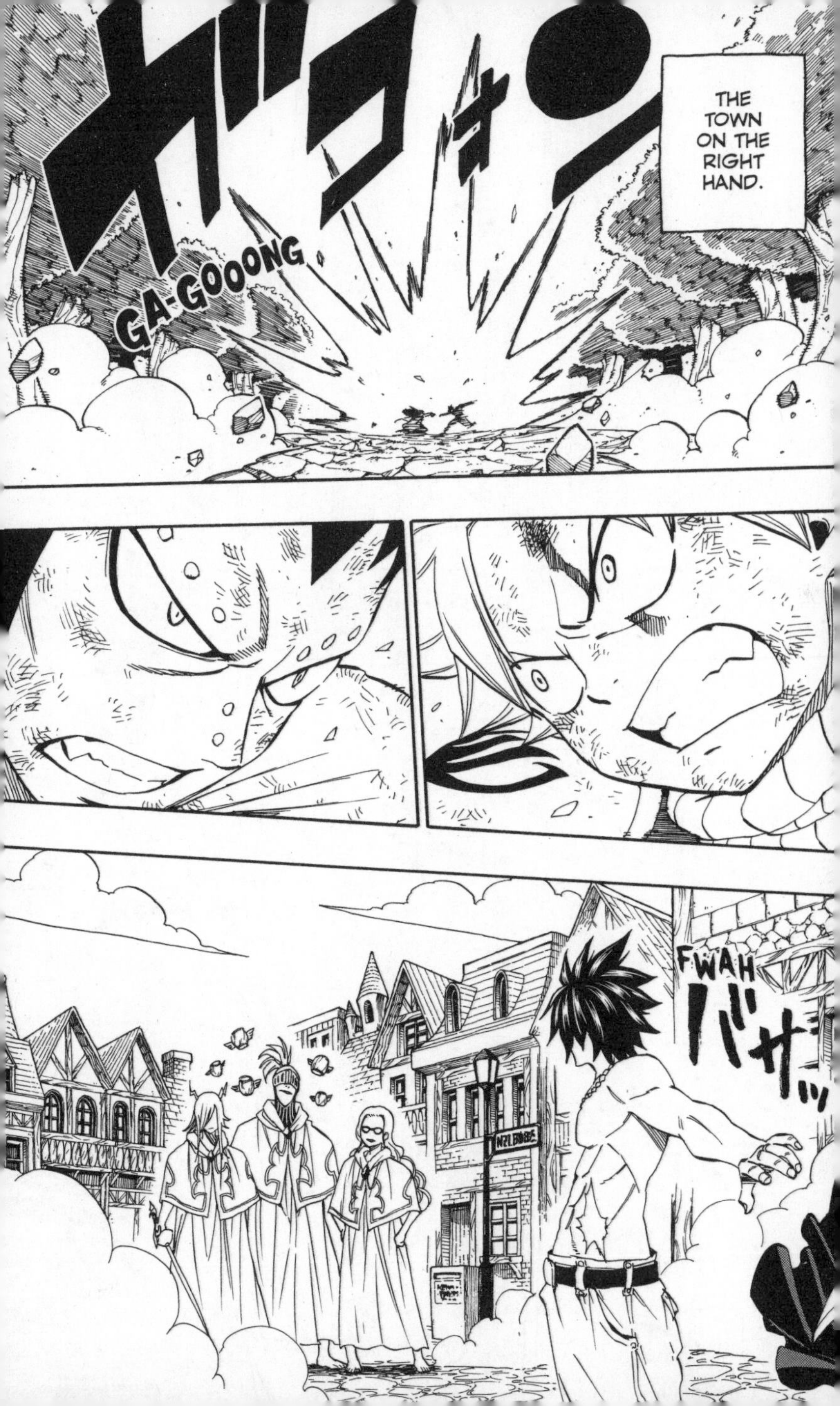

THE TOWN ON THE RIGHT HAND.
GA-GOOONG
FWAH

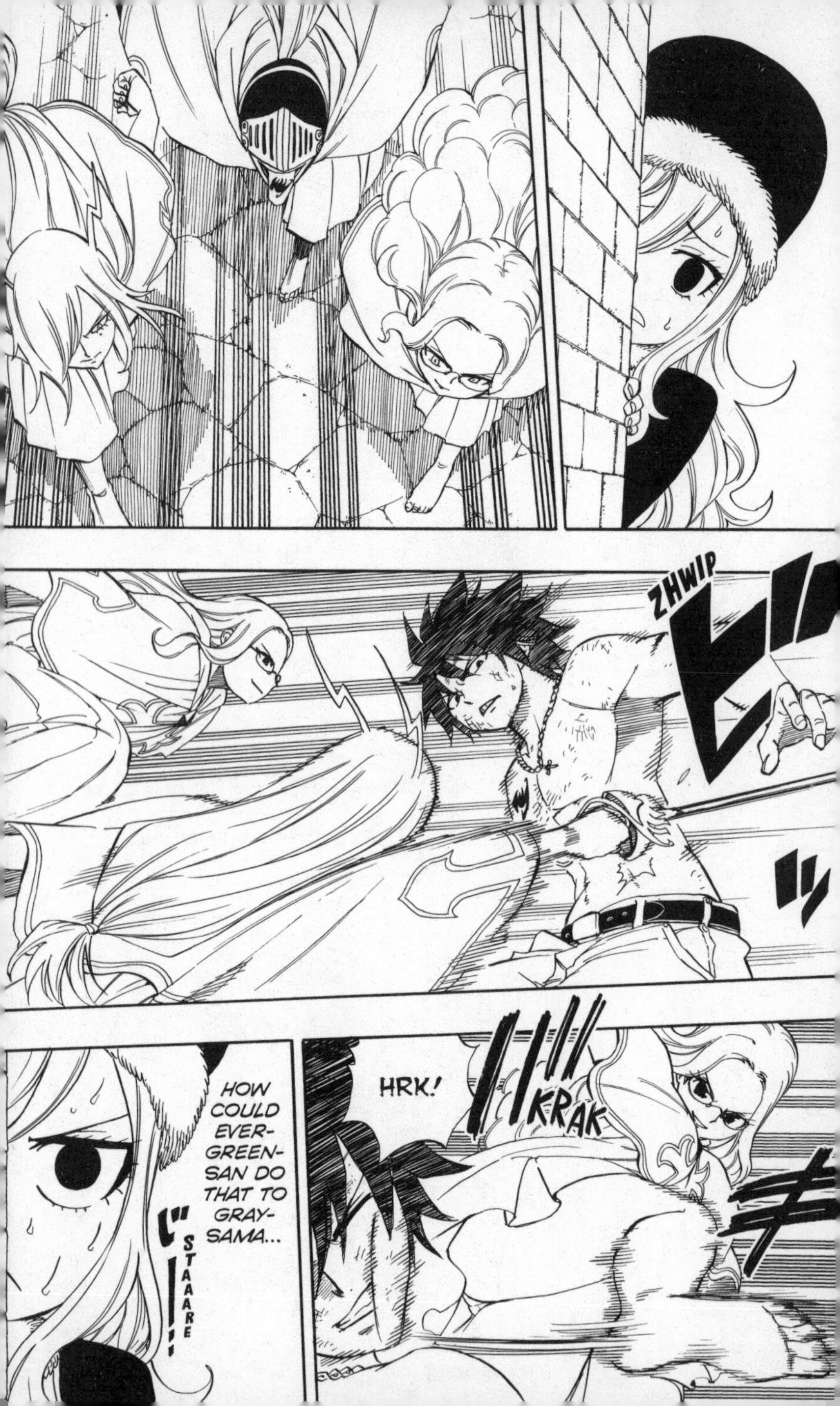
ZHWIP
HRK!
KRAK
HOW COULD EVER-GREEN-SAN DO THAT TO GRAY-SAMA...
STAAARE

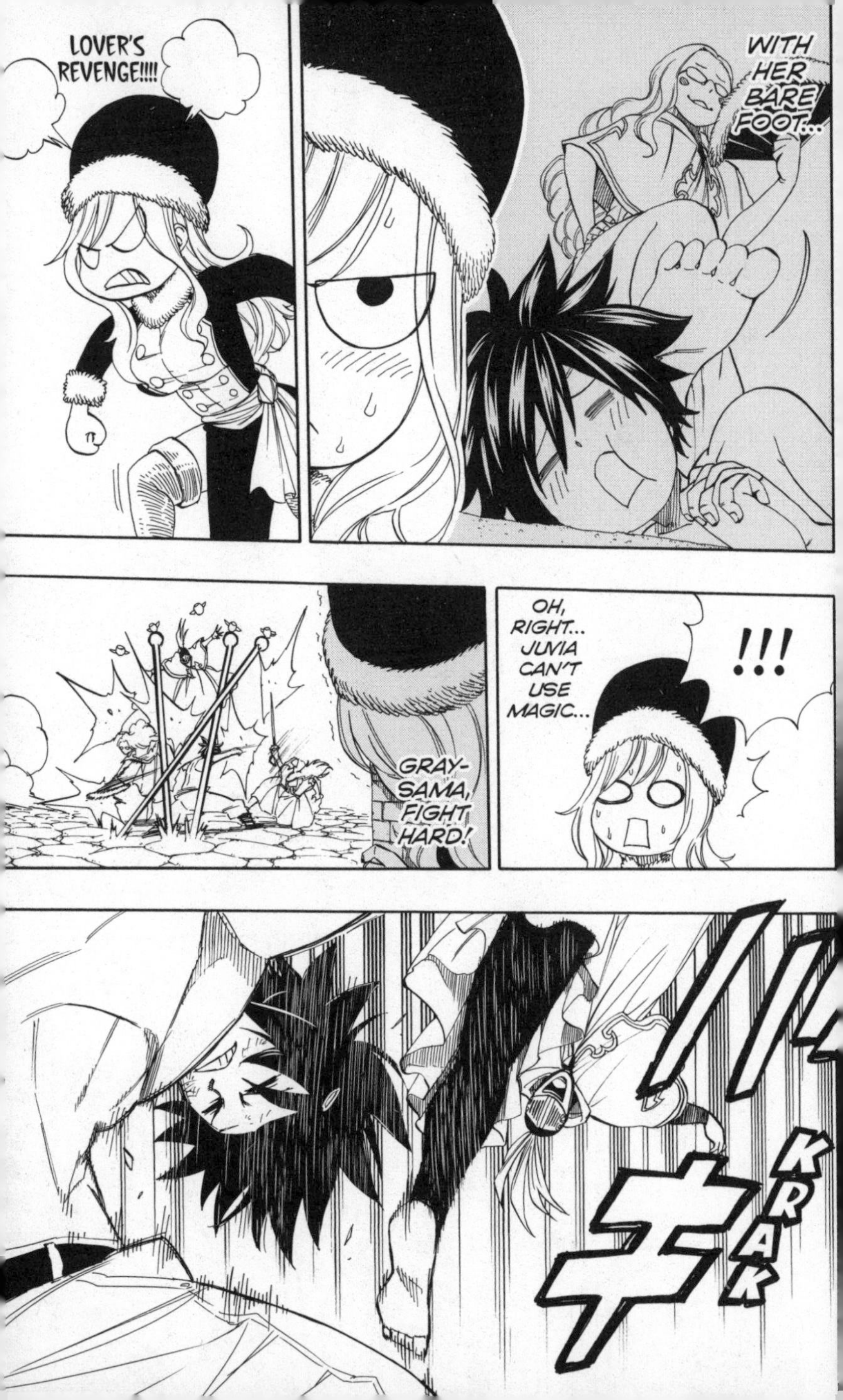
WITH HER BARE FOOT...
LOVER'S REVENGE!!!!
!!!
OH, RIGHT... JUVIA CAN'T USE MAGIC...
GRAY-SAMA, FIGHT HARD!
KRAK

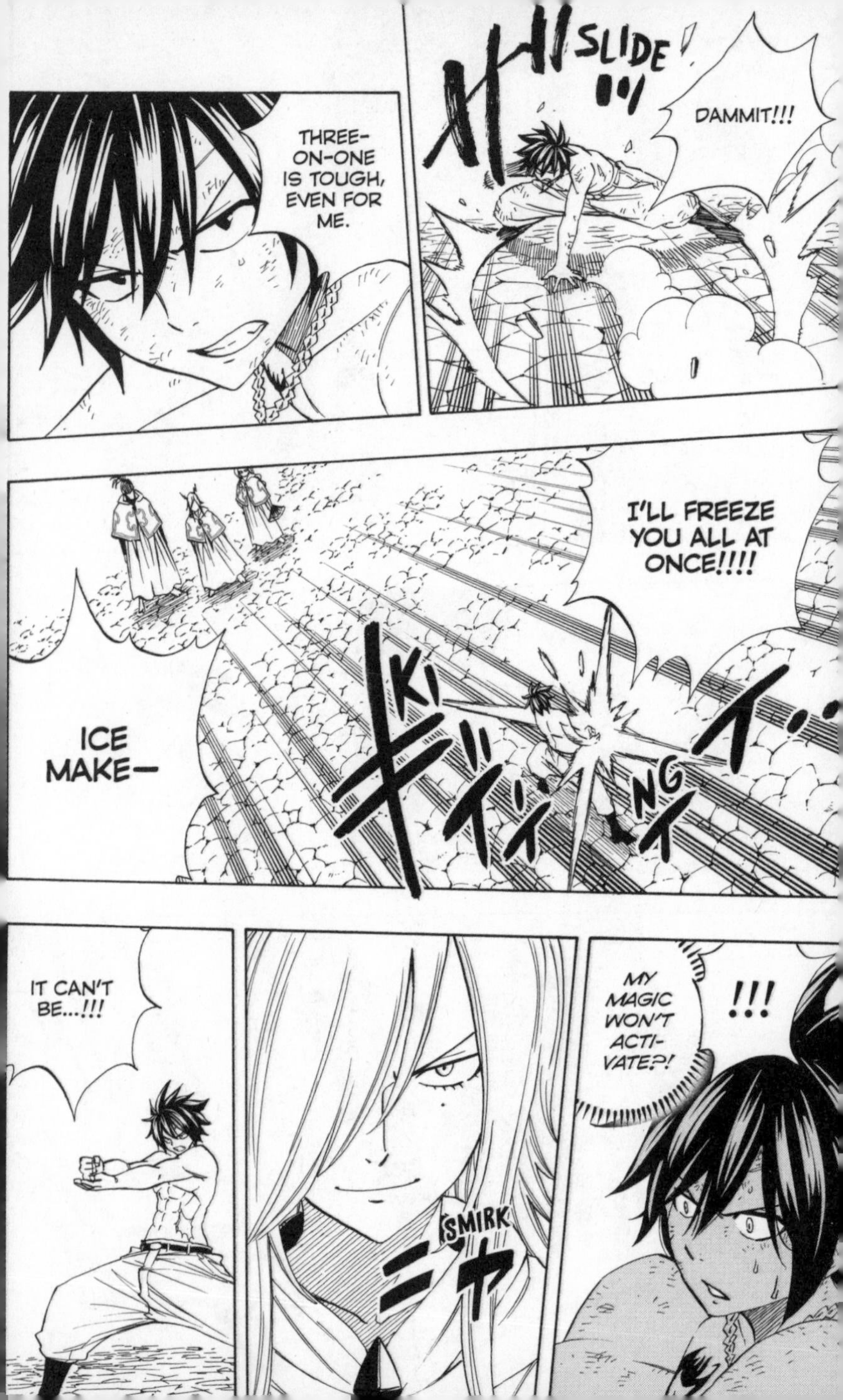
SLIDE
DAMMIT!!!
THREE-ON-ONE IS TOUGH, EVEN FOR ME.
I'LL FREEZE YOU ALL AT ONCE!!!!
KING
ICE MAKE—
!!!
MY MAGIC WON'T ACTI-VATE?!
SMIRK
IT CAN'T BE...!!!

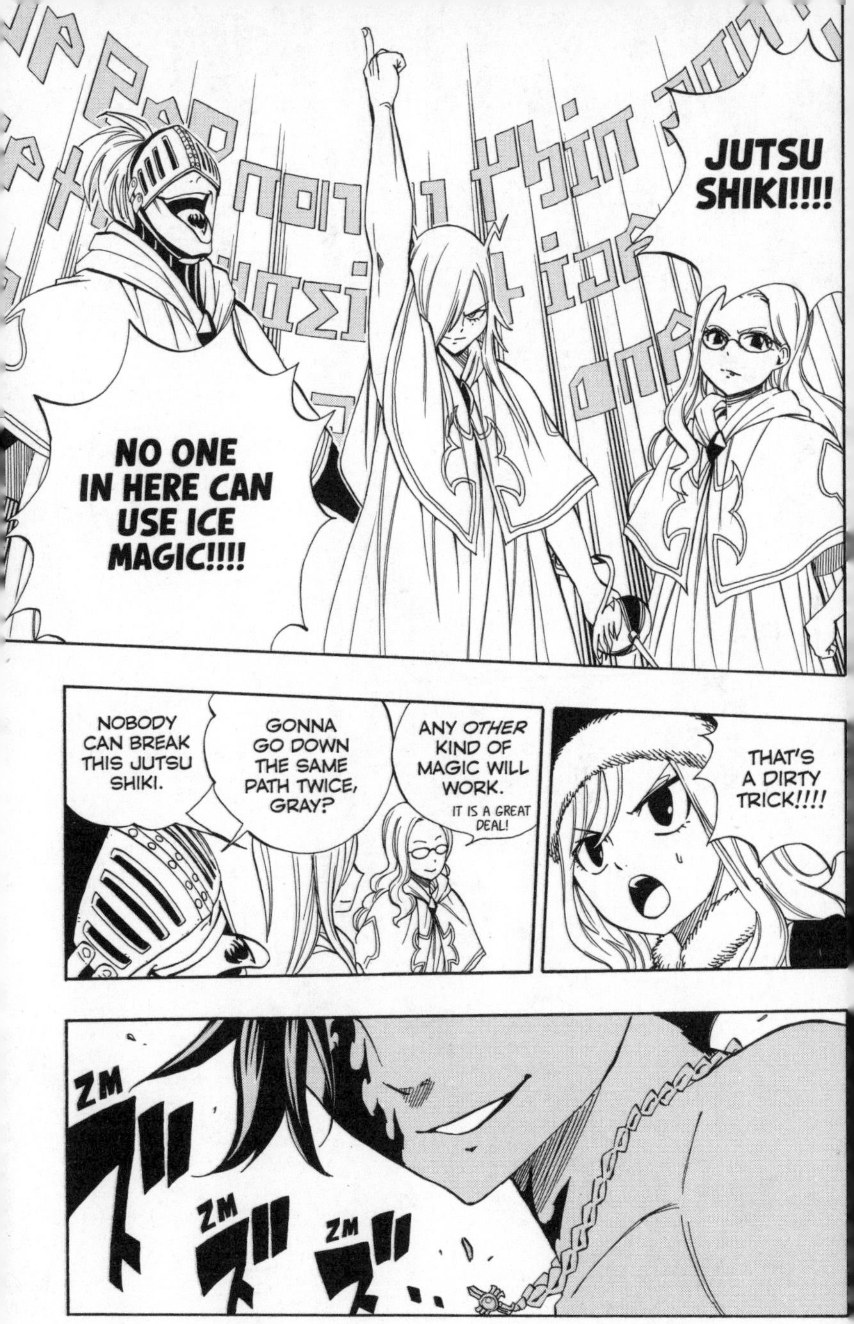

JUTSU SHIKI!!!!
NO ONE IN HERE CAN USE ICE MAGIC!!!!
THAT'S A DIRTY TRICK!!!!
ANY OTHER KIND OF MAGIC WILL WORK.
IT IS A GREAT DEAL!
GONNA GO DOWN THE SAME PATH TWICE, GRAY?
NOBODY CAN BREAK THIS JUTSU SHIKI.
ZM
ZM
ZM

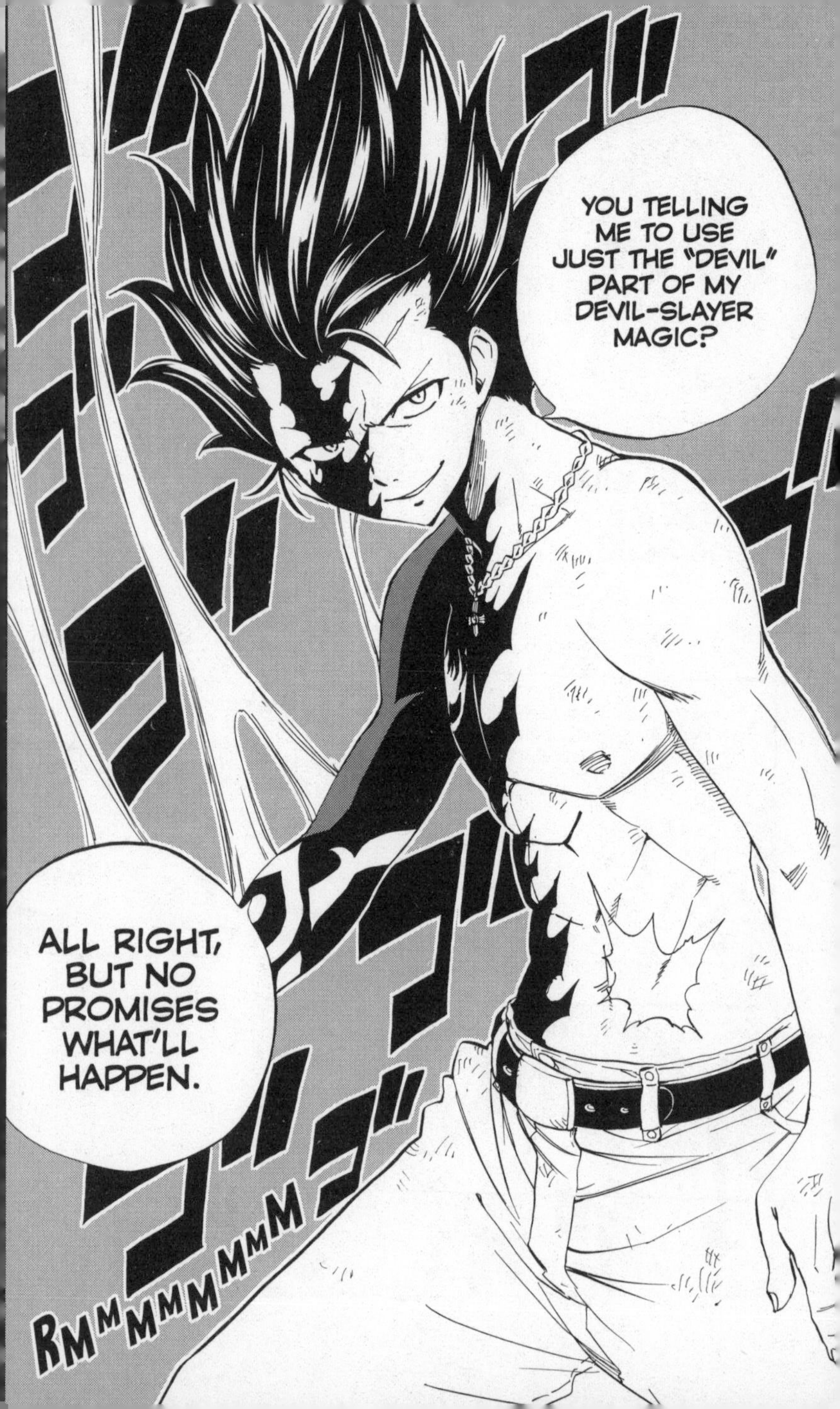
YOU TELLING ME TO USE JUST THE "DEVIL" PART OF MY DEVIL-SLAYER MAGIC?
ALL RIGHT, BUT NO PROMISES WHAT'LL HAPPEN.
RMMMMMMMMM

FAIRY TAIL 100 YEARS QUEST

Chapter 33: Pain

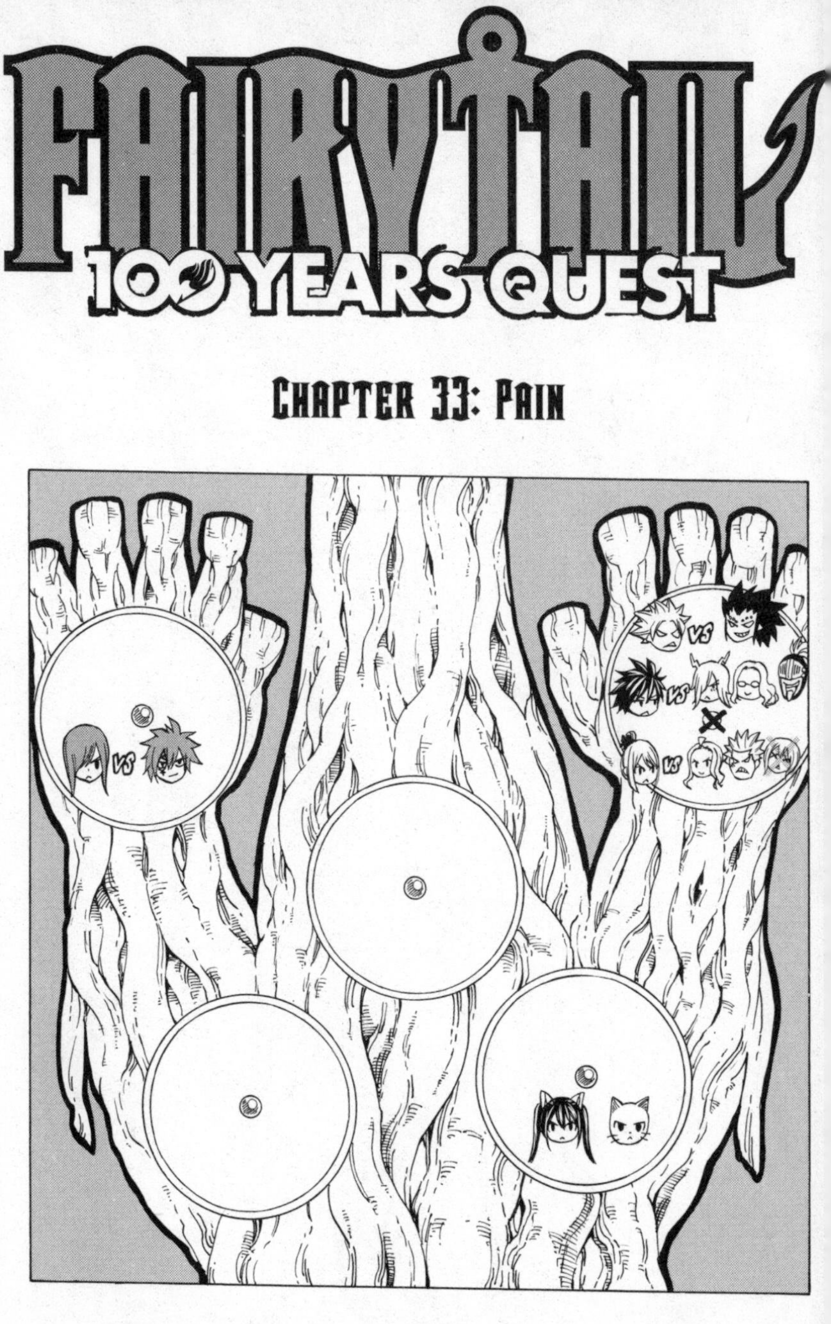
VS
VS
VS
VS

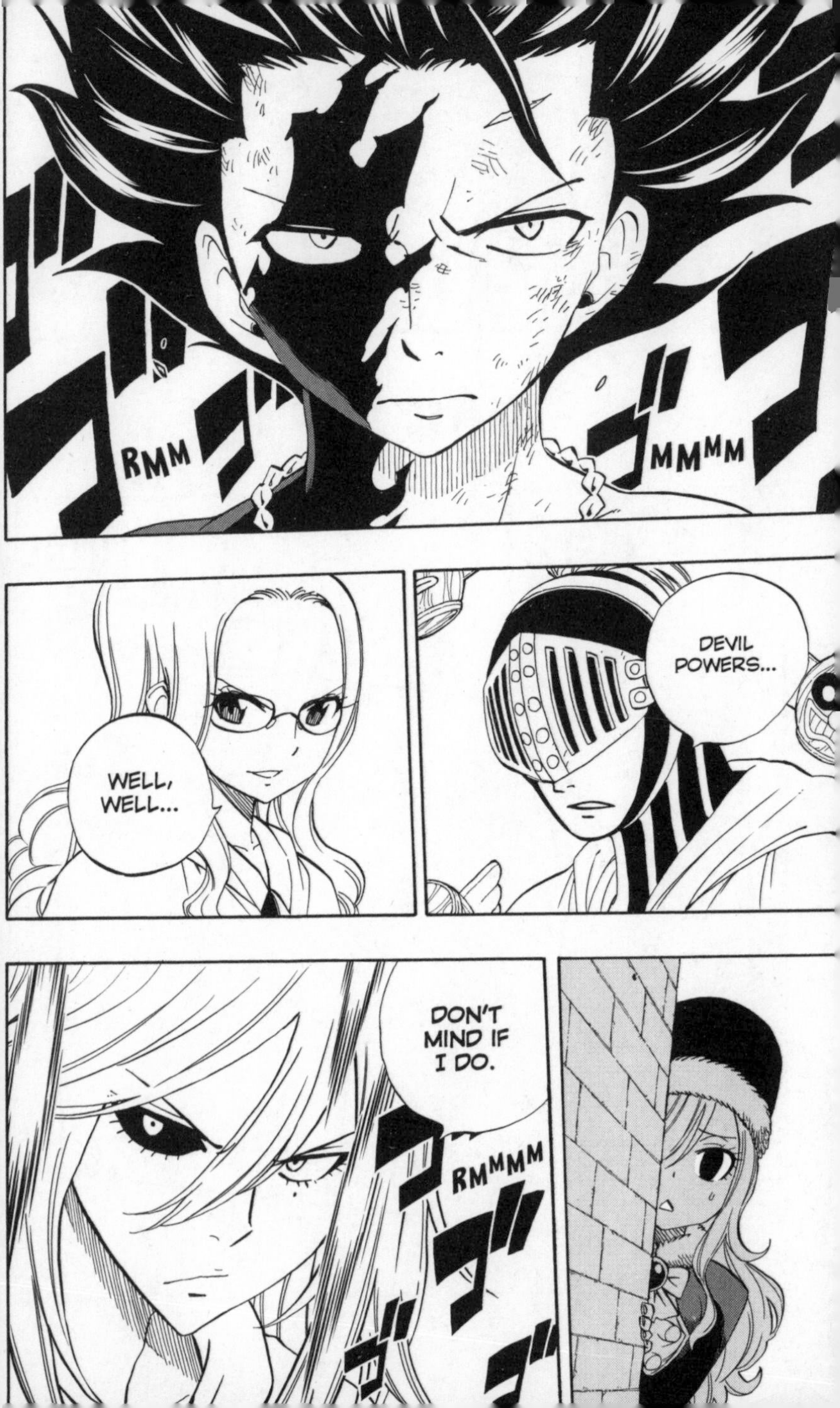
RMM
MMMM
DEVIL POWERS...
WELL, WELL...
DON'T MIND IF I DO.
RMMMM

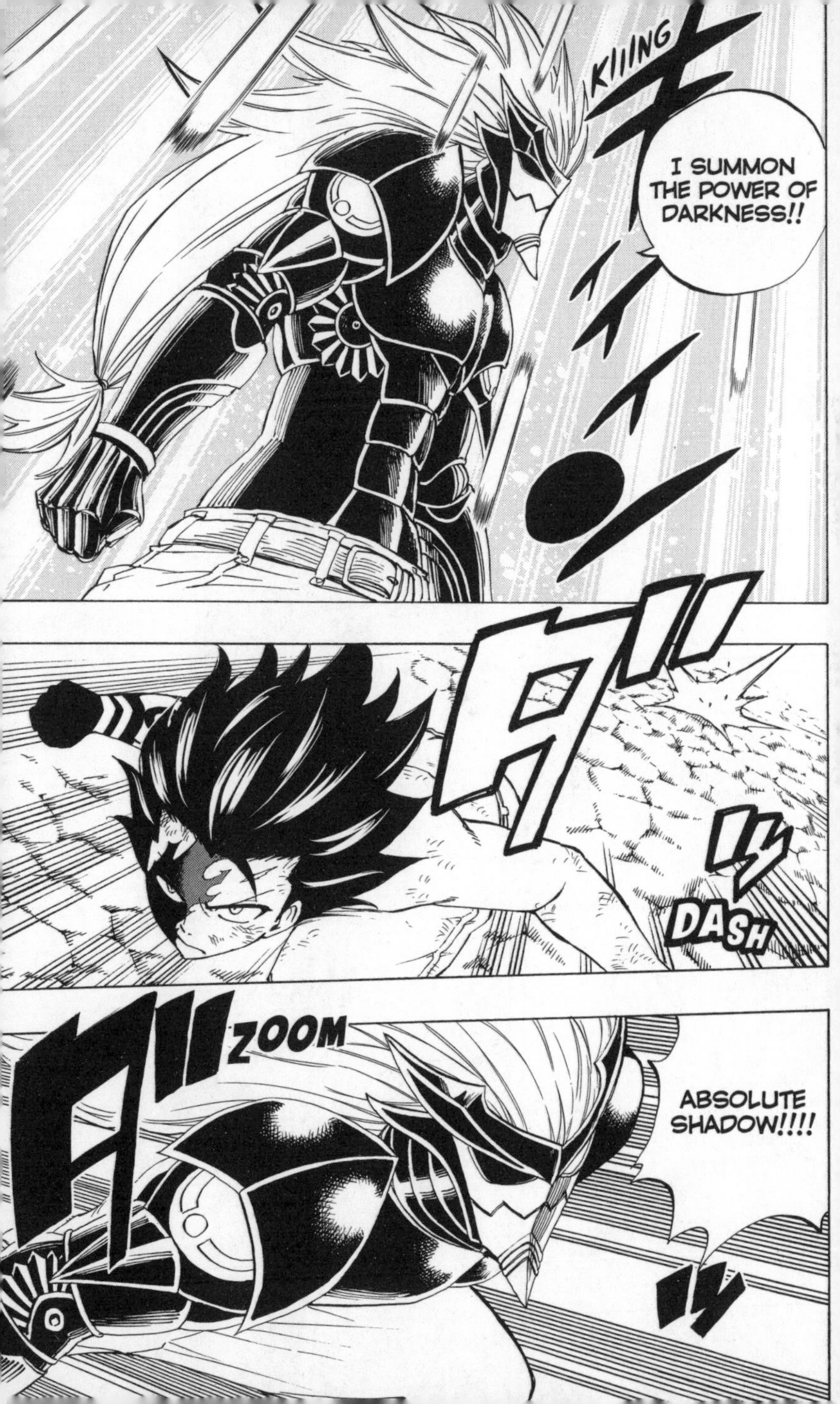
KIIIING
I SUMMON THE POWER OF DARKNESS!!
DASH
ZOOM
ABSOLUTE SHADOW!!!!

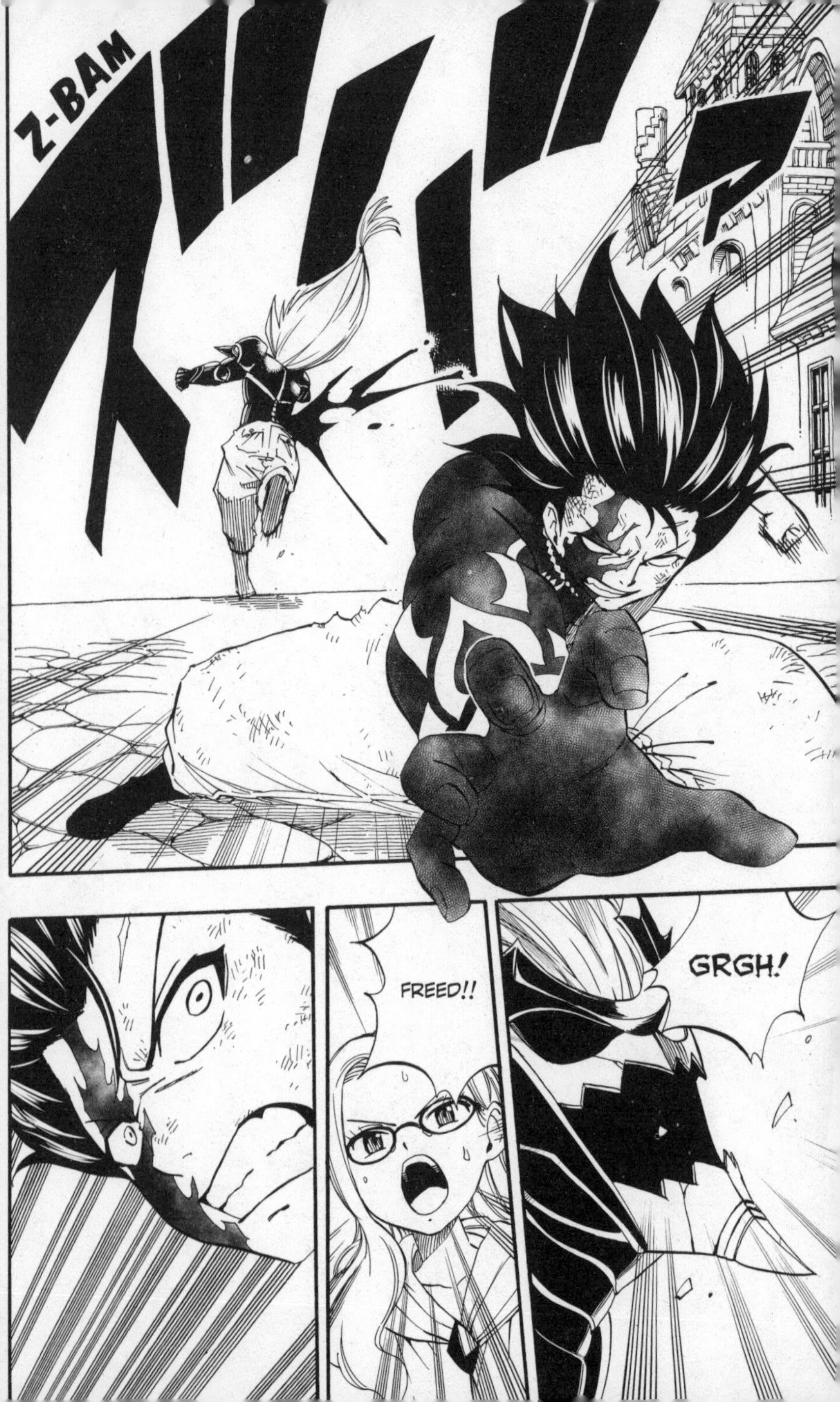
Z-BAM
GRGH!
FREED!!

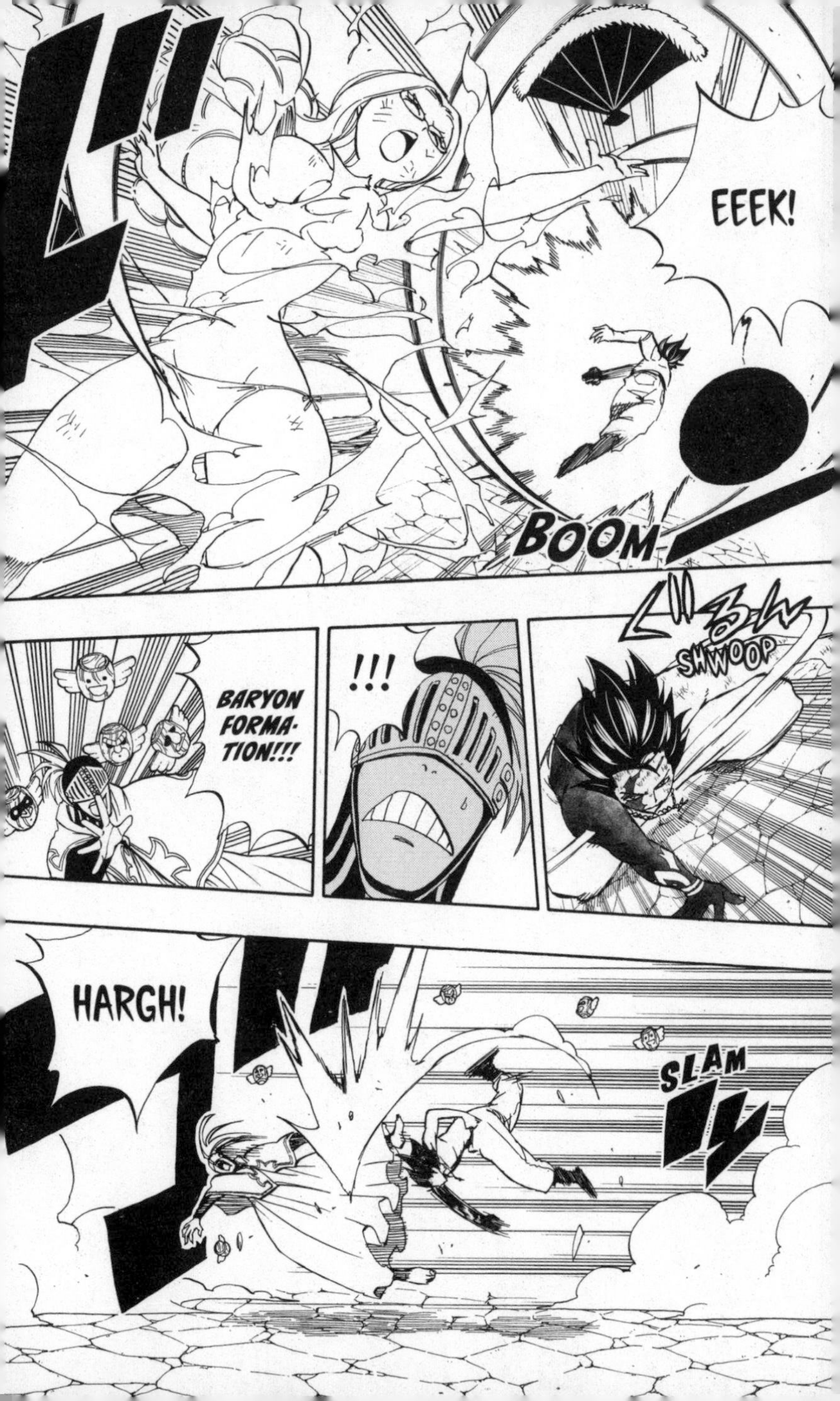
EEEK!
BOOM
SHWOOP
!!!
BARYON FORMA-TION!!!
HARGH!
SLAM

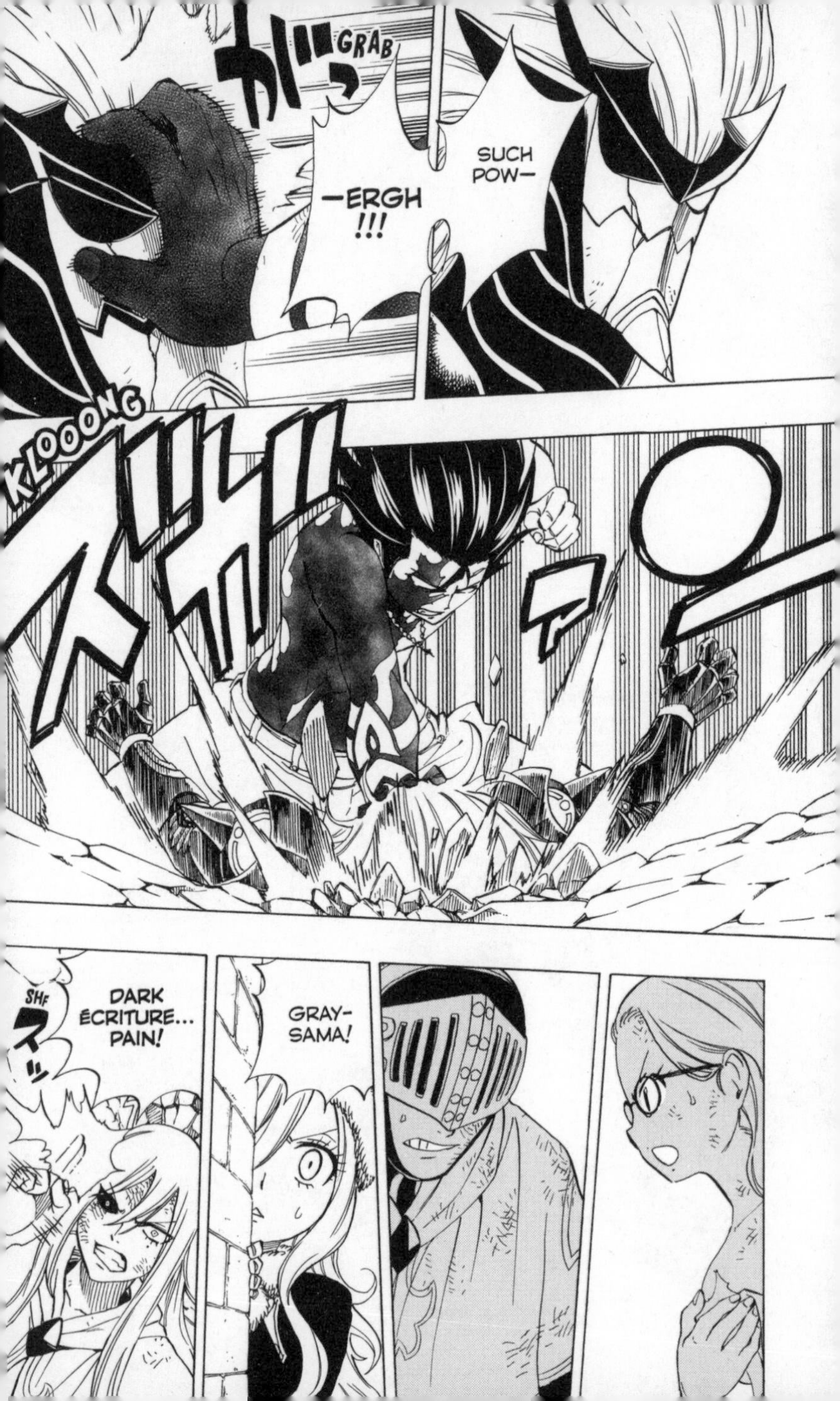
GRAB
SUCH POW—
—ERGH !!!
KLOOONG
GRAY-SAMA!
DARK ÉCRITURE... PAIN!
SHF

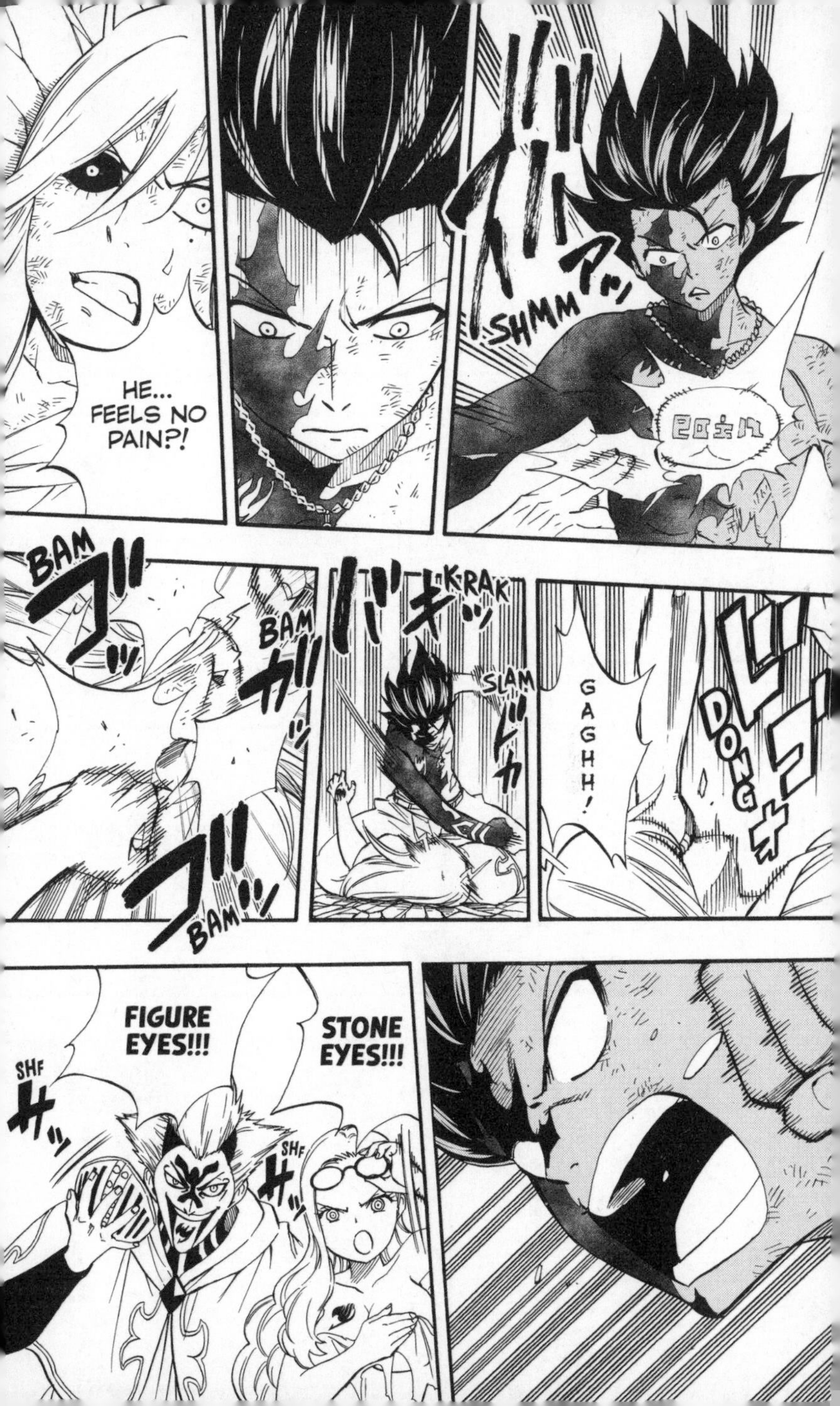

SHMM
HE... FEELS NO PAIN?!
DONG
GAGHH!
KRAK
SLAM
BAM
BAM
BAM
STONE EYES!!!
SHF
FIGURE EYES!!!
SHF

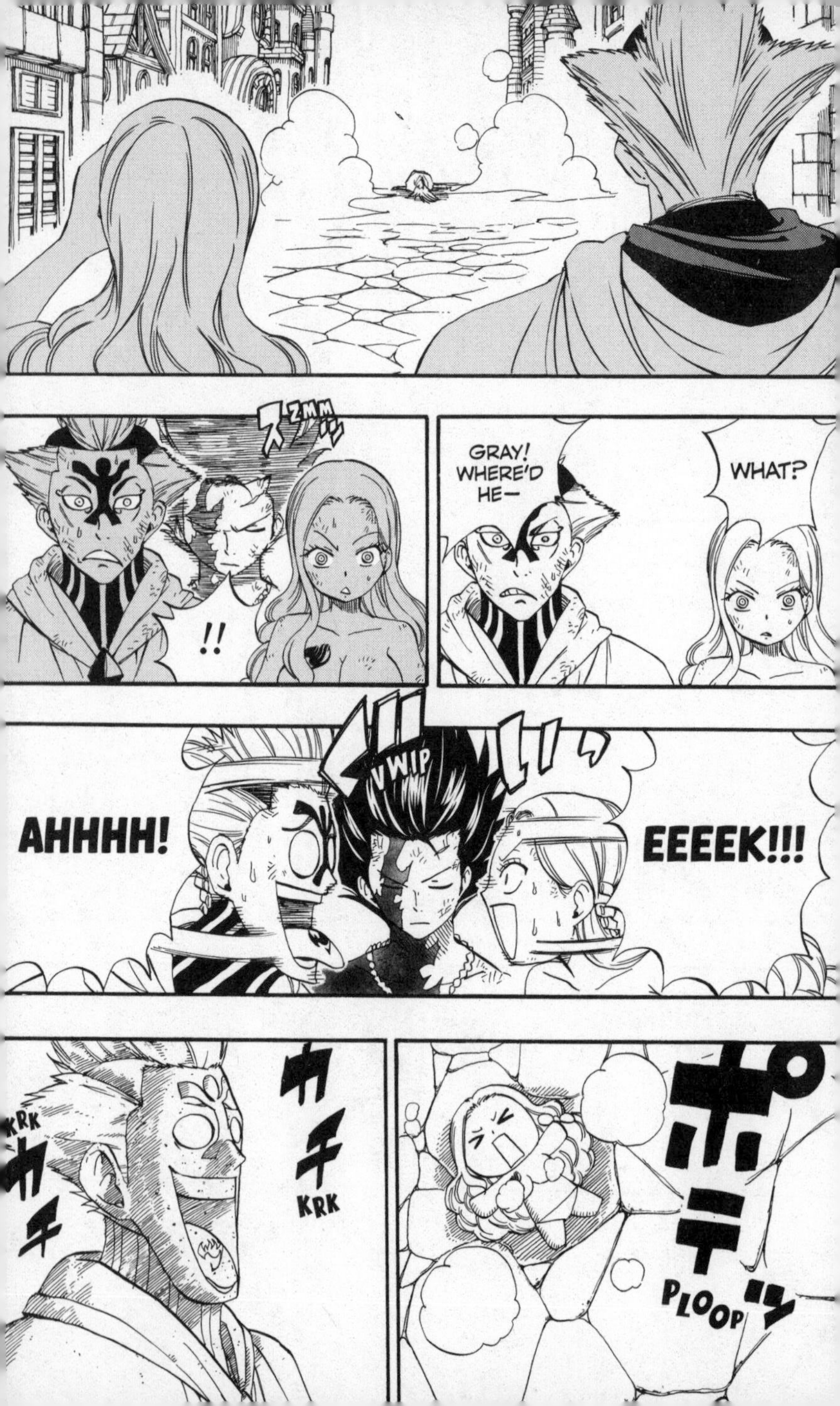

WHAT?
GRAY! WHERE'D HE—
ZMM
!!
VWIP
EEEEK!!!
AHHHH!
PLOOP
KRK
KRK

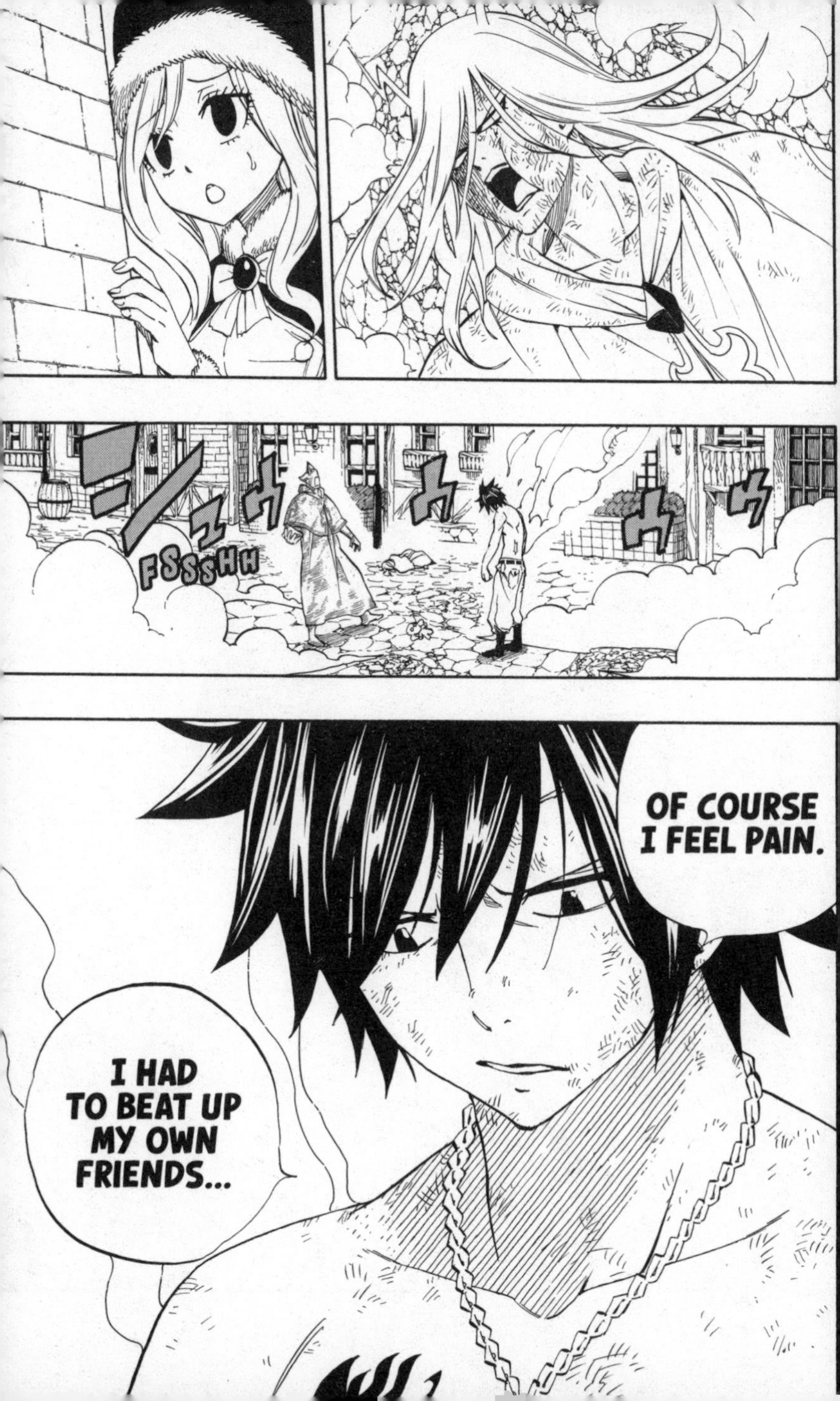
FSSSHH
OF COURSE I FEEL PAIN.
I HAD TO BEAT UP MY OWN FRIENDS...

BA-GOOOONG

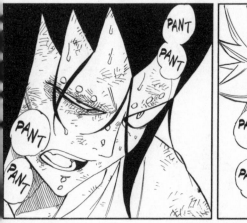

PANT

PANT

PANT

PANT

PANT

PANT

PANT

PANT

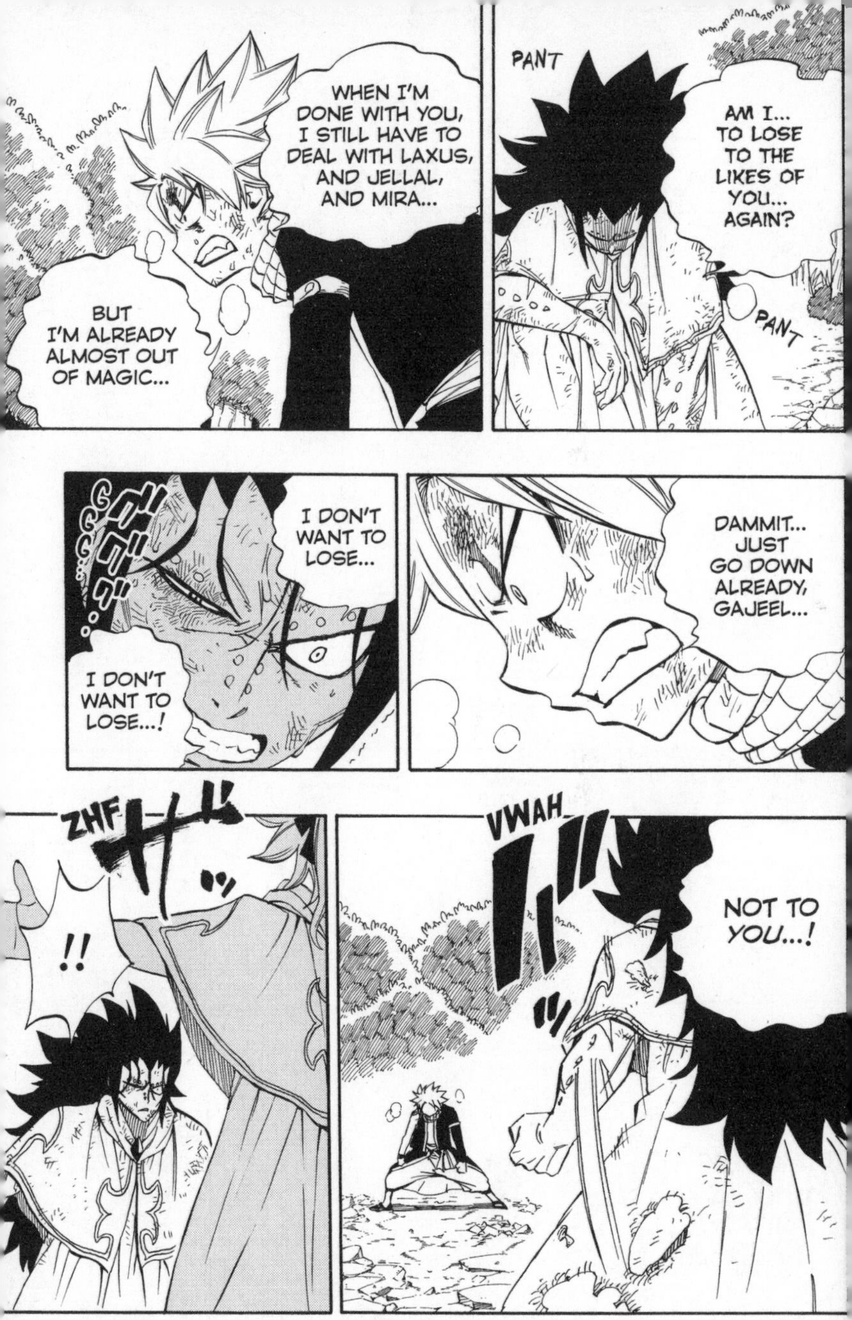
PANT
AM I... TO LOSE TO THE LIKES OF YOU... AGAIN?
PANT
WHEN I'M DONE WITH YOU, I STILL HAVE TO DEAL WITH LAXUS, AND JELLAL, AND MIRA...
BUT I'M ALREADY ALMOST OUT OF MAGIC...
DAMMIT... JUST GO DOWN ALREADY, GAJEEL...
I DON'T WANT TO LOSE...
I DON'T WANT TO LOSE...!
VWAH
NOT TO YOU...!
ZHF
!!

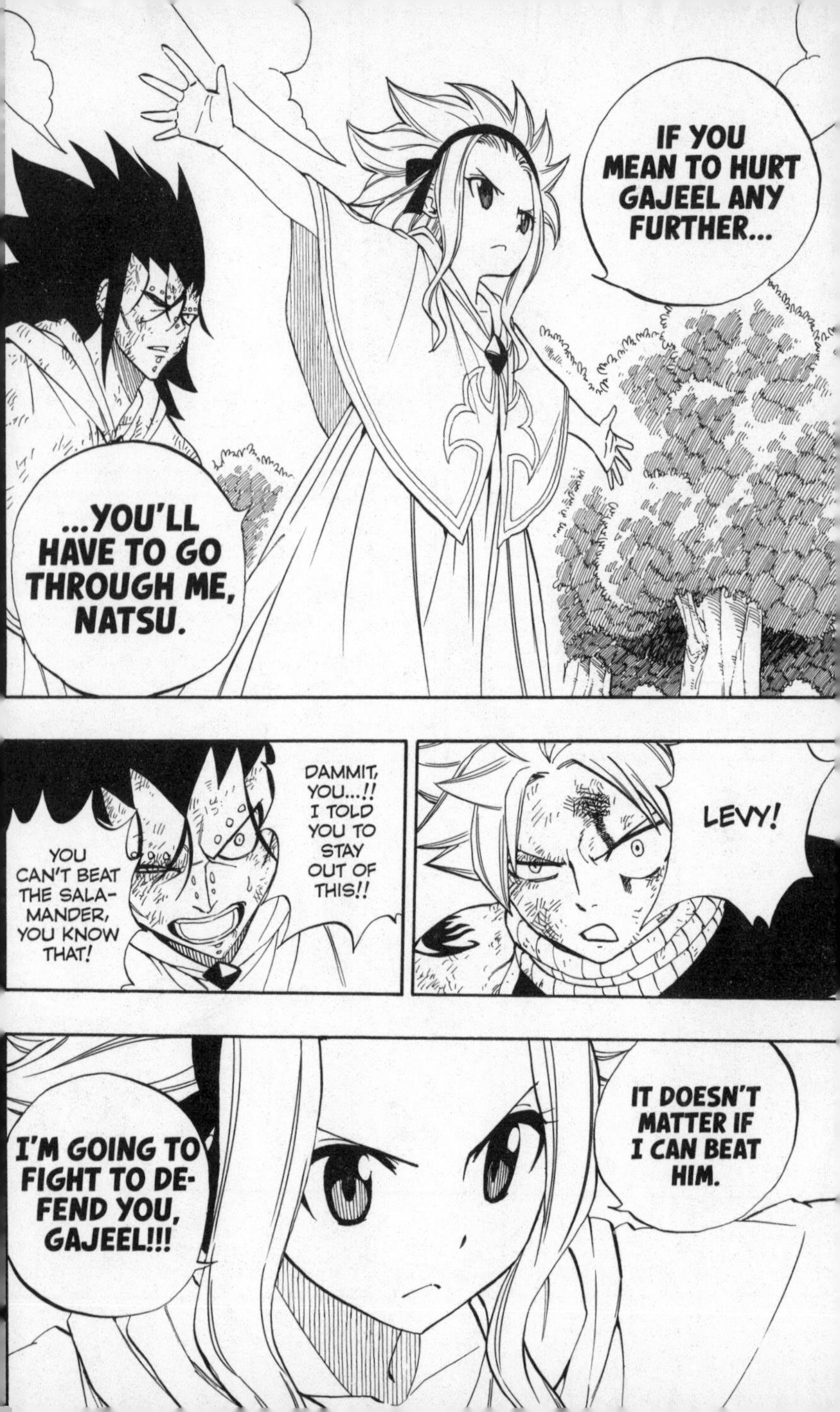
IF YOU MEAN TO HURT GAJEEL ANY FURTHER...
...YOU'LL HAVE TO GO THROUGH ME, NATSU.
LEVY!
DAMMIT, YOU...!! I TOLD YOU TO STAY OUT OF THIS!!
YOU CAN'T BEAT THE SALA- MANDER, YOU KNOW THAT!
IT DOESN'T MATTER IF I CAN BEAT HIM.
I'M GOING TO FIGHT TO DE- FEND YOU, GAJEEL!!!

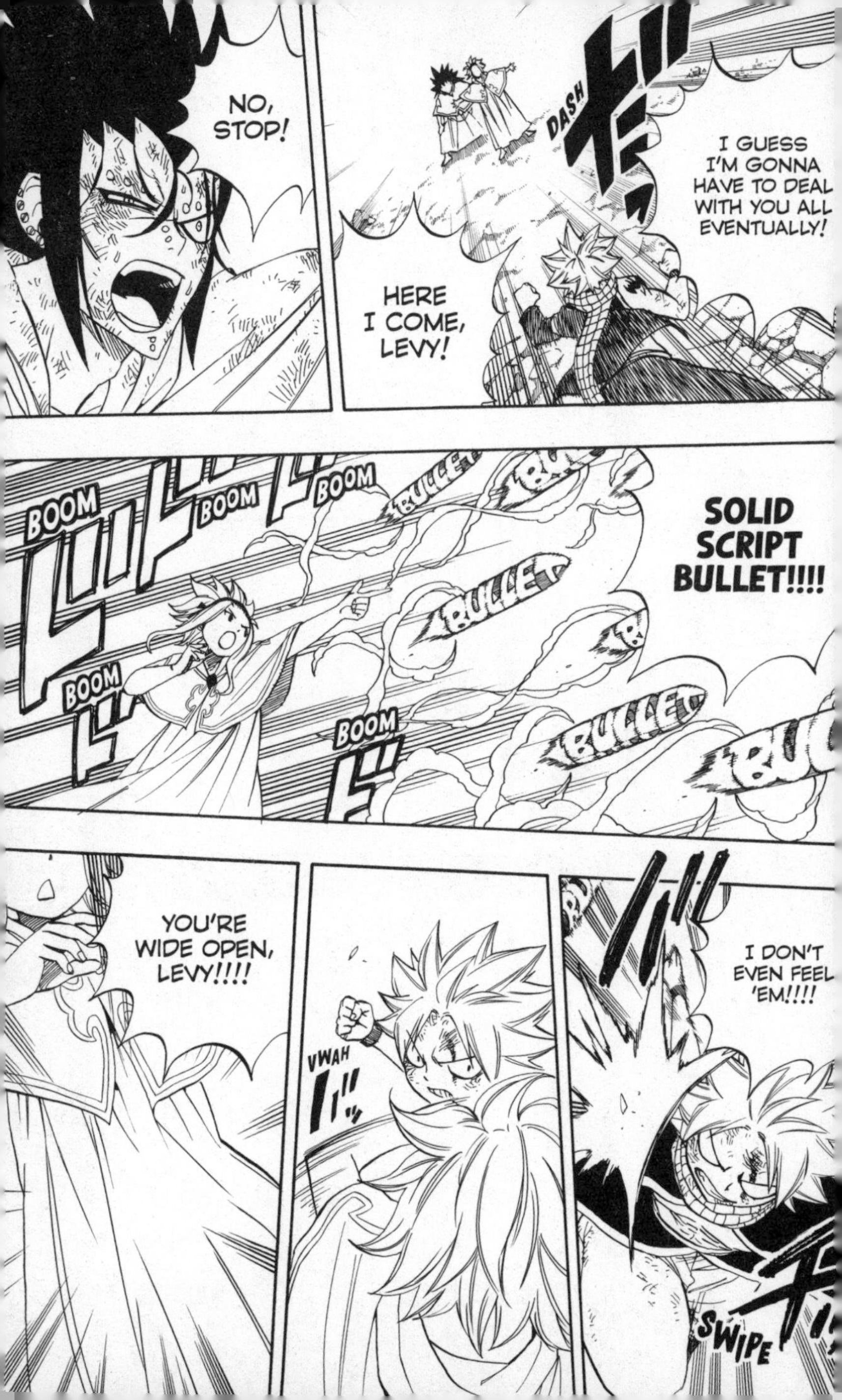
DASH
I GUESS I'M GONNA HAVE TO DEAL WITH YOU ALL EVENTUALLY!
HERE I COME, LEVY!
NO, STOP!
SOLID SCRIPT BULLET!!!!
BOOM
BOOM
BOOM
BOOM
BOOM
I DON'T EVEN FEEL 'EM!!!!
SWIPE
VWAH
YOU'RE WIDE OPEN, LEVY!!!!

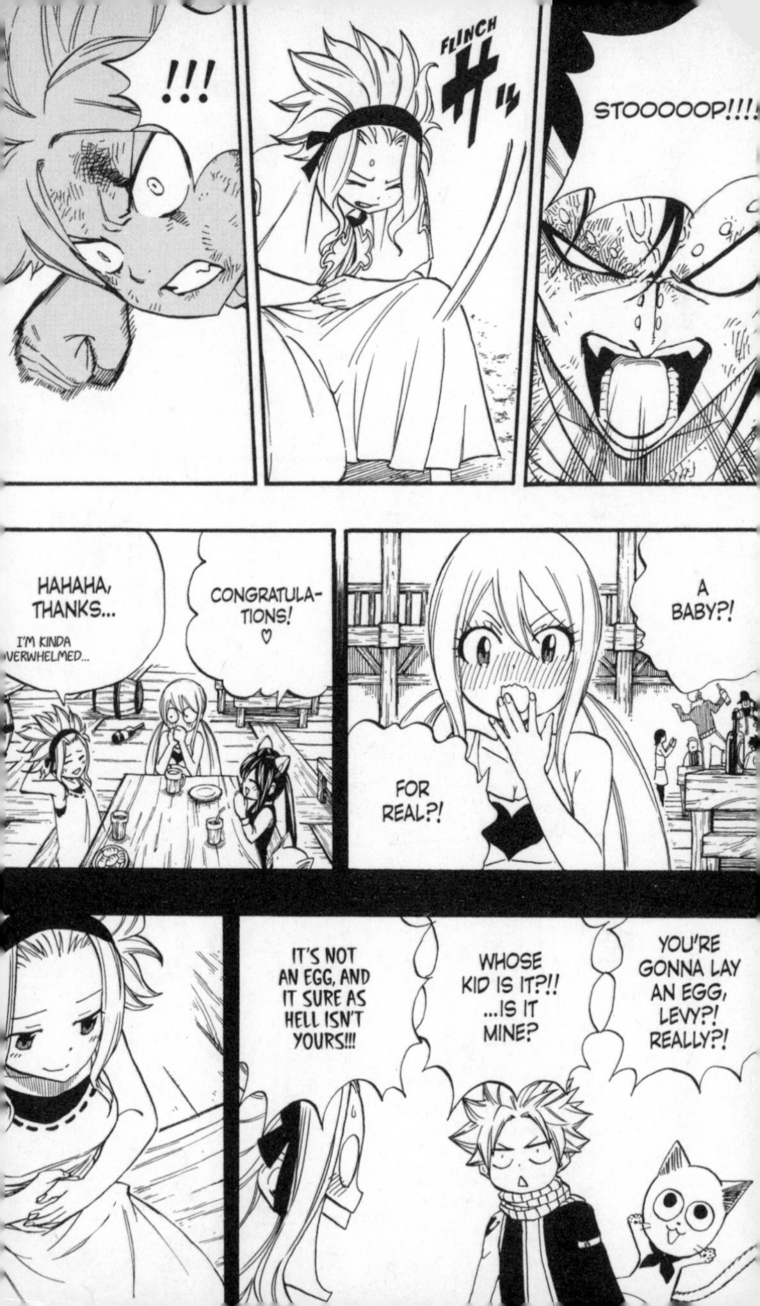
STOOOOOP!!!!
FLINCH
!!!
A BABY?!
FOR REAL?!
CONGRATULATIONS! ♡
HAHAHA, THANKS...
I'M KINDA VERWHELMED...
YOU'RE GONNA LAY AN EGG, LEVY?! REALLY?!
WHOSE KID IS IT?!! ...IS IT MINE?
IT'S NOT AN EGG, AND IT SURE AS HELL ISN'T YOURS!!!

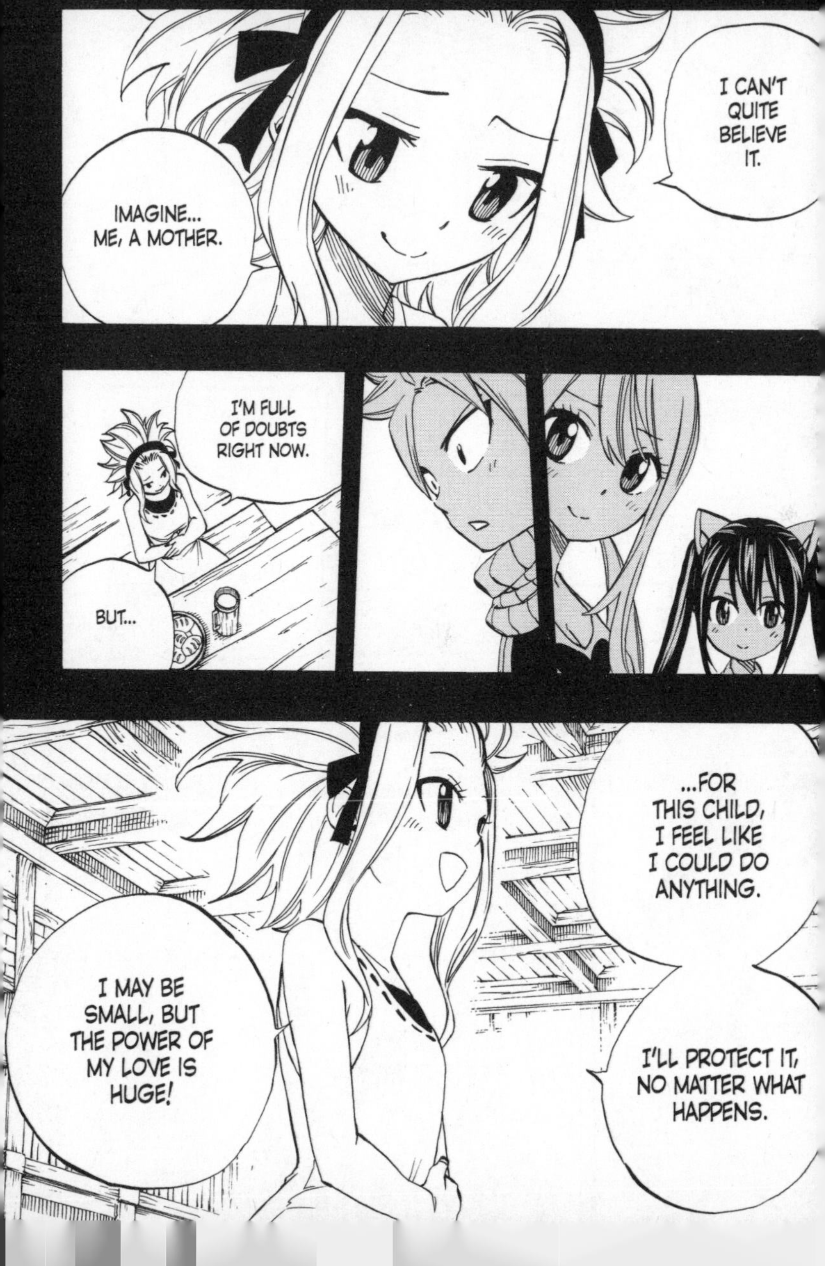
I CAN'T QUITE BELIEVE IT.
IMAGINE... ME, A MOTHER.
I'M FULL OF DOUBTS RIGHT NOW.
BUT...
...FOR THIS CHILD, I FEEL LIKE I COULD DO ANYTHING.
I'LL PROTECT IT, NO MATTER WHAT HAPPENS.
I MAY BE SMALL, BUT THE POWER OF MY LOVE IS HUGE!

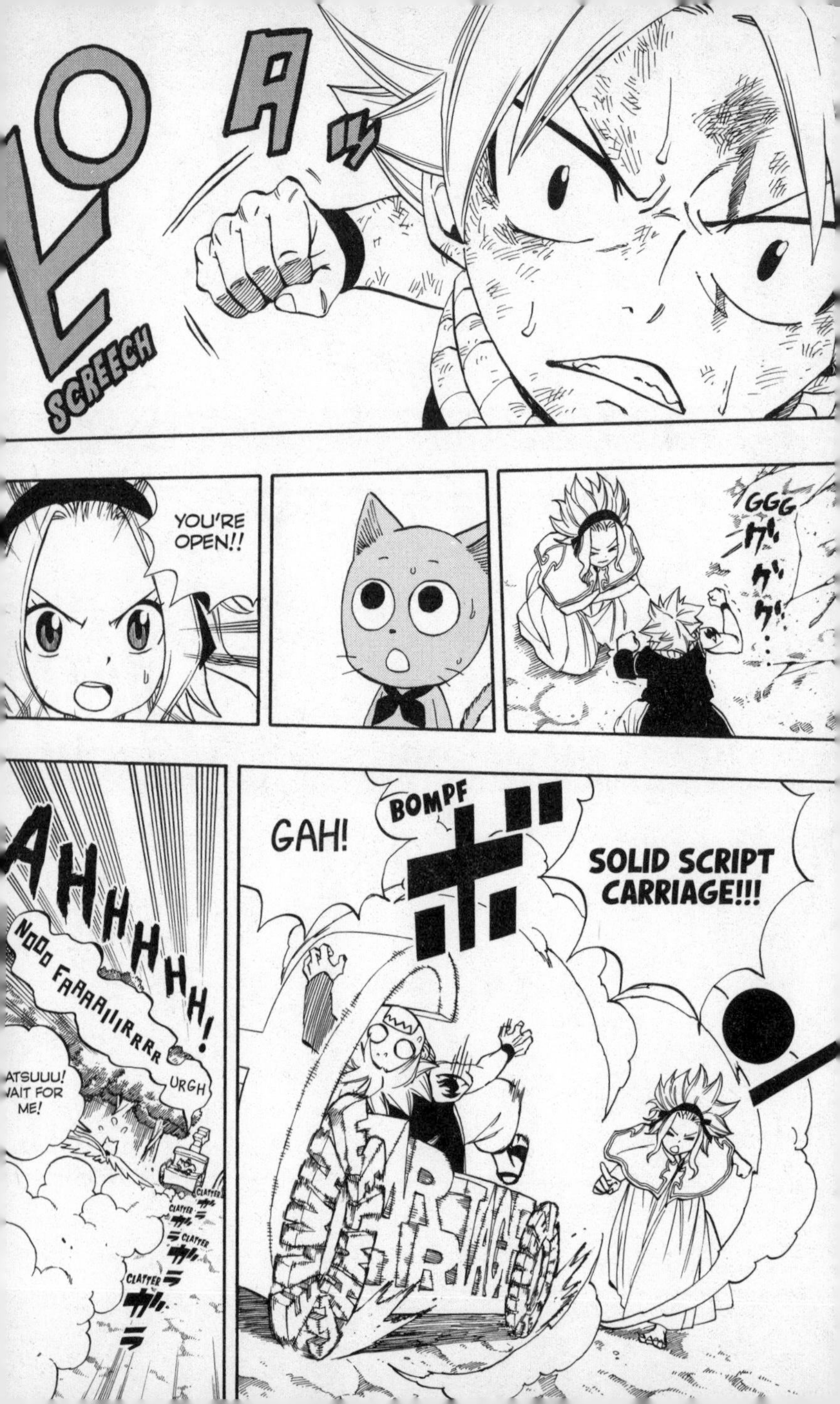
SCREECH
GGG
YOU'RE OPEN!!
SOLID SCRIPT CARRIAGE!!!
BOMPF
GAH!
AHHHHHHH!
NOOO FAAAAIIIRRRR
URGH
ATSUUU! WAIT FOR ME!
CLATTER
CLATTER
CLATTER
CLATTER

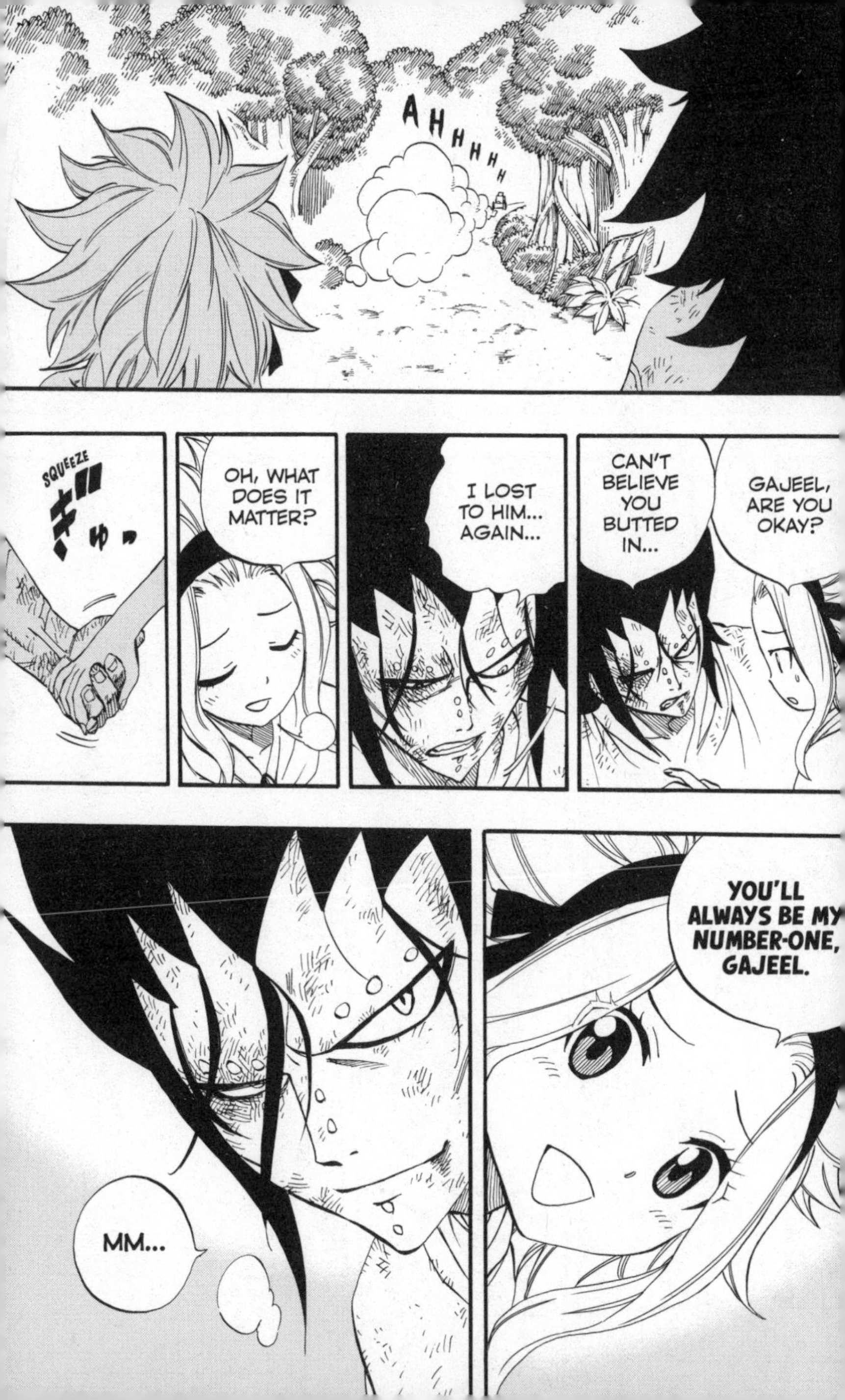
AHHHHHH
GAJEEL, ARE YOU OKAY?
CAN'T BELIEVE YOU BUTTED IN...
I LOST TO HIM... AGAIN...
OH, WHAT DOES IT MATTER?
SQUEEZE
ぎゅっ
YOU'LL ALWAYS BE MY NUMBER-ONE, GAJEEL.
MM...

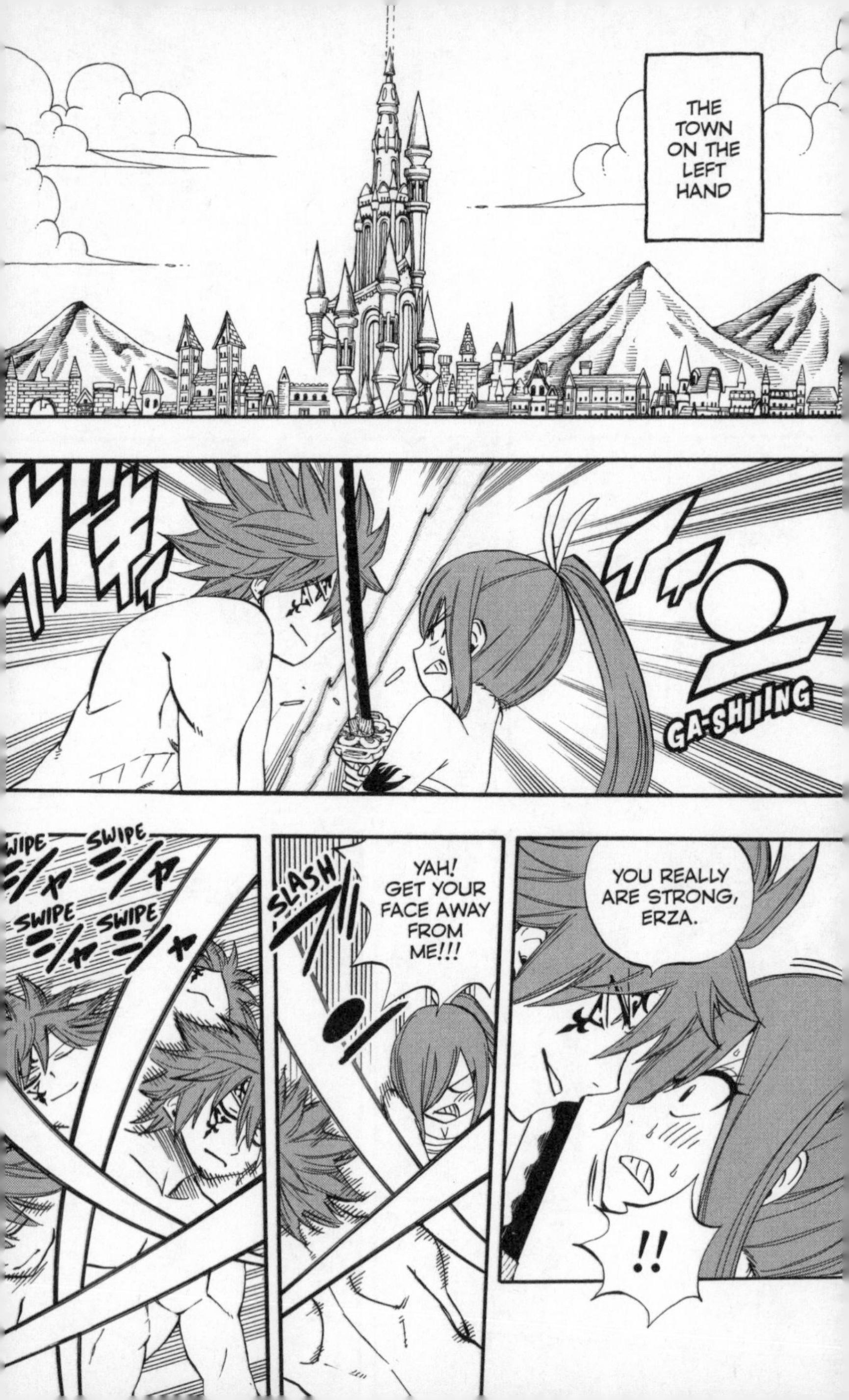
THE TOWN ON THE LEFT HAND
GA-SHIIIING
YOU REALLY ARE STRONG, ERZA.
!!
SLASH
YAH! GET YOUR FACE AWAY FROM ME!!!
SWIPE
SWIPE
SWIPE
SWIPE

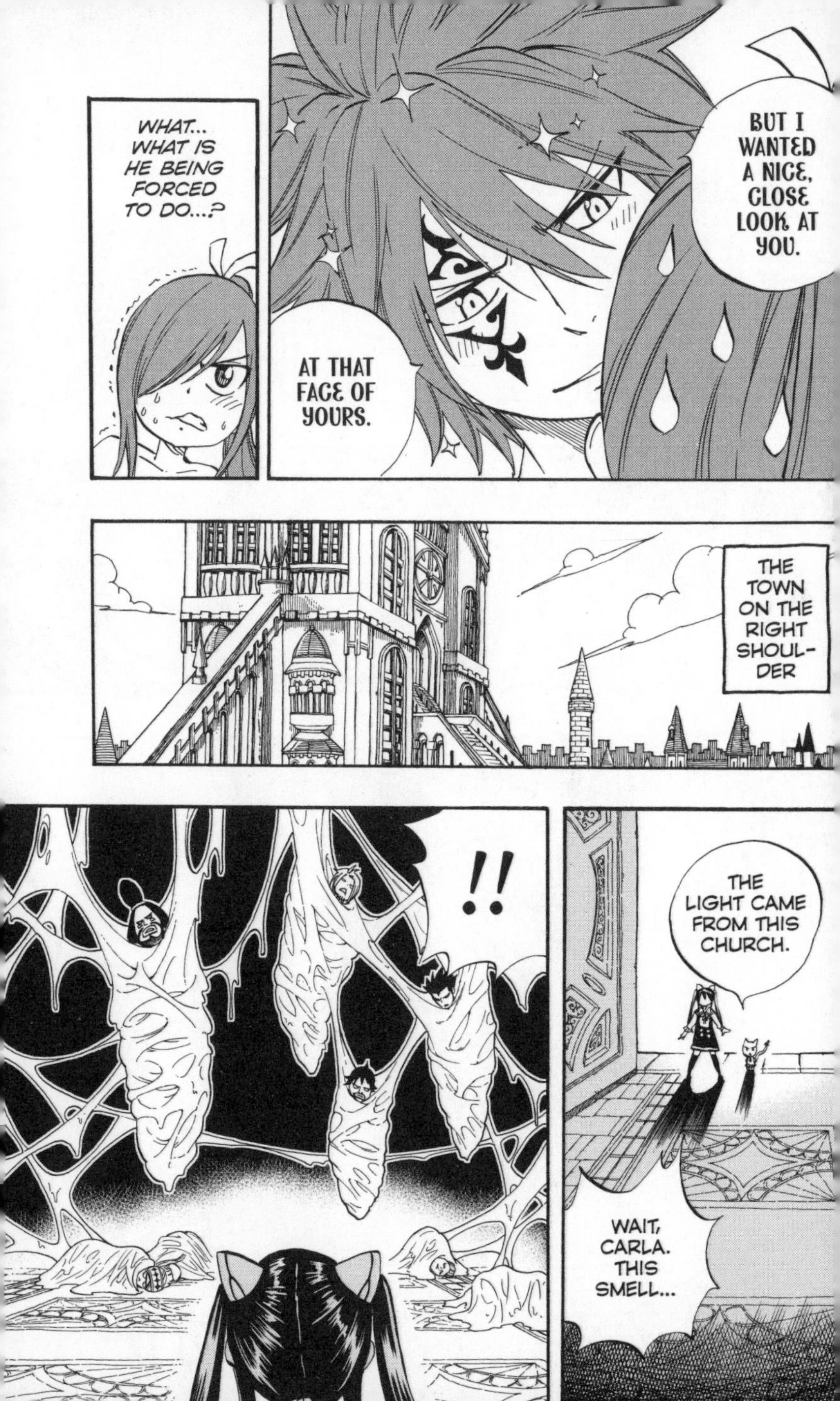
BUT I WANTED A NICE, CLOSE LOOK AT YOU.
AT THAT FACE OF YOURS.
WHAT... WHAT IS HE BEING FORCED TO DO...?
THE TOWN ON THE RIGHT SHOUL-DER
THE LIGHT CAME FROM THIS CHURCH.
WAIT, CARLA. THIS SMELL...
!!

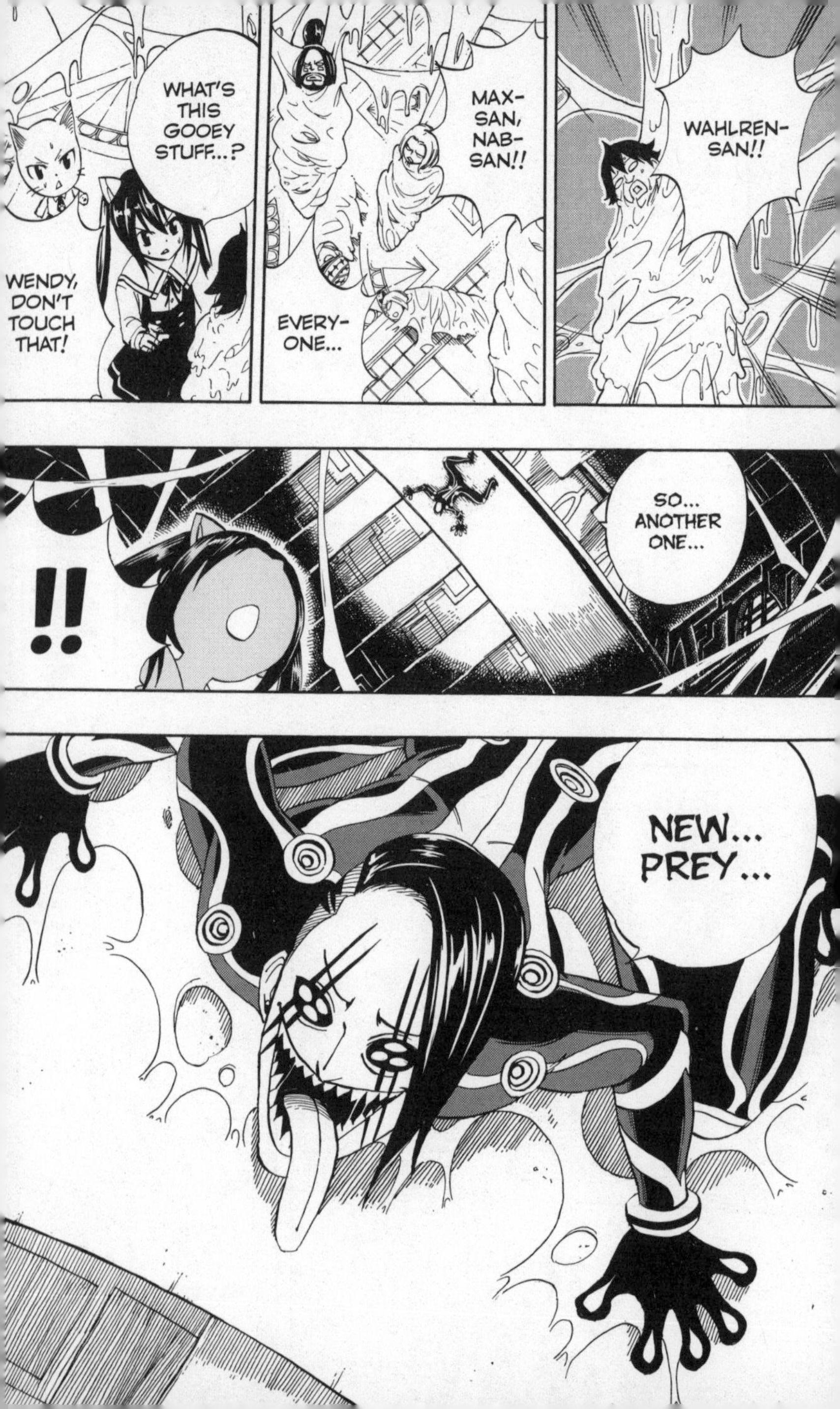
WAHLREN-SAN!!
MAX-SAN, NAB-SAN!!
EVERY-ONE...
WHAT'S THIS GOOEY STUFF...?
WENDY, DON'T TOUCH THAT!
SO... ANOTHER ONE...
!!
NEW... PREY...

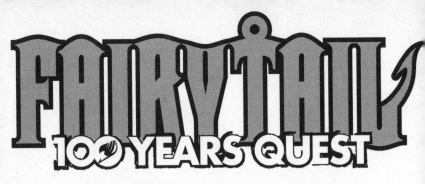

FAIRY TAIL
100 YEARS QUEST

CHAPTER 34: NEW FOES

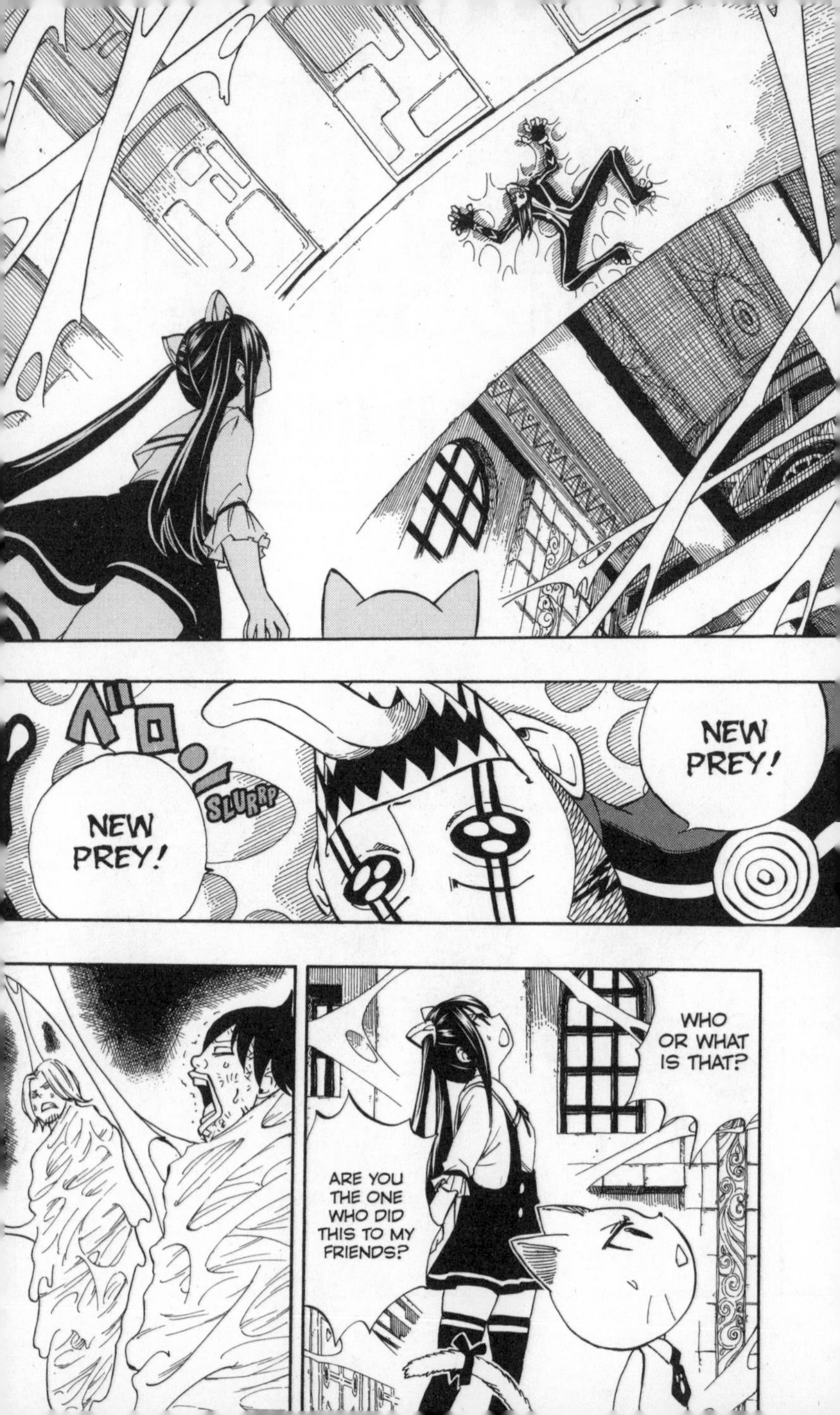
NEW PREY!
SLURRP
NEW PREY!
WHO OR WHAT IS THAT?
ARE YOU THE ONE WHO DID THIS TO MY FRIENDS?

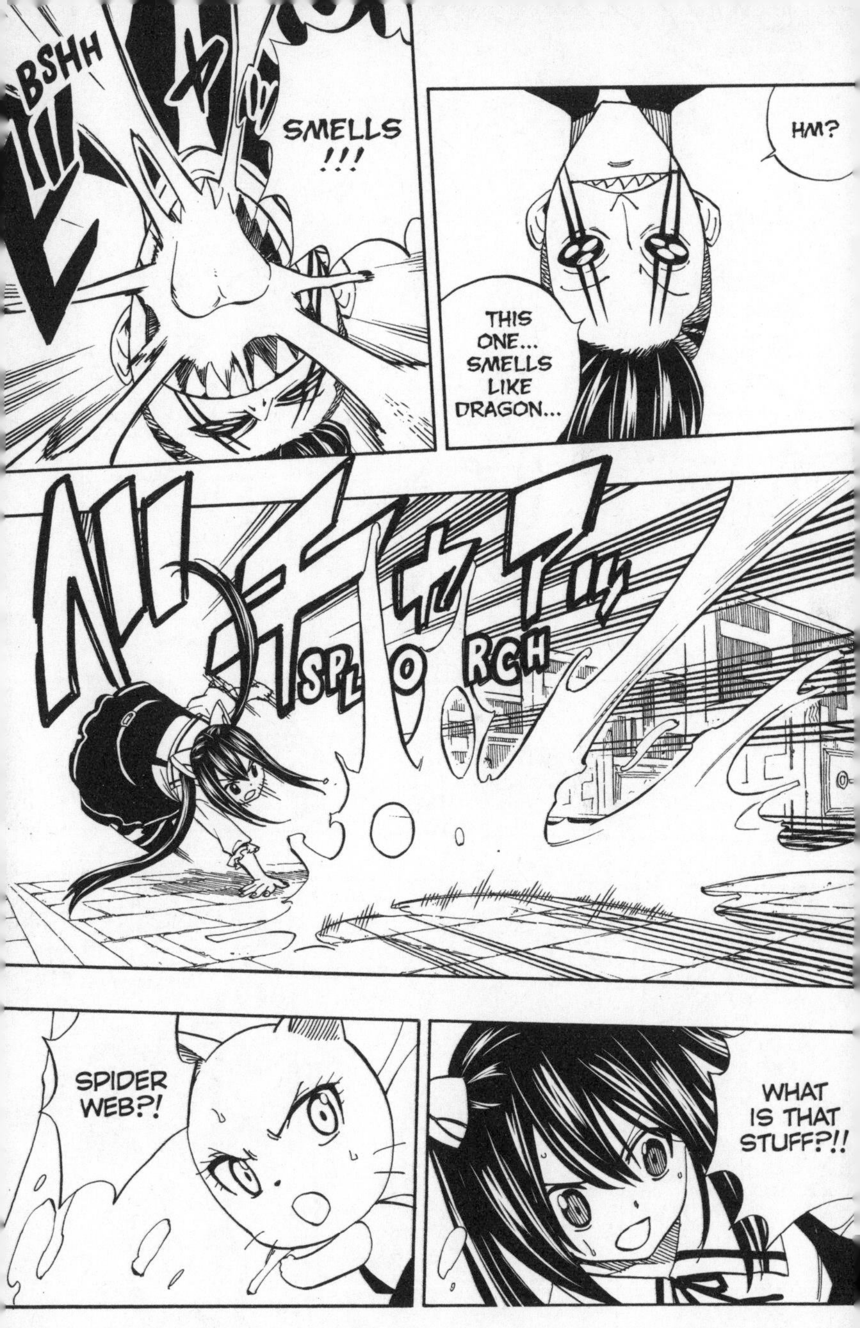
HM?
THIS ONE... SMELLS LIKE DRAGON...
BSHH
SMELLS !!!
SPLORCH
WHAT IS THAT STUFF?!!
SPIDER WEB?!

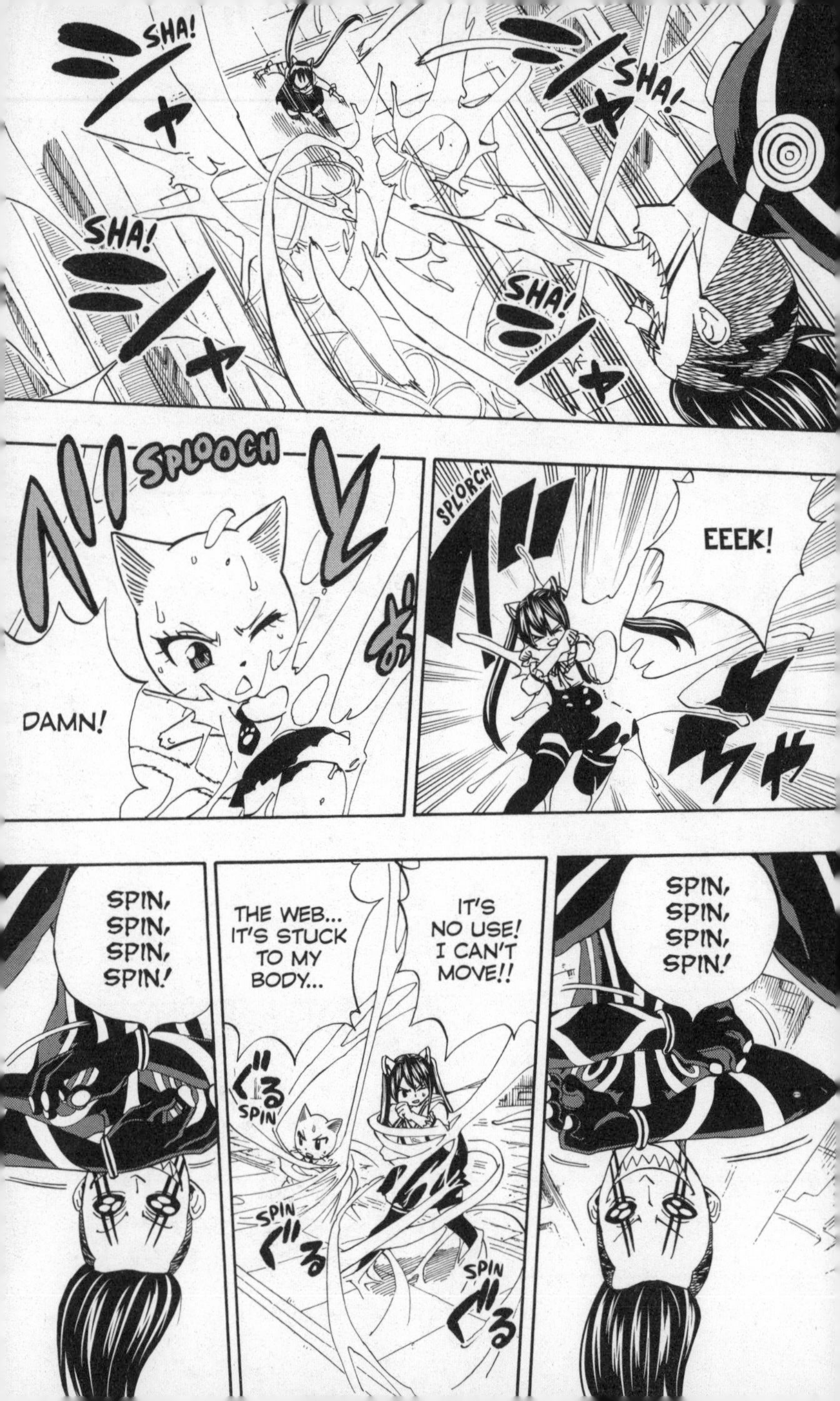
SHA!
SHA!
SHA!
SHA!
SPLORCH
EEEK!
SPLOOCH
DAMN!
SPIN, SPIN, SPIN, SPIN!
IT'S NO USE! I CAN'T MOVE!!
THE WEB... IT'S STUCK TO MY BODY...
SPIN
SPIN
SPIN
SPIN, SPIN, SPIN, SPIN!

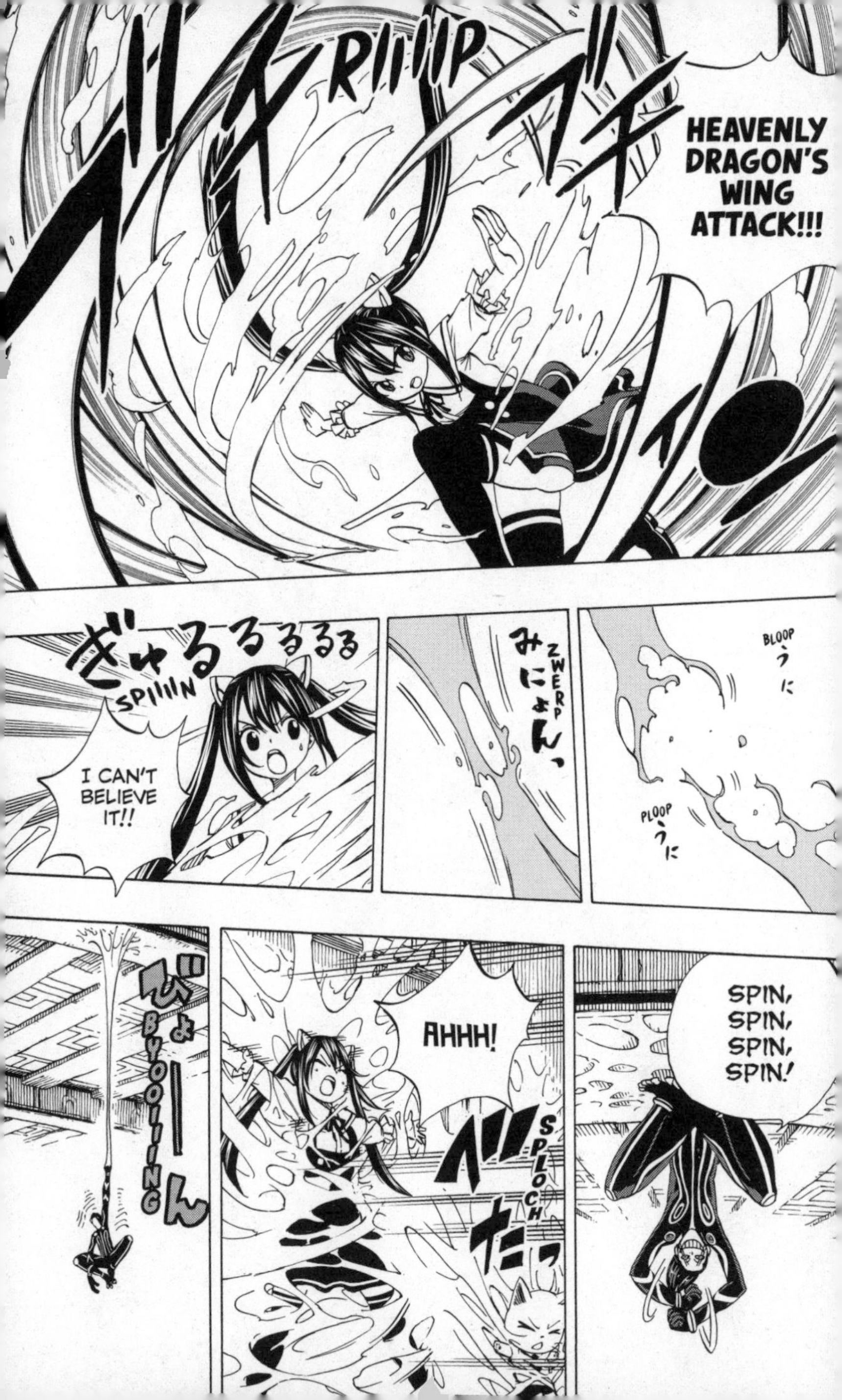

RIIIIP
HEAVENLY DRAGON'S WING ATTACK!!!
BLOOP うに
PLOOP うに
みにょん、
ZWERP
ぎゅるるるるる
SPIIIIN
I CAN'T BELIEVE IT!!
SPIN, SPIN, SPIN, SPIN!
AHHH!
SPLOCH
びょーーん
BYOOIIING

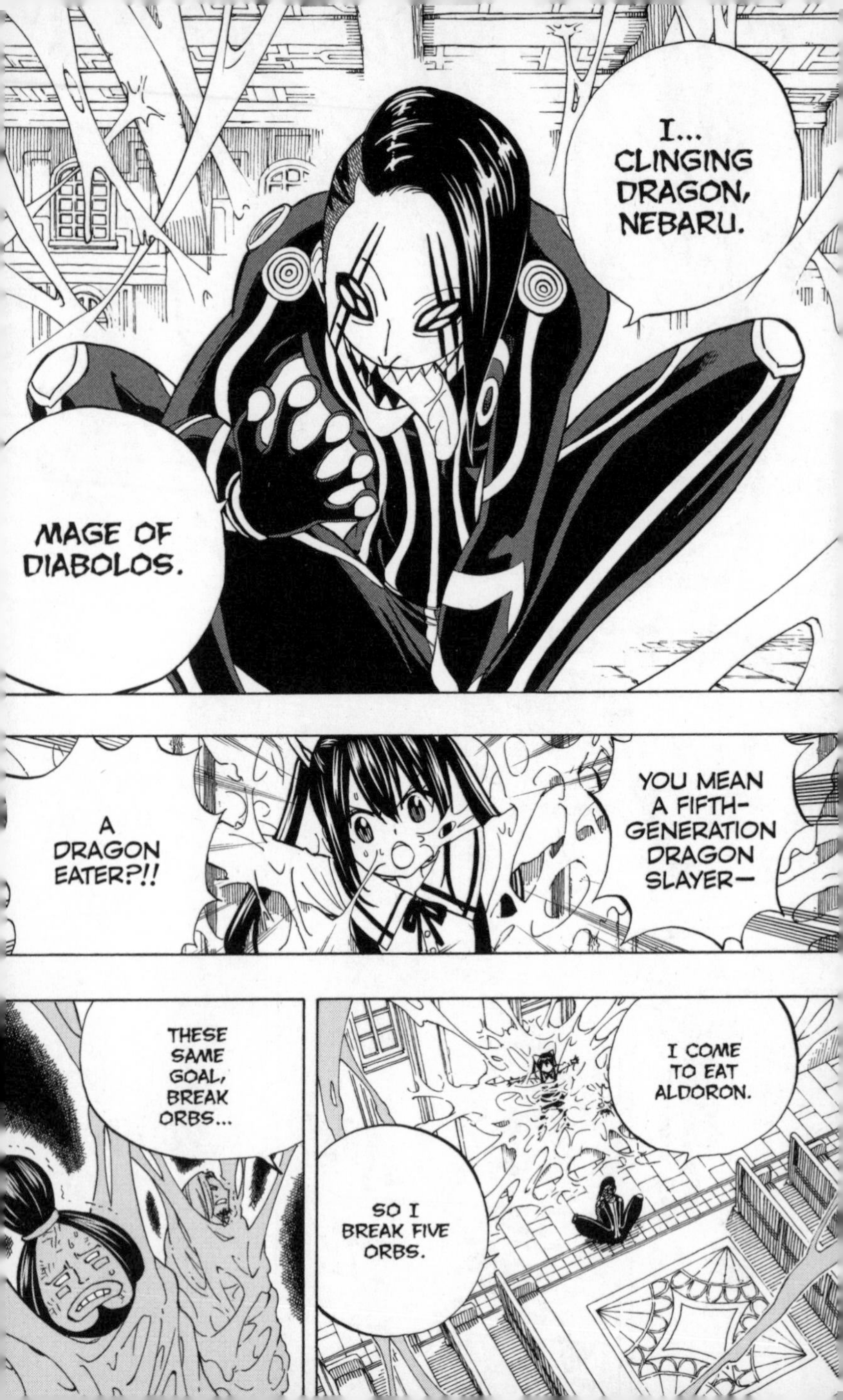
I... CLINGING DRAGON, NEBARU.
MAGE OF DIABOLOS.
YOU MEAN A FIFTH-GENERATION DRAGON SLAYER—
A DRAGON EATER?!!
I COME TO EAT ALDORON.
SO I BREAK FIVE ORBS.
THESE SAME GOAL, BREAK ORBS...

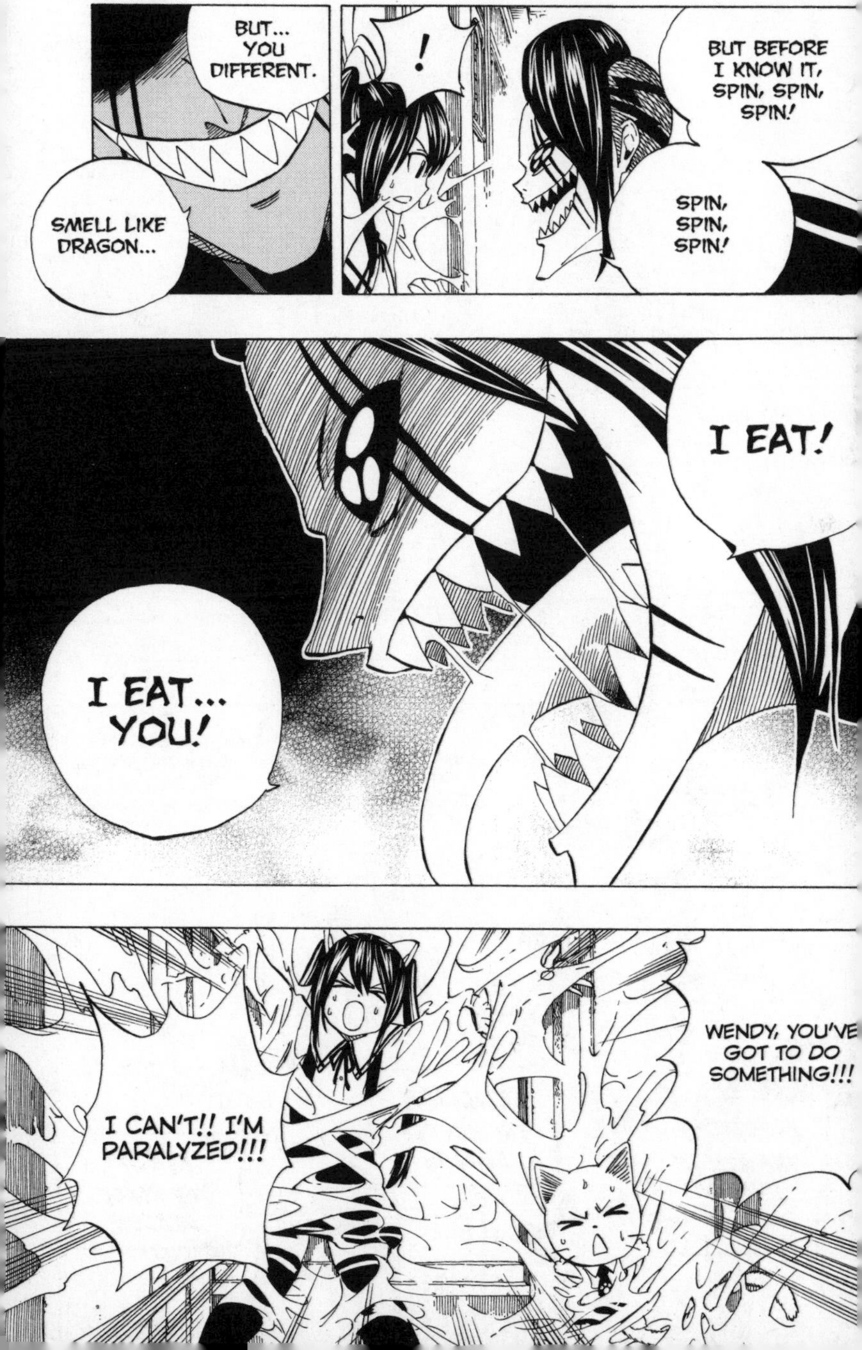
BUT BEFORE I KNOW IT, SPIN, SPIN, SPIN!
SPIN, SPIN, SPIN!
!
BUT... YOU DIFFERENT.
SMELL LIKE DRAGON...
I EAT!
I EAT... YOU!
WENDY, YOU'VE GOT TO DO SOMETHING!!!
I CAN'T!! I'M PARALYZED!!!

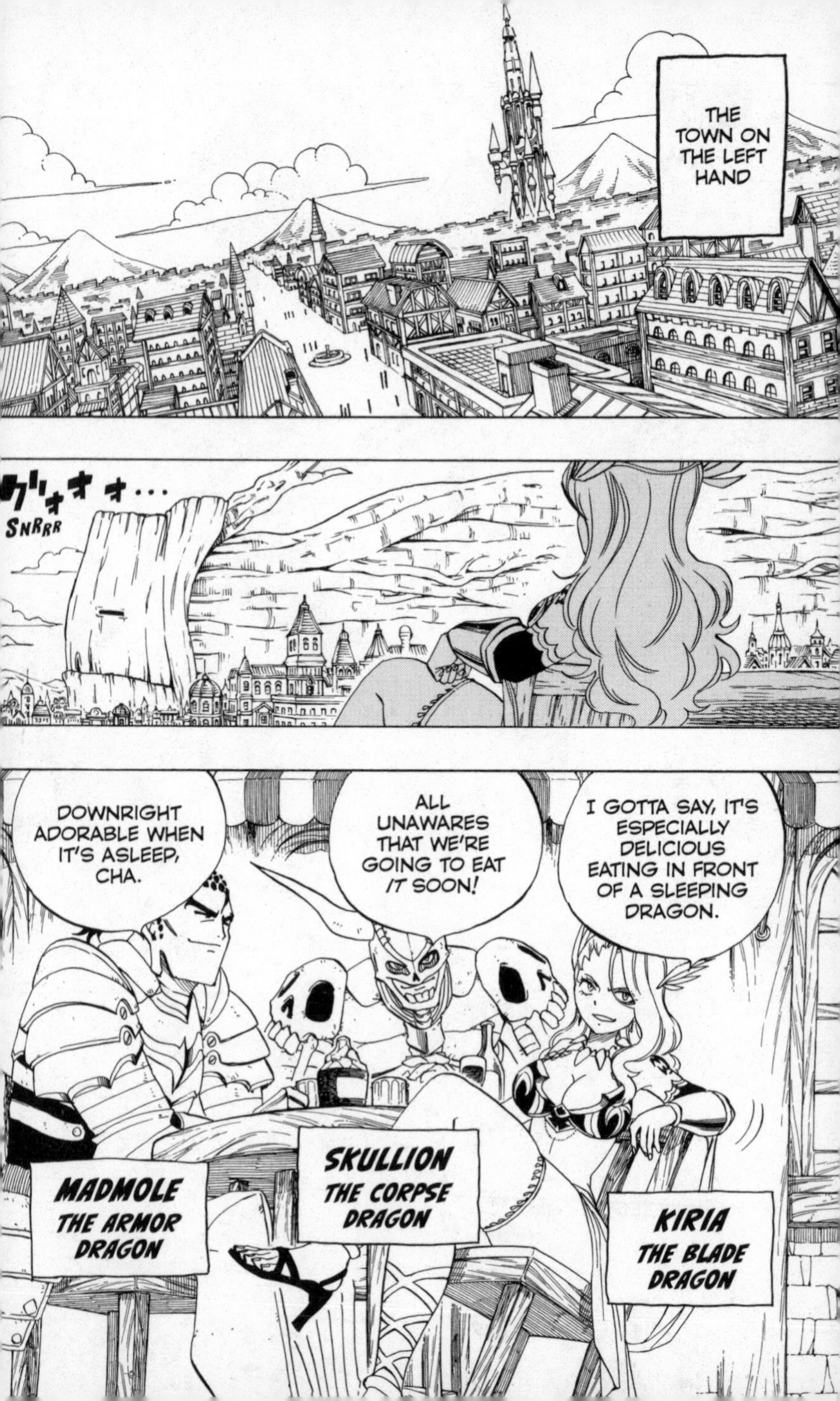
THE TOWN ON THE LEFT HAND
グリォオォ…
SNRRR
I GOTTA SAY, IT'S ESPECIALLY DELICIOUS EATING IN FRONT OF A SLEEPING DRAGON.
ALL UNAWARES THAT WE'RE GOING TO EAT IT SOON!
DOWNRIGHT ADORABLE WHEN IT'S ASLEEP, CHA.
KIRIA THE BLADE DRAGON
SKULLION THE CORPSE DRAGON
MADMOLE THE ARMOR DRAGON

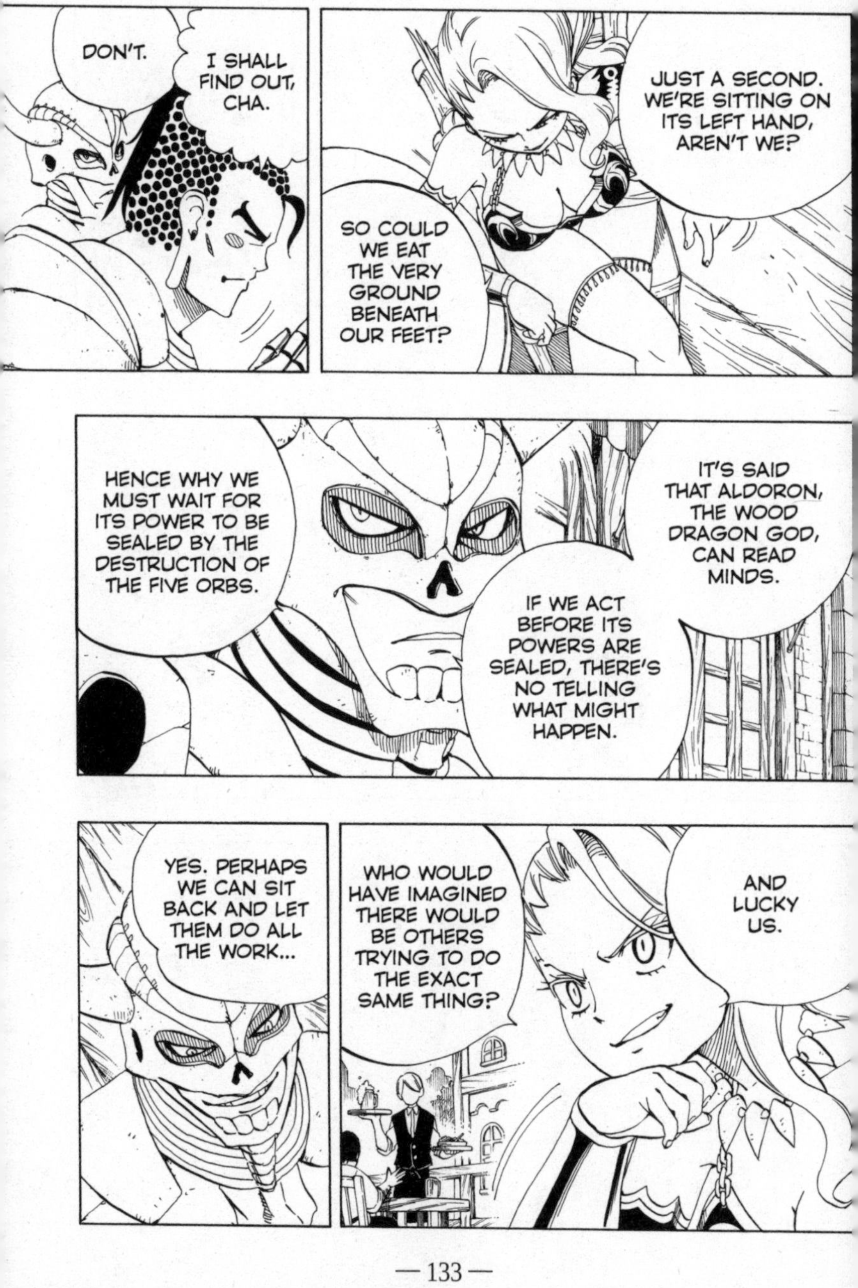
JUST A SECOND. WE'RE SITTING ON ITS LEFT HAND, AREN'T WE?
SO COULD WE EAT THE VERY GROUND BENEATH OUR FEET?
I SHALL FIND OUT, CHA.
DON'T.
IT'S SAID THAT ALDORON, THE WOOD DRAGON GOD, CAN READ MINDS.
IF WE ACT BEFORE ITS POWERS ARE SEALED, THERE'S NO TELLING WHAT MIGHT HAPPEN.
HENCE WHY WE MUST WAIT FOR ITS POWER TO BE SEALED BY THE DESTRUCTION OF THE FIVE ORBS.
AND LUCKY US.
WHO WOULD HAVE IMAGINED THERE WOULD BE OTHERS TRYING TO DO THE EXACT SAME THING?
YES. PERHAPS WE CAN SIT BACK AND LET THEM DO ALL THE WORK...

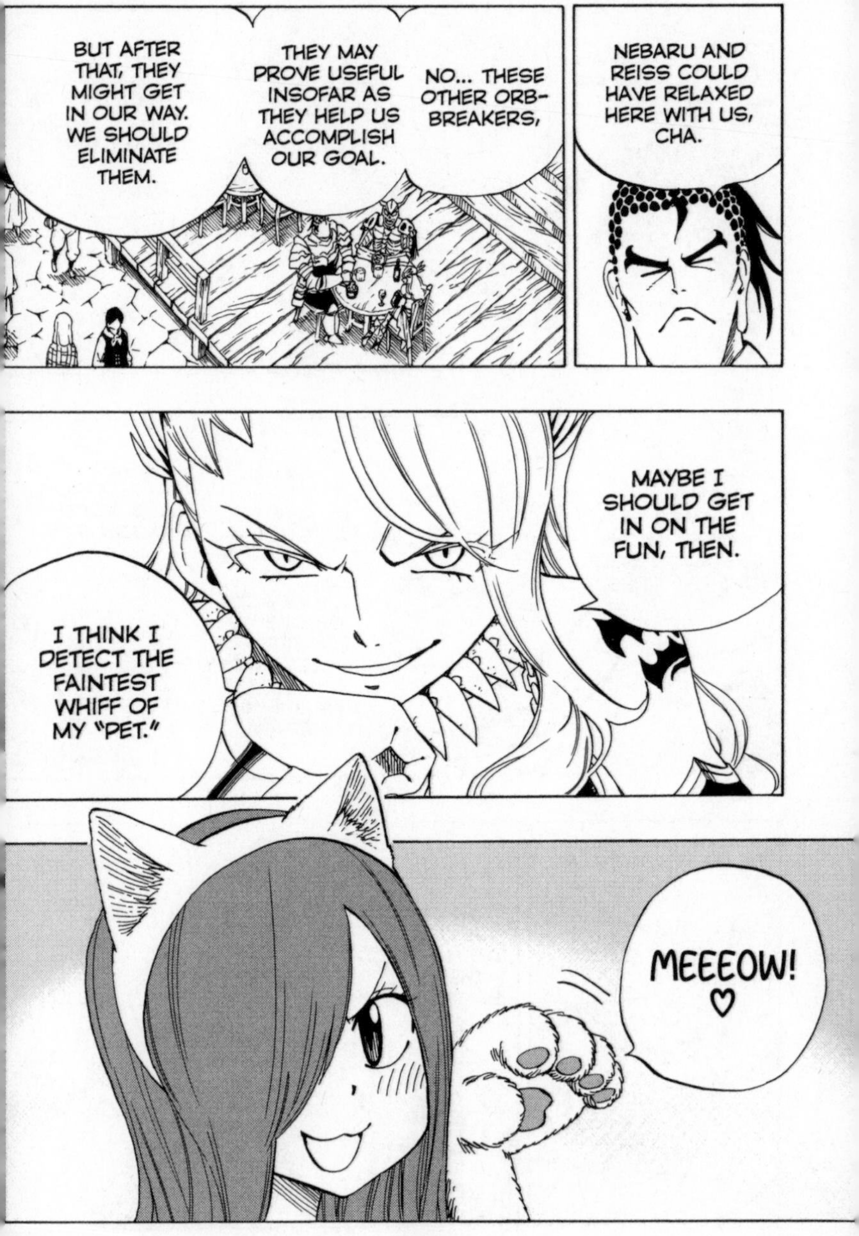
NEBARU AND REISS COULD HAVE RELAXED HERE WITH US, CHA.
NO... THESE OTHER ORB-BREAKERS,
THEY MAY PROVE USEFUL INSOFAR AS THEY HELP US ACCOMPLISH OUR GOAL.
BUT AFTER THAT, THEY MIGHT GET IN OUR WAY. WE SHOULD ELIMINATE THEM.
MAYBE I SHOULD GET IN ON THE FUN, THEN.
I THINK I DETECT THE FAINTEST WHIFF OF MY "PET."
MEEEOW! ♡

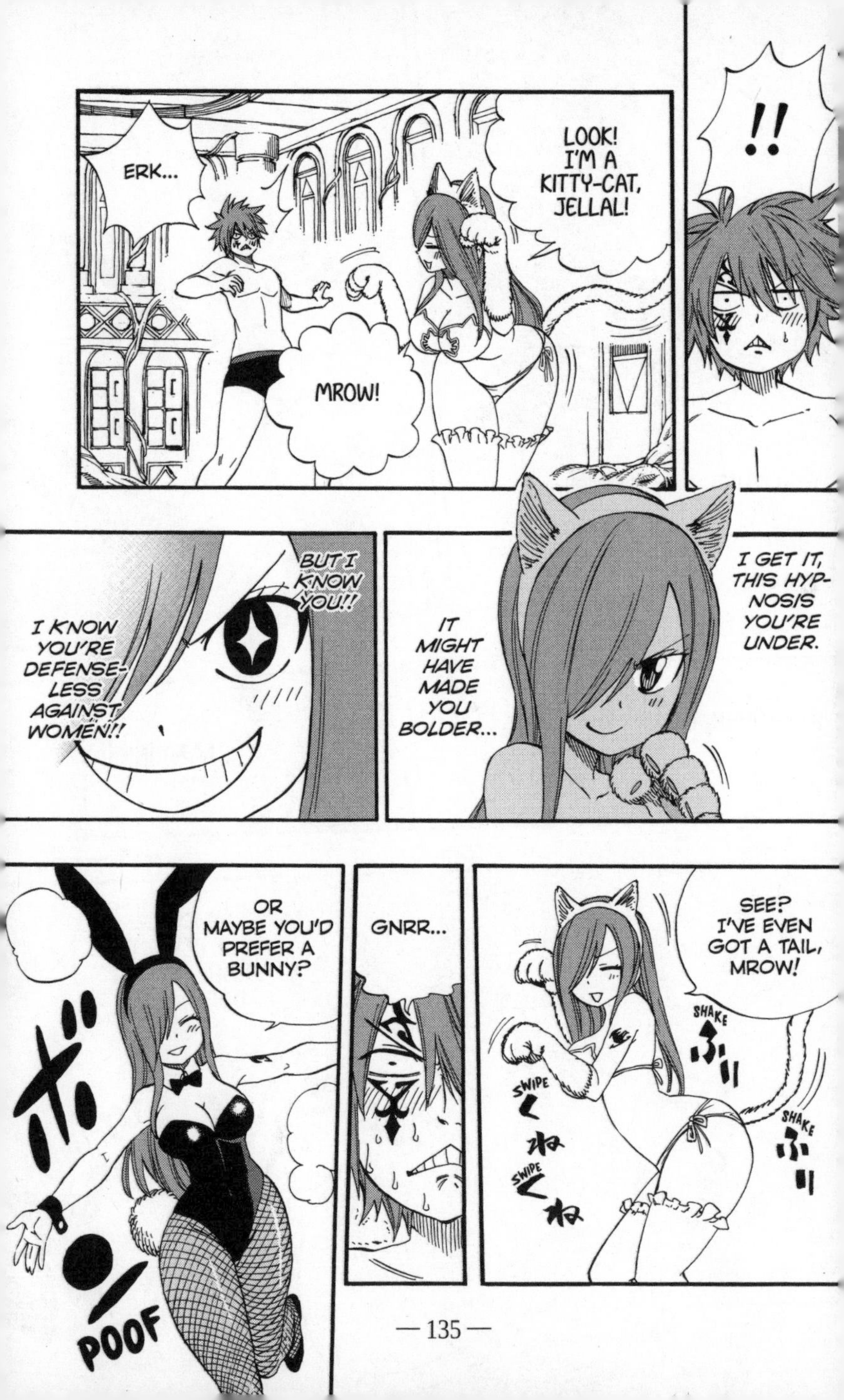
!!
LOOK! I'M A KITTY-CAT, JELLAL!
ERK...
MROW!
I GET IT, THIS HYPNOSIS YOU'RE UNDER.
IT MIGHT HAVE MADE YOU BOLDER...
BUT I KNOW YOU!!
I KNOW YOU'RE DEFENSELESS AGAINST WOMEN!!
SEE? I'VE EVEN GOT A TAIL, MROW!
SHAKE
SWIPE
SHAKE
SWIPE
GNRR...
OR MAYBE YOU'D PREFER A BUNNY?
POOF

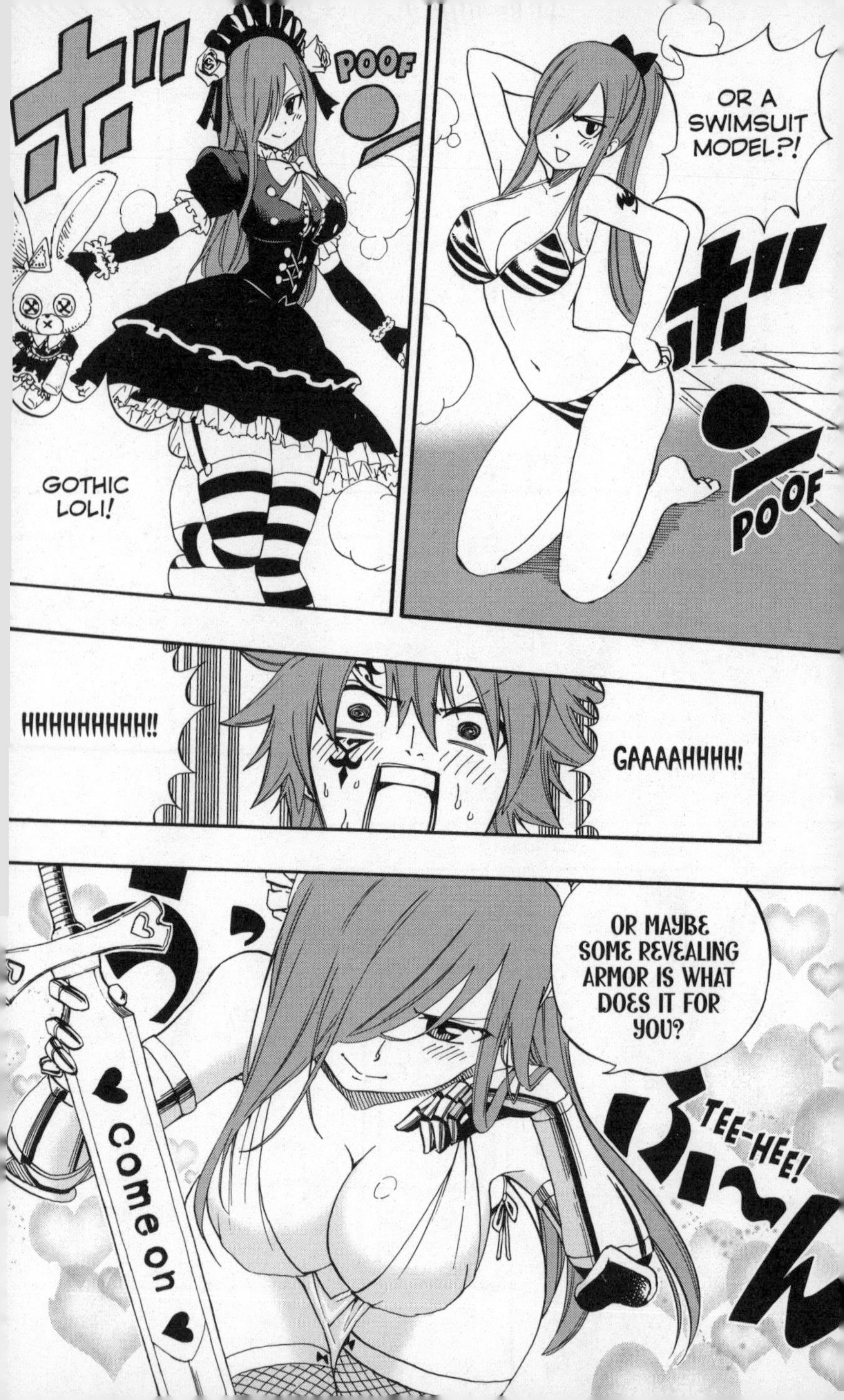
OR A SWIMSUIT MODEL?!
POOF
POOF
GOTHIC LOLI!
GAAAAHHHH!
HHHHHHHHH!!
OR MAYBE SOME REVEALING ARMOR IS WHAT DOES IT FOR YOU?
TEE-HEE!
come on

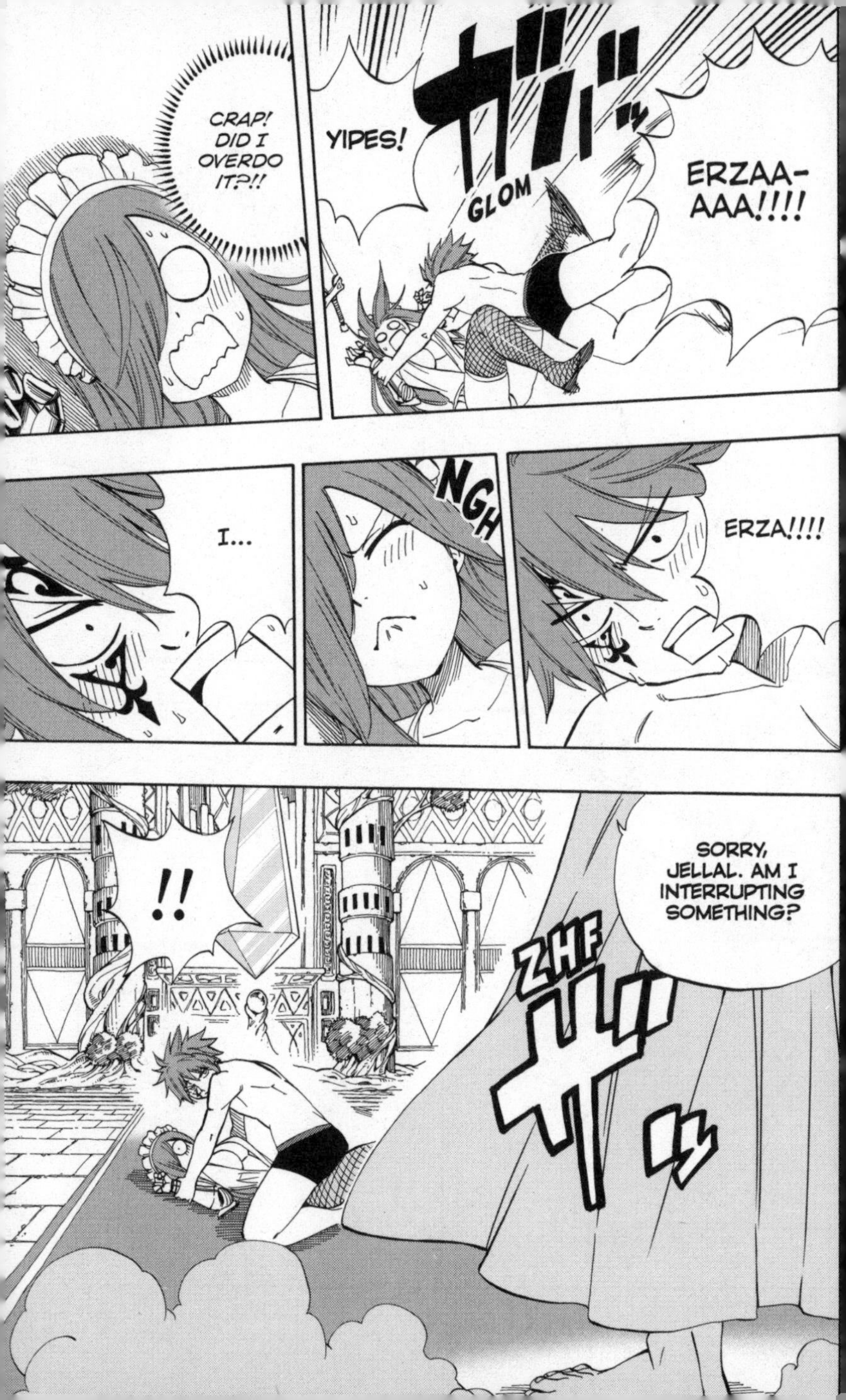
ERZAA-AAA!!!!
YIPES!
GLOM
CRAP! DID I OVERDO IT?!!
ERZA!!!!
NGH
I...
SORRY, JELLAL. AM I INTERRUPTING SOMETHING?
ZHF
!!

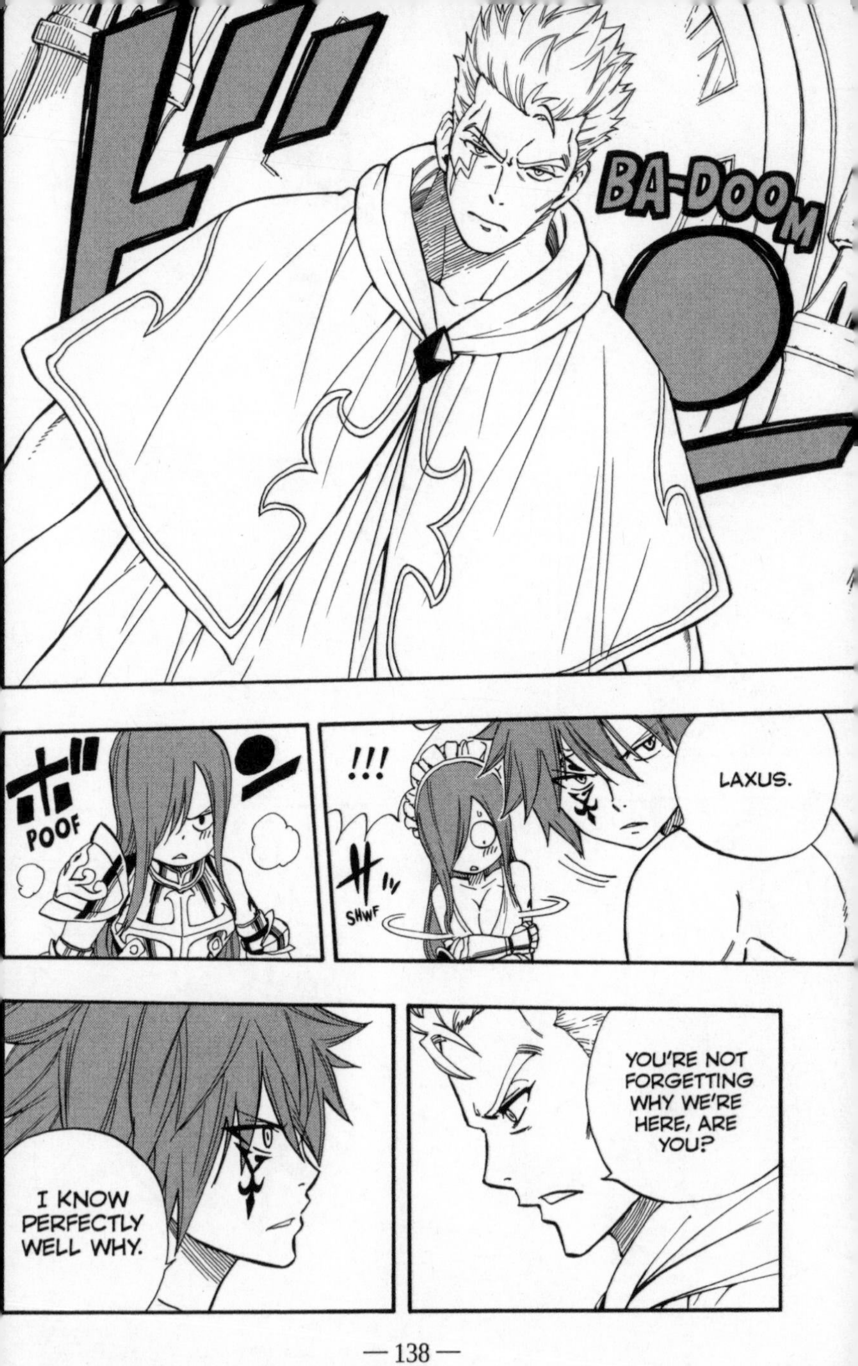
BA-DOOM
!!!
LAXUS.
SHWF
POOF
YOU'RE NOT FORGETTING WHY WE'RE HERE, ARE YOU?
I KNOW PERFECTLY WELL WHY.

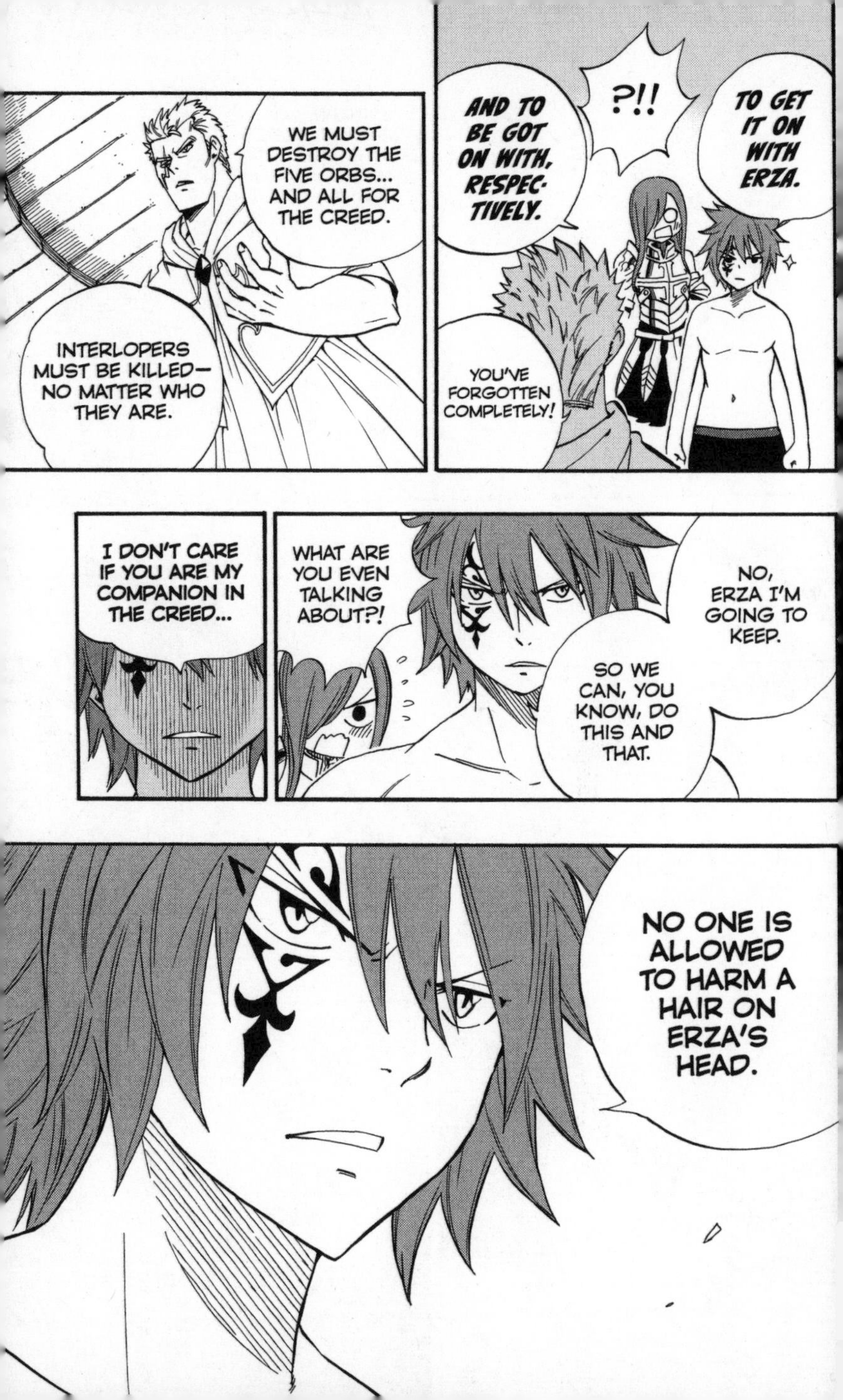
TO GET IT ON WITH ERZA.
?!!
AND TO BE GOT ON WITH, RESPECTIVELY.
YOU'VE FORGOTTEN COMPLETELY!
WE MUST DESTROY THE FIVE ORBS... AND ALL FOR THE CREED.
INTERLOPERS MUST BE KILLED— NO MATTER WHO THEY ARE.
NO, ERZA I'M GOING TO KEEP.
SO WE CAN, YOU KNOW, DO THIS AND THAT.
WHAT ARE YOU EVEN TALKING ABOUT?!
I DON'T CARE IF YOU ARE MY COMPANION IN THE CREED...
NO ONE IS ALLOWED TO HARM A HAIR ON ERZA'S HEAD.

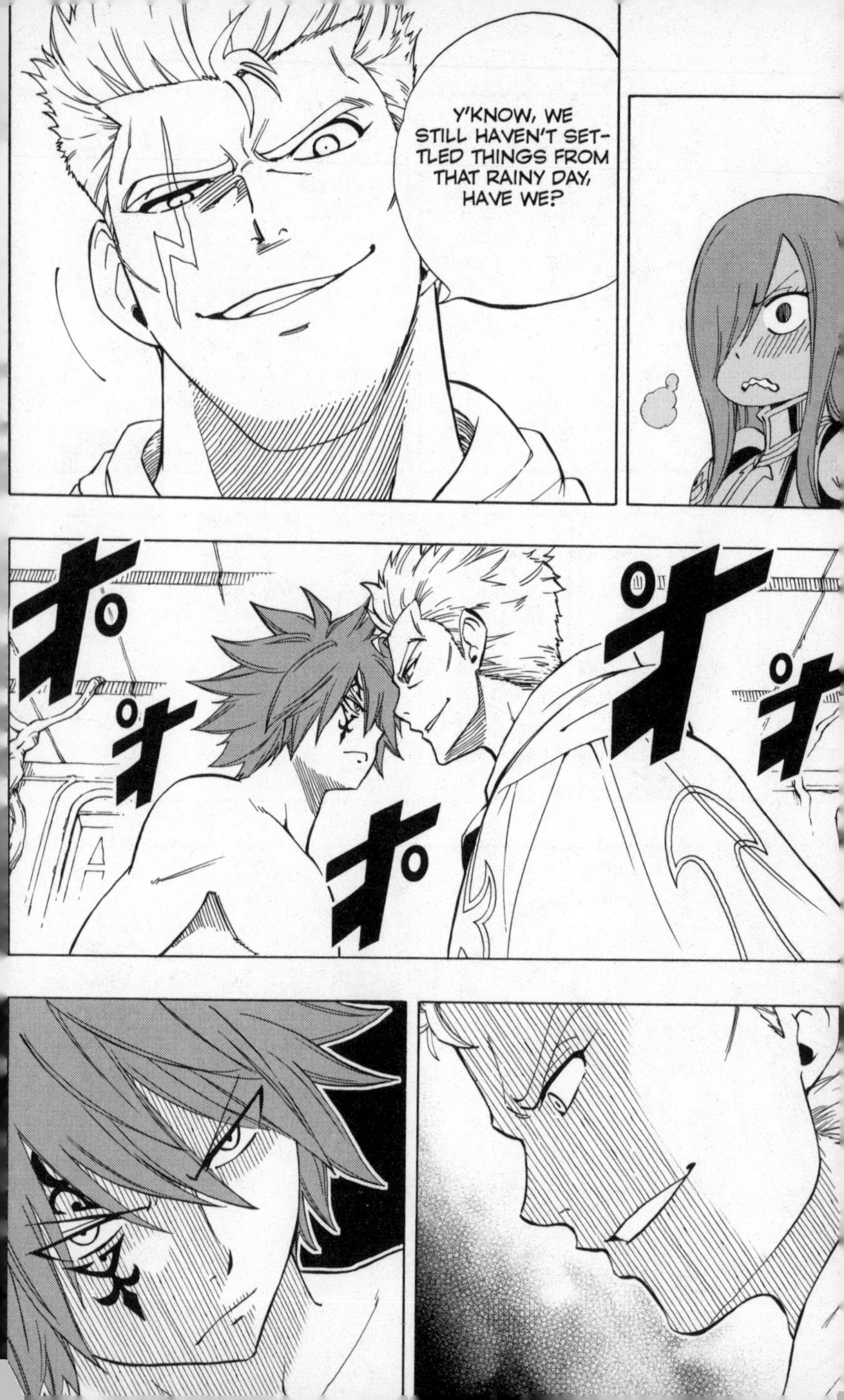
Y'KNOW, WE STILL HAVEN'T SET-TLED THINGS FROM THAT RAINY DAY, HAVE WE?

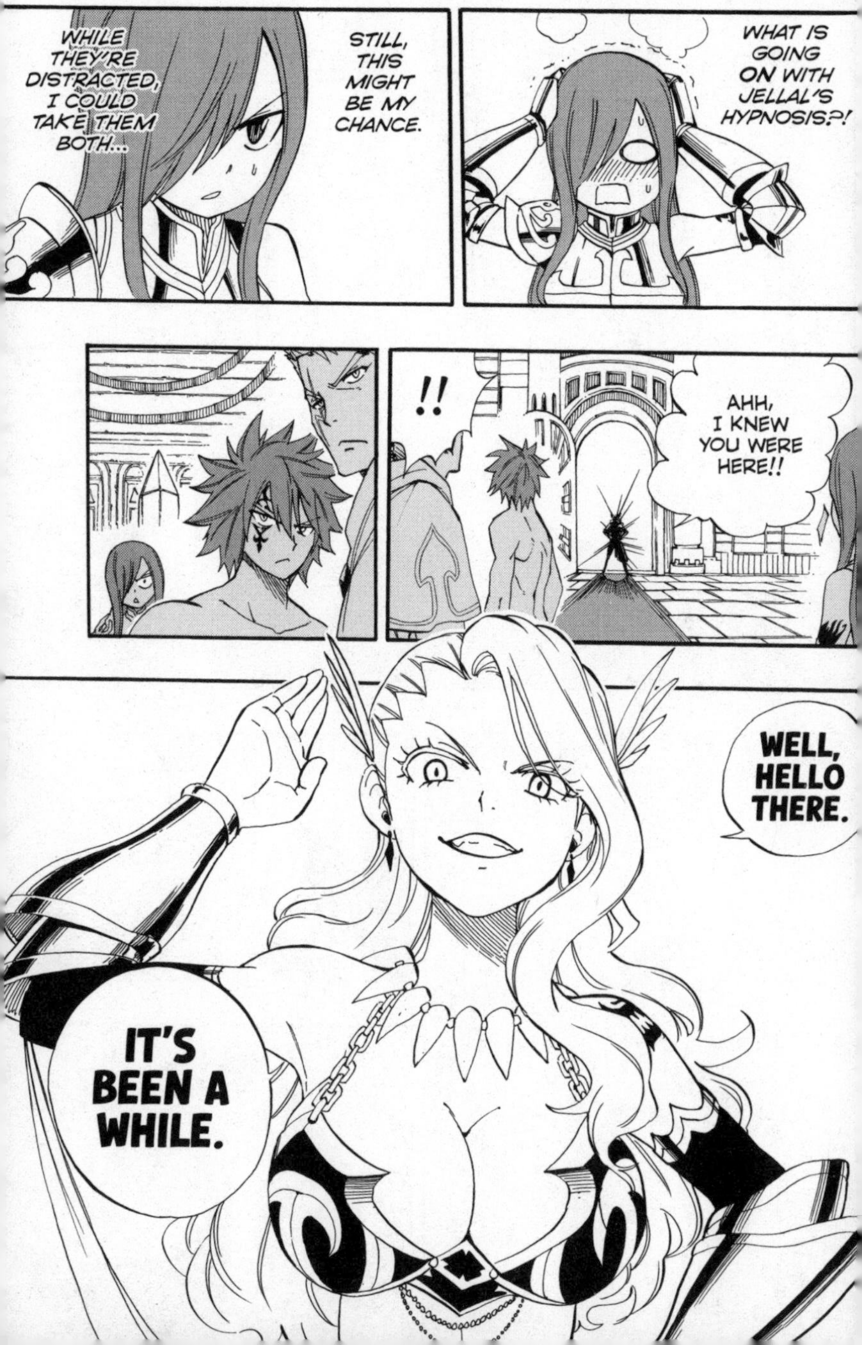
WHAT IS GOING ON WITH JELLAL'S HYPNOSIS?!
STILL, THIS MIGHT BE MY CHANCE.
WHILE THEY'RE DISTRACTED, I COULD TAKE THEM BOTH...
AHH, I KNEW YOU WERE HERE!!
!!
WELL, HELLO THERE.
IT'S BEEN A WHILE.

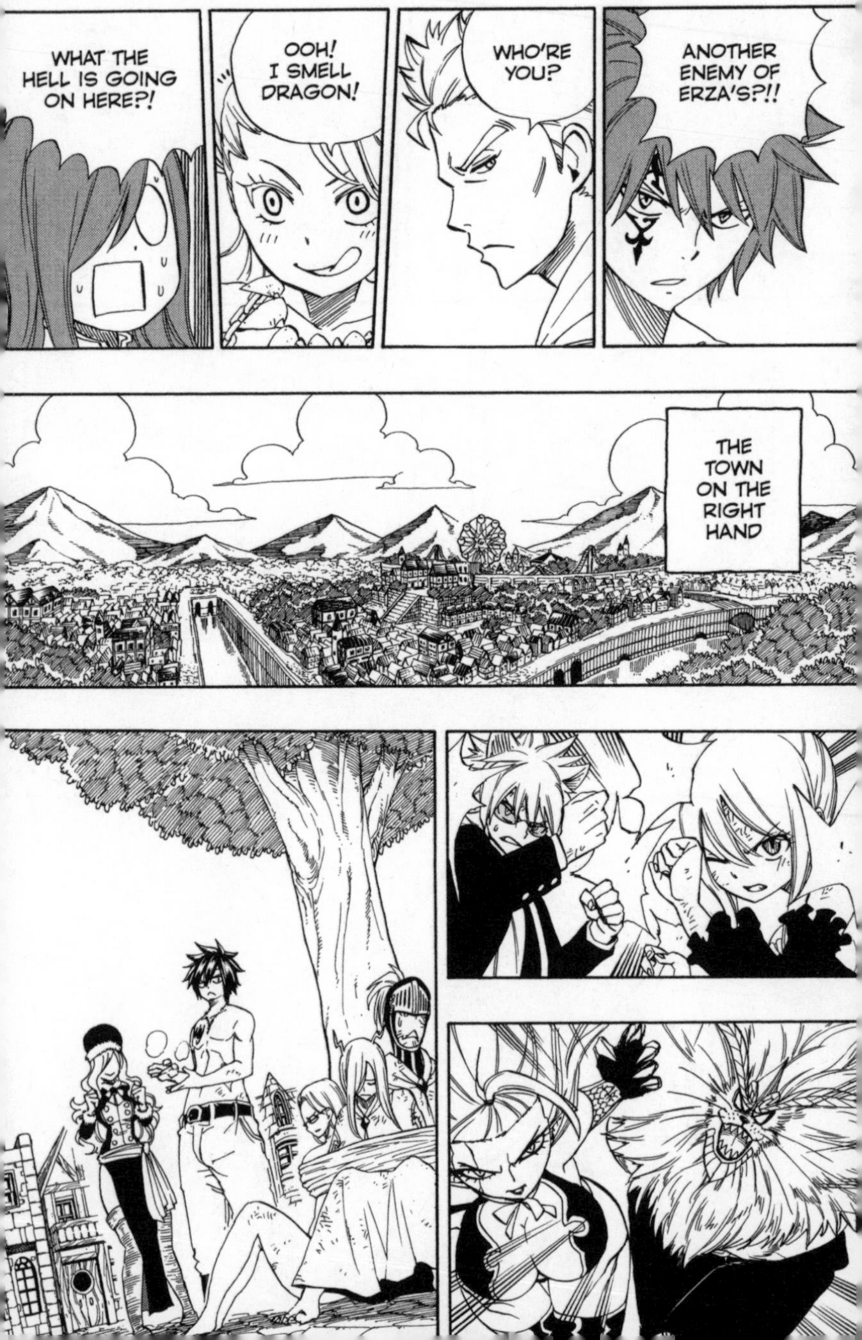
ANOTHER ENEMY OF ERZA'S?!!
WHO'RE YOU?
OOH! I SMELL DRAGON!
WHAT THE HELL IS GOING ON HERE?!
THE TOWN ON THE RIGHT HAND

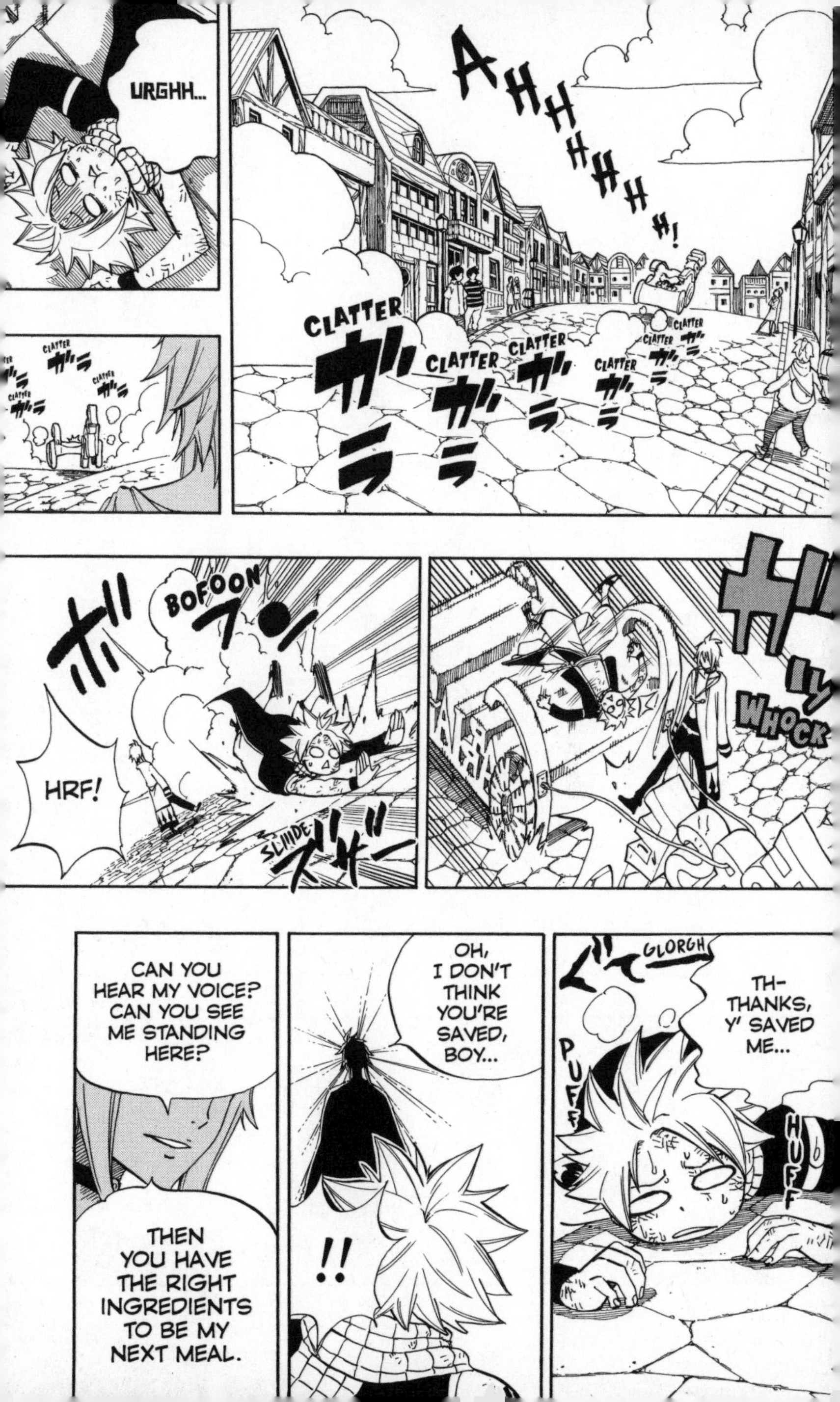
AHHHHHHHH!
CLATTER
CLATTER
CLATTER
CLATTER
CLATTER
CLATTER
URGHH...
CLATTER
CLATTER
CLATTER
WHOCK
BOFOON
HRF!
SLIIIDE
GLORGH
PUFF
HUFF
TH-THANKS, Y' SAVED ME...
OH, I DON'T THINK YOU'RE SAVED, BOY...
!!
CAN YOU HEAR MY VOICE? CAN YOU SEE ME STANDING HERE?
THEN YOU HAVE THE RIGHT INGREDIENTS TO BE MY NEXT MEAL.

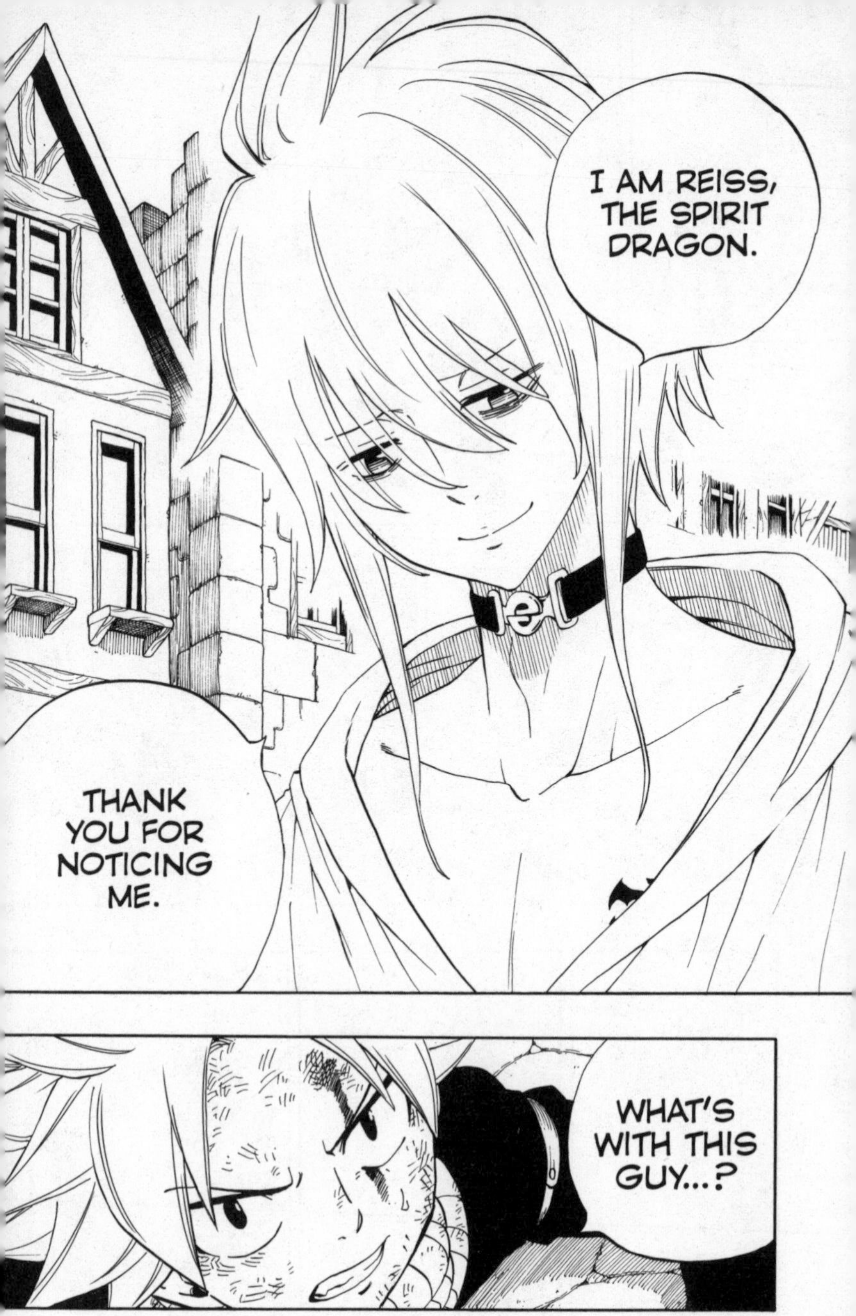
I AM REISS, THE SPIRIT DRAGON.
THANK YOU FOR NOTICING ME.
WHAT'S WITH THIS GUY...?

FAIRY TAIL 100 YEARS QUEST

Chapter 35: Reiss, the Spirit Dragon

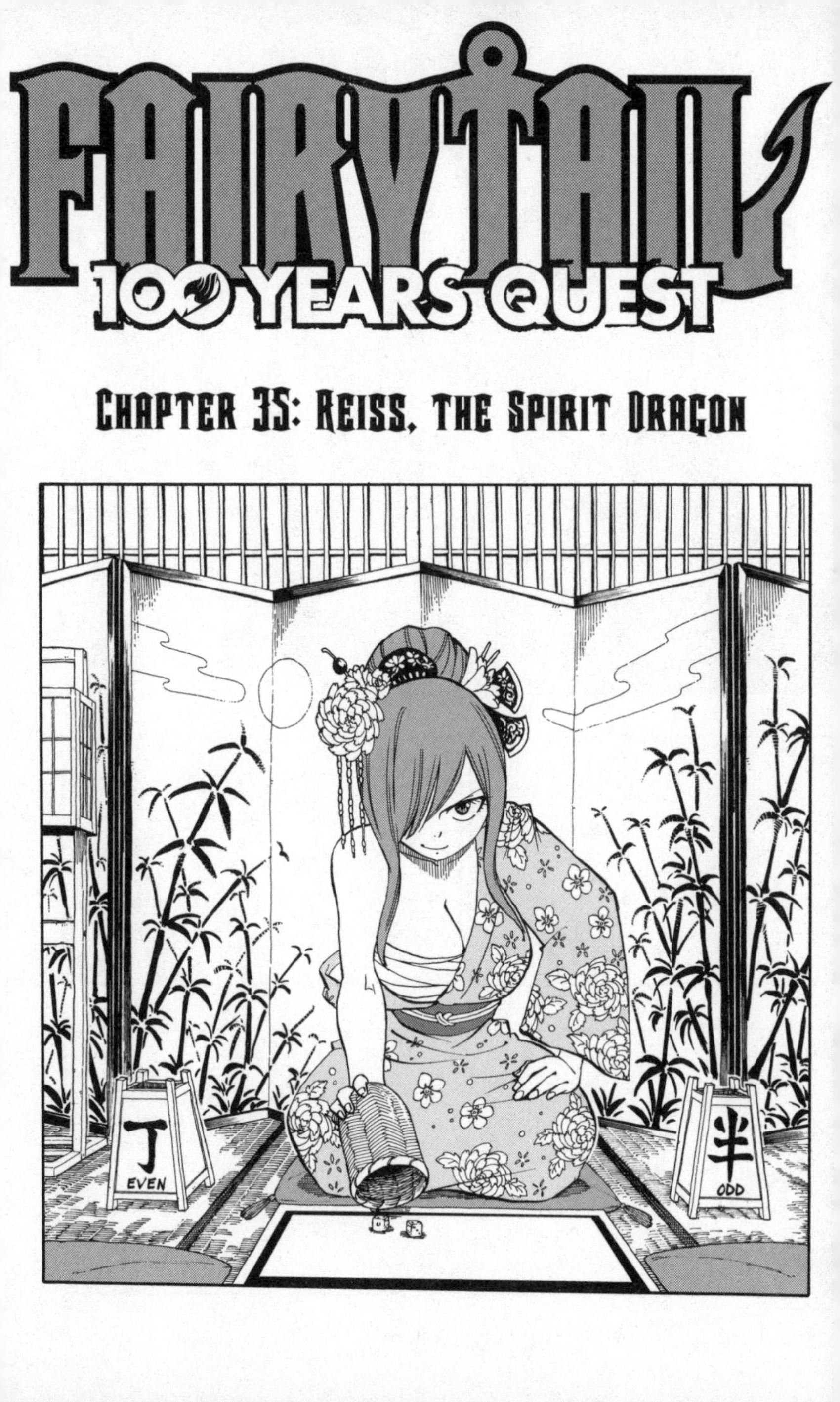
丁
EVEN
半
ODD

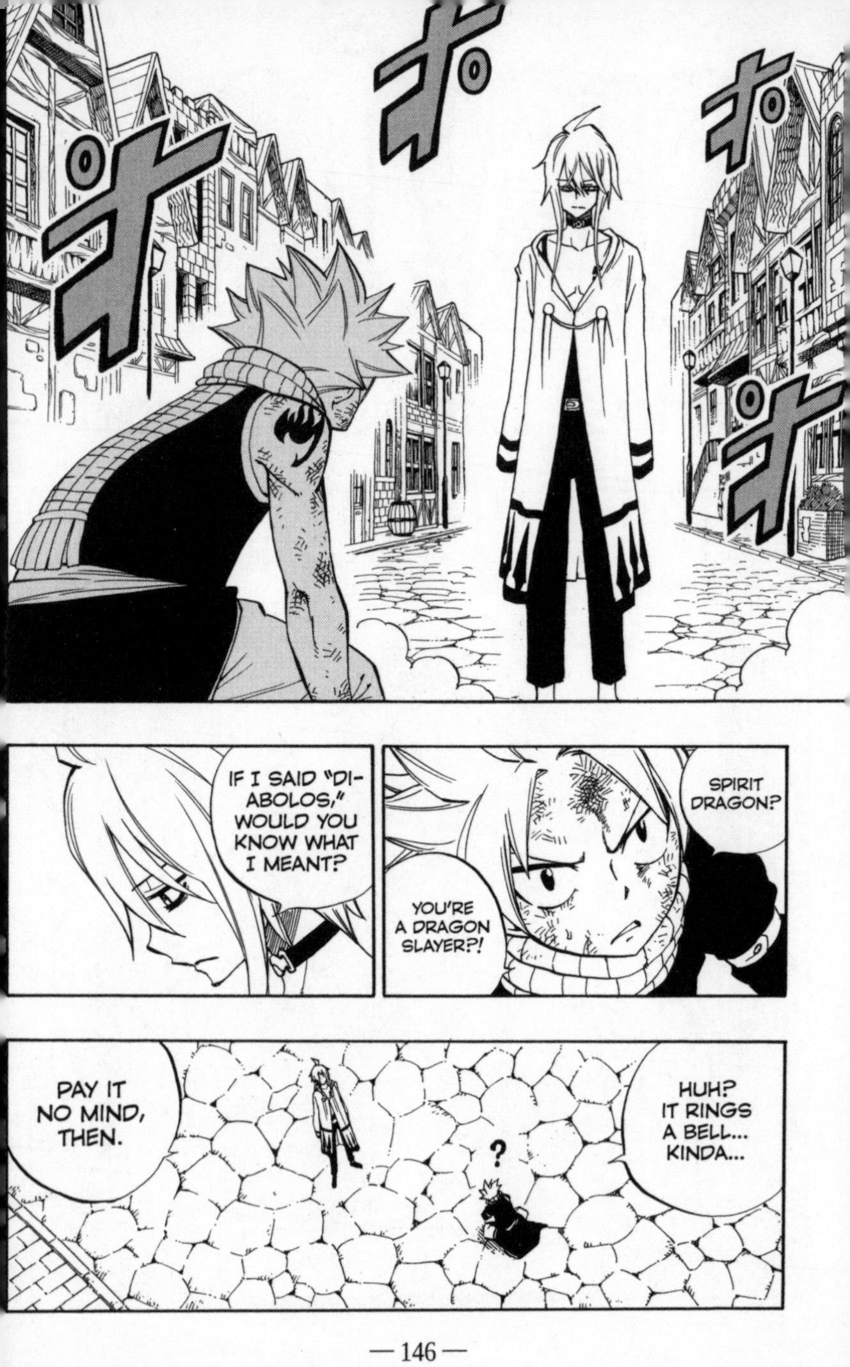
SPIRIT DRAGON?
YOU'RE A DRAGON SLAYER?!
IF I SAID "DI-ABOLOS," WOULD YOU KNOW WHAT I MEANT?
HUH? IT RINGS A BELL... KINDA...
?
PAY IT NO MIND, THEN.

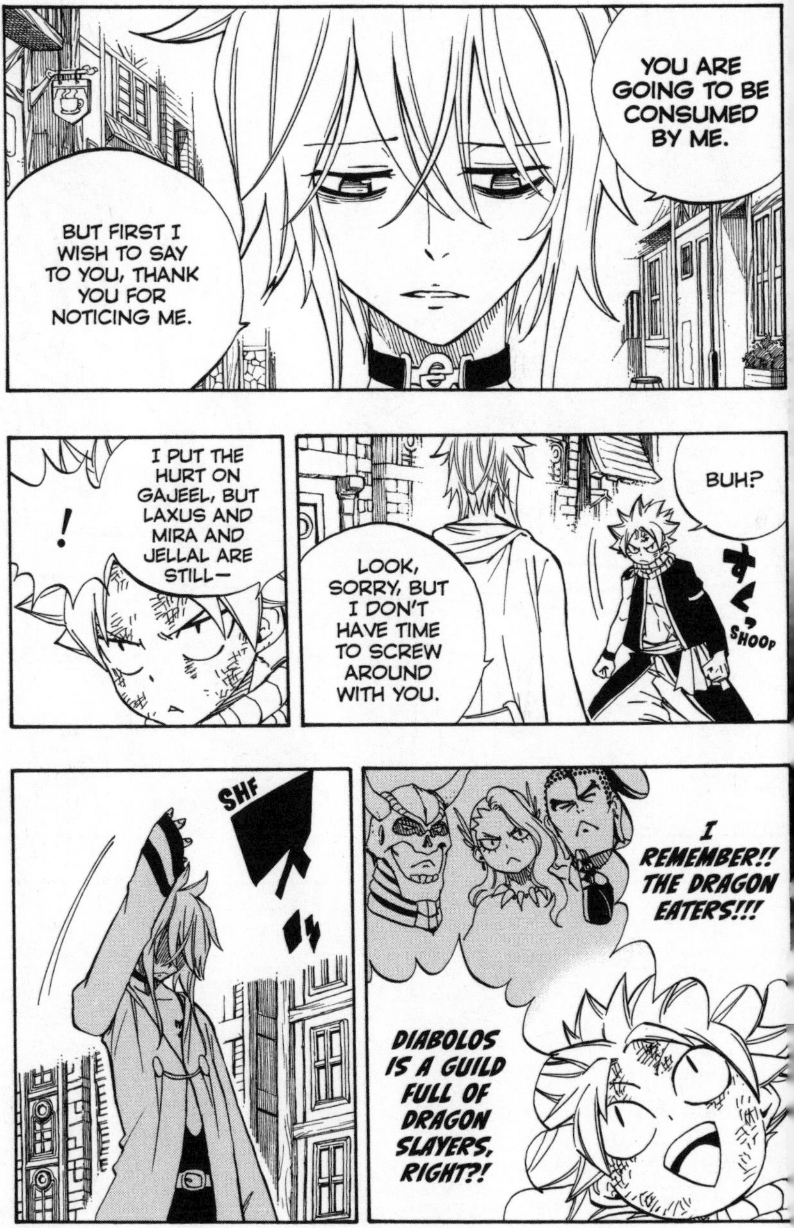

YOU ARE GOING TO BE CONSUMED BY ME.
BUT FIRST I WISH TO SAY TO YOU, THANK YOU FOR NOTICING ME.
BUH?
SHOOP
LOOK, SORRY, BUT I DON'T HAVE TIME TO SCREW AROUND WITH YOU.
I PUT THE HURT ON GAJEEL, BUT LAXUS AND MIRA AND JELLAL ARE STILL—
!
I REMEMBER!! THE DRAGON EATERS!!!
DIABOLOS IS A GUILD FULL OF DRAGON SLAYERS, RIGHT?!
SHF

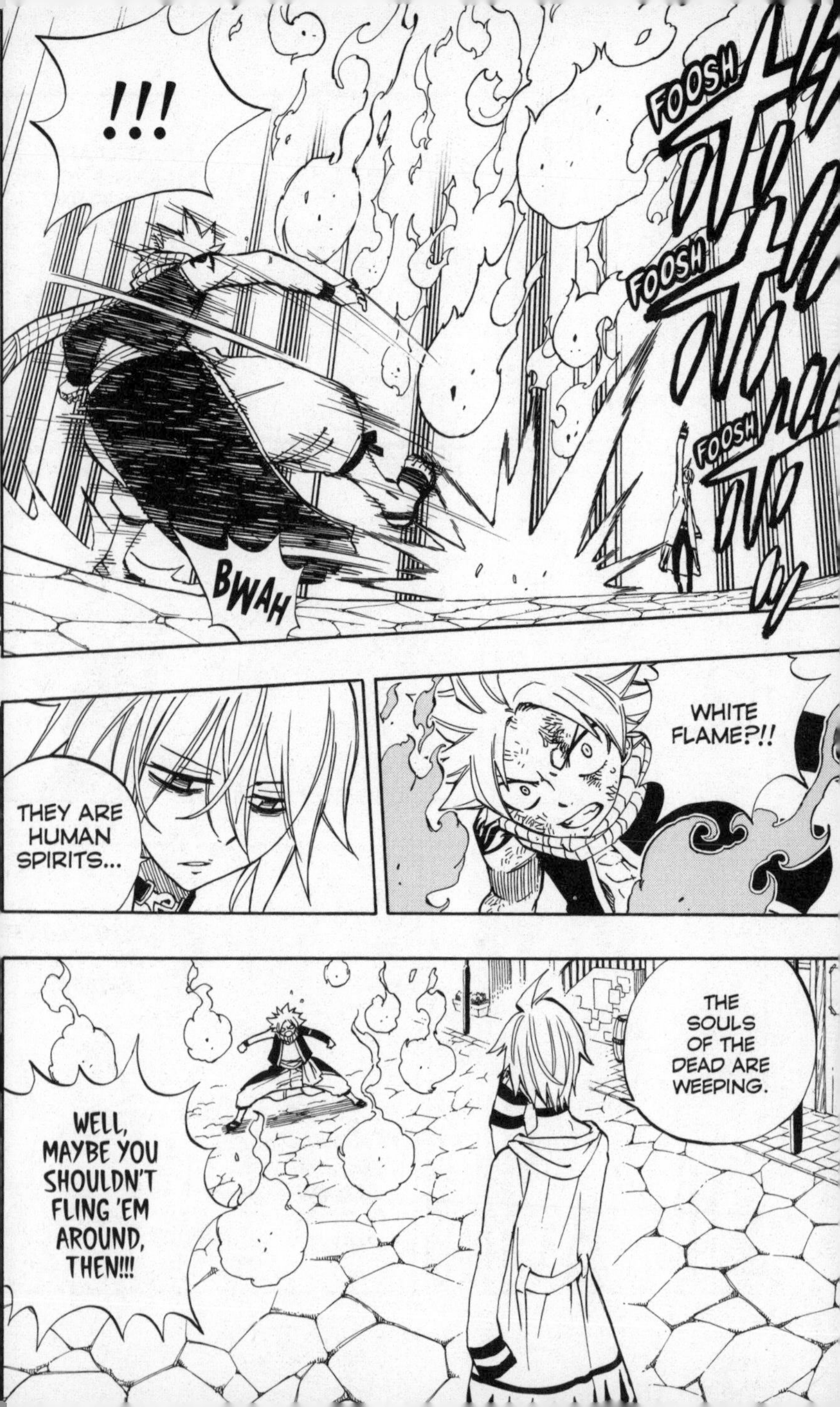
FOOSH
FOOSH
FOOSH
!!!
BWAH
WHITE FLAME?!!
THEY ARE HUMAN SPIRITS...
THE SOULS OF THE DEAD ARE WEEPING.
WELL, MAYBE YOU SHOULDN'T FLING 'EM AROUND, THEN!!!

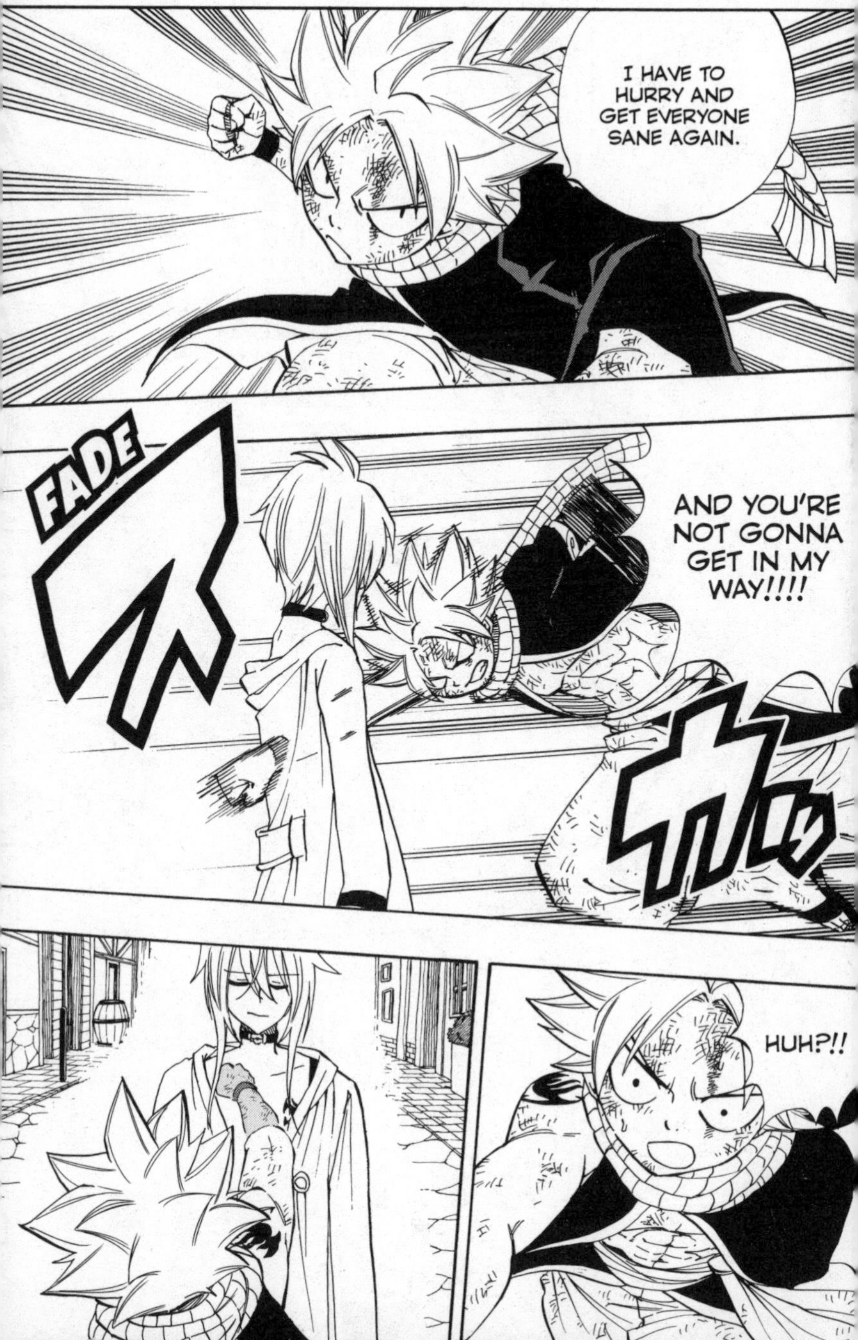
I HAVE TO HURRY AND GET EVERYONE SANE AGAIN.
AND YOU'RE NOT GONNA GET IN MY WAY!!!!
FADE
HUH?!!

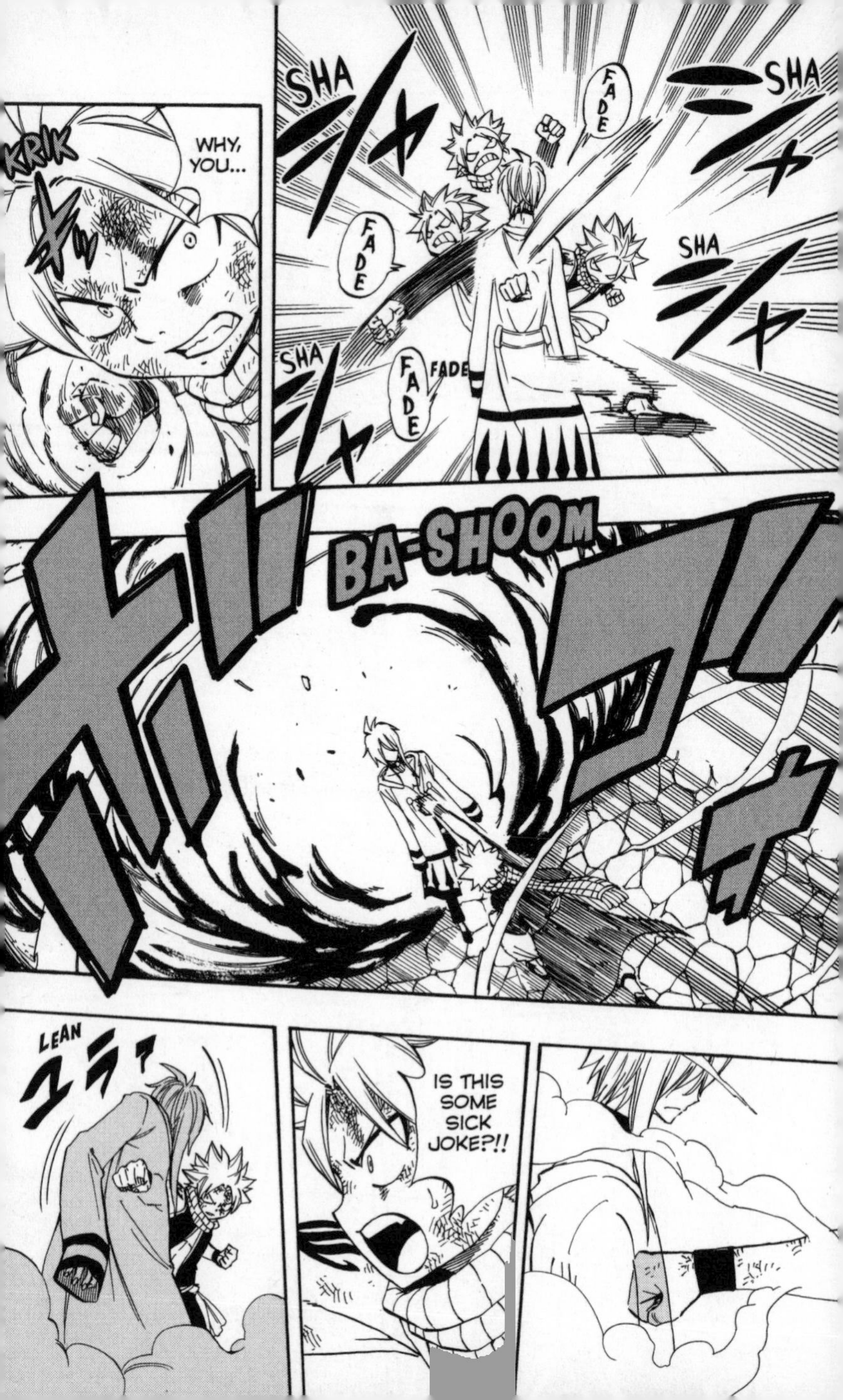
SHA
FADE
SHA
SHA
FADE
SHA
FADE
FADE
KRIK
WHY, YOU...
BA-SHOOM
IS THIS SOME SICK JOKE?!!
LEAN

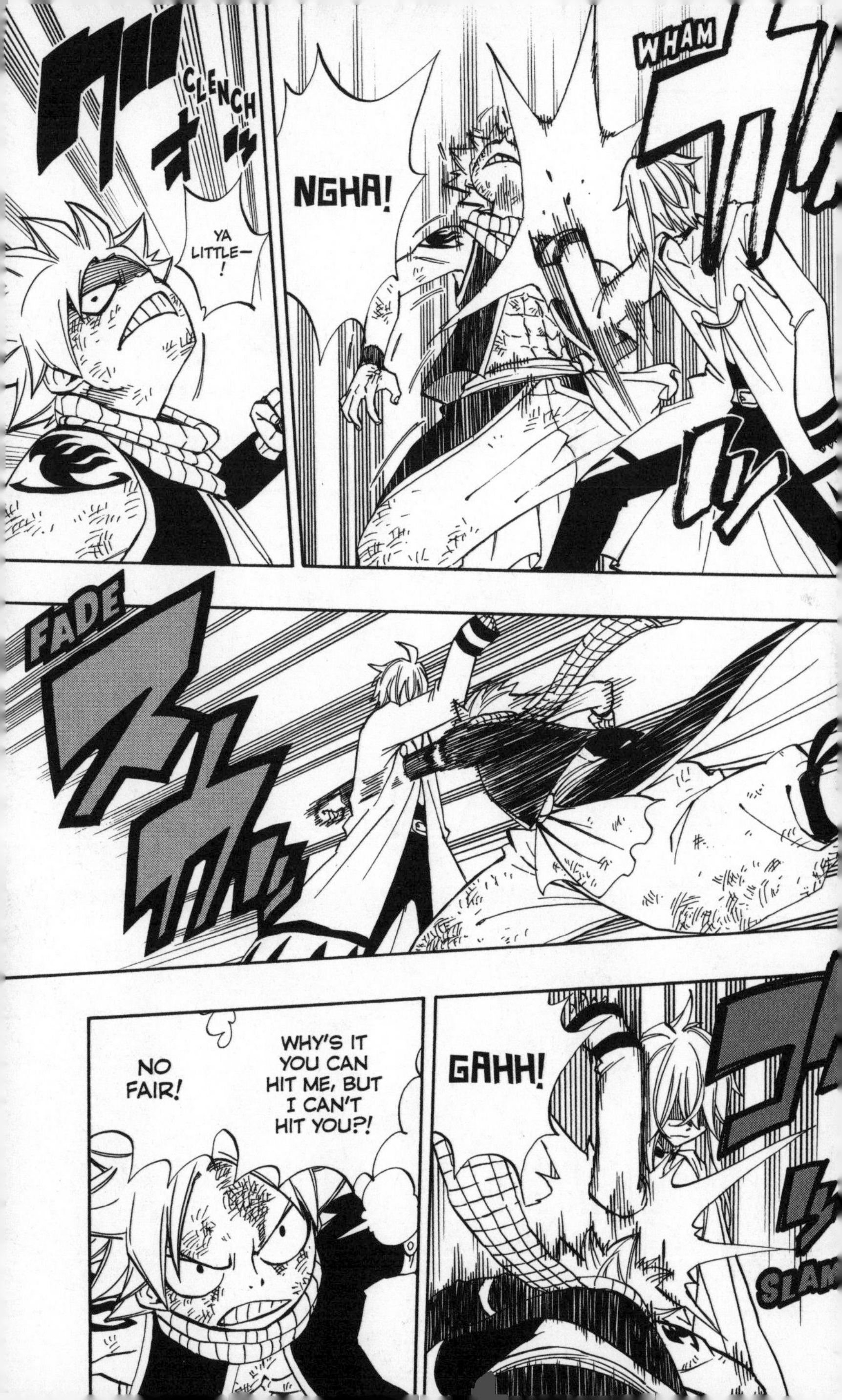
WHAM
NGHA!
CLENCH
YA LITTLE—!
FADE
GAHH!
SLAM
WHY'S IT YOU CAN HIT ME, BUT I CAN'T HIT YOU?!
NO FAIR!

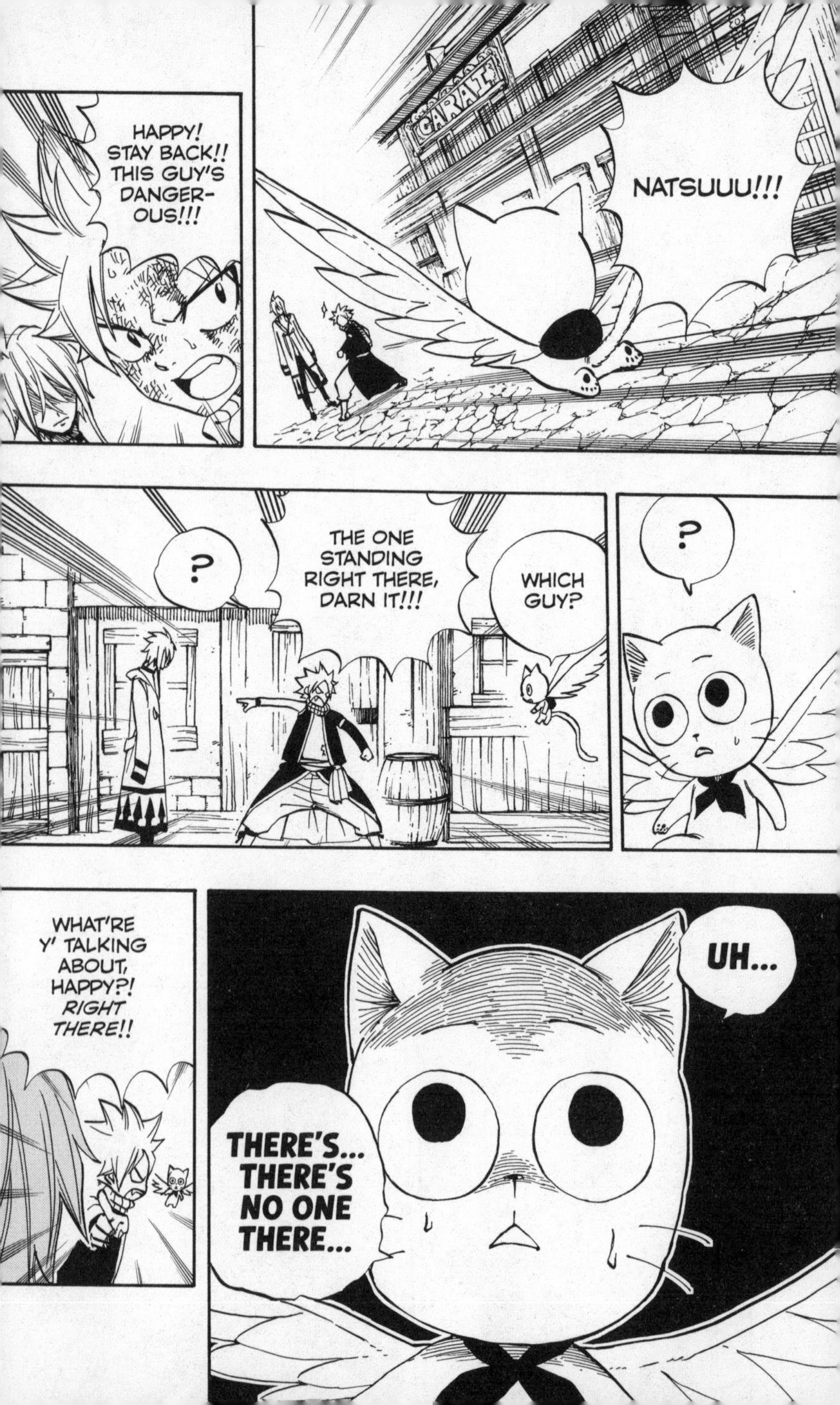
NATSUUU!!!
HAPPY! STAY BACK!! THIS GUY'S DANGER-OUS!!!
?
WHICH GUY?
THE ONE STANDING RIGHT THERE, DARN IT!!!
?
UH...
THERE'S... THERE'S NO ONE THERE...
WHAT'RE Y' TALKING ABOUT, HAPPY?! RIGHT THERE!!

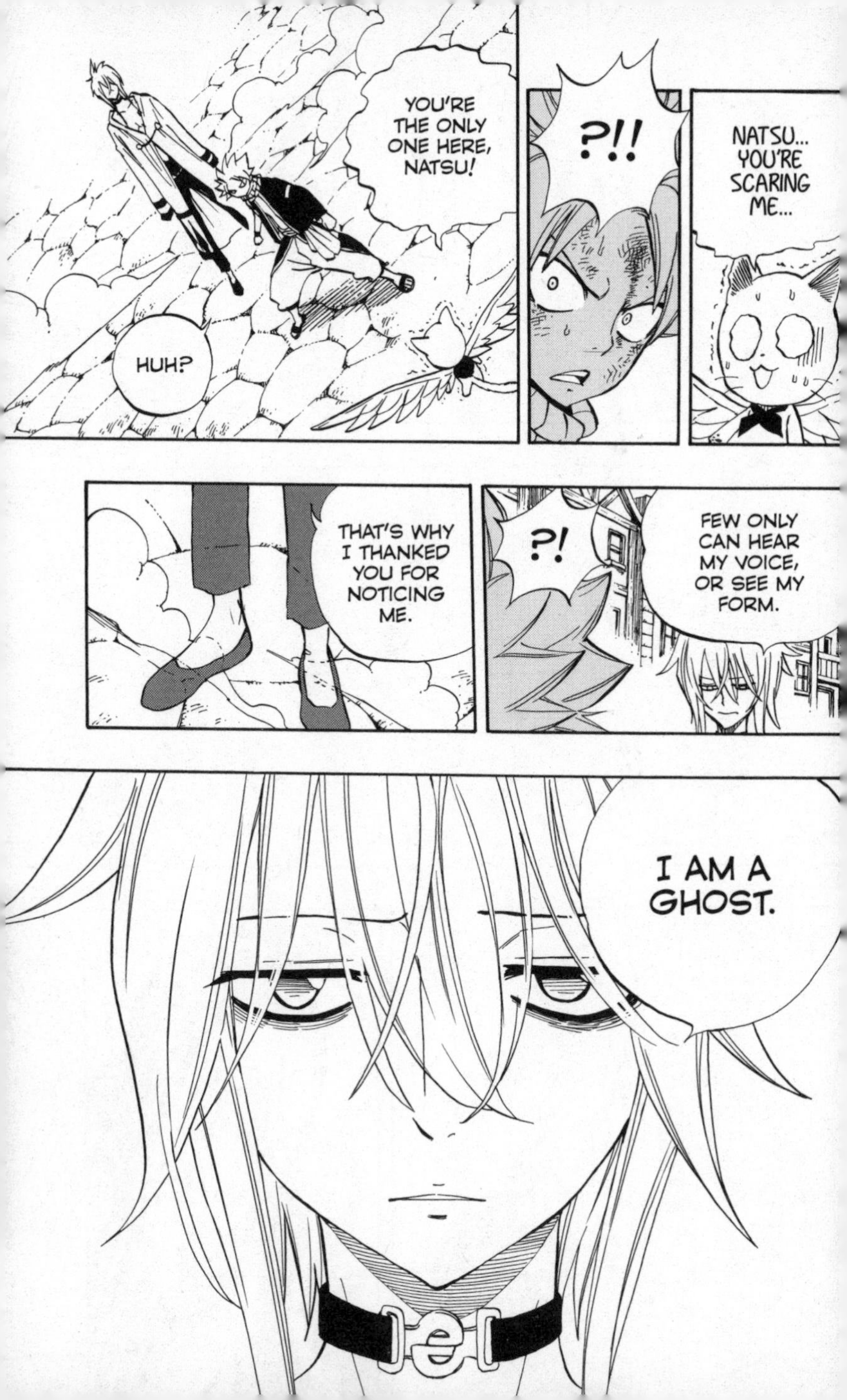
NATSU... YOU'RE SCARING ME...
?!!
YOU'RE THE ONLY ONE HERE, NATSU!
HUH?
FEW ONLY CAN HEAR MY VOICE, OR SEE MY FORM.
?!
THAT'S WHY I THANKED YOU FOR NOTICING ME.
I AM A GHOST.

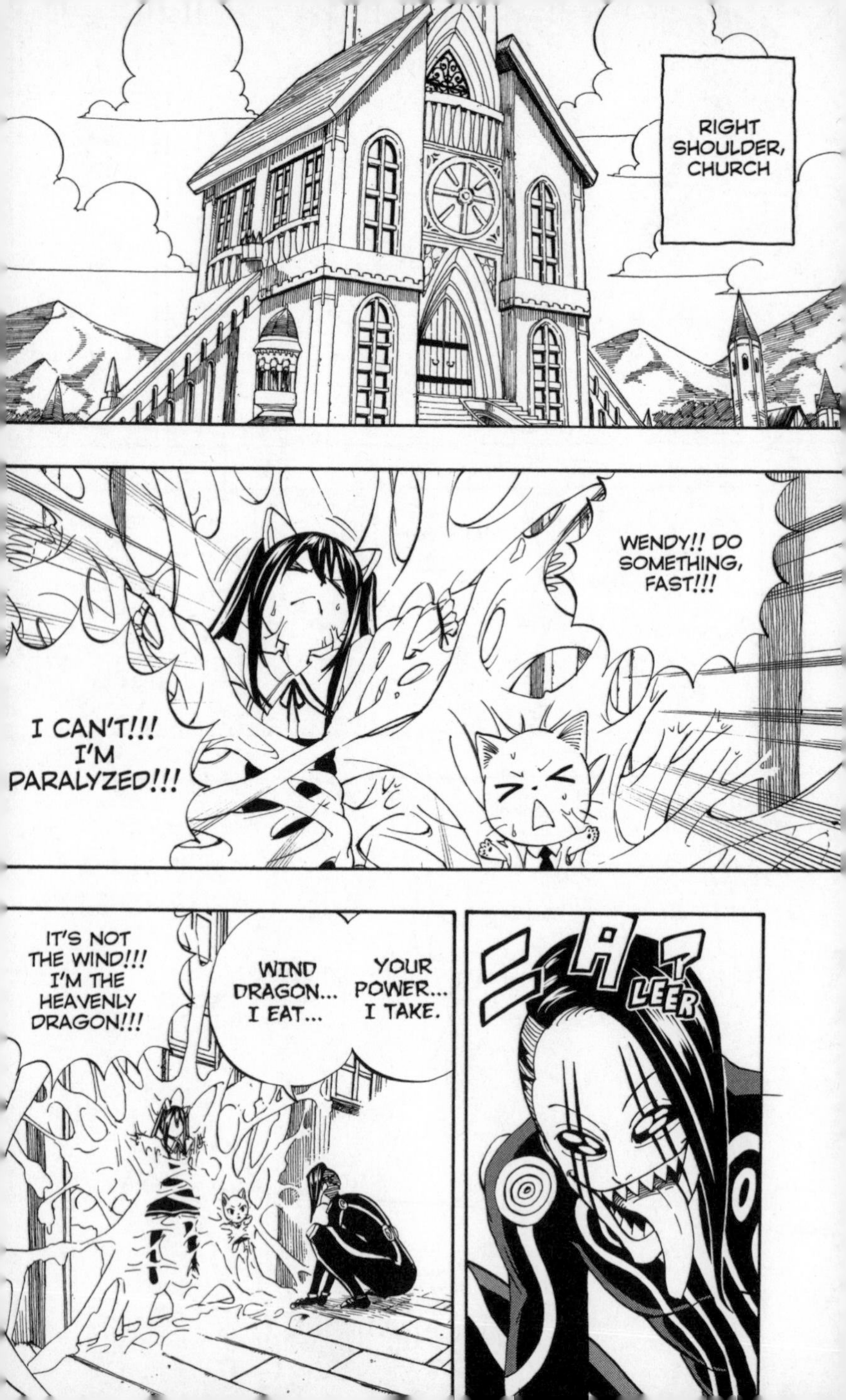
RIGHT SHOULDER, CHURCH
WENDY!! DO SOMETHING, FAST!!!
I CAN'T!!! I'M PARALYZED!!!
LEER
WIND DRAGON... I EAT...
YOUR POWER... I TAKE.
IT'S NOT THE WIND!!! I'M THE HEAVENLY DRAGON!!!

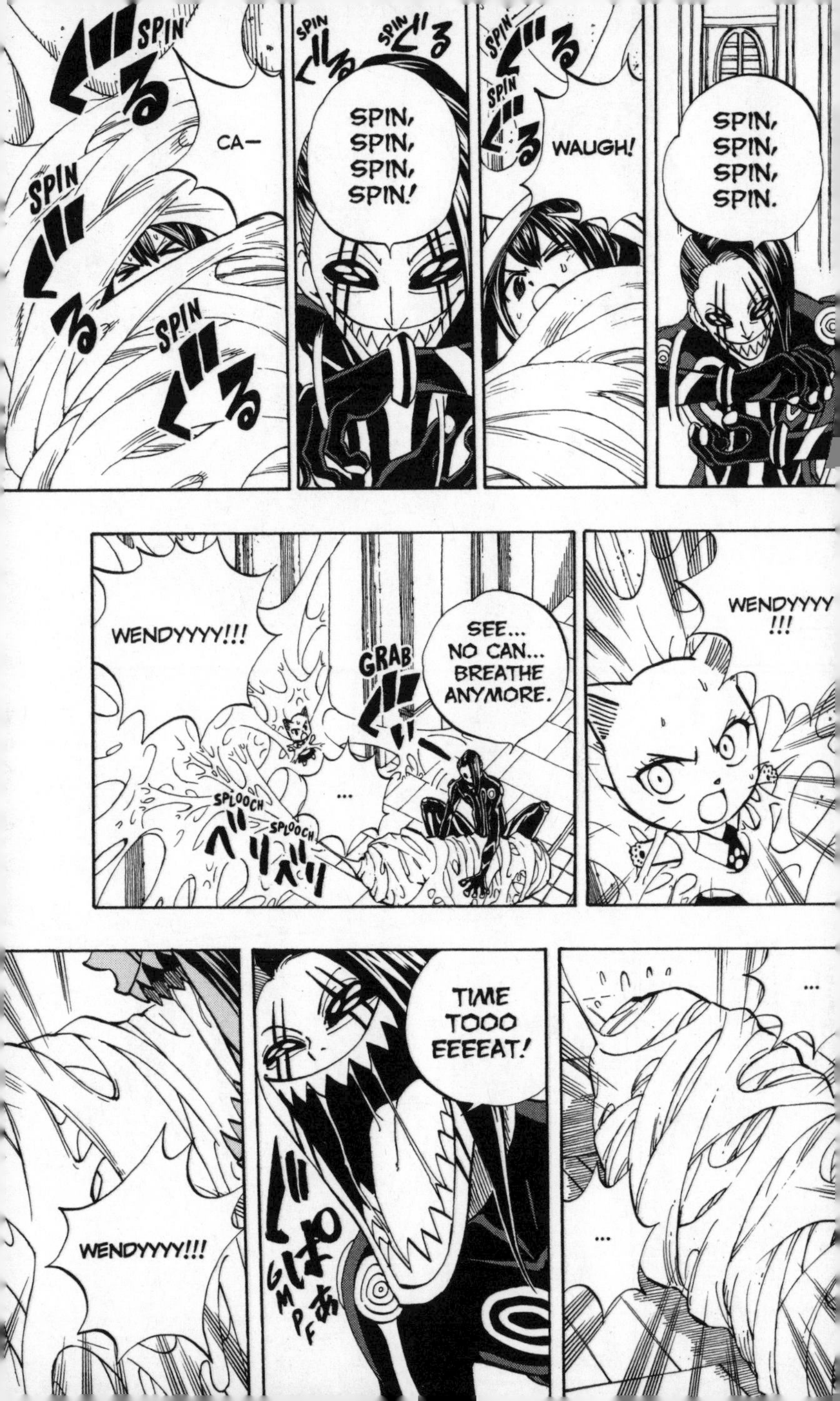

SPIN, SPIN, SPIN, SPIN.
SPIN
SPIN
WAUGH!
SPIN
SPIN
SPIN, SPIN, SPIN, SPIN!
SPIN
CA—
SPIN
SPIN
WENDYYYY !!!
SEE... NO CAN... BREATHE ANYMORE.
GRAB
WENDYYYY!!!
...
SPLOOCH
SPLOOCH
...
...
TIME TOOO EEEEAT!
GMPF
WENDYYYY!!!

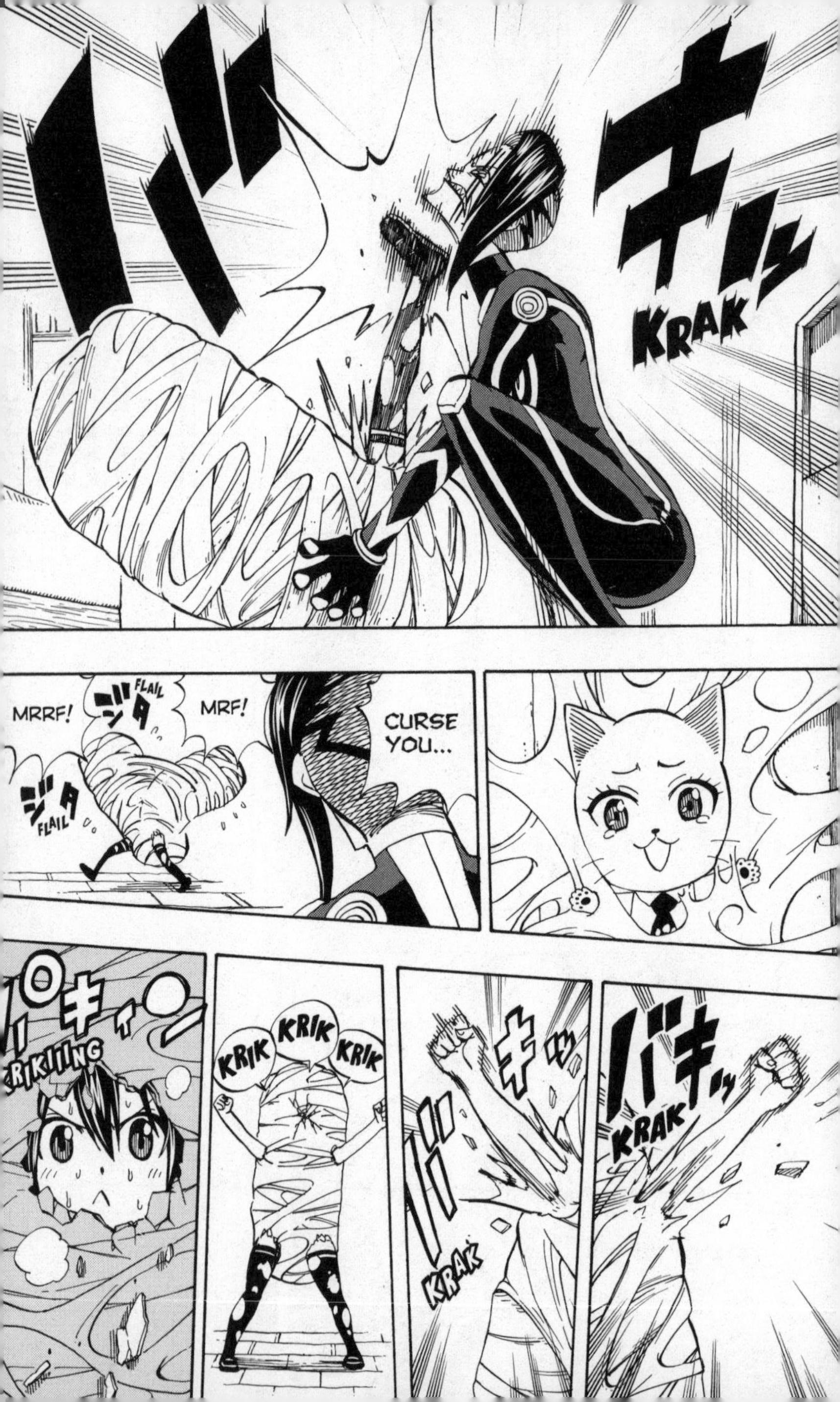

KRAK
CURSE YOU...
MRF!
FLAIL
MRRF!
FLAIL
KRAK
KRAK
KRIK
KRIK
KRIK
KRIKIIING

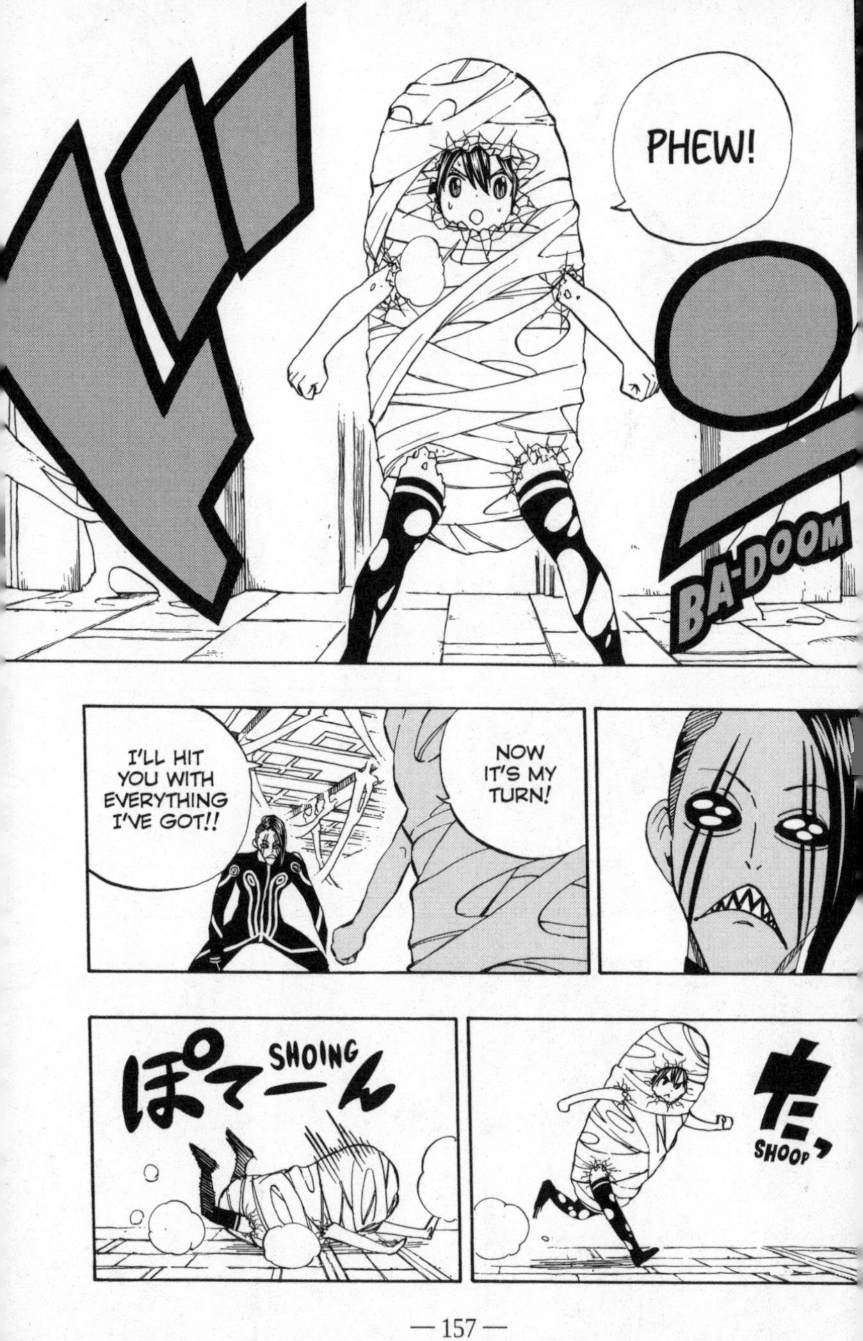
PHEW!
BA-DOOM
NOW IT'S MY TURN!
I'LL HIT YOU WITH EVERYTHING I'VE GOT!!
たっ
SHOOP
ぽてーん
SHOING

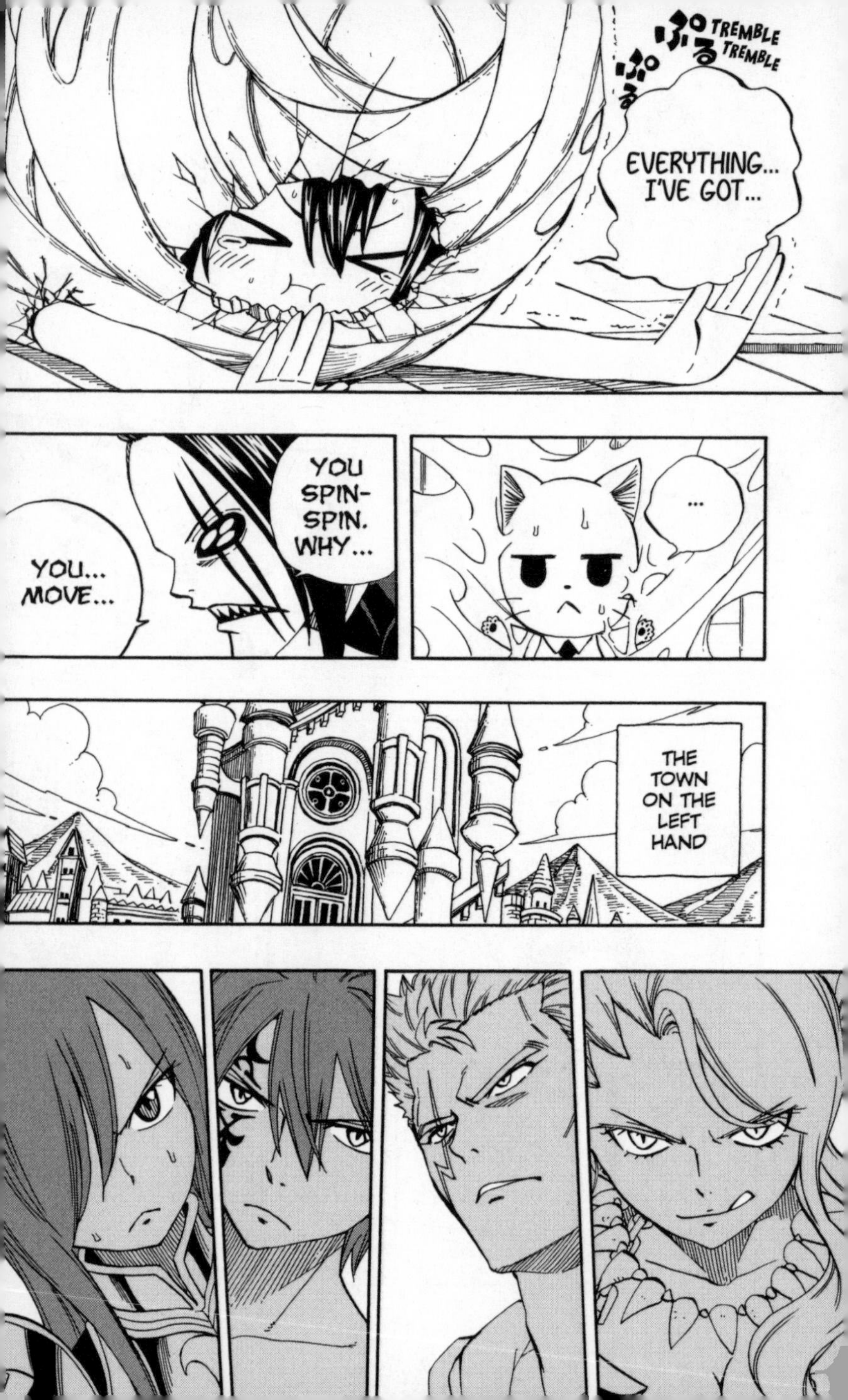
ぷる TREMBLE
ぷる TREMBLE
EVERYTHING... I'VE GOT...
...
YOU SPIN-SPIN. WHY...
YOU... MOVE...
THE TOWN ON THE LEFT HAND

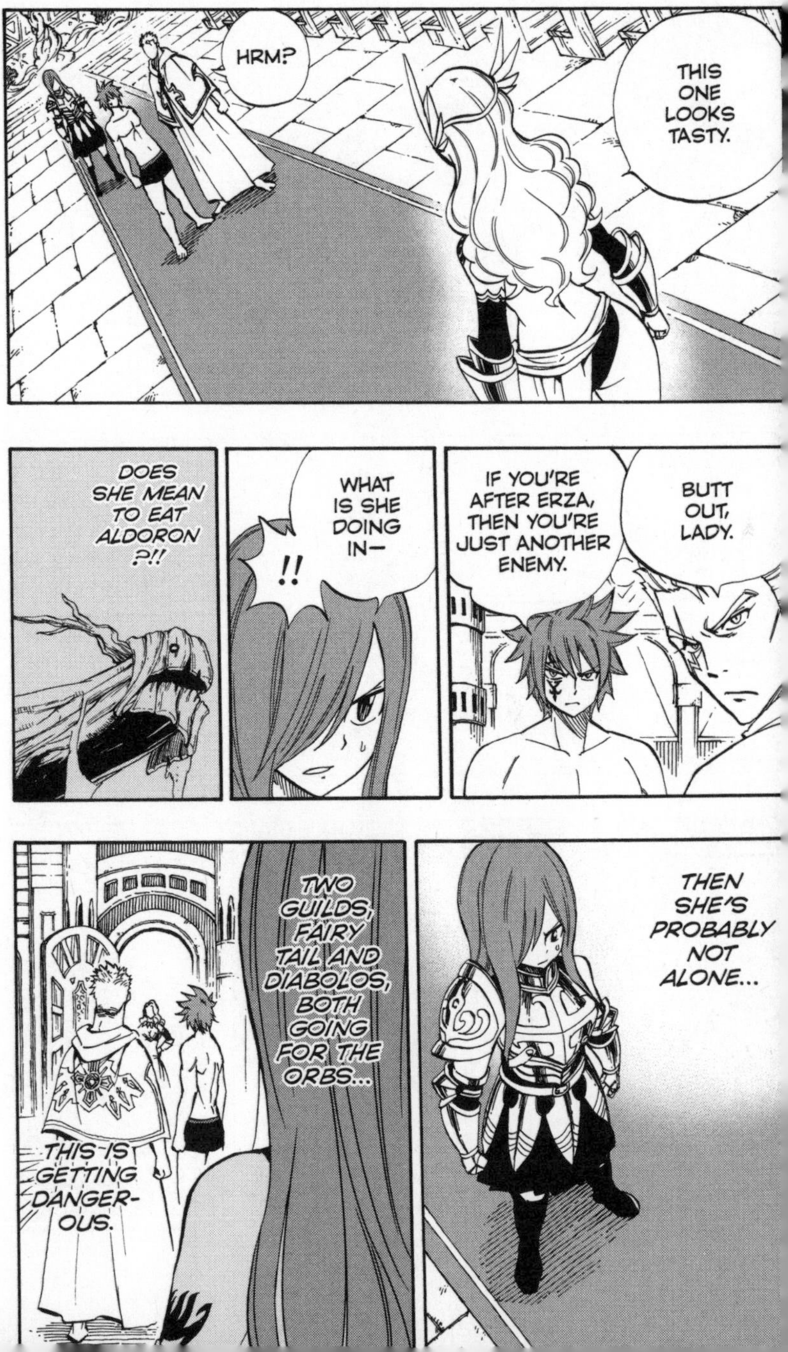
THIS ONE LOOKS TASTY.
HRM?
BUTT OUT, LADY.
IF YOU'RE AFTER ERZA, THEN YOU'RE JUST ANOTHER ENEMY.
WHAT IS SHE DOING IN—
!!
DOES SHE MEAN TO EAT ALDORON ?!!
THEN SHE'S PROBABLY NOT ALONE...
TWO GUILDS, FAIRY TAIL AND DIABOLOS, BOTH GOING FOR THE ORBS...
THIS IS GETTING DANGER-OUS.

ORBS?!

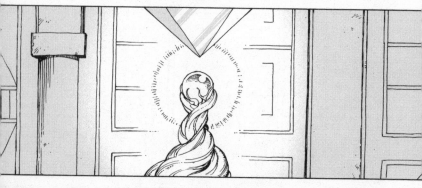

PRACTICALLY SMALL ENOUGH TO CARRY...

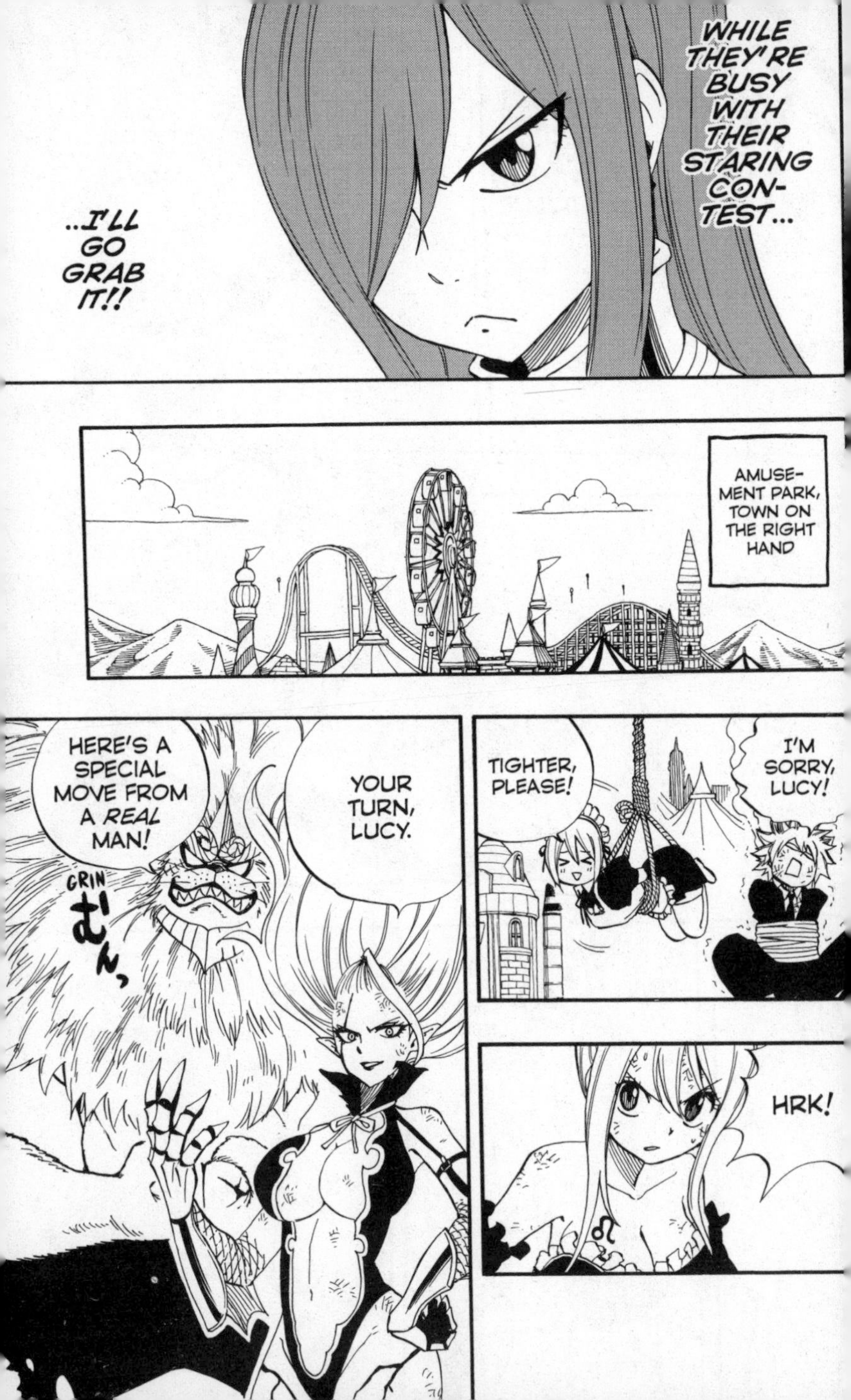
WHILE THEY'RE BUSY WITH THEIR STARING CON-TEST...
...I'LL GO GRAB IT!!
AMUSE-MENT PARK, TOWN ON THE RIGHT HAND
I'M SORRY, LUCY!
TIGHTER, PLEASE!
HRK!
YOUR TURN, LUCY.
HERE'S A SPECIAL MOVE FROM A *REAL* MAN!
GRIN
むん

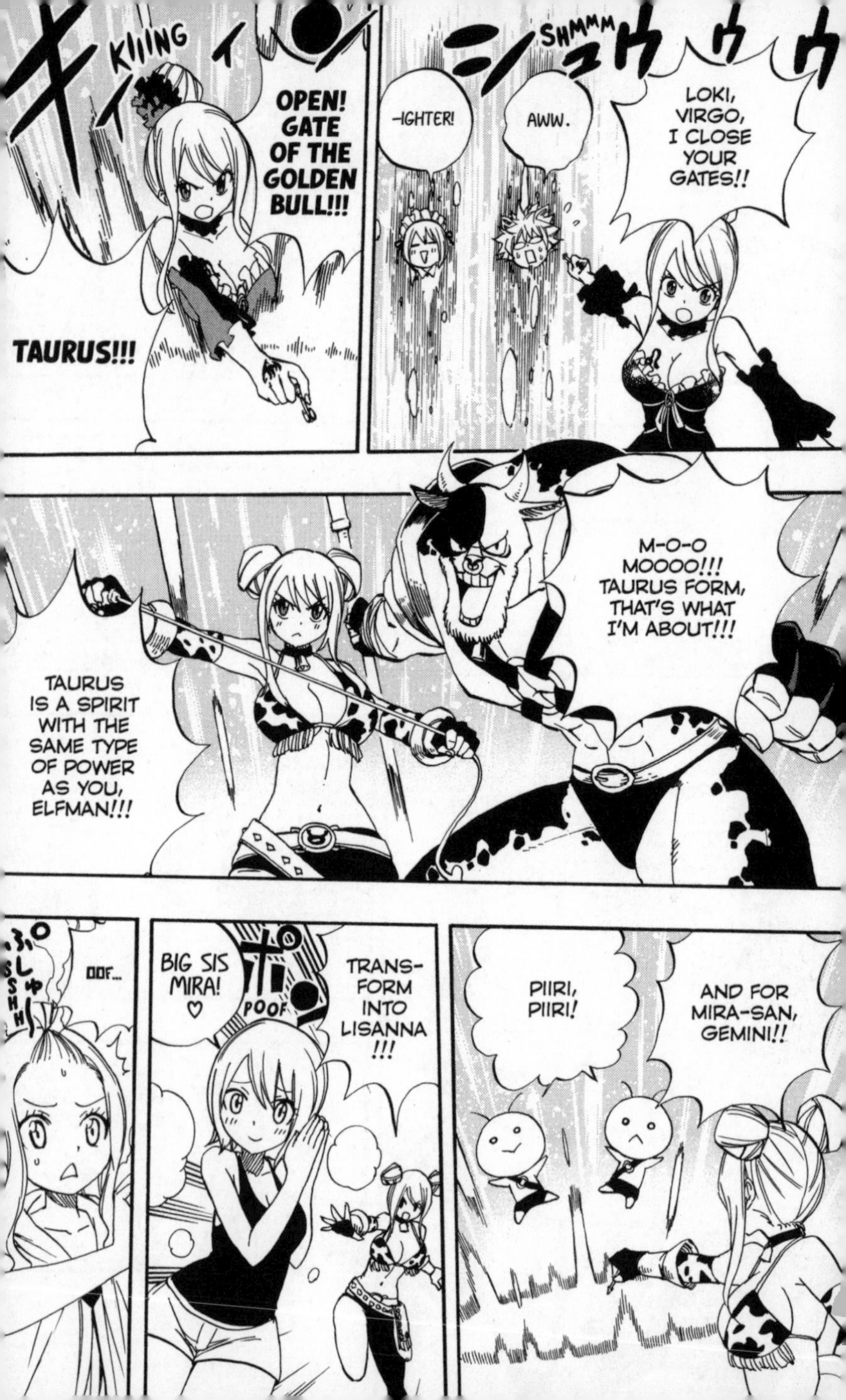
SHMMM
LOKI, VIRGO, I CLOSE YOUR GATES!!
AWW.
-IGHTER!
KIIING
OPEN! GATE OF THE GOLDEN BULL!!!
TAURUS!!!
M-O-O MOOOO!!! TAURUS FORM, THAT'S WHAT I'M ABOUT!!!
TAURUS IS A SPIRIT WITH THE SAME TYPE OF POWER AS YOU, ELFMAN!!!
AND FOR MIRA-SAN, GEMINI!!
PIIRI, PIIRI!
TRANS-FORM INTO LISANNA!!!
POOF
BIG SIS MIRA! ♡
SHHH
OOF...

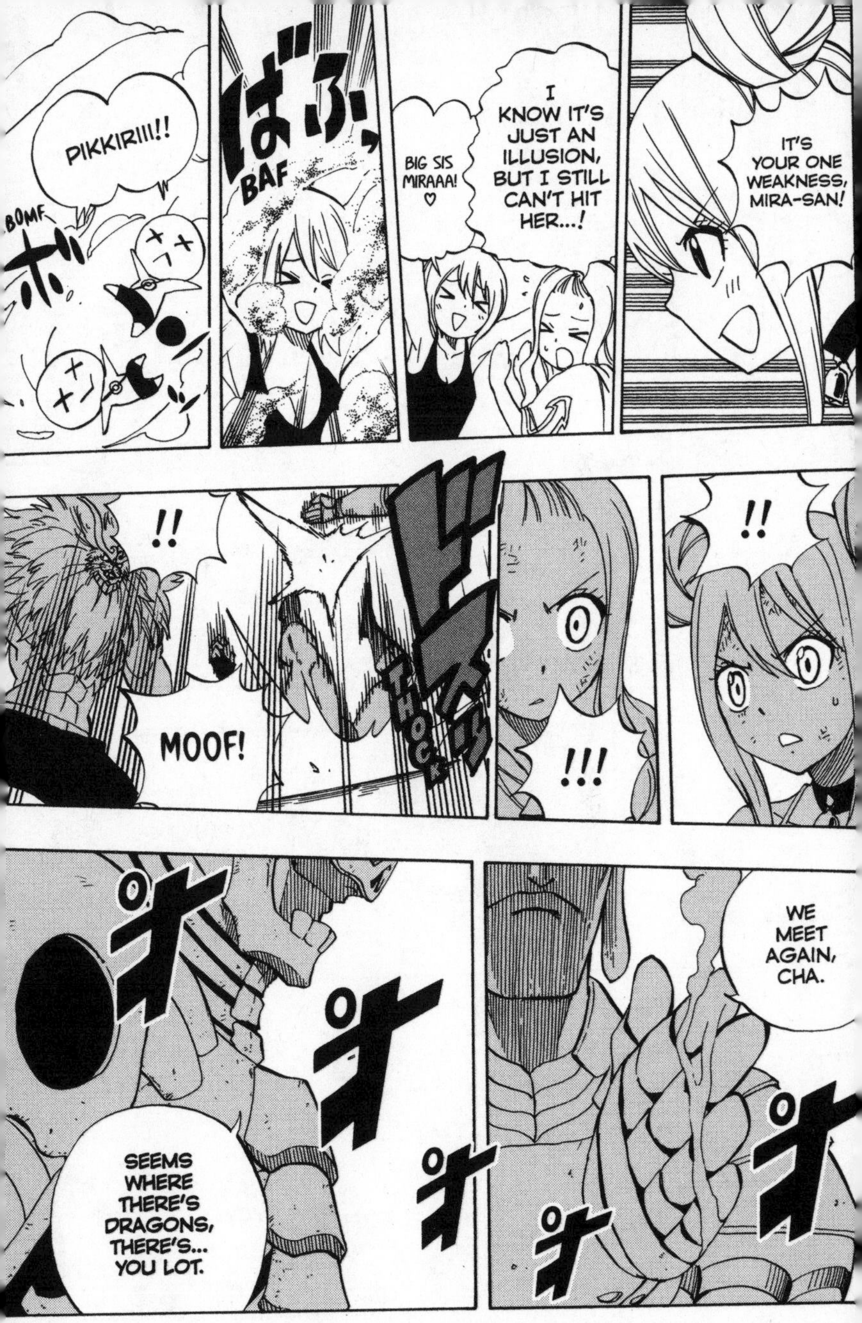
IT'S YOUR ONE WEAKNESS, MIRA-SAN!
I KNOW IT'S JUST AN ILLUSION, BUT I STILL CAN'T HIT HER...!
BIG SIS MIRAAA! ♡
ばふ
BAF
PIKKIRIII!!
BOMF
!!
!!!
THOCK
!!
MOOF!
WE MEET AGAIN, CHA.
SEEMS WHERE THERE'S DRAGONS, THERE'S... YOU LOT.

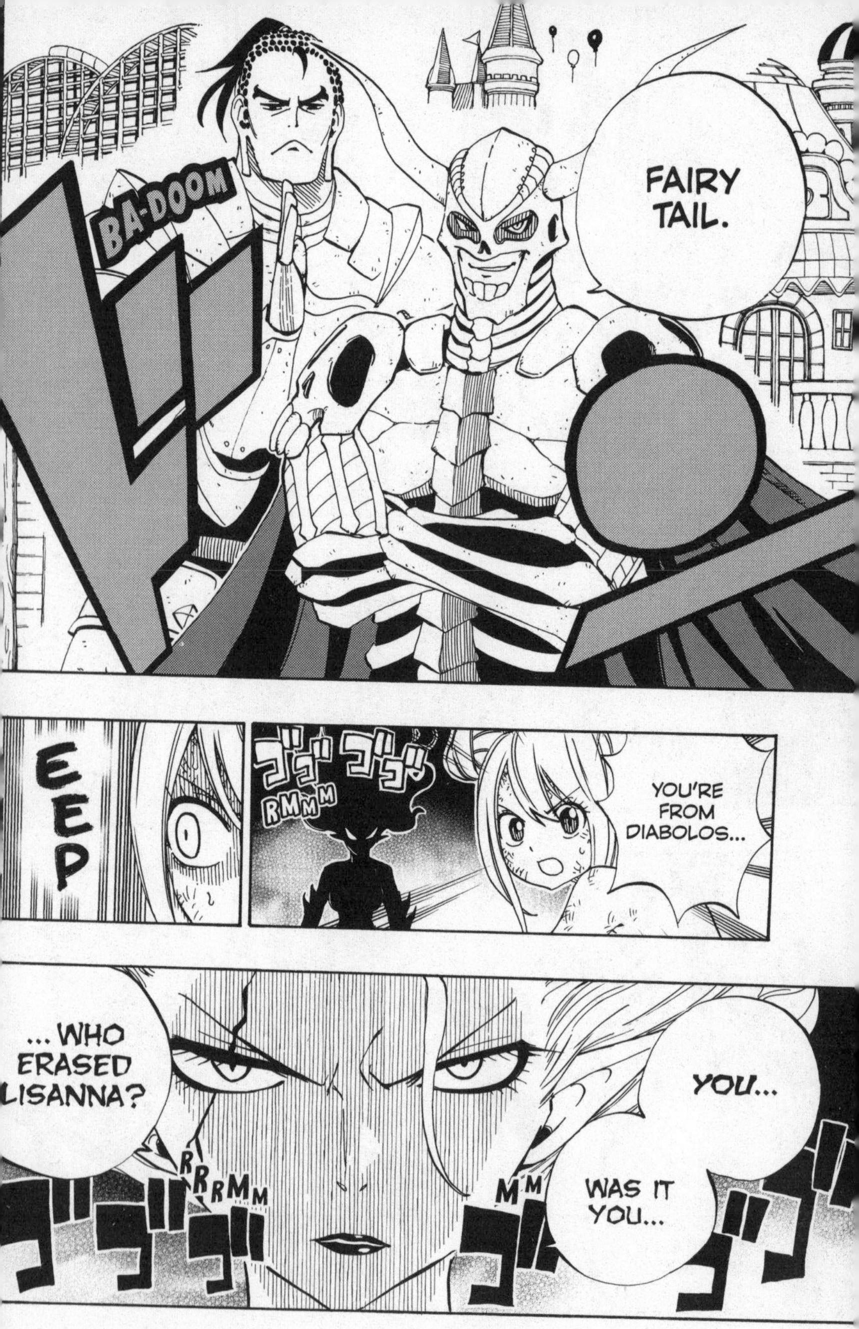
FAIRY TAIL.
BA-DOOM
YOU'RE FROM DIABOLOS...
RMMM
EEP
YOU...
WAS IT YOU...
MM
... WHO ERASED LISANNA?
RRRMM

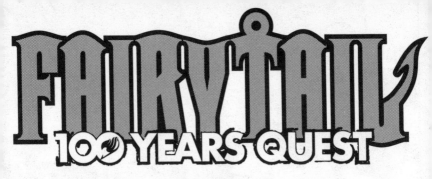

FAIRY TAIL
100 YEARS QUEST

Chapter 36: Rumble in Drasil

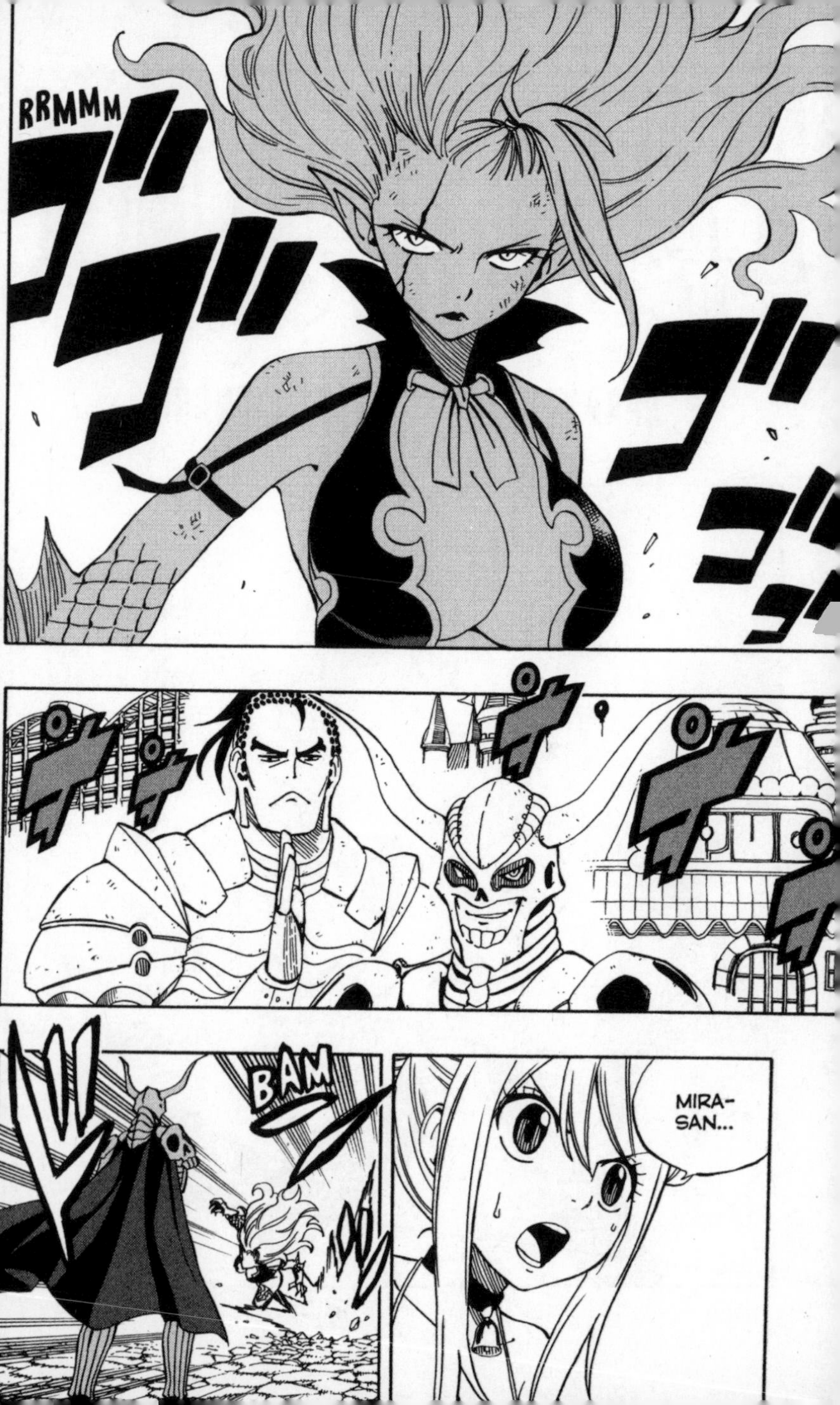
RRMMM
MIRA-SAN...
BAM

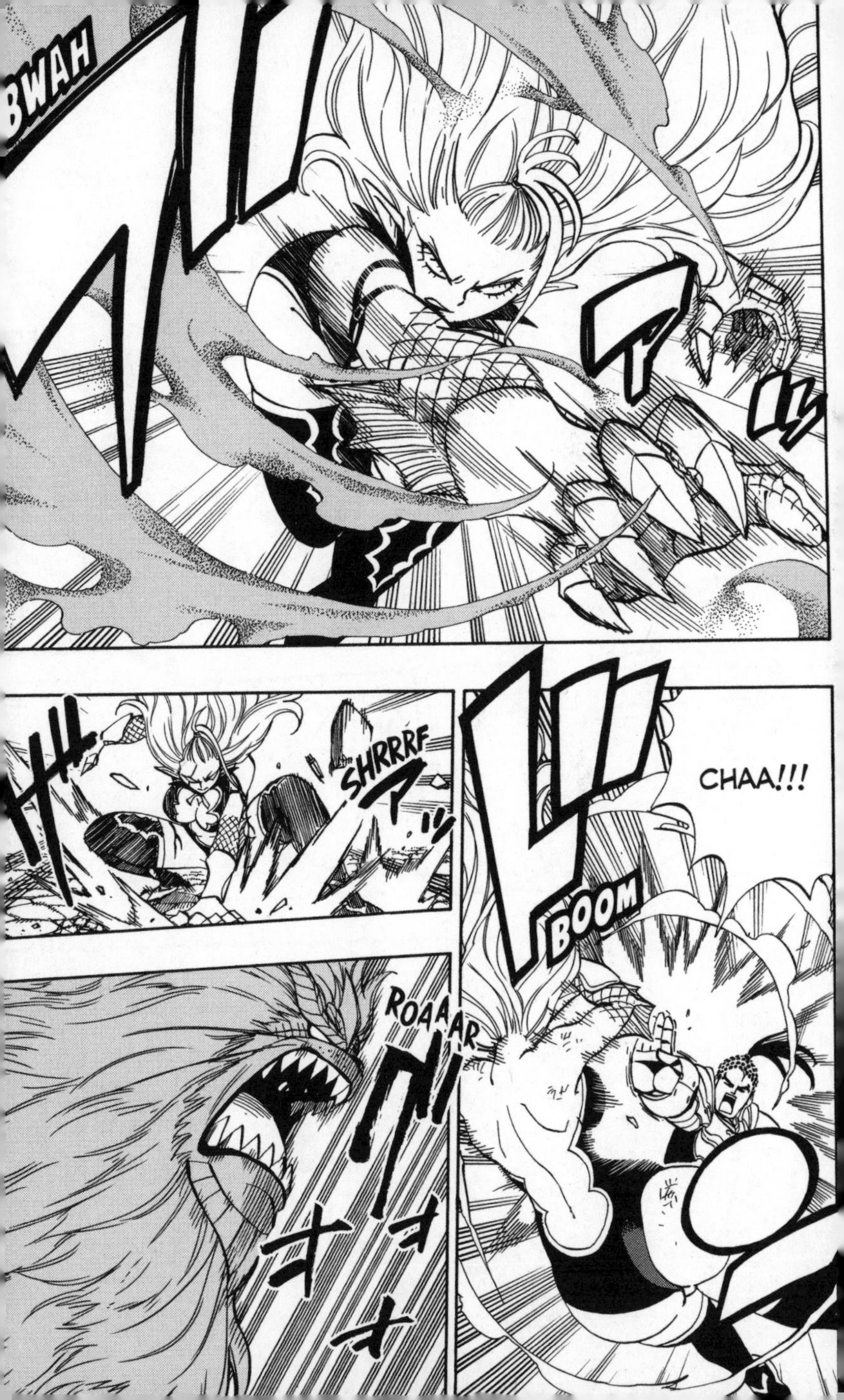
BWAH
CHAA!!!
BOOM
SHRRRF
ROAAAR

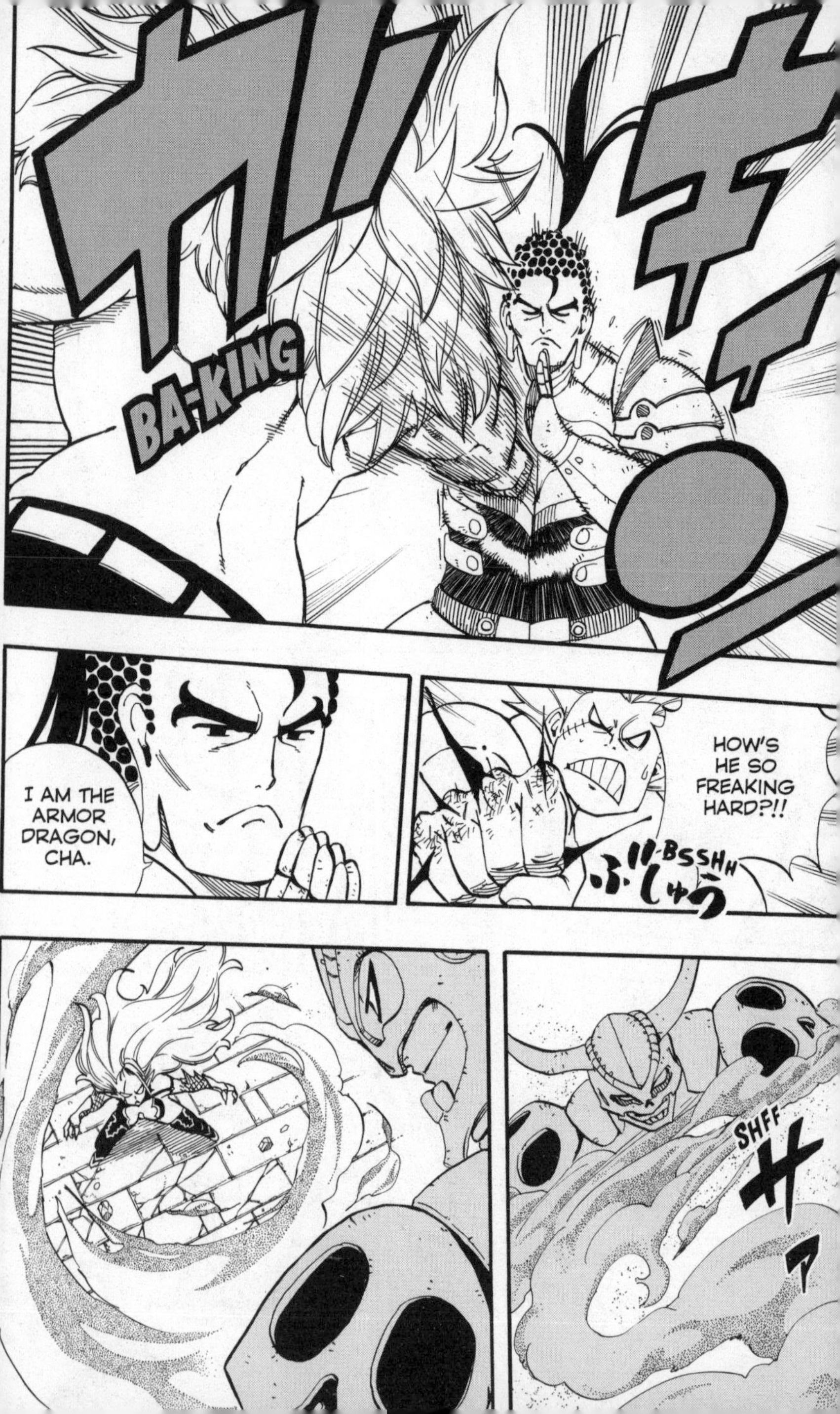
BA-KING
HOW'S HE SO FREAKING HARD?!!
B-BSSHH
I AM THE ARMOR DRAGON, CHA.
SHFF

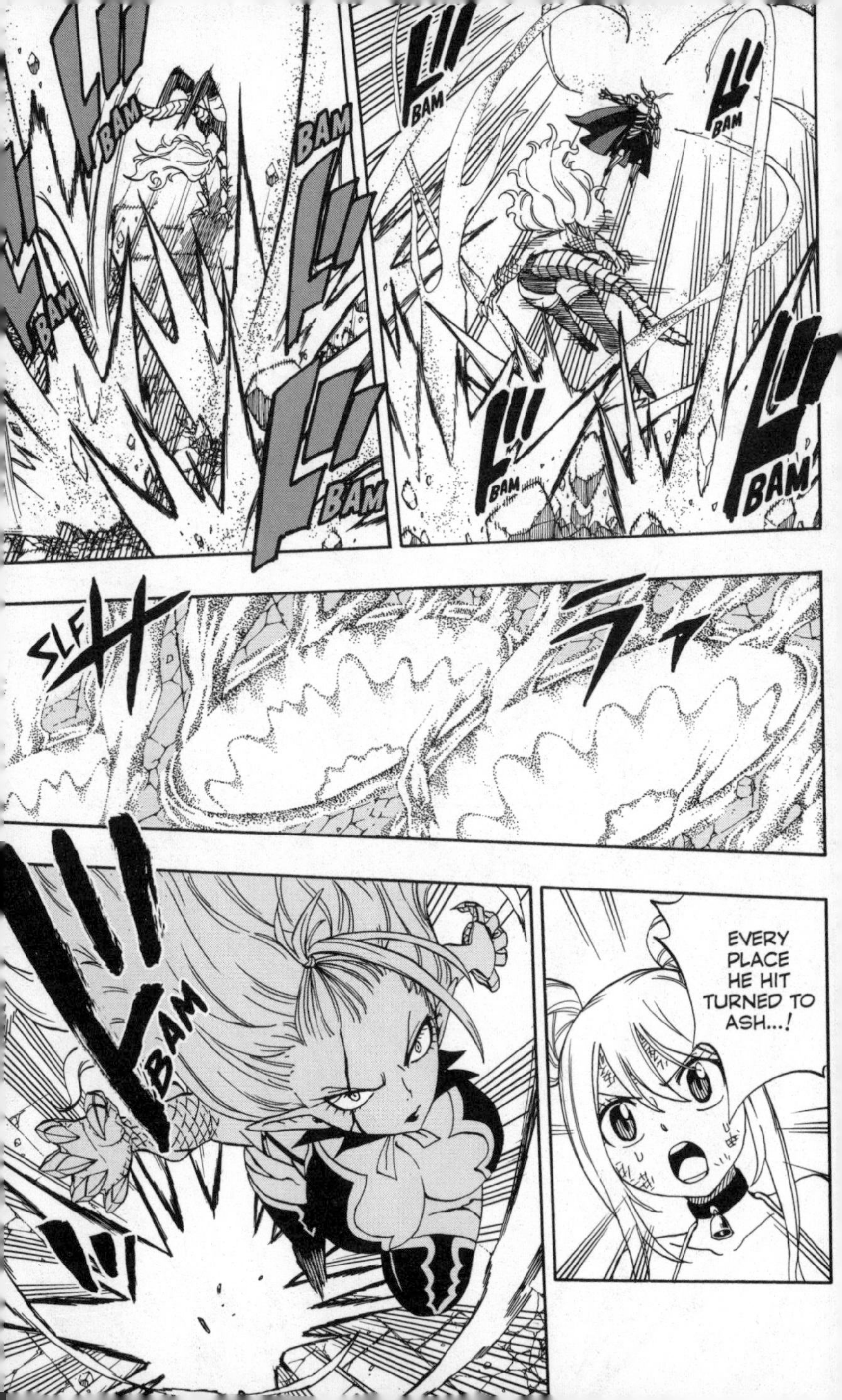
BAM
BAM
BAM
BAM
BAM
BAM
BAM
BAM
EVERY PLACE HE HIT TURNED TO ASH...!
BAM

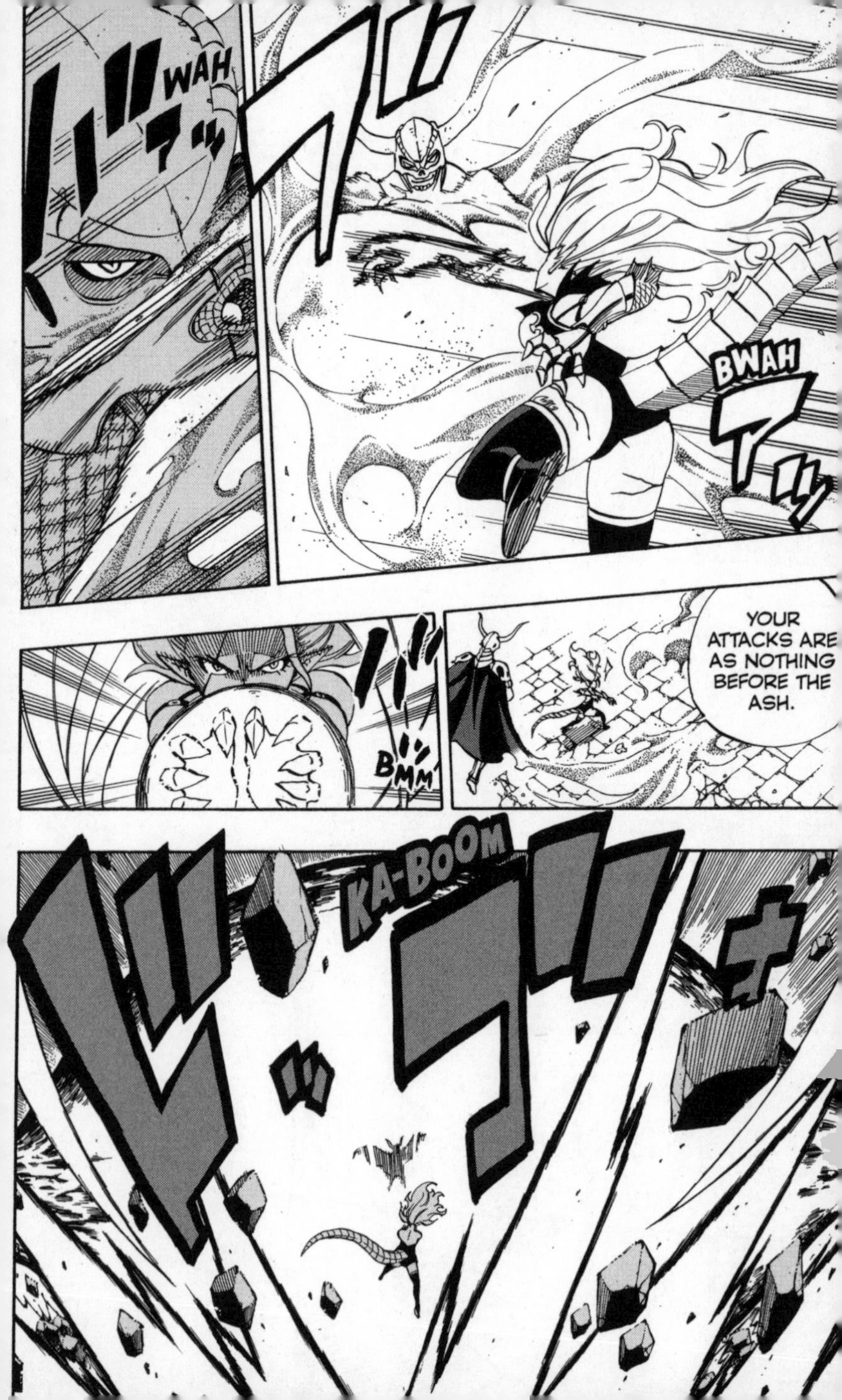
BWAH
WAH
YOUR ATTACKS ARE AS NOTHING BEFORE THE ASH.
BMM
KA-BOOM

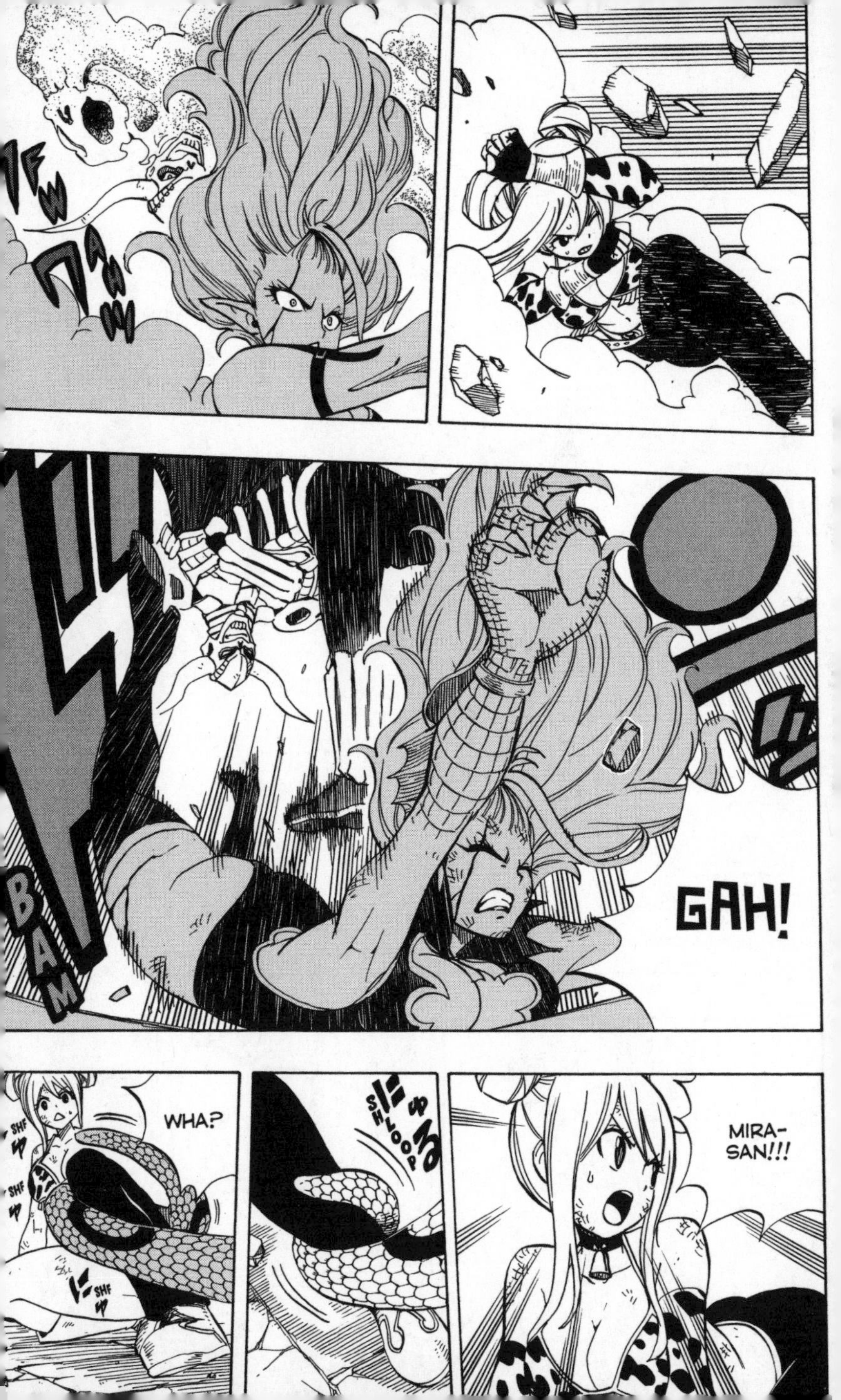
FWAHH
GAH!
BAM
MIRA-SAN!!!
SHLOOP
WHA?
SHF
SHF
SHF

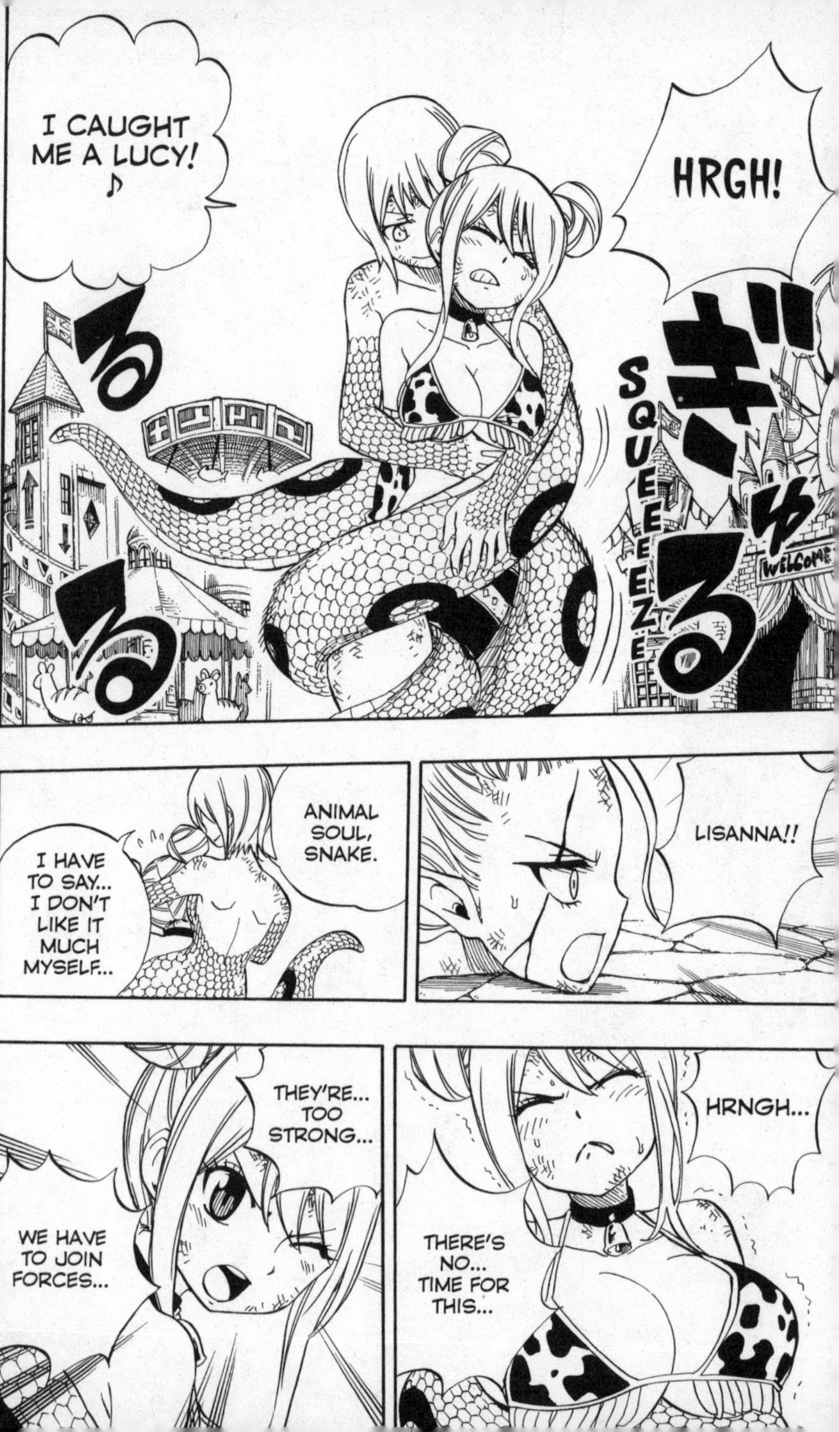
HRGH!
ぎゅるる
SQUEEEEZE
WELCOME
I CAUGHT ME A LUCY! ♪
るる
LISANNA!!
ANIMAL SOUL, SNAKE.
I HAVE TO SAY... I DON'T LIKE IT MUCH MYSELF...
HRNGH...
THERE'S NO... TIME FOR THIS...
THEY'RE... TOO STRONG...
WE HAVE TO JOIN FORCES...

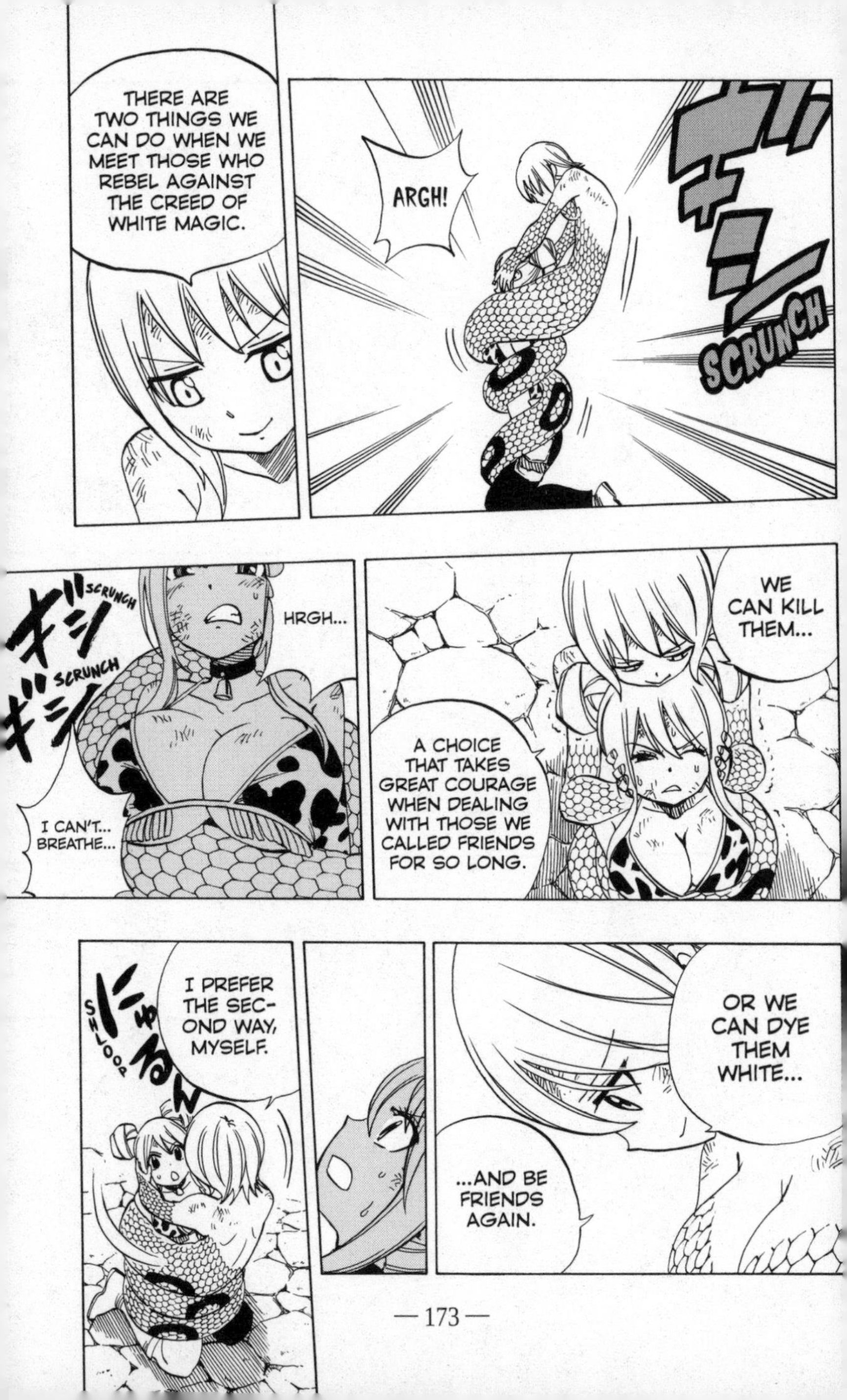
ARGH!
SCRUNCH
THERE ARE TWO THINGS WE CAN DO WHEN WE MEET THOSE WHO REBEL AGAINST THE CREED OF WHITE MAGIC.
WE CAN KILL THEM...
A CHOICE THAT TAKES GREAT COURAGE WHEN DEALING WITH THOSE WE CALLED FRIENDS FOR SO LONG.
HRGH...
SCRUNCH
SCRUNCH
I CAN'T... BREATHE...
OR WE CAN DYE THEM WHITE...
...AND BE FRIENDS AGAIN.
I PREFER THE SEC-OND WAY, MYSELF.
SHLOOP

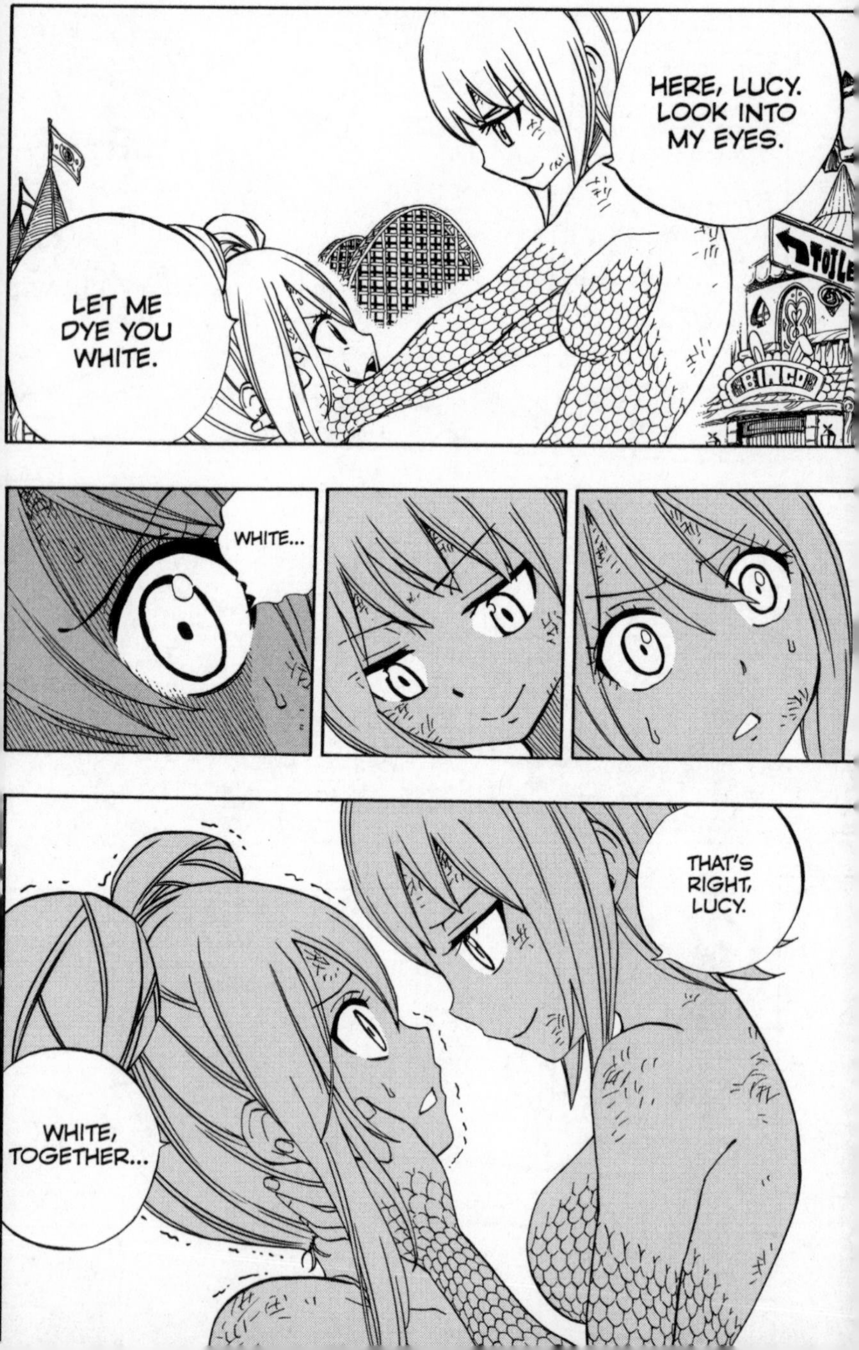
HERE, LUCY. LOOK INTO MY EYES.
LET ME DYE YOU WHITE.
WHITE...
THAT'S RIGHT, LUCY.
WHITE, TOGETHER...

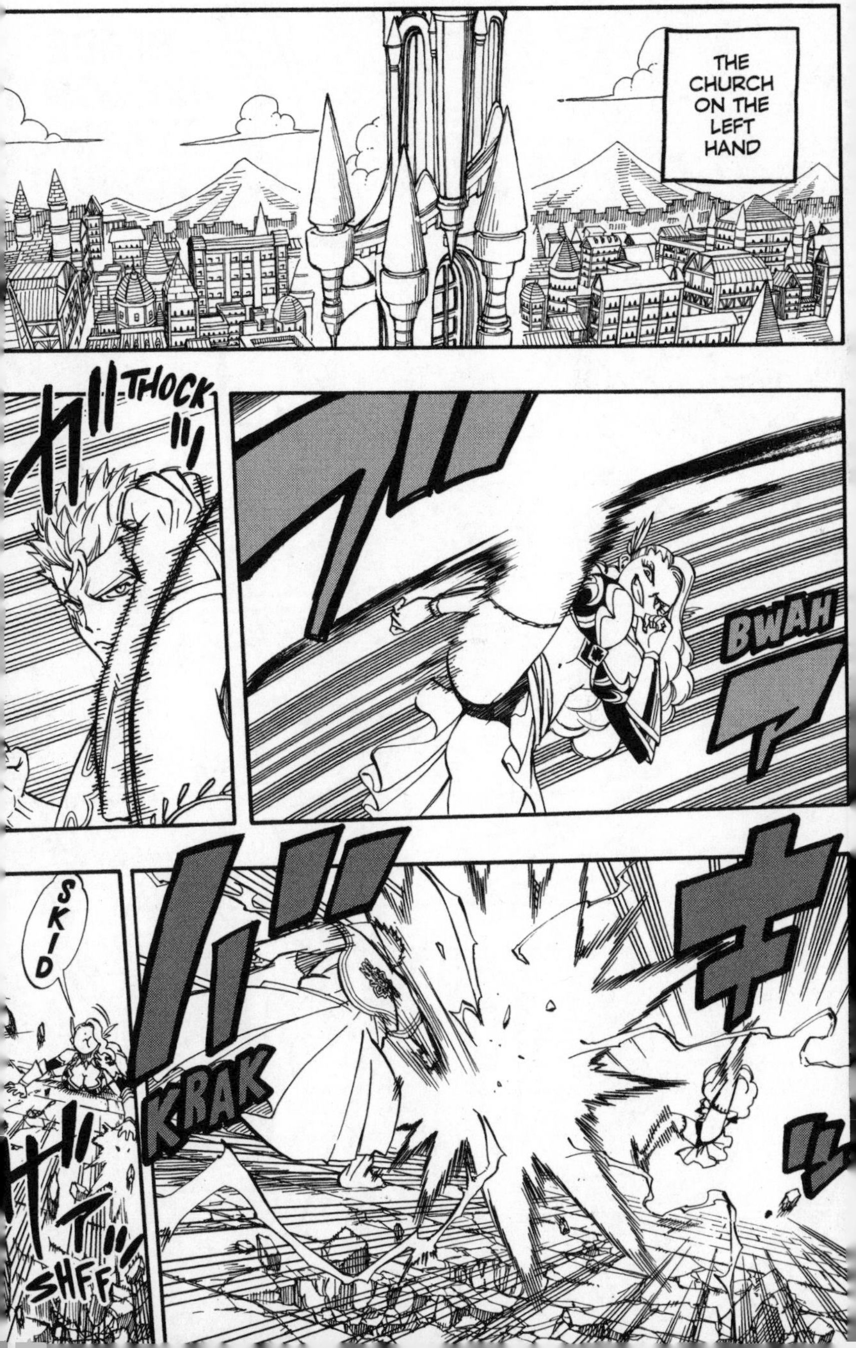
THE CHURCH ON THE LEFT HAND
BWAH
THOCK
KRAK
SKID
SHFF

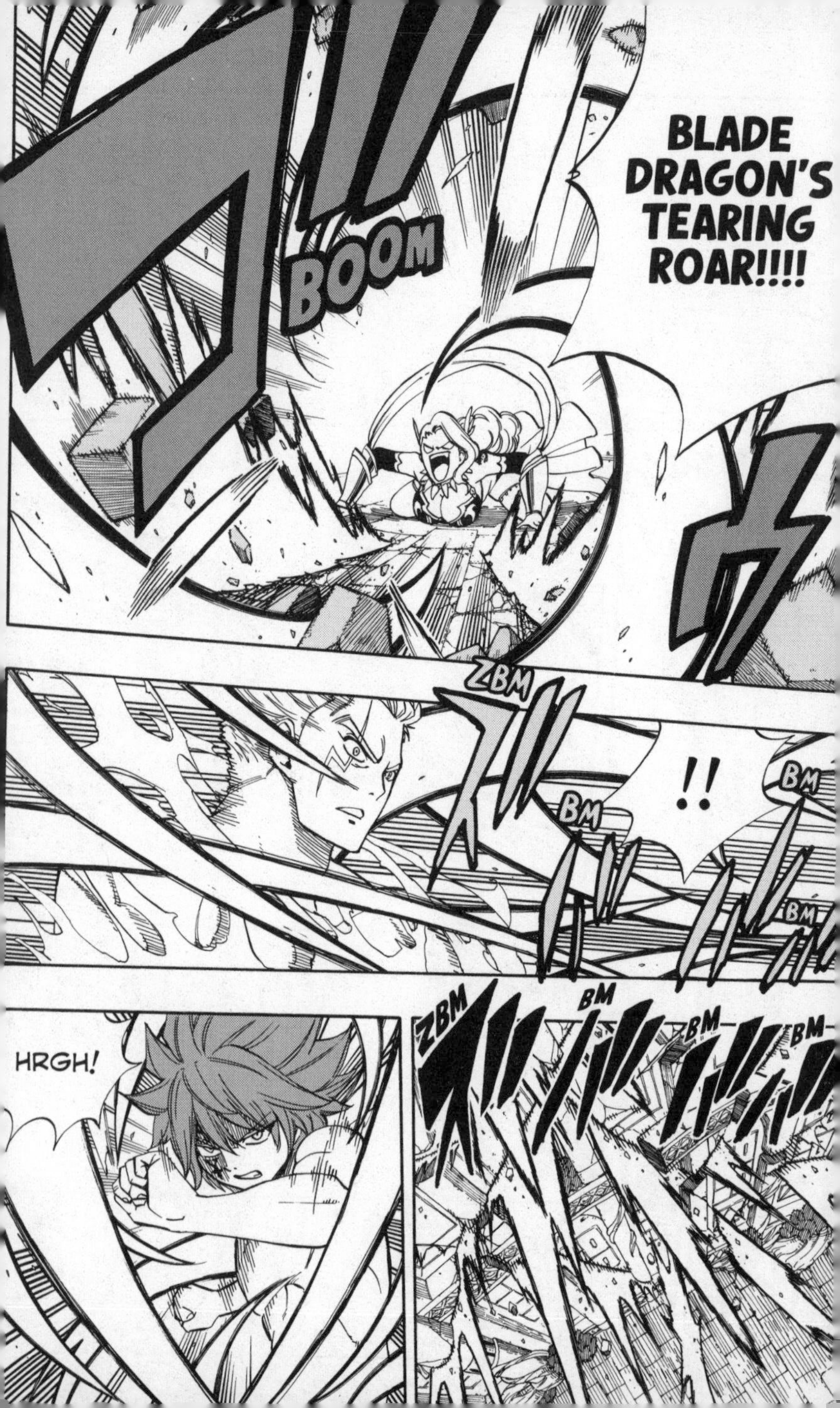
BLADE DRAGON'S TEARING ROAR!!!!
BOOM
ZBM
BM
!!
BM
BM
HRGH!
ZBM
BM
BM
BM

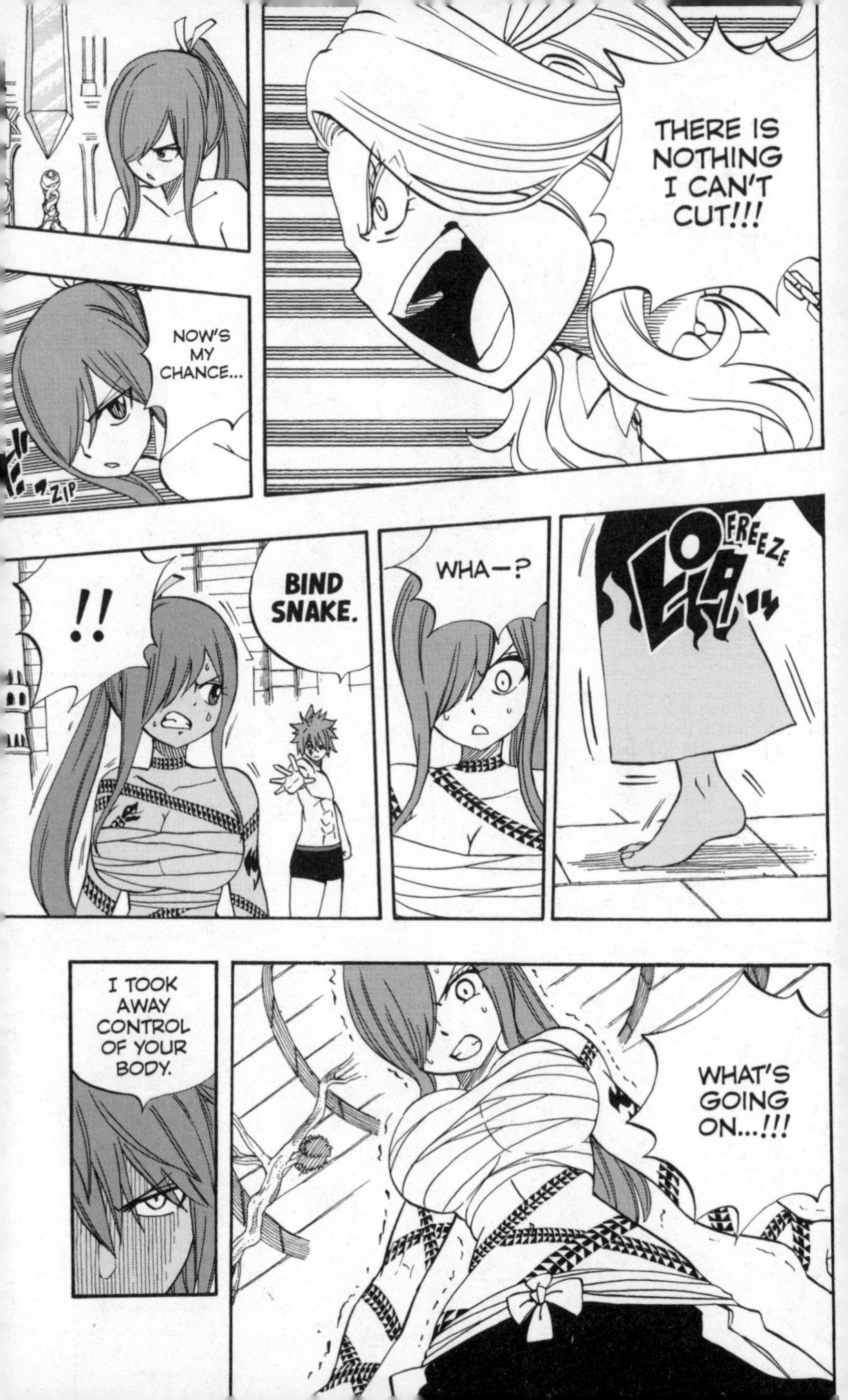
THERE IS NOTHING I CAN'T CUT!!!
NOW'S MY CHANCE...
ZIP
FREEZE
WHA—?
BIND SNAKE.
!!
WHAT'S GOING ON...!!!
I TOOK AWAY CONTROL OF YOUR BODY.

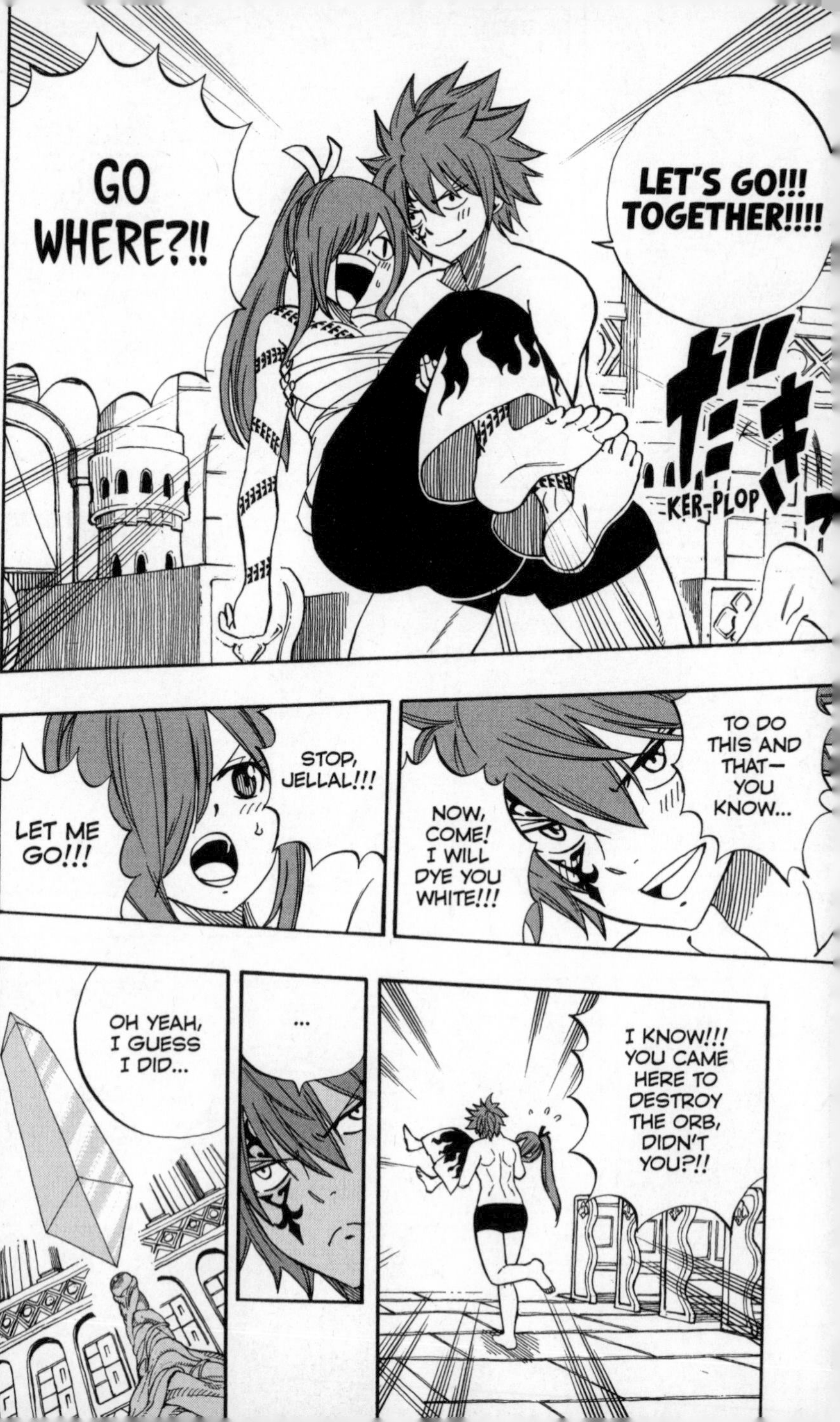
LET'S GO!!! TOGETHER!!!!
KER-PLOP
GO WHERE?!!
TO DO THIS AND THAT— YOU KNOW...
NOW, COME! I WILL DYE YOU WHITE!!!
STOP, JELLAL!!!
LET ME GO!!!
I KNOW!!! YOU CAME HERE TO DESTROY THE ORB, DIDN'T YOU?!!
...
OH YEAH, I GUESS I DID...

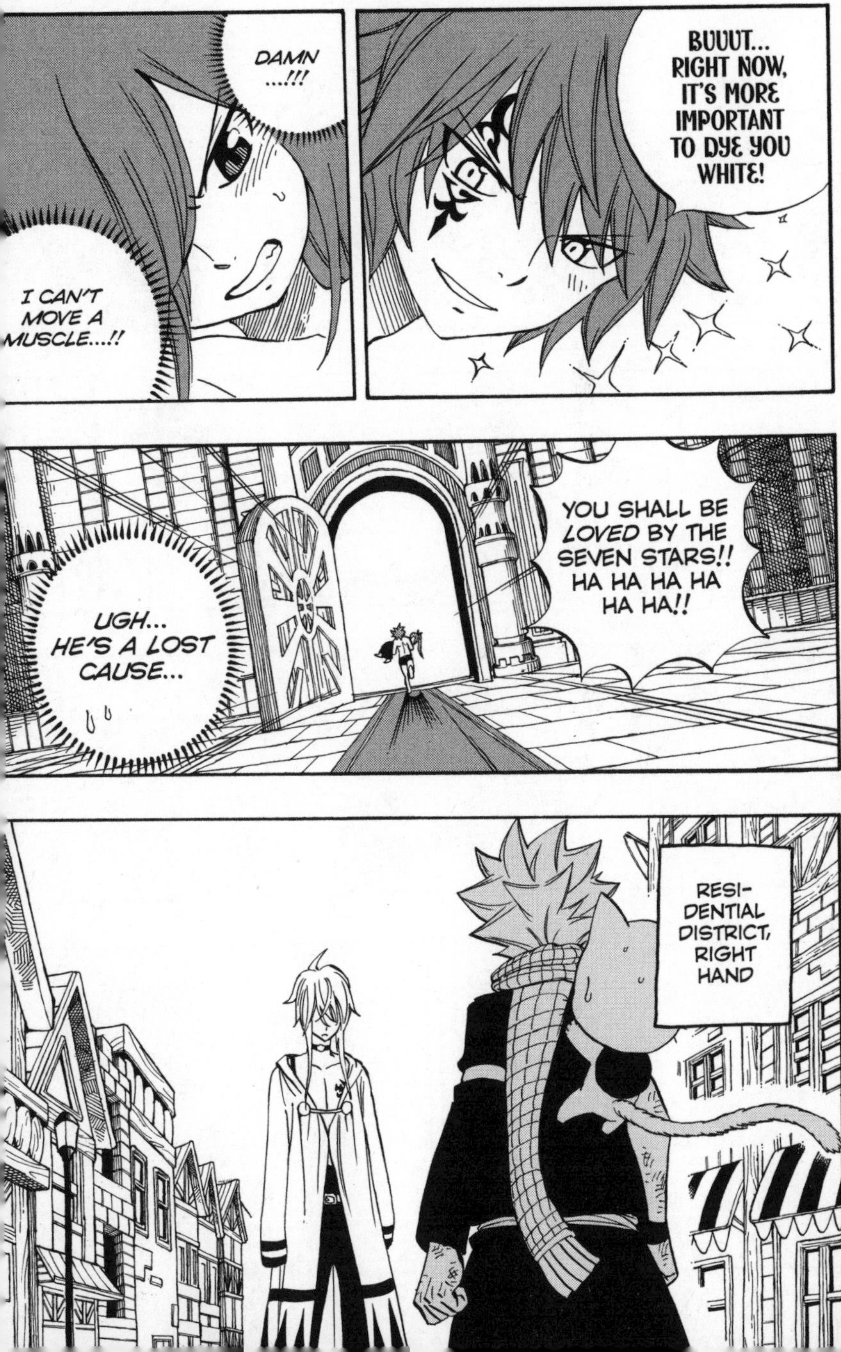
BUUUT... RIGHT NOW, IT'S MORE IMPORTANT TO DYE YOU WHITE!
DAMN ...!!!
I CAN'T MOVE A MUSCLE...!!
YOU SHALL BE LOVED BY THE SEVEN STARS!! HA HA HA HA HA HA!!
UGH... HE'S A LOST CAUSE...
RESI-DENTIAL DISTRICT, RIGHT HAND

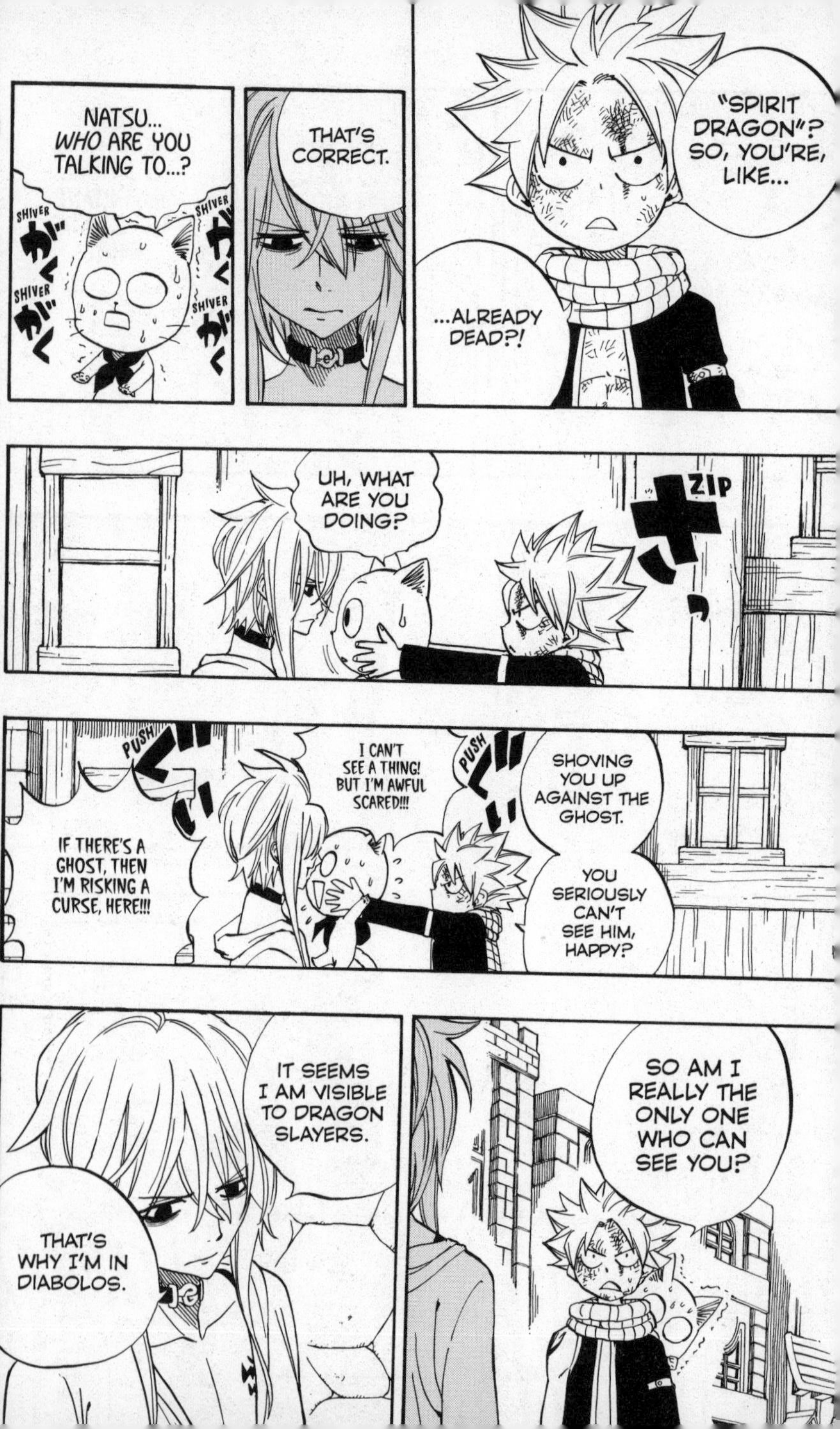
"SPIRIT DRAGON"? SO, YOU'RE, LIKE...
...ALREADY DEAD?!
THAT'S CORRECT.
NATSU... *WHO* ARE YOU TALKING TO...?
SHIVER
SHIVER
SHIVER
SHIVER
ZIP
UH, WHAT ARE YOU DOING?
PUSH
SHOVING YOU UP AGAINST THE GHOST.
YOU SERIOUSLY CAN'T SEE HIM, HAPPY?
I CAN'T SEE A THING! BUT I'M AWFUL SCARED!!!
PUSH
IF THERE'S A GHOST, THEN I'M RISKING A CURSE, HERE!!!
SO AM I REALLY THE ONLY ONE WHO CAN SEE YOU?
IT SEEMS I AM VISIBLE TO DRAGON SLAYERS.
THAT'S WHY I'M IN DIABOLOS.

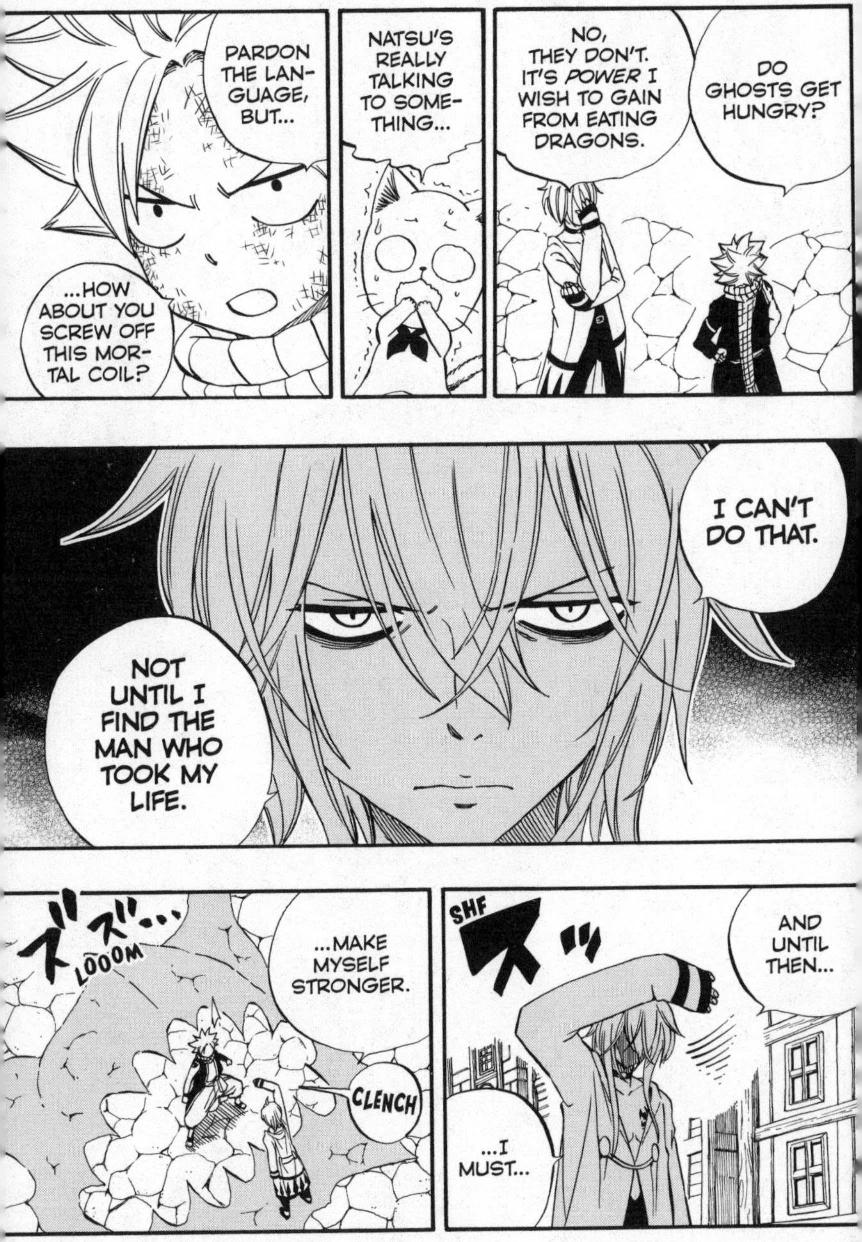
DO GHOSTS GET HUNGRY?
NO, THEY DON'T. IT'S *POWER* I WISH TO GAIN FROM EATING DRAGONS.
NATSU'S REALLY TALKING TO SOMETHING...
PARDON THE LANGUAGE, BUT...
...HOW ABOUT YOU SCREW OFF THIS MORTAL COIL?
I CAN'T DO THAT.
NOT UNTIL I FIND THE MAN WHO TOOK MY LIFE.
SHF
AND UNTIL THEN...
...I MUST...
...MAKE MYSELF STRONGER.
LOOOM
CLENCH

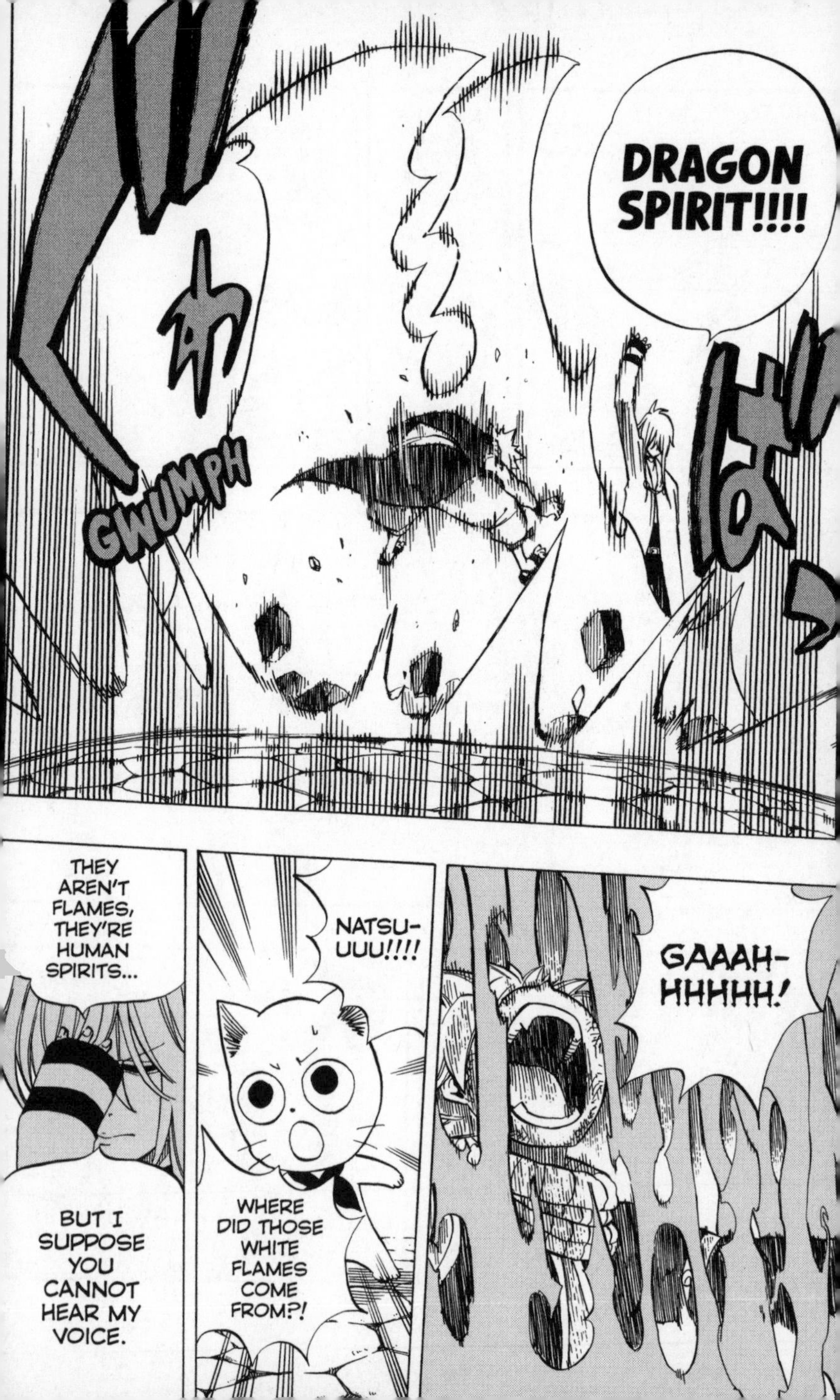
DRAGON SPIRIT!!!!
GWUMPH
GAAAH-HHHHH!
NATSU-UUU!!!!
WHERE DID THOSE WHITE FLAMES COME FROM?!
THEY AREN'T FLAMES, THEY'RE HUMAN SPIRITS...
BUT I SUPPOSE YOU CANNOT HEAR MY VOICE.

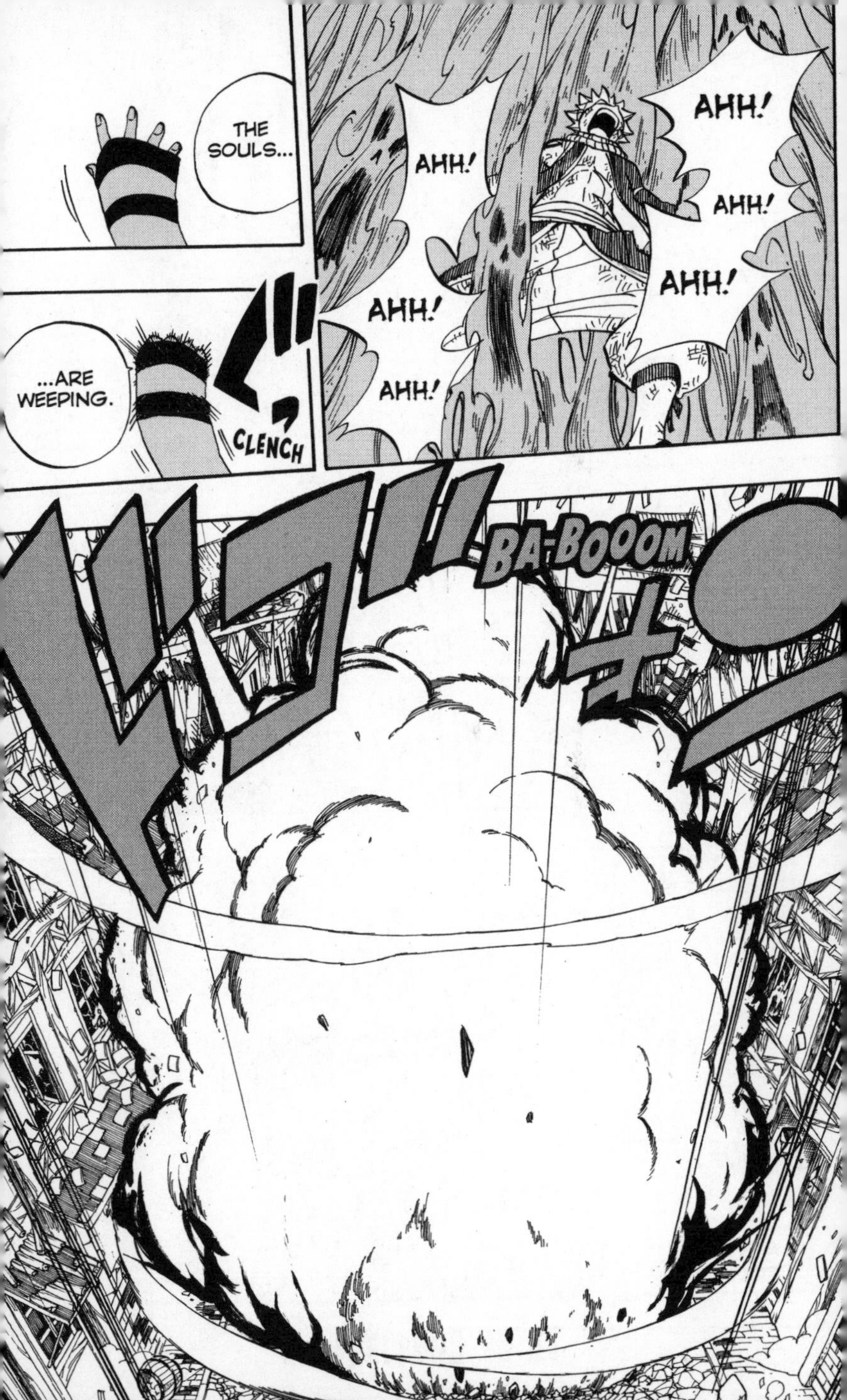
AHH!
AHH!
AHH!
AHH!
AHH!
AHH!
THE SOULS...
...ARE WEEPING.
CLENCH
BA-BOOOM

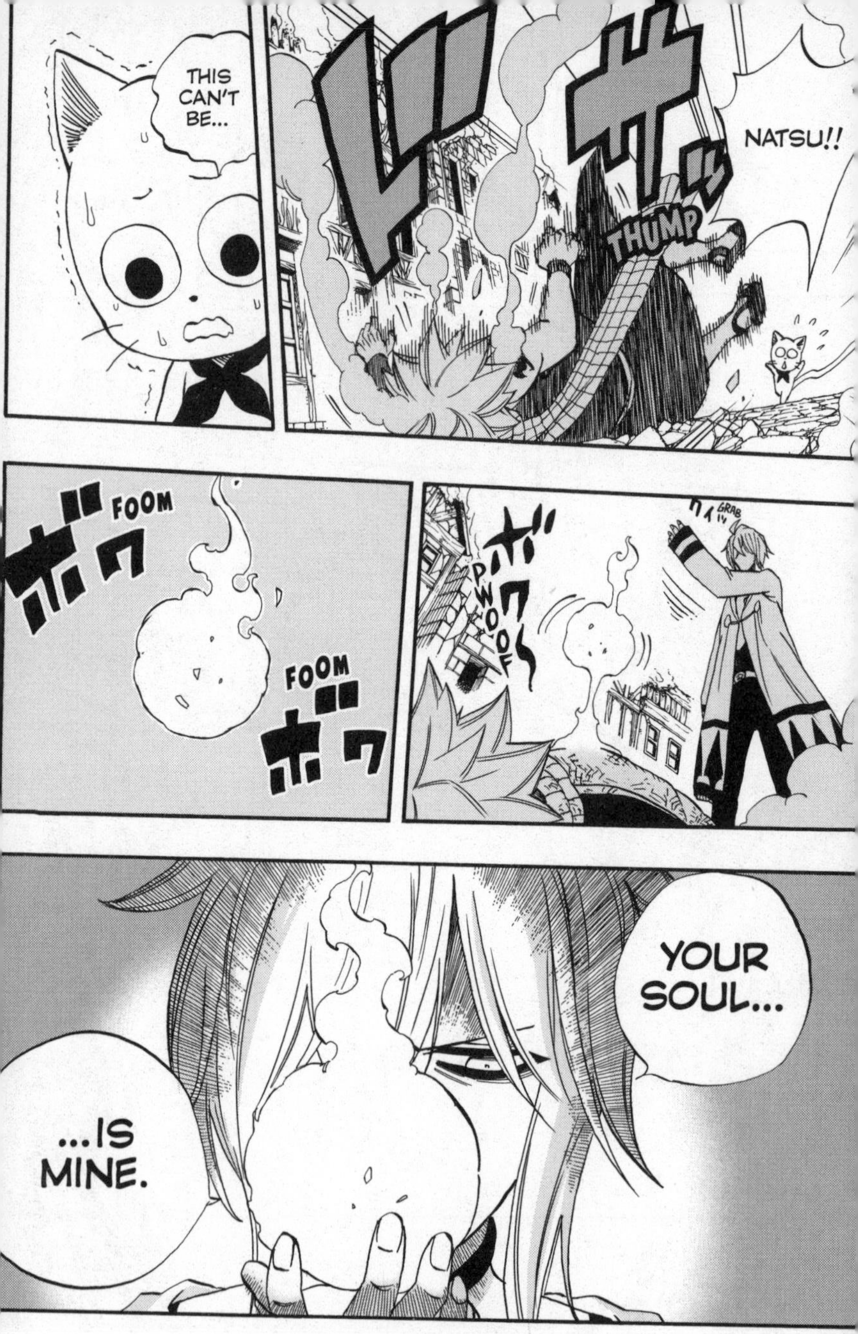
NATSU!!
THUMP
THIS CAN'T BE...
GRAB
PWOOF
FOOM
FOOM
YOUR SOUL...
...IS MINE.

TO BE CONTINUED

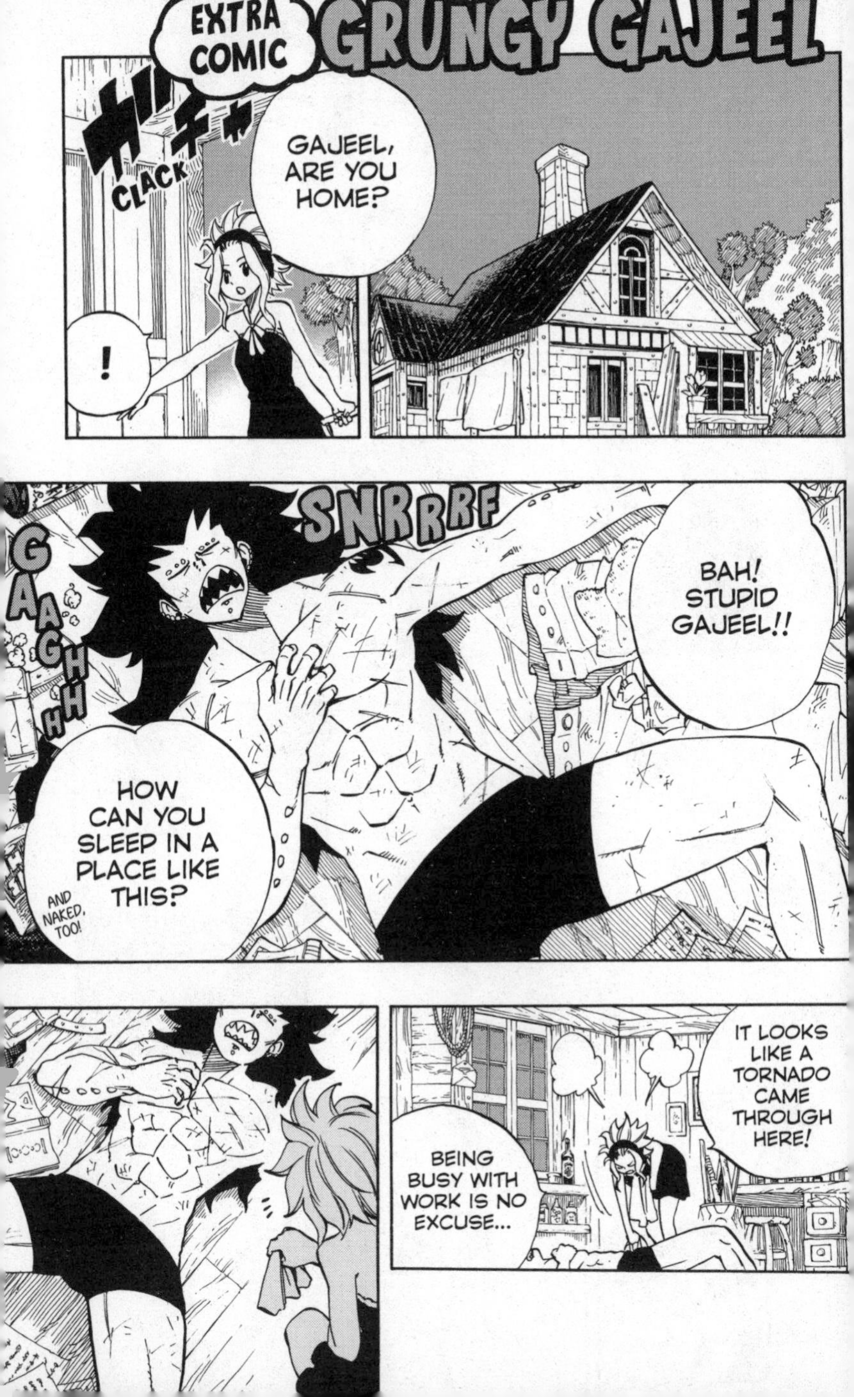

EXTRA COMIC
GRUNGY GAJEEL
ガチャ
CLACK
GAJEEL, ARE YOU HOME?
!
SNRRRF
BAH! STUPID GAJEEL!!
GAAGHHH
HOW CAN YOU SLEEP IN A PLACE LIKE THIS?
AND NAKED, TOO!
IT LOOKS LIKE A TORNADO CAME THROUGH HERE!
BEING BUSY WITH WORK IS NO EXCUSE...

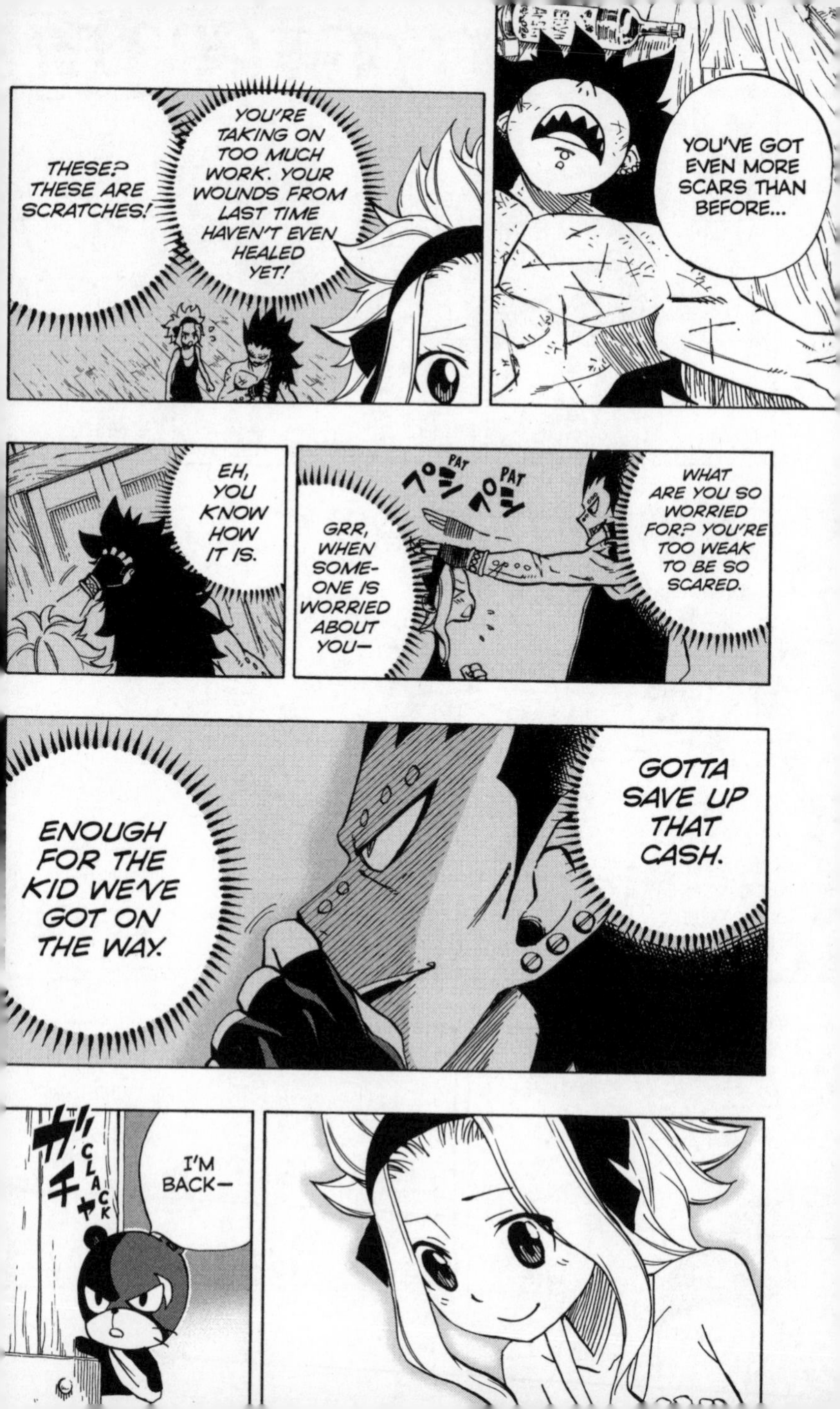
YOU'VE GOT EVEN MORE SCARS THAN BEFORE...
YOU'RE TAKING ON TOO MUCH WORK. YOUR WOUNDS FROM LAST TIME HAVEN'T EVEN HEALED YET!
THESE? THESE ARE SCRATCHES!
WHAT ARE YOU SO WORRIED FOR? YOU'RE TOO WEAK TO BE SO SCARED.
PAT
PAT
GRR, WHEN SOMEONE IS WORRIED ABOUT YOU—
EH, YOU KNOW HOW IT IS.
GOTTA SAVE UP THAT CASH.
ENOUGH FOR THE KID WE'VE GOT ON THE WAY.
CLACK
I'M BACK—

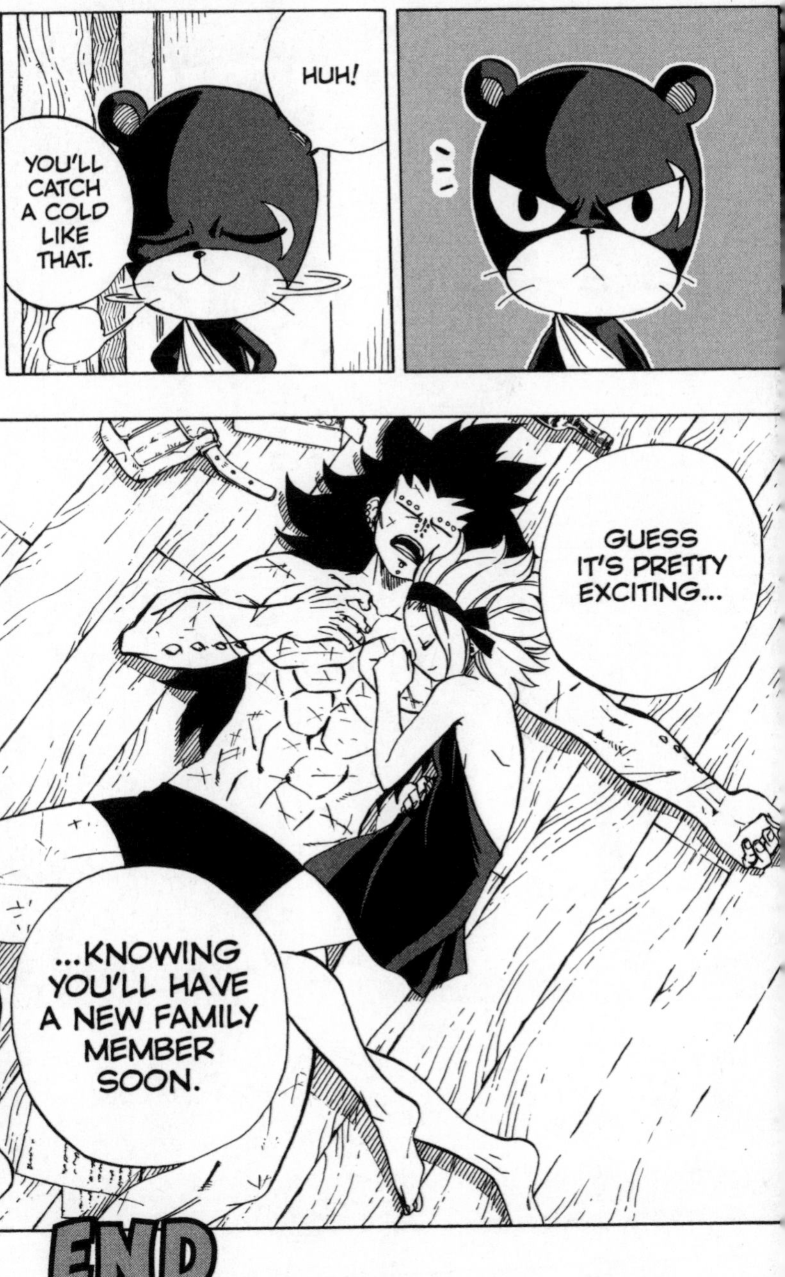
HUH!
YOU'LL CATCH A COLD LIKE THAT.
GUESS IT'S PRETTY EXCITING...
...KNOWING YOU'LL HAVE A NEW FAMILY MEMBER SOON.
END

DE ART RETURNS

(GIFU PREFECTURE aya)

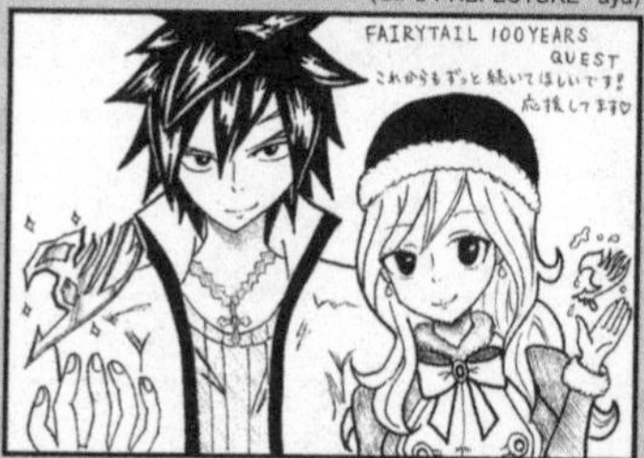
FAIRYTAIL 100YEARS QUEST
これからもずっと続いてほしいです!
応援してます♡

▲ TOGETHER AGAIN, FINALLY.
WONDER WHERE THEY GO FROM HERE?

(TOKYO PREFECTURE A.U.)

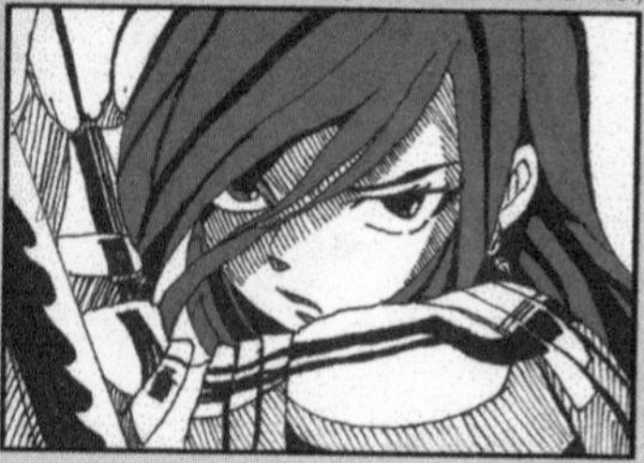

▲ THIS ERZA IS SO COOL! THAT PIERCING
GAZE JUST KILLS ME!

(SHIZUOKA PREFECTURE MAO SHIBUTANI)

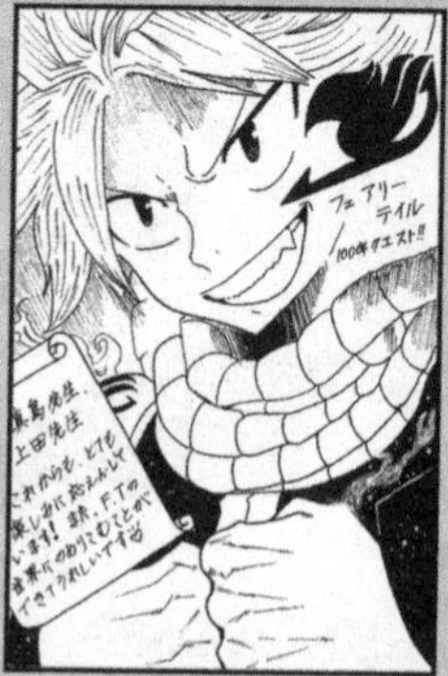
フェアリーテイル
100年クエスト!!

▲ OOH! COOL!
LOOKING POWERFUL.

▼ THIS PICTURE IS SOOO CUTE!
I LOVE IT.

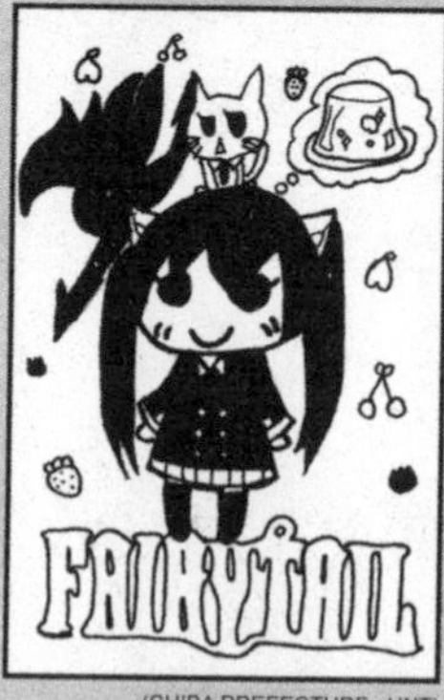
FAIRYTAIL

(CHIBA PREFECTURE HNT)

(MIE PREFECTURE YUI SAKADA)

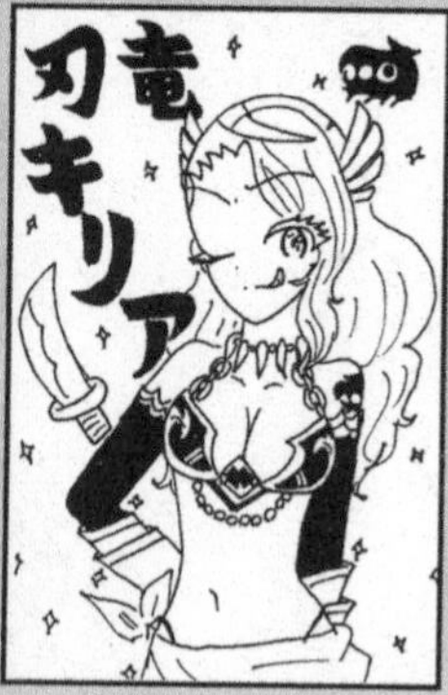
刃竜キリア

▲ K-KIRIA CAN BE C-CUTE...?
THIS IS KIND OF GREAT...!

FAIRY TAIL 100 YEARS QUEST GUILD

(AICHI PREFECTURE SOUSAI)

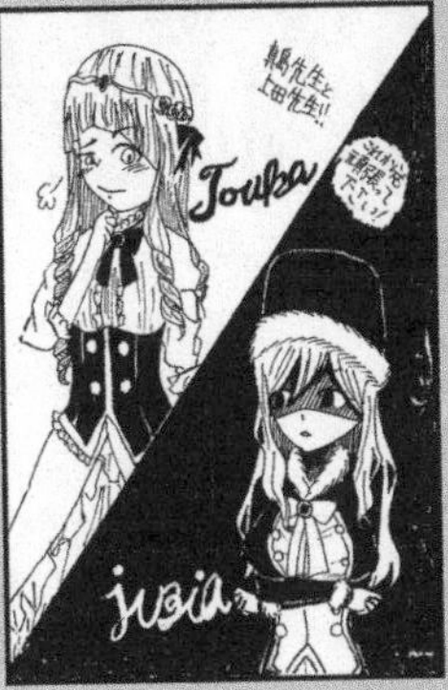

juvia

▼ YOU CAN ALMOST SEE THE SPARKS. PLAY NICE, GIRLS... PLEASE?

(YAMANASHI PREFECTURE YUU)

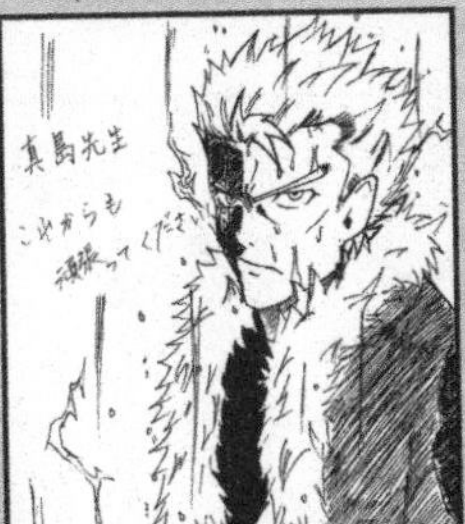

真島先生
これからも
頑張ってください
ラクサス☆

▼ NOTHING SAYS MANLY LIKE DRIPPING WATER... CAREFUL OF ELECTRICITY!

(GIFU PREFECTURE WAYAJO SAKAI)

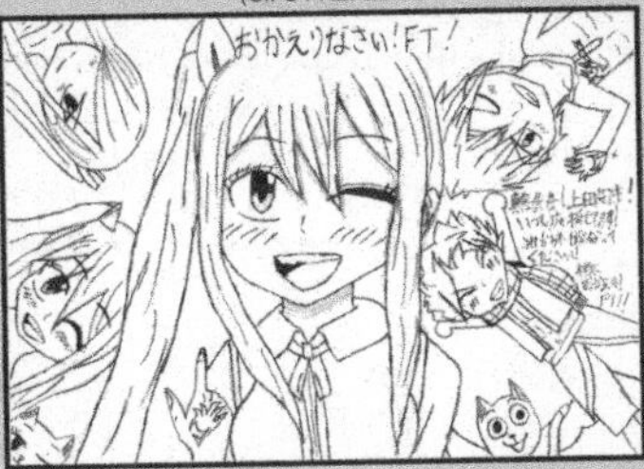

おかえりなさい！FT！

▼ WHAT GREAT SMILES! LOOKS LIKE THEY'RE HAVING FUN!

(IBARAKI PREFECTURE SUKAI)

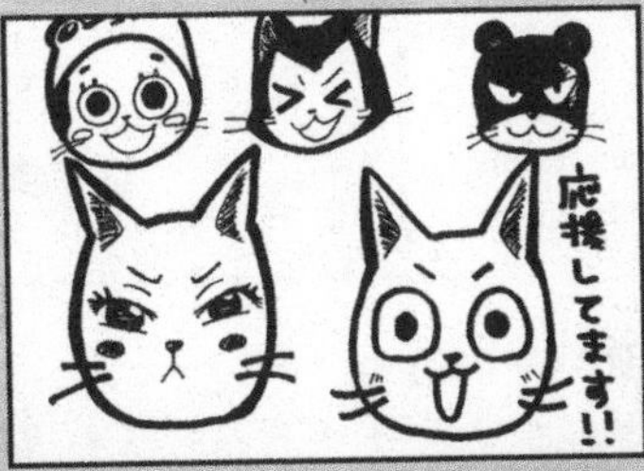

応援してます!!

▼ EXCEEDS UNITE! GREAT WORK.

OVERSEAS CORNER

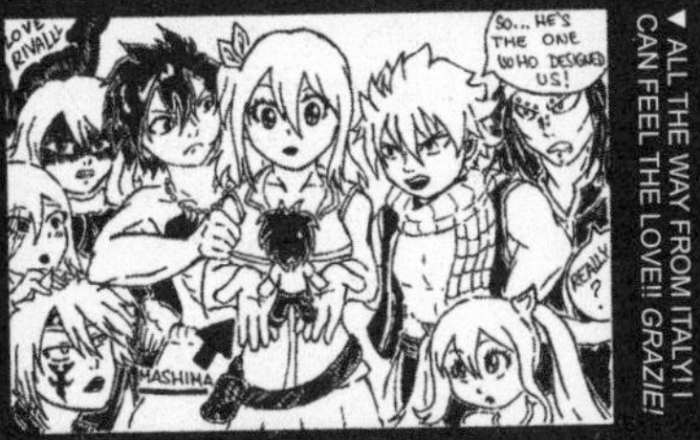

LOVE RIVALLY
SO... HE'S THE ONE WHO DESIGNED US!
REALLY ?
MASHIMA

▼ ALL THE WAY FROM ITALY! I CAN FEEL THE LOVE!! GRAZIE!

(ITALY SVEVA CESCHIA)

HERE'S OUR FOURTH BATCH OF FAN DRAWINGS! ENJOY!

EDITOR'S NOTE: DRAWING SUBMISSIONS LIMITED TO JAPAN.

TRANSLATION NOTES

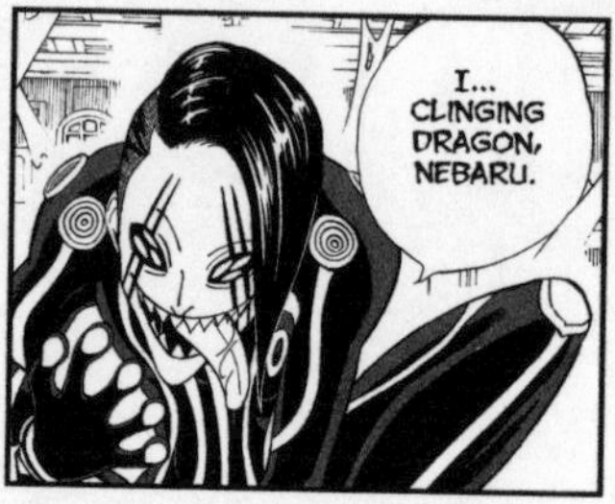
I... CLINGING DRAGON, NEBARU.

Nebaru, page 130

Nebaru's name transparently derives from the Japanese verb *nebaru*, meaning "to cling" or "to stick to." His sobriquet is *nenryuu*, composed of the characters for "cling" (the kanji that is actually read *nebaru* as a verb) and "dragon." Nebaru speaks in half-formed phrases punctuated by long pauses, a tendency we've tried to replicate in the English.

Reiss, page 144

Reiss's nickname, *reiryuu*, is pretty straightforward: it translates directly as "spirit dragon." It's possible the syllable *rei* in the character's name is a reference to the kanji 霊 (*rei*, spirit). Unfortunately, there isn't a very good way to communicate this pun in English without completely changing the name, even though, by sheer and strange coincidence, the rendering "Reiss" happens to preserve the Japanese syllable in translation.

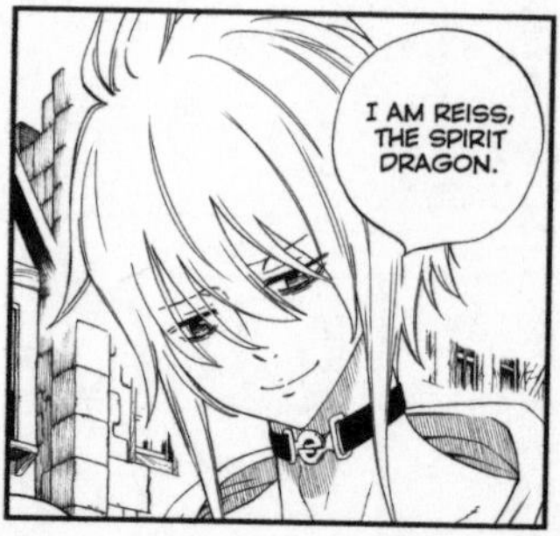
I AM REISS, THE SPIRIT DRAGON.

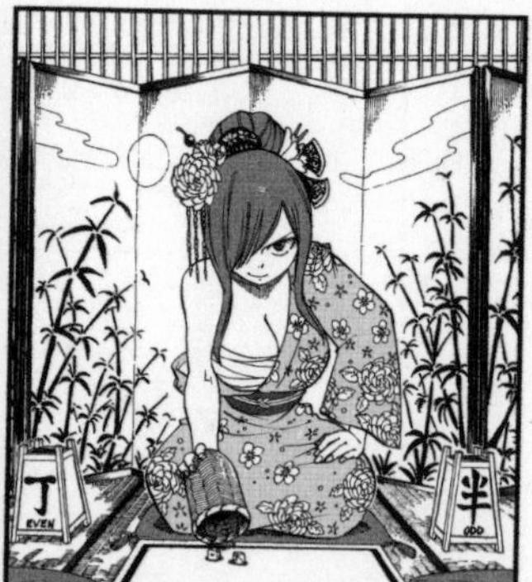
半
ODD
丁
EVEN

Lanterns, page 145

The legends in the lanterns to Erza's right and left read *han* (odd) and *cho* (even). She's playing a popular dice game in which dice are put into a wicker cup and shaken, and participants bet on whether the total number of pips displayed on the faces will come out even or odd. It's a simple but long-standing game, though it's often associated with gangsters and ne'er-do-wells.

Human Spirits, page 148

"Human spirits" (or souls) is the literal translation of the Japanese *hitodama*, but this word often refers to little glowing flames like the ones in the fourth panel on this page. Usually depicted as bluish-white, they're sometimes called foxfire or spirit flames, and are indeed believed to be the souls of the dead.

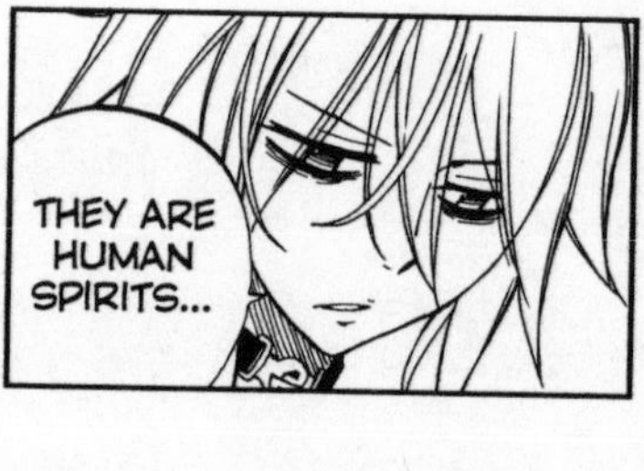
THEY ARE HUMAN SPIRITS...

FAIRY TAIL
100 YEARS QUEST

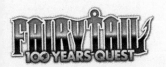

A Kodansha Comics Trade Paperback Original
FAIRY TAIL: 100 Years Quest 4 copyright © 2019 Hiro Mashima/Atsuo Ueda
English translation copyright © 2020 Hiro Mashima/Atsuo Ueda

Published in the United States by Kodansha Comics, an imprint of
Kodansha USA Publishing, LLC, New York.

Publication rights for this English edition arranged through
Kodansha Ltd., Tokyo.

First published in Japan in 2019 by Kodansha Ltd., Tokyo.

ISBN 978-1-63236-948-2

Original cover design by Hisao Ogawa (Blue in Green)

Printed in Mexico.

www.kodansha.us

9 8 7 6 5 4
Translation: Kevin Steinbach
Lettering: Phil Christie
Editing: Nathaniel Gallant
Kodansha Comics edition cover design by Phil Balsman

Publisher: Kiichiro Sugawara
Vice president of marketing & publicity: Naho Yamada

Director of publishing services: Ben Applegate
Associate director of operations: Stephen Pakula
Publishing services managing editor: Noelle Webster
Assistant production manager: Emi Lotto, Angela Zurlo